W9-CED-839
It's YOUR country. Learn it. Love it. Explore it.

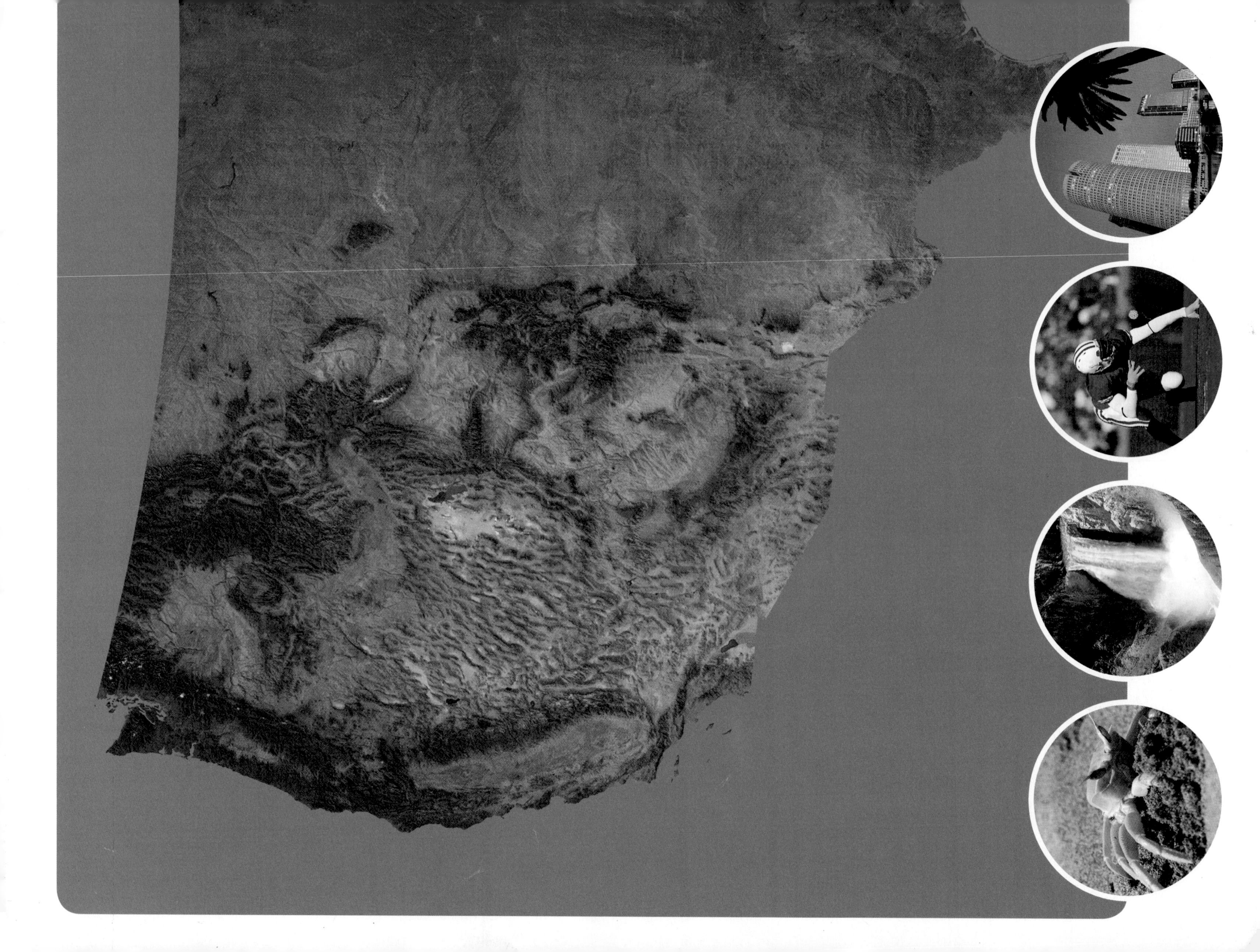

NATIONAL GEOGRAPHIC KIDS™

UNITED STATES ATLAS

NATIONAL GEOGRAPHIC
SCHOLASTIC INC.

TABLE OF CONTENTS

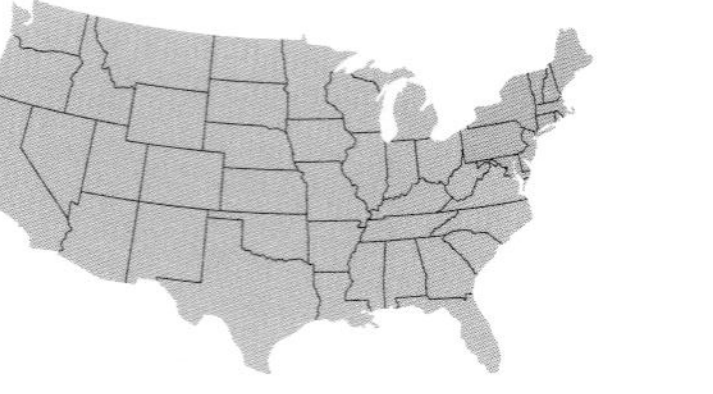
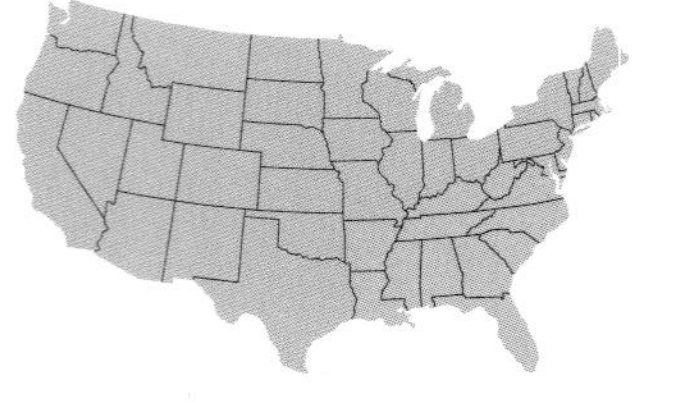
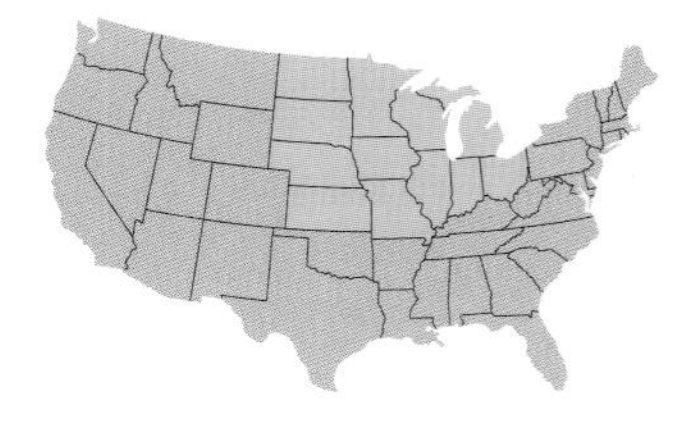

FRONT OF THE BOOK

GETTING STARTED
How to Use This Atlas 6
How to Use the Atlas Web Site 8

THE PHYSICAL UNITED STATES 10
Natural Environment 12
Natural Hazards 14

THE POLITICAL UNITED STATES 16
Population 18
People on the Move 20
Getting Green 22
The National Capital 24

THE NORTHEAST 26

PHYSICAL & POLITICAL MAPS 28
About the Northeast 30
Connecticut 32
Delaware 34
Maine 36
Maryland 38
Massachusetts 40
New Hampshire 42
New Jersey 44
New York 46
Pennsylvania 48
Rhode Island 50
Vermont 52

THE SOUTHEAST 54

PHYSICAL & POLITICAL MAPS 56
About the Southeast 58
Alabama 60
Arkansas 62
Florida 64
Georgia 66
Kentucky 68
Louisiana 70
Mississippi 72
North Carolina 74
South Carolina 76
Tennessee 78
Virginia 80
West Virginia 82

THE MIDWEST 84

PHYSICAL & POLITICAL MAPS 86
About the Midwest 88
Illinois 90
Indiana 92
Iowa 94
Kansas 96
Michigan 98
Minnesota 100
Missouri 102
Nebraska 104
North Dakota 106
Ohio 108
South Dakota 110
Wisconsin 112

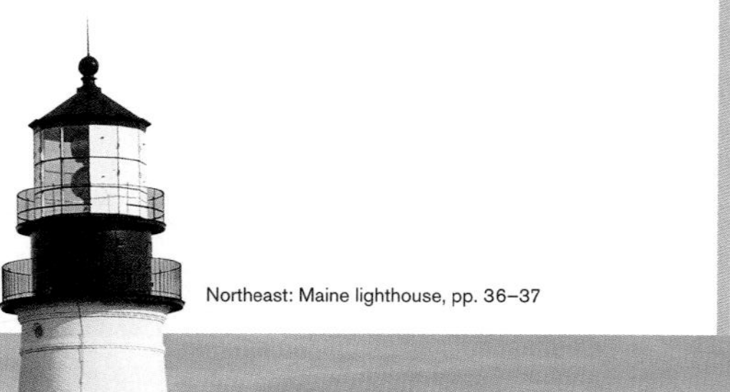

Northeast: Maine lighthouse, pp. 36–37

Southeast:
Florida manatee, p. 64

Midwest: Illinois hay field with tractor, pp. 90–91

Title page: Atlantic sand crab; Lower Falls of the Yellowstone, MT; football player; Tampa, FL; sage grouse; skyline, Seattle, WA; Organ Pipe Cactus National Monument, AZ.

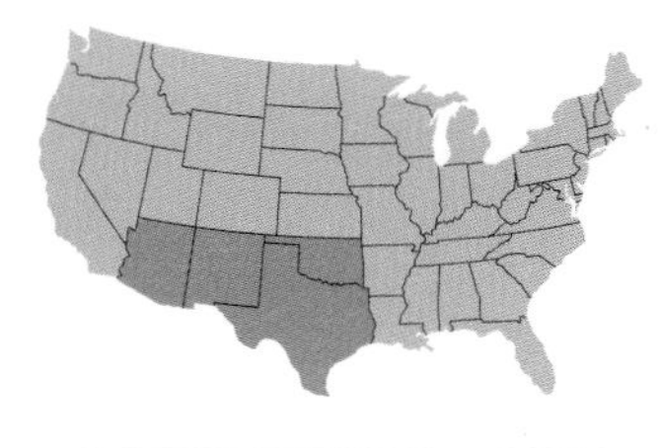

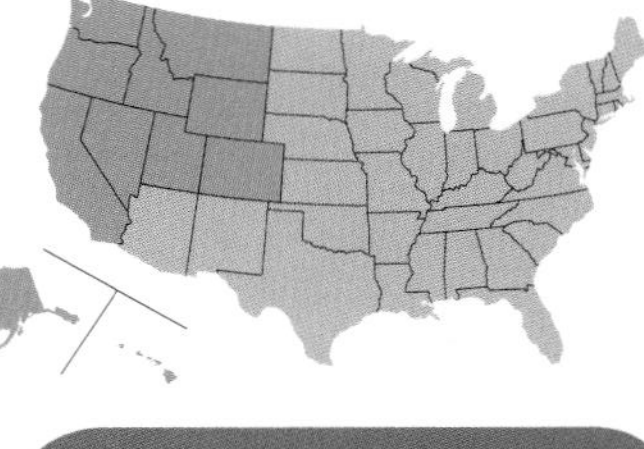

THE SOUTHWEST 114

PHYSICAL & POLITICAL MAPS 116
About the Southwest 118
Arizona 120
New Mexico 122
Oklahoma 124
Texas 126

THE WEST 128

PHYSICAL & POLITICAL MAPS 130
About the West 132
Alaska 134
California 136
Colorado 138
Hawai‘i 140
Idaho 142
Montana 144
Nevada 146
Oregon 148
Utah 150
Washington 152
Wyoming 154

THE TERRITORIES 156

POLITICAL MAP & FACT BOXES 156
U.S. Caribbean Territories
Puerto Rico, Virgin Islands
U.S. Pacific Territories
American Samoa, Guam, Northern Mariana Islands
Other U.S. Territories
Baker Is., Howland Is., Jarvis Is., Johnston Atoll, Kingman Reef, Midway Islands, Navassa Is., Palmyra Atoll, Wake Is.
About the Territories 158

BACK OF THE BOOK

U.S. FACTS & FIGURES 160
GLOSSARY 161
OUTSIDE WEB SITES 161
PLACE-NAME INDEX 162
CREDITS 176

Territories: Festival dancers, American Samoa, pp. 158–159

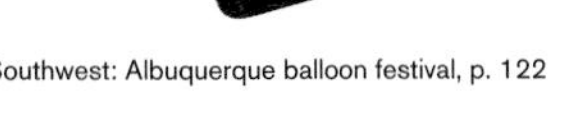

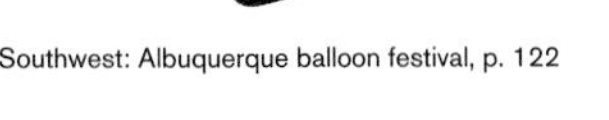

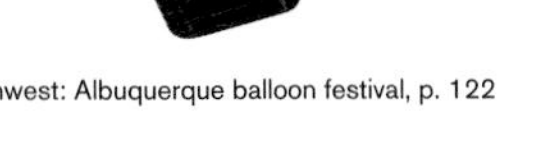

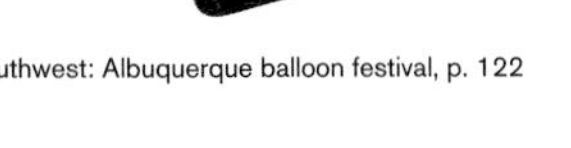

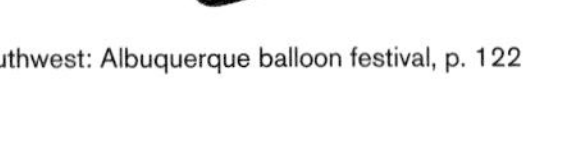

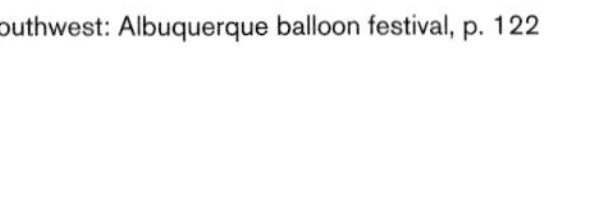

Southwest: Albuquerque balloon festival, p. 122

West: Wyoming ranch, p. 154

GETTING STARTED

HOW TO USE THIS ATLAS

This atlas is much more than just another book of maps about the United States. Of course you'll find all the things you'd expect to find—country, regional, and state maps, essays, photos, flags, graphs, and fact boxes—for the country as a whole as well as for each region and state (even the territories). But there's much more. This atlas, through a specially designed Web site (see pages 8–9), not only leads you to places where you can find more information and keep up-to-date about all kinds of things, it also allows you to go beyond the flat page and experience the sights and sounds of the country through the multimedia archives of National Geographic.

COLOR BARS

Each section of the atlas has its own color to make it easy to move from one to another. Look for the color in the Table of Contents and across the top of the pages in the atlas. The name of the section and the title for each topic or map is in the color bar.

- The Northeast
- The Southeast
- The Midwest
- The Southwest
- The West
- The Territories

46 | THE NORTHEAST

THE EMPIRE STATE: NEW YORK

NEW YORK

When Englishman Henry Hudson explored New York's Hudson River Valley in 1609, the territory was already inhabited by large tribes of Native Americans, including the powerful Iroquois. In 1624 a Dutch trading company established the New Netherland colony, but after just 40 years the colony was taken over by the English and renamed for England's Duke of York. In 1788 New York became the 11th state. The state can be divided into two parts. The powerful port city of New York, center of trade and commerce and gateway to immigrants, is the largest city in the U.S. Its metropolitan area has more than 18 million people. Everything north of the city is simply referred to as "Upstate." Cities such as Buffalo and Rochester are industrial centers, while Ithaca and Syracuse boast major universities. Agriculture is also important in New York. With almost 5 million acres in cropland, the state is a major producer of dairy products, fruits, and vegetables.

LADY LIBERTY. Standing in New York Harbor, the Statue of Liberty, a gift from the people of France, is a symbol of freedom and democracy.

NATURAL WONDER. As many as 12 million tourists annually visit Niagara Falls on the U.S.-Canada border. Visitors in rain slickers trek through the mists below Bridal Veil Falls on the American side.

URBAN GIANT

With more than twice the population of the next largest city, New York—known as the Big Apple—is the country's largest city.

STATE FACT BOX

The fact box has all the key information you need at a glance about a state, its flag and nickname, statistics about area, cities, population, ethnic and racial makeup,* statehood, industry, and agriculture, plus some fun Geo Whiz facts and the state bird and flower.

*The ethnic/racial percentages total more than 100 percent because Hispanics can be included with any race or ethnic group.

WEB LINKS

Throughout the atlas you will find black-and-yellow Web link icons for photos, videos, sounds, games, and more information. You can get to all of these links through one URL: **www.nationalgeographic.com/kids-usa-atlas.** This link will take you to the Web site specially designed to go with this atlas (see pages 8–9). Bookmark it so you can use it often.

WHERE ARE THE PICTURES?

If you want to know where a picture in any of the regional sections in the atlas was taken, check the map in the regional photo essay. Find the label that describes the photograph you are curious about, and follow the line to its location.

CHARTS AND GRAPHS

The photo essay for each state includes a chart or graph that highlights economic, physical, cultural, or some other type of information related to the state.

BAR SCALE
Each map has a bar scale in miles and kilometers to help you find out how far it is from one place to another on the map.

"YOU ARE HERE"
Locator maps show you where each region and state within the region is in relation to the rest of the United States. Regions are shown in the regional color; featured states are in yellow.

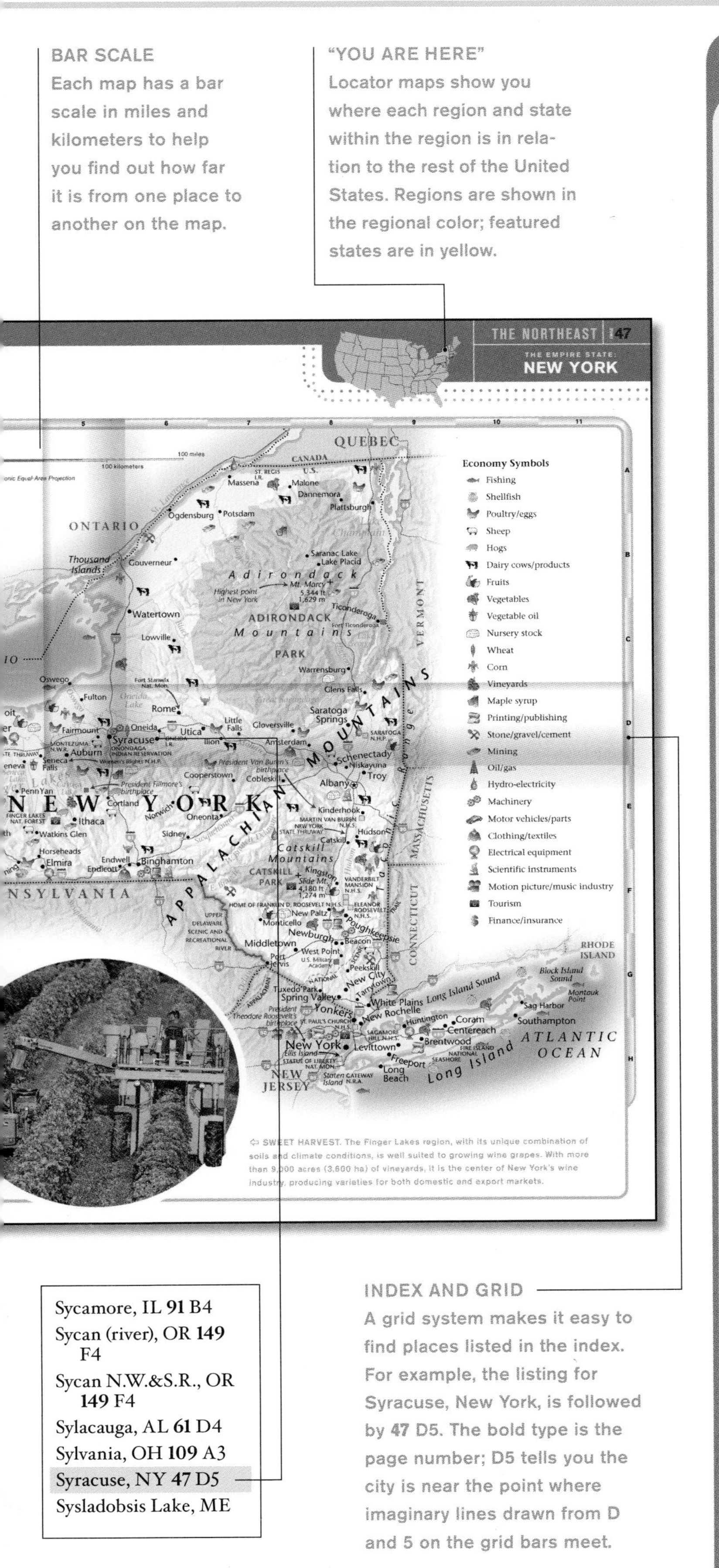

⇦ SWEET HARVEST. The Finger Lakes region, with its unique combination of soils and climate conditions, is well suited to growing wine grapes. With more than 9,000 acres (3,600 ha) of vineyards, it is the center of New York's wine industry, producing varieties for both domestic and export markets.

Sycamore, IL **91** B4
Sycan (river), OR **149** F4
Sycan N.W.&S.R., OR **149** F4
Sylacauga, AL **61** D4
Sylvania, OH **109** A3
Syracuse, NY **47** D5
Sysladobsis Lake, ME

INDEX AND GRID
A grid system makes it easy to find places listed in the index. For example, the listing for Syracuse, New York, is followed by **47** D5. The bold type is the page number; D5 tells you the city is near the point where imaginary lines drawn from D and 5 on the grid bars meet.

MAP ICONS

Maps use symbols to stand for many physical, political, and economic features. Below is a complete list of the map symbols used in this atlas. In addition, each state map has its own key featuring symbols for major economic activities. Additional abbreviations used in this atlas as well as metric conversion tables are listed on the endsheets at the back of the book.

- •Aspen ....*town of under 25,000 residents*
- •Frankfort ....*town of 25,000 to 99,999*
- •San Jose ....*city of 100,000 to 999,999*
- •New York .....*city of 1,000,000 and over*
- National capital
- State capital
- Point of interest
- Mountain peak with elevation above sea level
- Low point with elevation below sea level
- River
- Intermittent river
- Canal
- Interstate or selected other highway
- Trail
- State or national boundary
- Continental divide
- Lake and dam
- Intermittent lake
- Dry lake
- Swamp
- Glacier
- National Wild & Scenic River, **N.W.&S.R.**
- Sand
- Lava
- Area below sea level
- Indian Reservation, **I.R.**
- State Park, **S.P.**
  State Historical Park, **S.H.P.**
  State Historic Site, **S.H.S.**
- National Battlefield, **N.B.**
  National Battlefield Park, **N.B.P.**
  National Battlefield Site, **N.B.S.**
  National Historic Site, **N.H.S.**
  National Historical Area, **N.H.A.**
  National Historical Park, **N.H.P.**
  National Lakeshore
  National Military Park, **N.M.P.**
  National Memorial, **NAT. MEM.**
  National Monument, **NAT. MON.**
  National Park, **N.P.**
  National Parkway
  National Preserve
  National Recreation Area, **N.R.A.**
  National River
  National Riverway
  National Scenic Area
  National Seashore
  National Volcanic Monument
- National Forest, **N.F.**
- National Grassland, **N.G.**
- National Wildlife Refuge, **N.W.R.**

Economy Symbols

- Fishing
- Lobster fishing
- Shellfish
- Poultry/eggs
- Sheep
- Hogs
- Dairy cows/products
- Beef cattle
- Fruits
- Vegetables
- Vegetable oil
- Peanuts
- Nursery stock
- Wheat
- Corn
- Rice
- Soybeans
- Sugarcane
- Cotton
- Tobacco
- Coffee
- Vineyards
- Maple syrup
- Timber/forest products
- Furniture
- Printing/publishing
- Stone/gravel/cement
- Mining
- Coal
- Oil/gas
- Hydro-electricity
- Machinery
- Metal manufacturing
- Metal products
- Shipbuilding
- Railroad equipment
- Motor vehicles/parts
- Rubber/plastics
- Chemistry
- Food processing
- Clothing/textiles
- Leather products
- Glass/clay products
- Jewelry
- Electrical equipment
- Computers/electronics
- Scientific instruments
- Aircraft/parts
- Aerospace
- Motion picture/music industry
- Tourism
- Finance/insurance

GETTING STARTED

HOW TO USE THE ATLAS WEB SITE

As you can see by flipping through the pages, this atlas is chock full. There are photographs, statistics, quick facts, and—most of all—lots of charts and detailed maps. Plus there is a companion Web site that adds even more. You can watch videos of animals in their natural surroundings or of a volcano erupting; listen to the sounds of people, places, and animals; find lots of state information; download pictures and maps for school reports; and play games that allow you to explore the United States. You can even send e-postcards to your friends. The Web site provides added value to specific subjects in the atlas and also helps you explore on your own, taking you deep into the resources of National Geographic and beyond. Throughout the atlas you will find these icons.

The icons are placed near pictures, on maps, or next to text. Each icon tells you that you can find more on that subject on the Web site. To follow any icon link, go to www.nationalgeographic.com/kids-usa-atlas.

⇨START HERE.

There are three ways to find what you are looking for from the Home Page:

1. BY ATLAS PAGE NUMBER
2. BY TOPIC
3. BY ICON

www.nationalgeographic.com/kids-usa-atlas

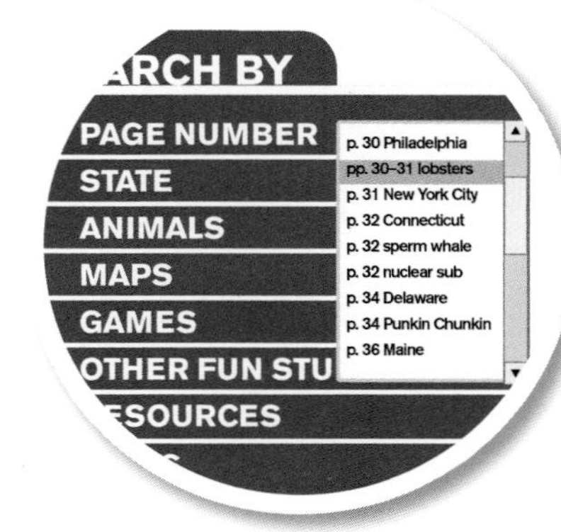

1. SEARCH BY ATLAS PAGE NUMBER

⇦ **PAGE NUMBER PULL-DOWN MENU.** If you find an icon in the atlas and want to go directly to that link, use the page number pull-down menu. Just drag and click.

2. SEARCH BY TOPIC

⇨ **LIST OF TOPICS.** If you want to explore a specific topic, click on the entry in the topic list. This list is your portal to vast quantities of National Geographic information, photos, videos, games, and more, all arranged by subject. Say you're interested in Animals. One click takes you to the Animals choice page (below).

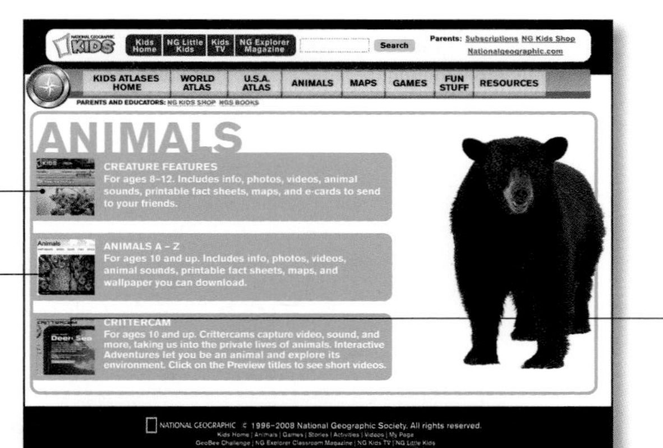

⇩ **CREATURE FEATURES.** Click to go to the National Geographic Kids' animal site. Click on an animal, and you will find a full feature about it, including photos, video, a range map, and other fun info.

⇦ **ANIMALS A–Z.** This choice takes you to the animal site for adults and older kids. Use the list of animals in the upper right-hand corner of the page. Clicking on an animal name takes you to the profile of that animal.

⇩ **CRITTERCAM.** Scientists put video cameras on animals to learn about the animal from its point of view. Click to see those videos, learn about the project, play games such as exploring the virtual world of a seal, and more.

3. SEARCH BY ICON

⇦ **SELECT ONE OF FIVE ICONS.** If you want to find all the videos referenced in the atlas, or all of the audios, photos, or games, click on one of the icons. A list will drop down. Choose from the list, and you're there! Clicking on Blackbeard takes you to a trailer for a National Geographic Channel film.

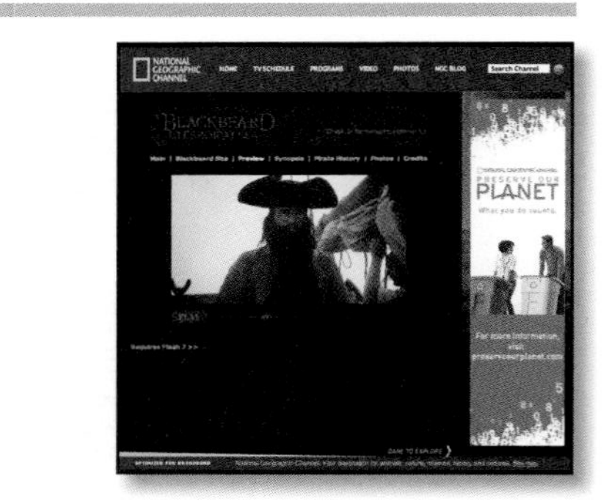

PHYSICAL MAP

THE PHYSICAL UNITED STATES

Stretching from the Atlantic in the east to the Pacific in the west, the United States is the third largest country in area in the world. Its physical diversity ranges from mountains to fertile plains and dry deserts. Shading on the map indicates changes in elevation, while colors suggest different vegetation patterns.

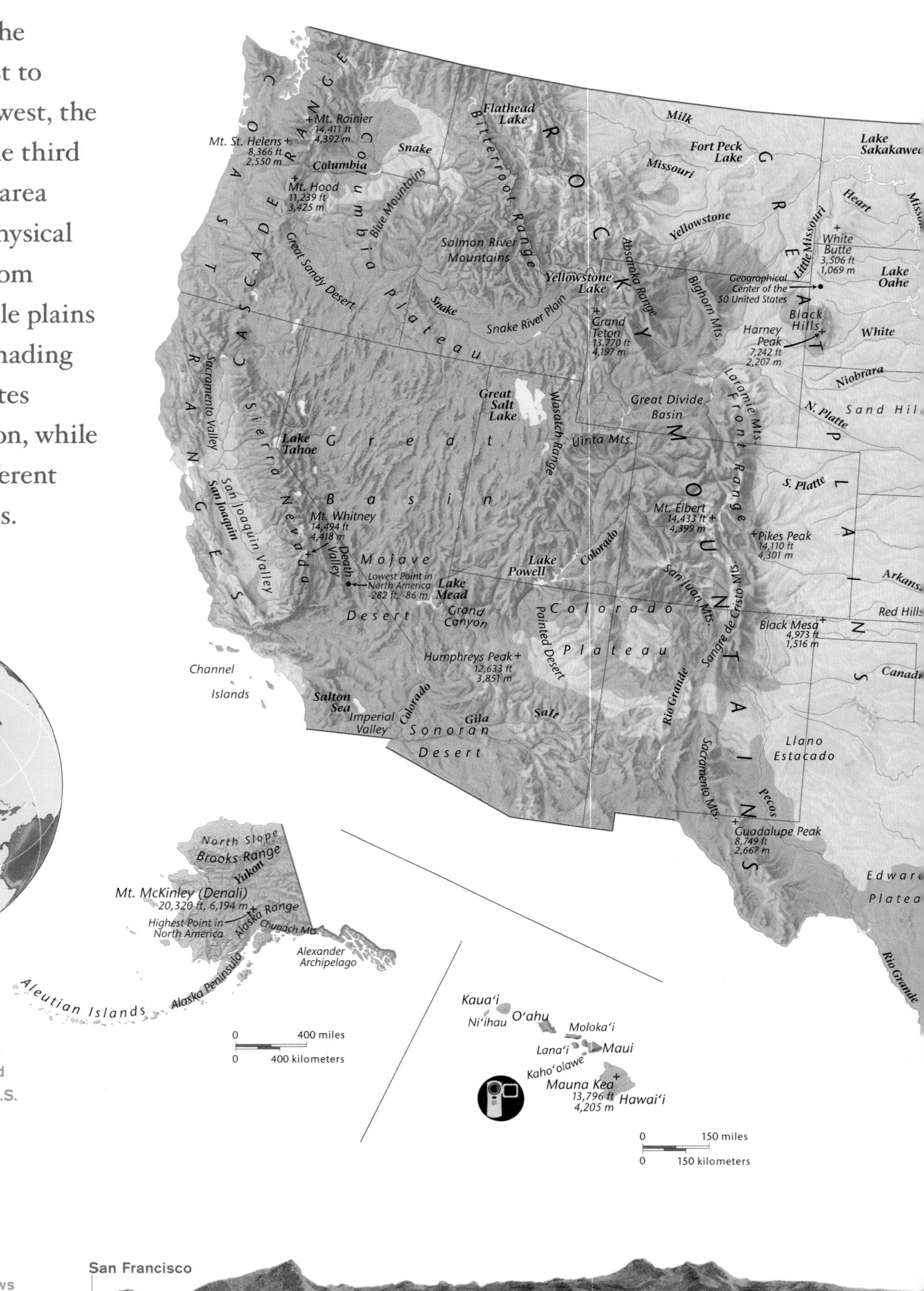

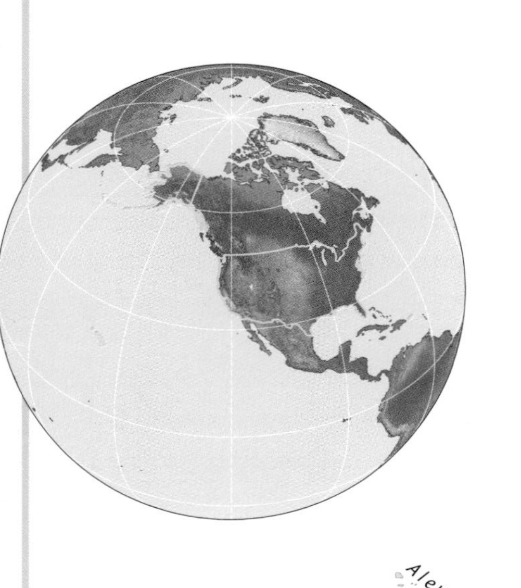

⇨ ALASKA AND HAWAI'I. In addition to the states located on the main landmass, the U.S. has two states—Alaska and Hawai'i—that are not directly connected to the other 48 states. If Alaska and Hawai'i were shown in their correct relative sizes and locations, the map would not fit on the page. The locator globe shows the correct relative size and location of each.

PHYSICAL MAP

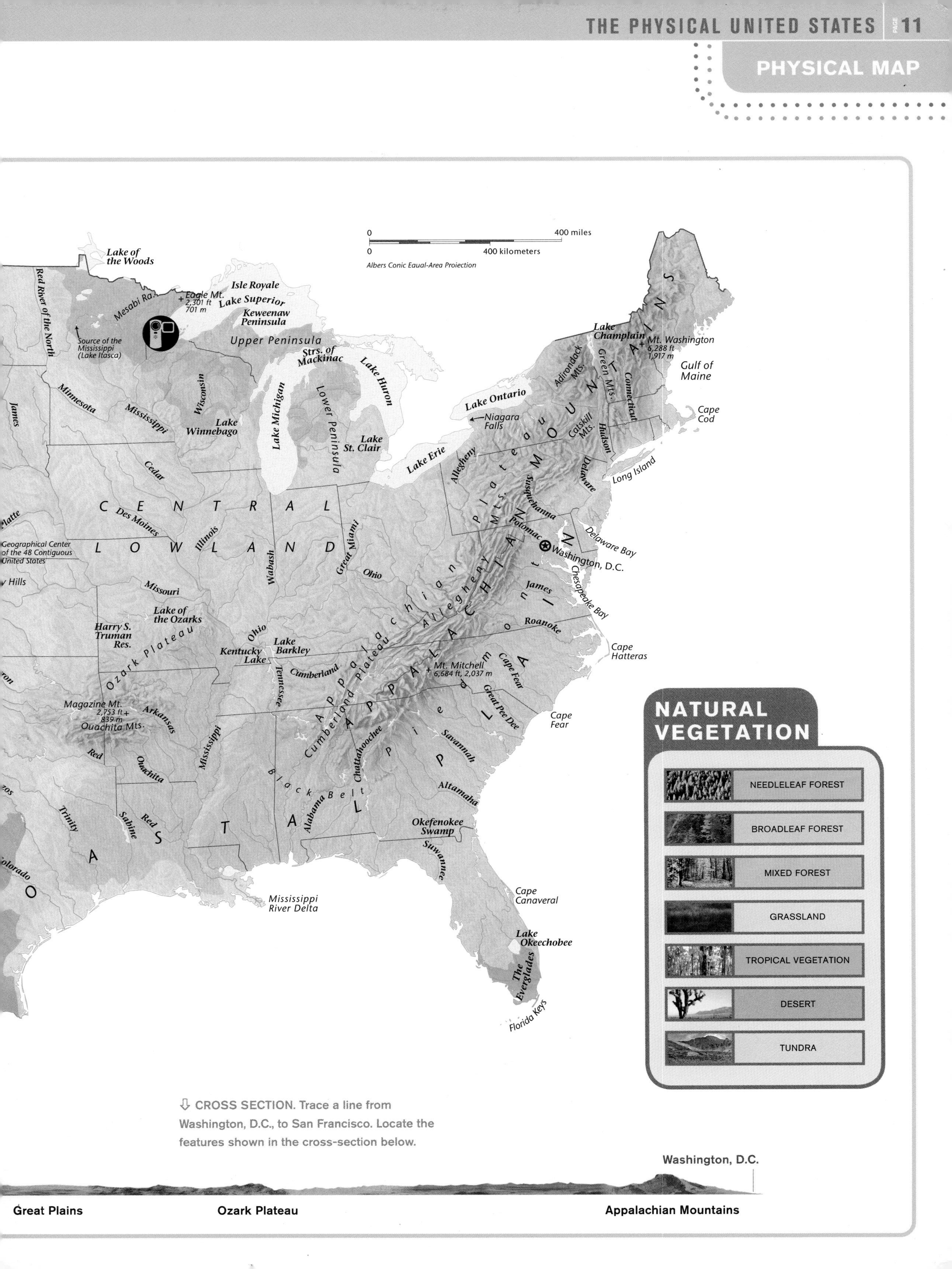

NATURAL VEGETATION

- NEEDLELEAF FOREST
- BROADLEAF FOREST
- MIXED FOREST
- GRASSLAND
- TROPICAL VEGETATION
- DESERT
- TUNDRA

⇩ CROSS SECTION. Trace a line from Washington, D.C., to San Francisco. Locate the features shown in the cross-section below.

NATURAL ENVIRONMENT

A big part of the natural environment of the United States is the climate. With humid areas near the coasts, dry interior regions far from any major water body, and land areas that extend from northern Alaska to southern Florida and Hawai'i, the country experiences great variation in climate. Location is the key. Distance from the Equator, nearness to water, wind patterns, temperature of nearby water bodies, and elevation are things that influence temperature and precipitation. Climate affects the types of vegetation that grow in a particular place and plays a part in soil formation.

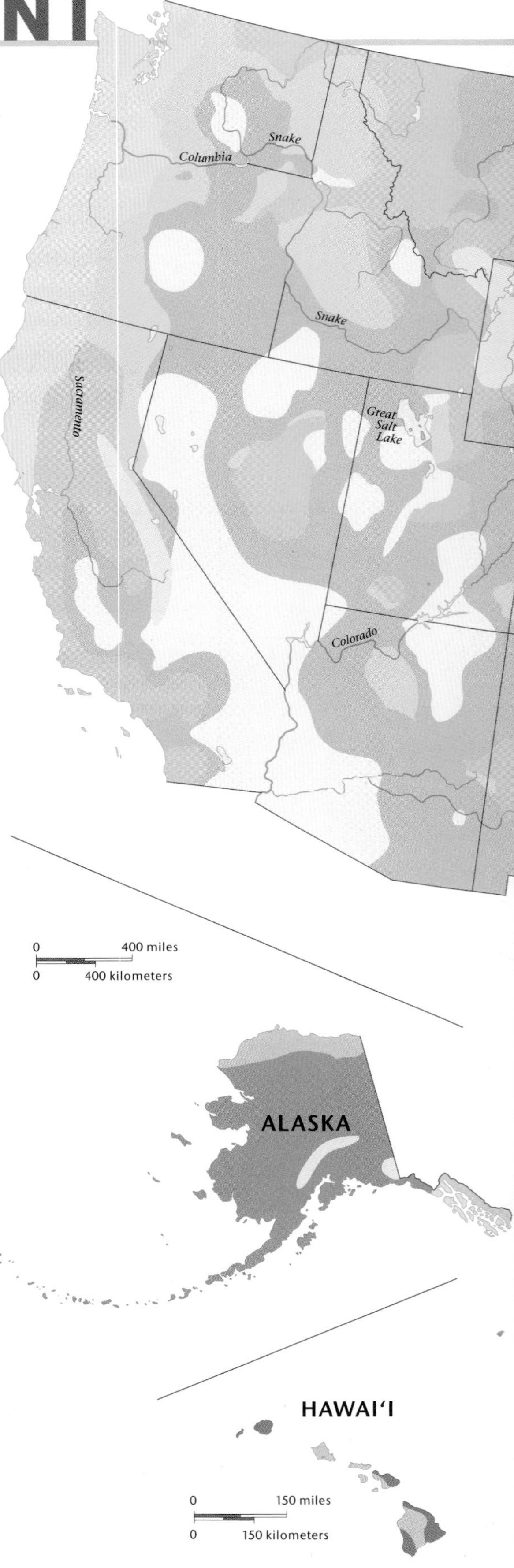

CHANGING CLIMATE

Scientists are concerned that a recent warming trend may be more than a natural cycle and that human activity may be a contributing factor. An increase in average temperatures could result in more severe storms, changes in precipitation patterns, and the spread of deserts. Rising temperatures may also play a part in the melting of glaciers, which could lead to a rise in ocean levels and the shrinking of the Arctic ice cover. NASA satellite images indicate that Arctic ice is shrinking as much as 9 percent each decade. Many believe that this puts polar bears at risk, since they normally hunt and raise their young on ice floes.

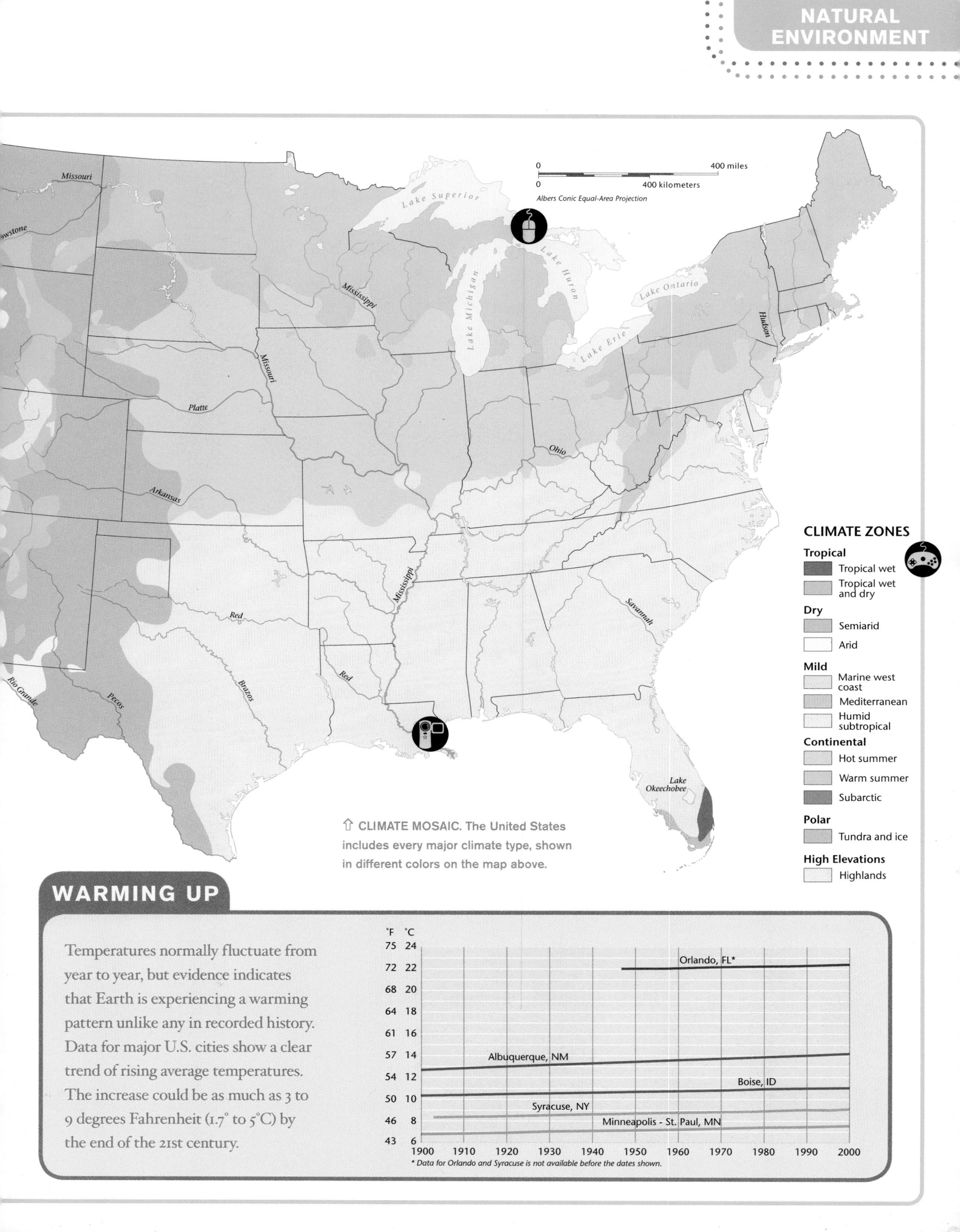

⇧ CLIMATE MOSAIC. The United States includes every major climate type, shown in different colors on the map above.

WARMING UP

Temperatures normally fluctuate from year to year, but evidence indicates that Earth is experiencing a warming pattern unlike any in recorded history. Data for major U.S. cities show a clear trend of rising average temperatures. The increase could be as much as 3 to 9 degrees Fahrenheit (1.7° to 5°C) by the end of the 21st century.

* Data for Orlando and Syracuse is not available before the dates shown.

NATURAL HAZARDS

The natural environment of the United States provides much diversity, but it also poses many dangers, especially when people locate homes and businesses in places at risk of natural disasters. Tornadoes bring destructive winds, and hurricanes bring strong winds, rain, and more; shifting of Earth's crust along fault lines rattles buildings; flood waters and wildfires threaten lives and property. More than one-third of the U.S. population lives in hazard-prone areas. Compare this natural disasters map to the population map on pages 18–19.

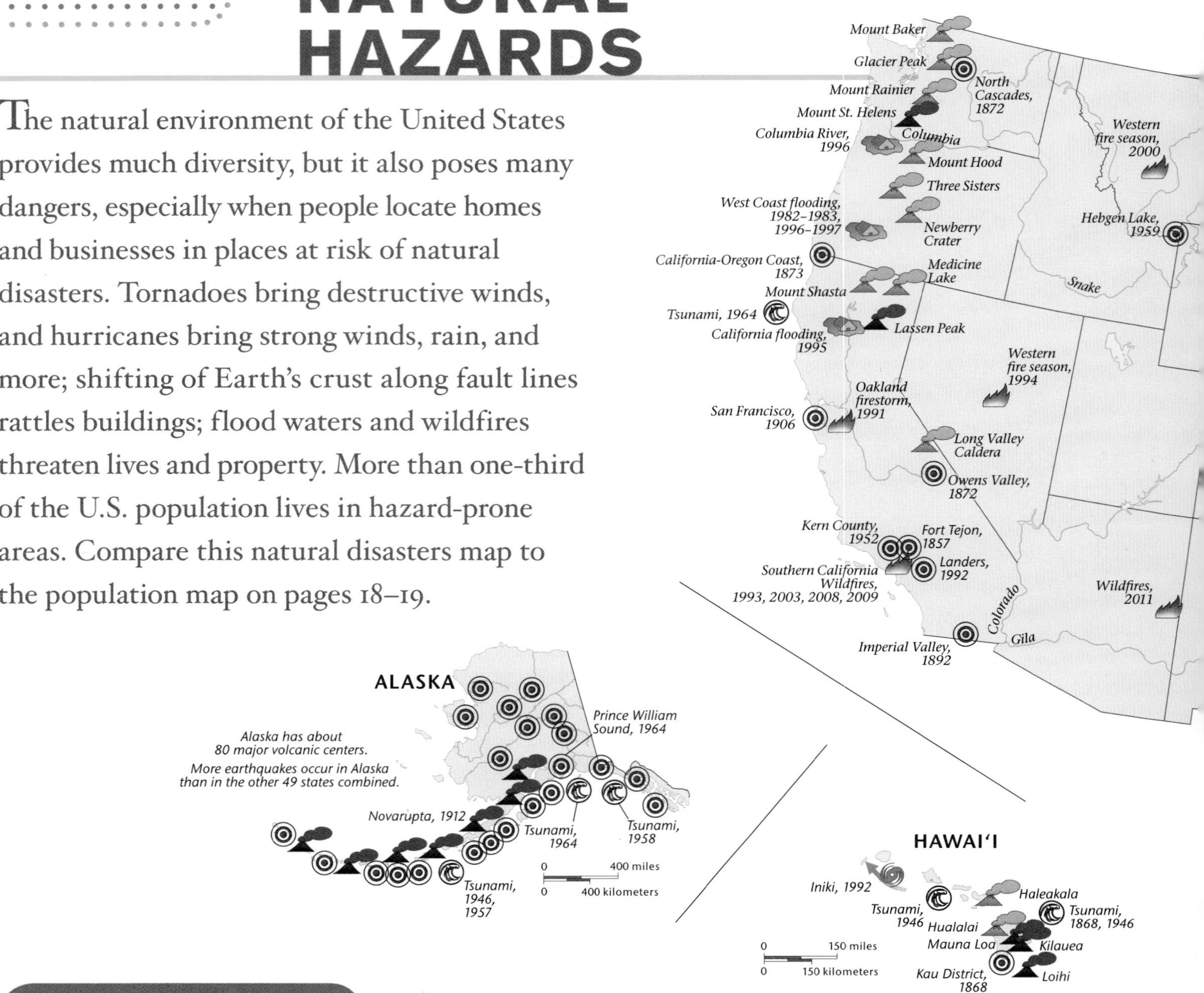

NATURAL HAZARDS

BLIZZARD. Severe storm with bitter cold temperatures and wind-whipped snow and ice particles that reduce visibility to less than 650 feet (198 m), paralyzing transportation systems

FLOOD. Inundation of buildings or roadways caused by overflow of a river or stream swollen by heavy rainfall or rapid snowmelt; may involve displacement of people

DROUGHT. Long and continuous period of abnormally low precipitation, resulting in water shortages that negatively impact people, animals, and plant life; may result in crop loss

HURRICANE. Tropical storm in the Atlantic, Caribbean, Gulf of Mexico, or eastern Pacific with a minimum sustained wind speed of 74 miles per hour (119 kmph)

ICE STORM. Damaging accumulations of ice associated with freezing rain; may pull down trees or utility lines, causing extensive damage and creating dangerous travel conditions

NATURAL HAZARDS

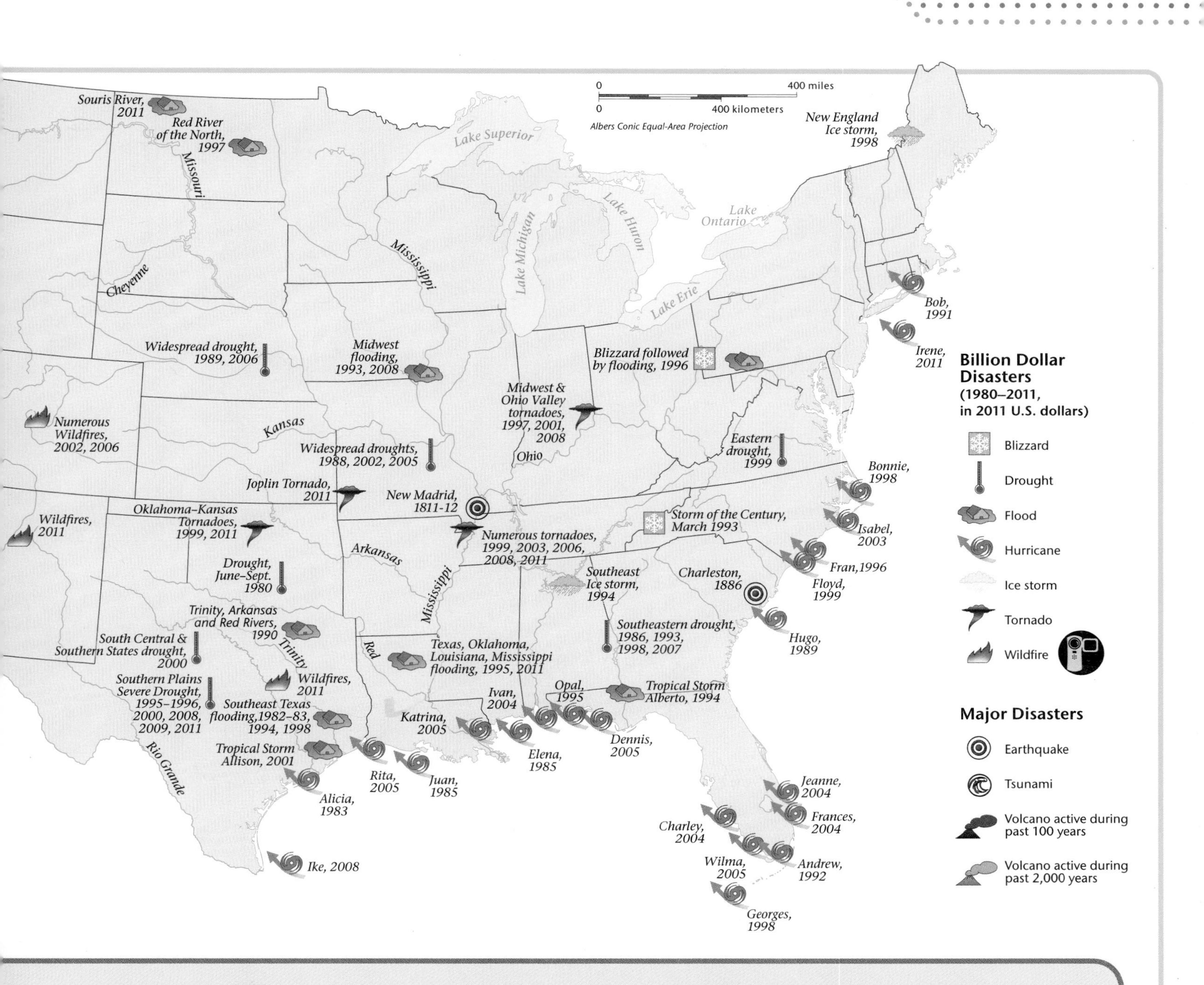

TORNADO. Violently rotating column of air that, when it reaches the ground, is the most damaging of all atmospheric phenomena; most common in the central U.S.

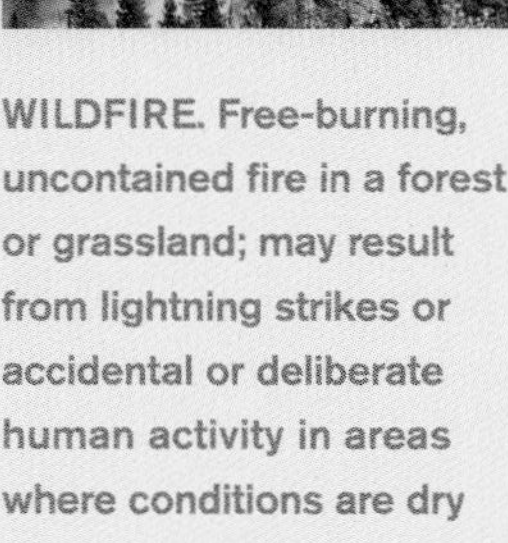

WILDFIRE. Free-burning, uncontained fire in a forest or grassland; may result from lightning strikes or accidental or deliberate human activity in areas where conditions are dry

EARTHQUAKE. Shaking or vibration created by the energy released by movement of Earth's crust along plate boundaries; can cause structural damage and loss of life

TSUNAMI. Series of unusually large ocean waves caused by an underwater earthquake, landslide, or volcanic eruption; very destructive in coastal areas

VOLCANO. Vent or opening in Earth's surface through which molten rock called lava, ash, and gases are released; often associated with tectonic plate boundaries

POLITICAL MAP

THE POLITICAL UNITED STATES

Like a giant patchwork quilt, the United States is made up of 50 states, each uniquely different but together making a national fabric held together by a Constitution and a federal government. State boundaries, outlined in various colors on the map, set apart internal political units within the country. The national capital—Washington, D.C.—is marked by a star in a double circle on the map. The capital of each state is marked by a star in a single circle.

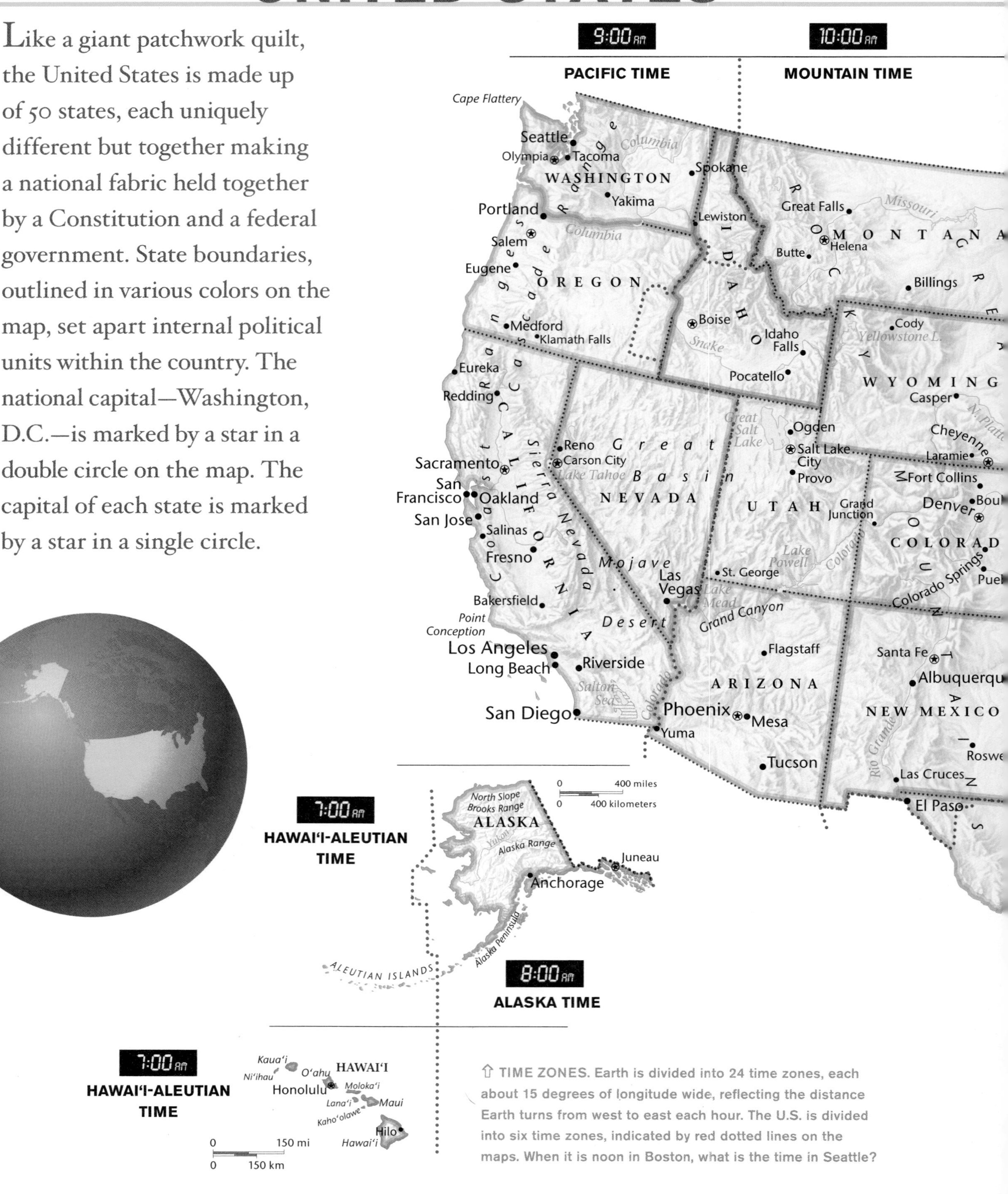

⇧ TIME ZONES. Earth is divided into 24 time zones, each about 15 degrees of longitude wide, reflecting the distance Earth turns from west to east each hour. The U.S. is divided into six time zones, indicated by red dotted lines on the maps. When it is noon in Boston, what is the time in Seattle?

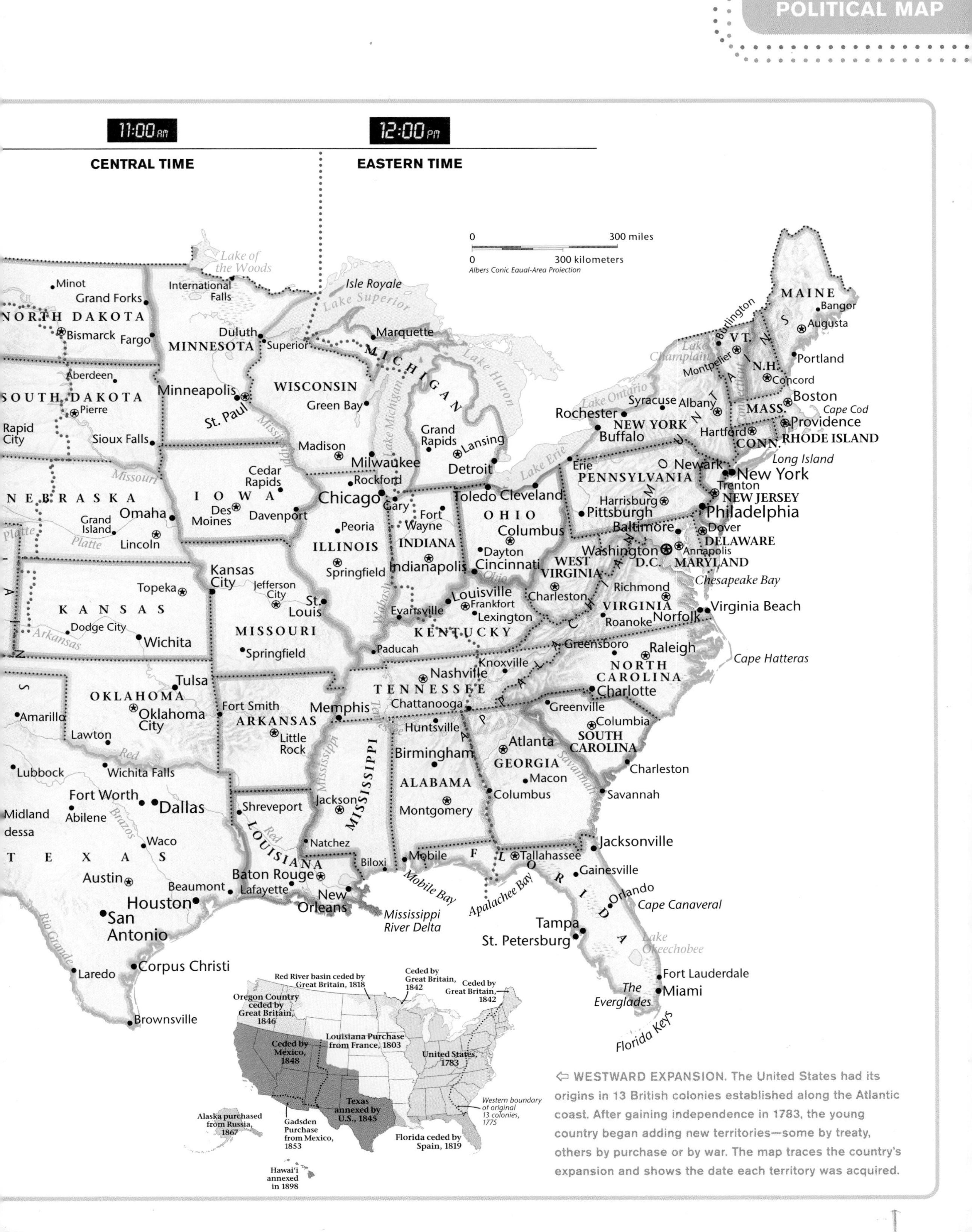

⇦ **WESTWARD EXPANSION.** The United States had its origins in 13 British colonies established along the Atlantic coast. After gaining independence in 1783, the young country began adding new territories—some by treaty, others by purchase or by war. The map traces the country's expansion and shows the date each territory was acquired.

POPULATION

More than 312 million and growing! The population of the United States topped the 300 million mark in 2006, and it continues to grow by more than 600,000 people each year. Before the arrival of European settlers, the population consisted of Native Americans living in tribal groups scattered across the country. In the 16th and 17th centuries, Europeans, some with slaves from Africa, settled first along the eastern seaboard and later moved westward. In 1790 the U.S. population was not quite 4 million people. Today, New York City alone has a population more than double that number. The country's population is unevenly distributed. The map shows the number of people per square mile for each county in every state. Greatest densities are in the East and along the West Coast, especially around major cities. The most rapid growth is occurring in the South and the West—an area referred to as the Sunbelt—as well as in suburban areas around cities.

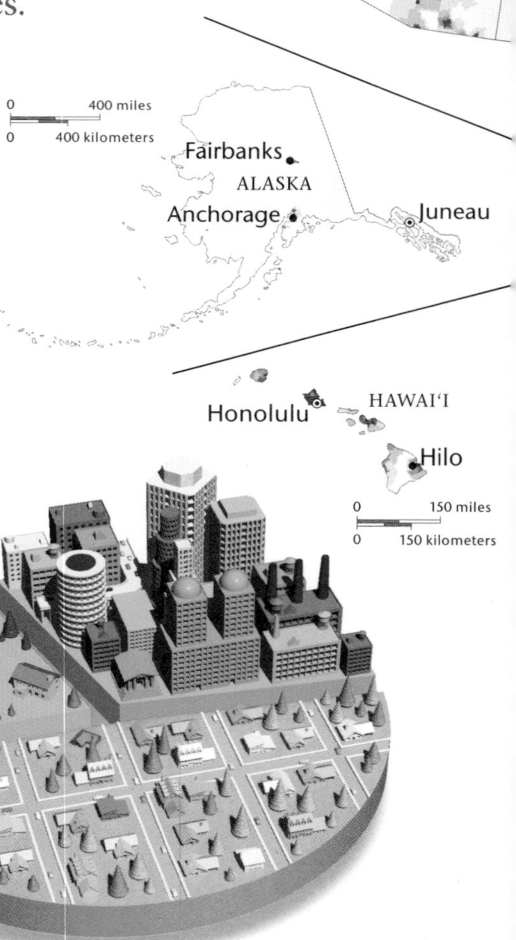

⇧ COMMUTER RUSH HOUR. Crowds of people press toward trains in New York City's Grand Central Station. With more than three-quarters of the population living in urban areas, commuter transportation poses a major challenge to cities in the United States.

⇨ WHERE WE LIVE. The first U.S. census in 1790 revealed that only 5 percent of people lived in towns. As industry has grown and agriculture has become increasingly mechanized, people have left farms (green), moving to urban places (blue) and their surrounding suburbs (orange).

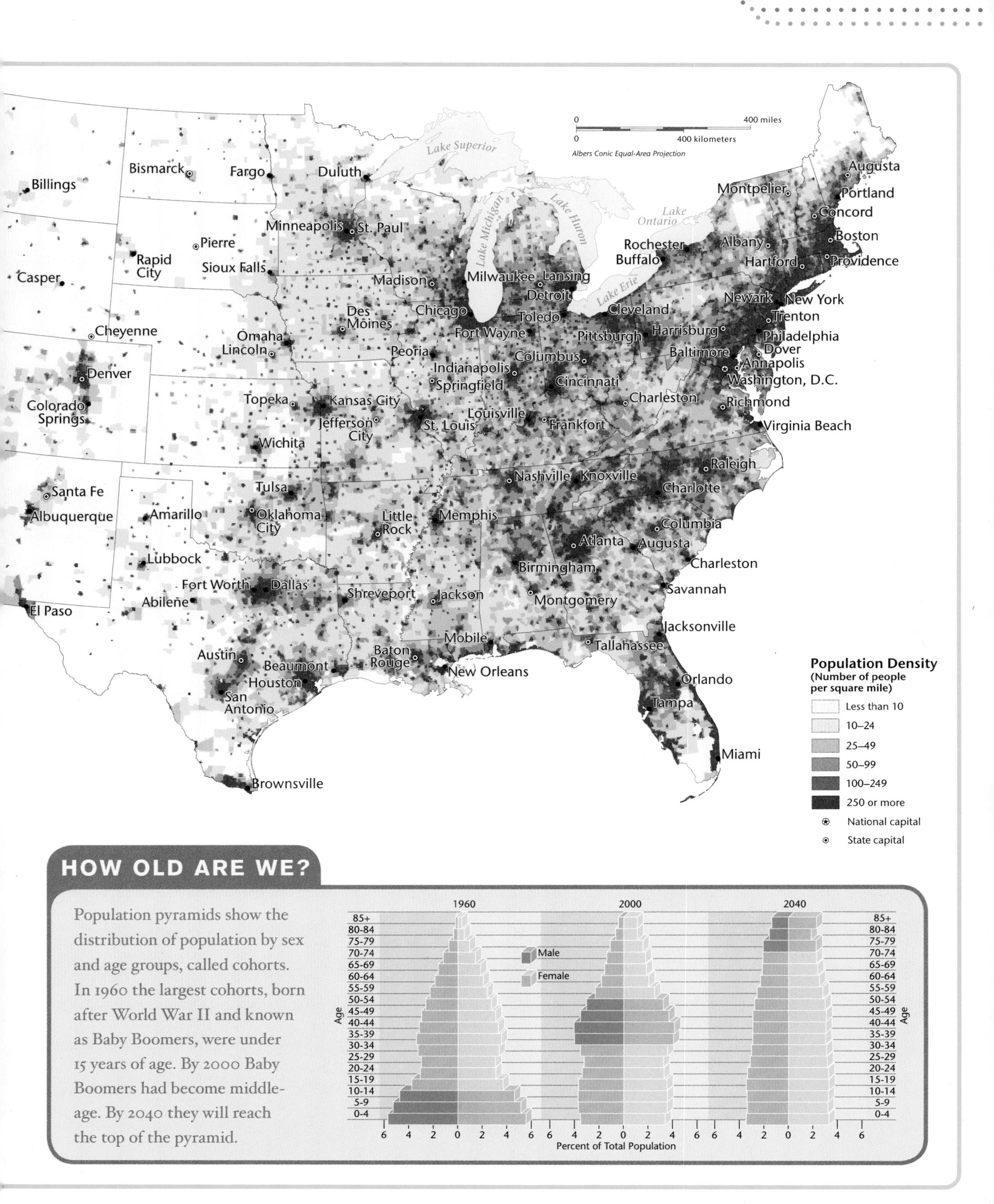

HOW OLD ARE WE?

Population pyramids show the distribution of population by sex and age groups, called cohorts. In 1960 the largest cohorts, born after World War II and known as Baby Boomers, were under 15 years of age. By 2000 Baby Boomers had become middle-age. By 2040 they will reach the top of the pyramid.

PEOPLE ON THE MOVE

From earliest human history, the land of the United States has been a focus of migration. Native peoples arrived thousands of years ago. The first European settlers came in the 16th and 17th centuries, and slave ships brought people from Africa. Today, people are still on the move. Since the mid-20th century, most international migrants have come from Latin America—especially Mexico and countries of Central America and the Caribbean—and Asia, particularly China, the Philippines, and India. While most of the population is still of European descent, certain regions have large minority concentrations, as shown on the map, that influence local cultural landscapes.

San Francisco
San Jose
Los Angeles
San Diego
Phoenix
0 400 miles
0 400 kilometers
0 150 miles
0 150 kilometer

⇧ BRIDGE OF HOPE. Many Mexicans enter the U.S. (foreground) by bridges across the Rio Grande, such as this one between Nuevo Laredo, Mexico, and Laredo, Texas.

⇧ IMMIGRANT INFLUENCE. With Hispanics making up over 16 percent of the population, signs in Spanish are popping up everywhere—even at voting areas.

⇧ SUNBELT SPRAWL. Spreading suburbs are becoming a common feature of the desert Southwest as people flock to the Sunbelt.

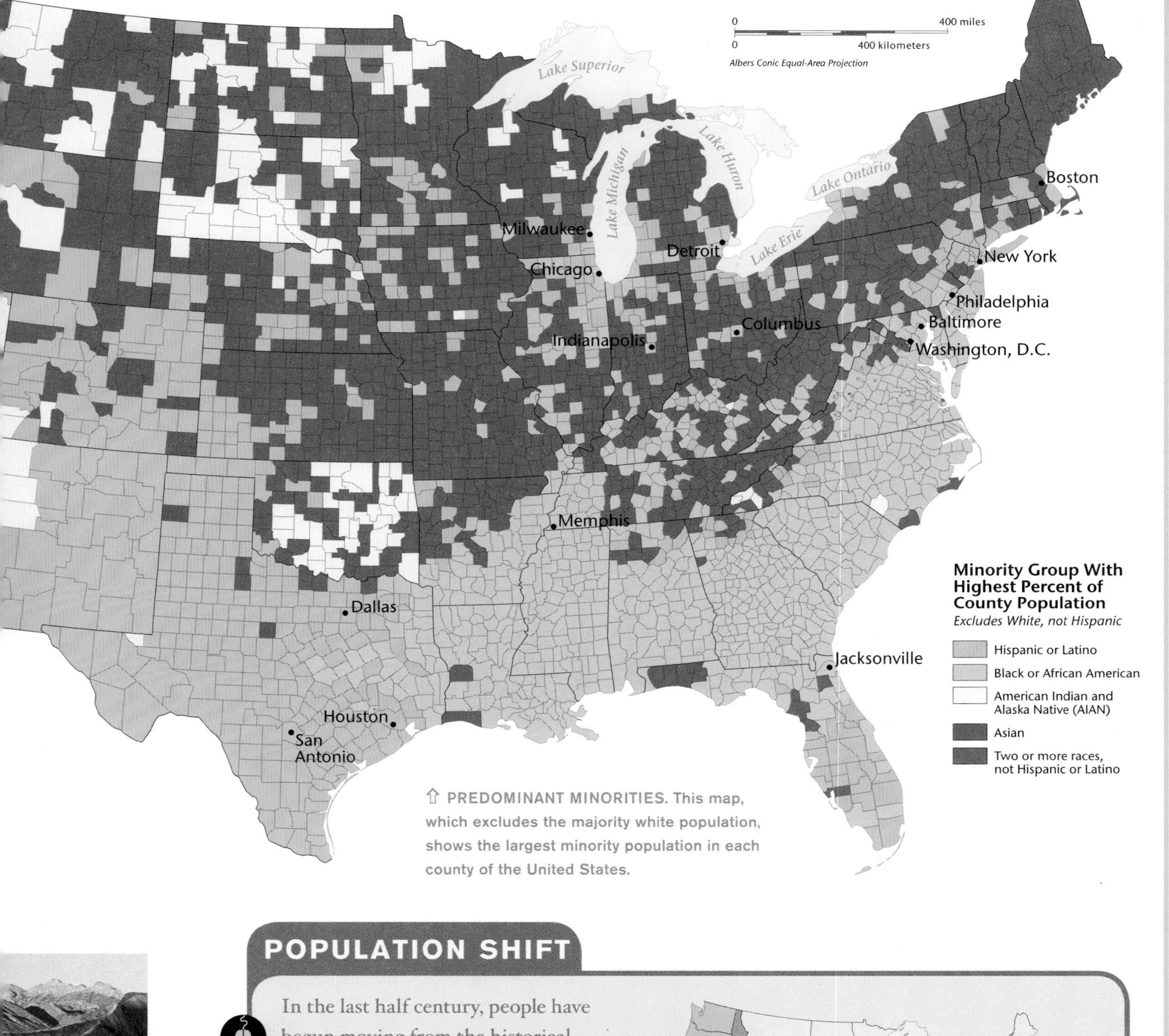

⇧ **PREDOMINANT MINORITIES.** This map, which excludes the majority white population, shows the largest minority population in each county of the United States.

POPULATION SHIFT

In the last half century, people have begun moving from the historical industrial and agricultural regions of the Northeast and Midwest toward the South and West, attracted by the promise of jobs, generally lower living costs, and a more relaxed way of life. This trend can be seen in the population growth patterns shown in the map at right.

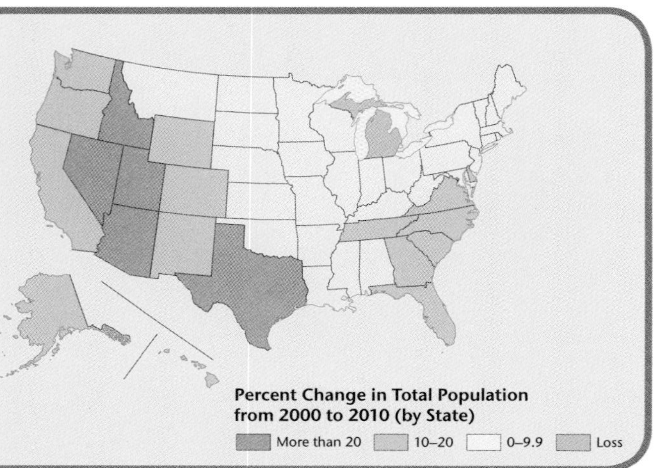

GETTING GREEN

Every day the media are filled with stories about global warming, pollution, and dwindling resources. Headlines warn of environmental risks that may threaten our way of life. The United States is the source of a quarter of the world's greenhouse gas emissions, and Americans generate more than 250 million tons of trash each year. The average American also uses 32 times more resources than a person in the African country of Kenya. But there's a bright side to these grim statistics: We can make a positive difference to the environment by making simple lifestyle changes. Scientists and engineers have developed energy-efficient appliances, cars that run on alternative fuels, and products made from recycled paper and plastics. But it is up to each of us to make changes that take advantage of these environment-friendly developments.

THINGS YOU CAN DO

Each year the average American household generates more than 80 tons of carbon dioxide gases, uses 102,000 gallons (386,111 l) of water, and creates 3.3 tons of landfill waste. Improving the health of our environment begins with you. You can make a difference if you practice the 3 R's of "getting green."

- REDUCE resource consumption by turning off lights, the TV, computers, and other electronic devices when you leave the room. Close the faucet when you are not using the water. Avoid buying things you do not need.
- REUSE items whenever possible, rather than throwing things away. Consider whether a container can be used again or a pair of shoes repaired.
- RECYCLE paper, plastic, glass, and aluminum cans. Recycling makes for less landfill trash, plus it preserves resources by reusing old products to make new ones.

Visit the library or go online to learn what your community is doing to protect the environment.

Share the Road

⇧ GREEN STREETS. Biking to work or school reduces use of gasoline, a source of greenhouse gases, and it is healthy, too.

Columbia
Snake
Colorado
Gila
0 400 miles
0 400 kilometers
0 150 mi
0 150 km

GETTING GREEN

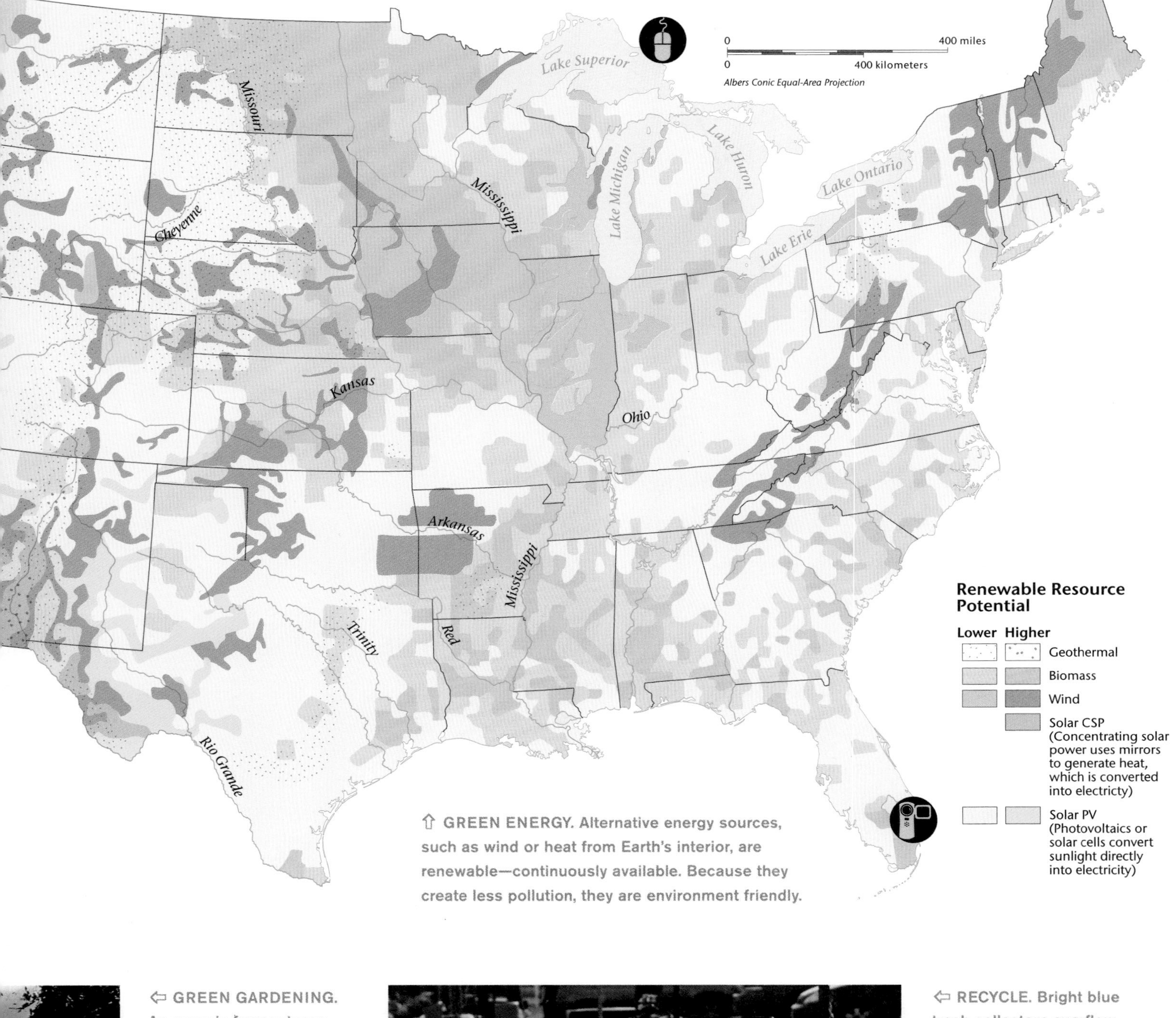

⇧ **GREEN ENERGY.** Alternative energy sources, such as wind or heat from Earth's interior, are renewable—continuously available. Because they create less pollution, they are environment friendly.

⇦ **GREEN GARDENING.** An organic farmer turns a compost pile with a pitchfork. Compost is a natural fertilizer made from decayed plant material. It is good for the environment because it reuses natural materials and avoids the use of chemicals that can pollute soil and water.

⇦ **RECYCLE.** Bright blue trash collectors overflow with plastic containers waiting to go to a recycling center. Citizen participation is an important step toward reducing landfill waste and restoring the health of the environment.

THE NATIONAL CAPITAL

THE BASICS

STATS

Area
68 sq mi (177 sq km)

Population
601,723

Ethnic/racial groups
50.7% African American; 38.5% white; 3.5% Asian; .3% Native American. Hispanic (any race) 9.1%

Industry
Government, services, tourism

Founded
1790–91

GEO WHIZ

License plates in the District of Columbia bear the slogan "Taxation Without Representation," reflecting the fact that residents of the District have no voting representative in either house of the U.S. Congress.

The flag of the District of Columbia, with its three red stars and two red stripes, is based on the shield in George Washington's family coat of arms.

In 1790 Benjamin Banneker, a free black, helped survey the land that would become the capital city. The 40 stones that were placed at one-mile intervals to mark the boundaries were set according to his celestial measurements.

WOOD THRUSH
AMERICAN BEAUTY ROSE

THE NATIONAL CAPITAL

Chosen as a compromise location between Northern and Southern interests and built on land ceded by Virginia and Maryland in the late 1700s, Washington, D.C., sits on a bank of the Potomac River. It is the seat of U.S. government and symbol of the country's history. Pierre L'Enfant, a French architect, was appointed by President George Washington to design the city, which is distinguished by a grid pattern cut by diagonal avenues. At the city's core is the National Mall, a broad park lined by monuments, museums, and stately government buildings.

FOGGY BOTTOM
Watergate Complex
George Washington University
Pan American Health Organization
John F. Kennedy Center for the Performing Arts
Department of State
Office of Personnel Management
General Services Administration
World Bank
Federal Reserve Board
Department of the Interior
National Academy of Sciences
Organization of American States
Vietnam Veterans Memorial
Vietnam Women's Memorial
Lincoln Memorial
Reflecting Pool
WEST POTOMAC PARK
Korean War Veterans Memorial
FRANKLIN DELANO ROOSEVELT MEMORIAL PARK
Franklin Delano Roosevelt Memorial
Georgetown Channel
Potomac River
THEODORE ROOSEVELT MEMORIAL BRIDGE
ARLINGTON MEMORIAL BRIDGE
ROCK CREEK AND POTOMAC PARKWAY
GEORGE WASHINGTON MEMORIAL PARKWAY
LADY BIRD JOHNSON PARK
WASHINGTON CIRCLE
K STREET
I (EYE) STREET
H STREET
F STREET
E STREET
C STREET
PENNSYLVANIA AVENUE
NEW HAMPSHIRE AVENUE
VIRGINIA AVENUE
CONSTITUTION AVENUE
INDEPENDENCE AVENUE
OHIO DRIVE
24TH STREET
23RD STREET
22ND STREET
21ST STREET
20TH STREET
19TH STREET
18TH STREET
D.C.
VA.
0 0.25 mile
0 0.25 kilometer

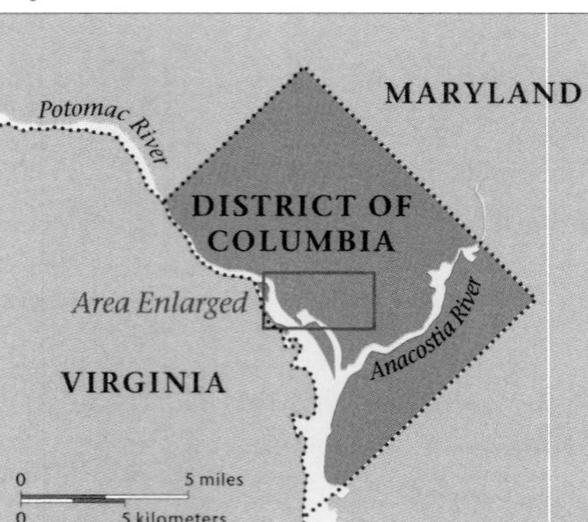

⇦ DISTRICT OF COLUMBIA. Originally on both sides of the Potomac River, the city returned land to Virginia in 1846.

⇦ GREAT LEADER. Abraham Lincoln, who was president during the Civil War and a strong opponent of slavery, is remembered in a monument that houses this seated statue at the west end of the National Mall.

THE NATIONAL CAPITAL

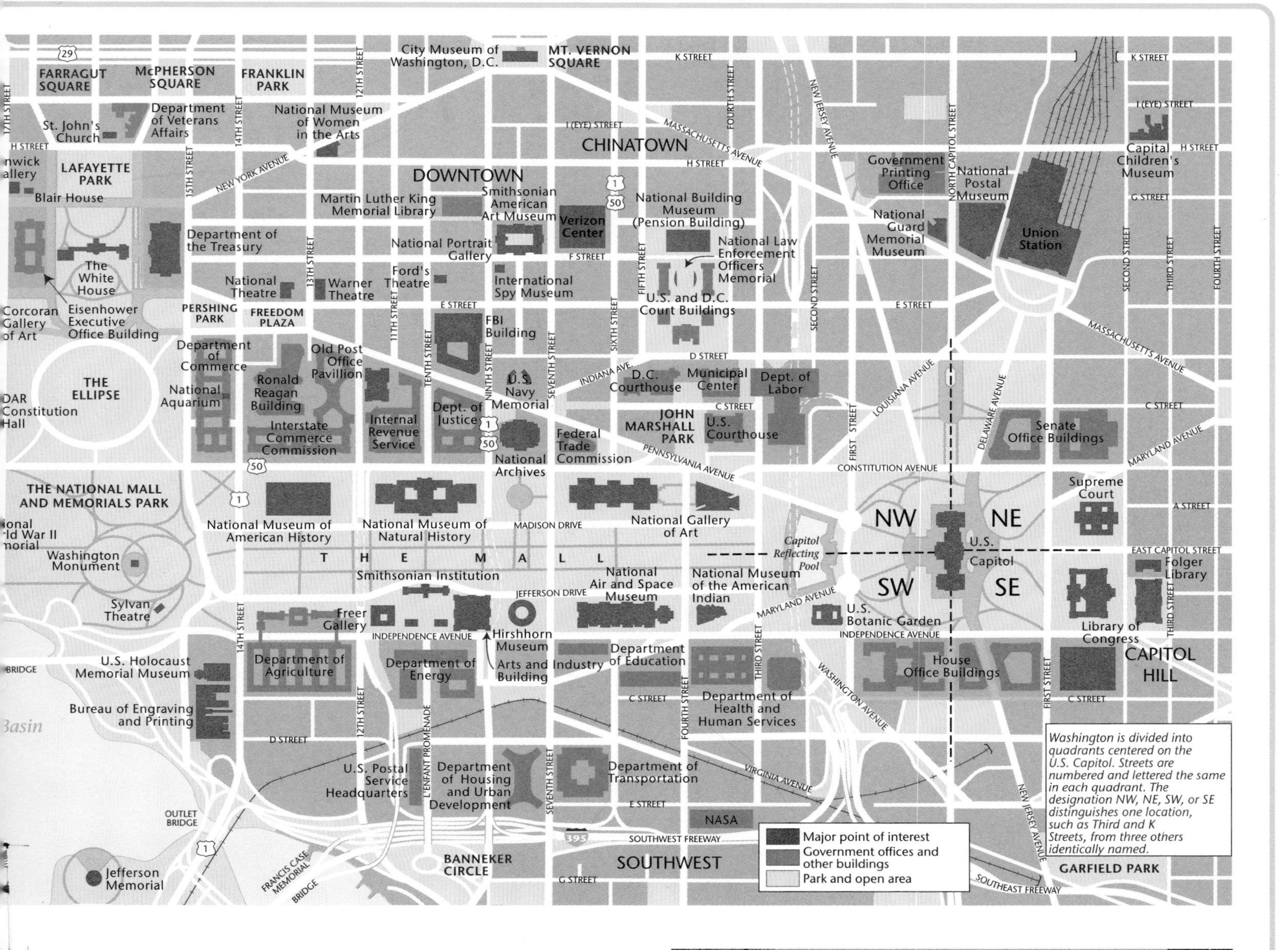

⇦ KEEPER OF HISTORY. The Smithsonian Institution, the world's largest museum, is actually made up of 19 museums. Established in 1846, the Smithsonian is sometimes referred to as the nation's attic because of its large collections.

⇧ NATIONAL ICON. The gleaming dome of the U.S. Capitol, home to the Senate and House of Representatives, is a familiar symbol of Washington's main business—the running of the country's government.

THE REGION

PHYSICAL

Total area
196,220 sq mi
(508,209 sq km)

Highest point
Mount Washington, NH
6,288 ft (1,917 m)

Lowest point
Sea level, shores of the Atlantic Ocean

Longest rivers
St. Lawrence, Susquehanna, Connecticut, Hudson

Largest lakes
Erie, Ontario, Champlain

Vegetation
Needleleaf, broadleaf, and mixed forest

Climate
Continental to mild, with cool to warm summers, cold winters, and moderate precipitation throughout the year

POLITICAL

Total population
61,988,726

States (11):
Connecticut, Delaware, Maine, Maryland, Massachusetts, New Hampshire, New Jersey, New York, Pennsylvania, Rhode Island, Vermont

Largest state
New York: 54,556 sq mi (141,300 sq km)

Smallest state
Rhode Island: 1,545 sq mi (4,002 sq km)

Most populous state
New York: 19,378,102

Least populous state
Vermont: 625,741

Largest city proper
New York, NY: 8,175,133

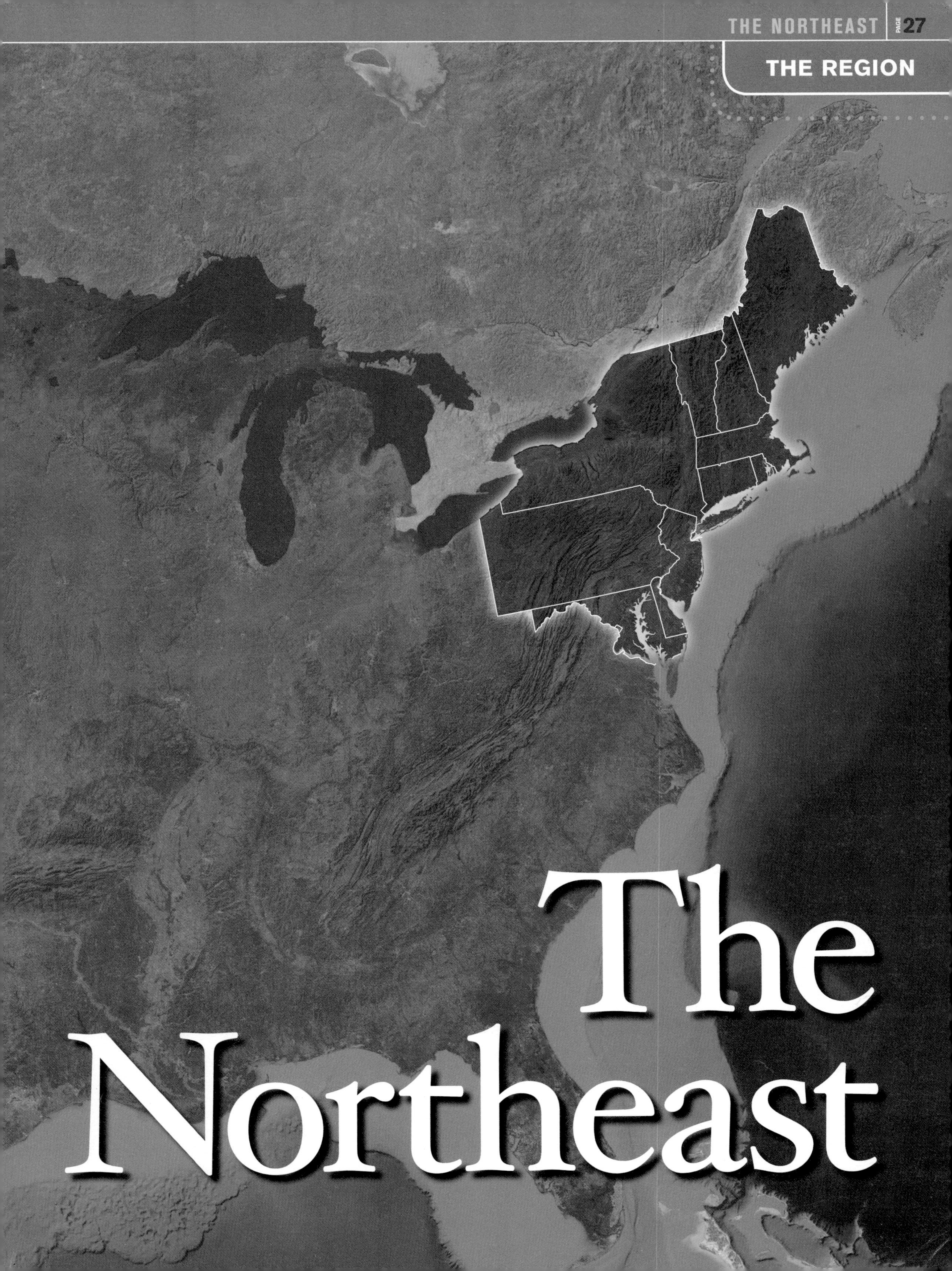

The Northeast

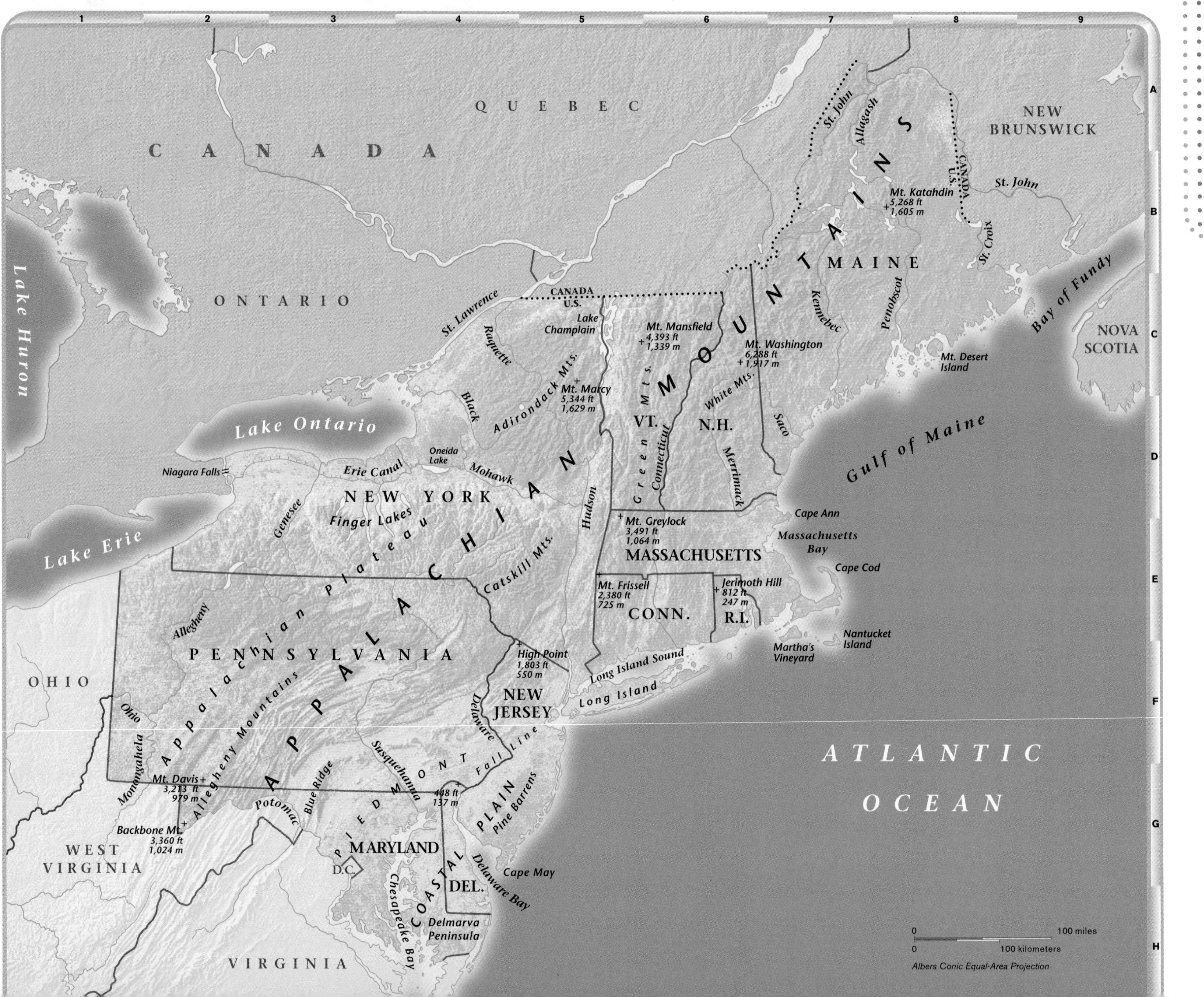
QUEBEC
CANADA
ONTARIO
Lake Huron
Lake Ontario
Lake Erie
NEW BRUNSWICK
NOVA SCOTIA
MAINE
St. John
Allagash
Mt. Katahdin
5,268 ft
1,605 m
CANADA
U.S.
St. Croix
Bay of Fundy
Kennebec
Penobscot
Mt. Desert Island
Mt. Washington
6,288 ft
1,917 m
White Mts.
Saco
N.H.
Merrimack
Gulf of Maine
Mt. Mansfield
4,393 ft
1,339 m
Green Mts.
VT.
Connecticut
St. Lawrence
Lake Champlain
Raquette
Black
Adirondack Mts.
Mt. Marcy
5,344 ft
1,629 m
Oneida Lake
Mohawk
Erie Canal
Niagara Falls
NEW YORK
Finger Lakes
Genesee
Hudson
Catskill Mts.
APPALACHIAN MOUNTAINS
Appalachian Plateau
Allegheny Mountains
Mt. Greylock
3,491 ft
1,064 m
MASSACHUSETTS
Cape Ann
Massachusetts Bay
Cape Cod
Mt. Frissell
2,380 ft
725 m
CONN.
Jerimoth Hill
812 ft
247 m
R.I.
Nantucket Island
Martha's Vineyard
Long Island Sound
Long Island
High Point
1,803 ft
550 m
NEW JERSEY
Delaware
PENNSYLVANIA
Allegheny
OHIO
Ohio
Monongahela
Mt. Davis
3,213 ft
979 m
Backbone Mt.
3,360 ft
1,024 m
WEST VIRGINIA
Potomac
Blue Ridge
PIEDMONT
Susquehanna
Fall Line
448 ft
137 m
COASTAL PLAIN
Pine Barrens
MARYLAND
D.C.
DEL.
Cape May
Delaware Bay
Chesapeake Bay
Delmarva Peninsula
VIRGINIA
ATLANTIC OCEAN
0
100 miles
0
100 kilometers
Albers Conic Equal-Area Projection
1
2
3
4
5
6
7
8
9
A
B
C
D
E
F
G
H

THE NORTHEAST
POLITICAL MAP

THE GRANITE STATE: NEW HAMPSHIRE

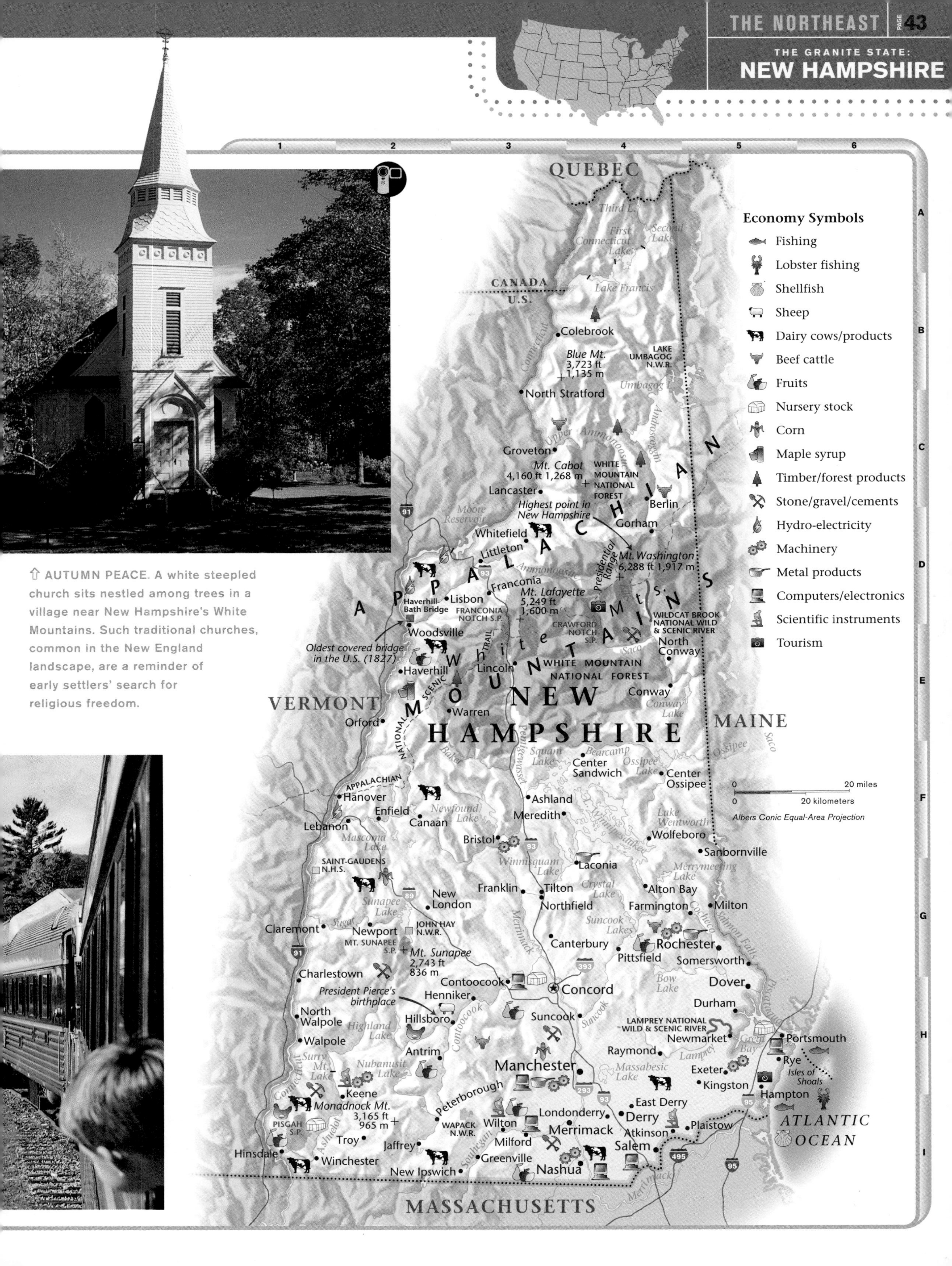

⇧ AUTUMN PEACE. A white steepled church sits nestled among trees in a village near New Hampshire's White Mountains. Such traditional churches, common in the New England landscape, are a reminder of early settlers' search for religious freedom.

THE GARDEN STATE:
NEW JERSEY

NEW JERSEY

THE BASICS

STATS

Area
8,721 sq mi (22,588 sq km)

Population
8,791,894

Capital
Trenton
Population 84,913

Largest city
Newark
Population 277,140

Ethnic/racial groups
68.6% white; 13.7% African American; 8.3% Asian; .3% Native American. Hispanic (any race) 17.1%.

Industry
Machinery, electronics, metal products, chemicals

Agriculture
Nursery stock, poultry and eggs, fruits and nuts, vegetables

Statehood
December 18, 1787; 3rd state

GEO WHIZ

Site of a one-time trash heap, the Meadowlands, a swampy lowland on either side of the Hackensack River, is now home to a major sports complex, bustling suburban neighborhoods, and congested roadways. Parts of it are isolated enough to allow days of quiet canoeing.

In 1930 New Jerseyite Charles Darrow developed the game Monopoly. He named Boardwalk and other streets in the game after those in Atlantic City.

The first dinosaur skeleton found in North America was excavated at Haddonfield in 1858. It was named *Hadrosaurus* in honor of its discovery site.

AMERICAN GOLDFINCH
VIOLET

Long before Europeans settled in New Jersey, the region was home to hunting and farming communities of Delaware Indians. The Dutch set up a trading post in northern New Jersey in 1618, calling it New Netherland, but yielded the land in 1664 to the English, who named it New Jersey after the English Channel Isle of Jersey. New Jersey saw more than 90 battles during the Revolutionary War. It became the 3rd U.S. state in 1787 and the first to sign the Bill of Rights. In the 19th century southern New Jersey remained largely agricultural, while the northern part of the state rapidly industrialize. Today highways and railroads link the state to urban centers along the Atlantic seaboard. More than 10,000 farms grow fruits and vegetables for nearby urban markets. Industries as well as services and trade are thriving. Beaches along the Atlantic coast attract thousands of tourists each year.

⇧ HOLD ON! New Jersey's Atlantic coast is lined with sandy beaches that attract vacationers from near and far. Amusement parks, such as this one in Wildwood, add to the fun.

⇨ HEADED TO MARKET. New Jersey is a leading producer of fresh fruits and vegetables. These organic vegetables are headed for urban markets in the Northeast.

⇦ SUBURBAN SPRAWL. With more than 90 percent of the state's population living in urban areas, housing developments, with close-set, look-alike houses, are a common characteristic of the suburban landscape. Residents commute to jobs in the city.

THE GARDEN STATE: NEW JERSEY

⇧ PLAY BALL! Fans pack the seats at Newark's Bear and Eagles Riverfront Stadium to watch a minor league baseball game. Built in 1999, the stadium is a part of Newark's plan to revitalize the downtown area, drawing people into the city.

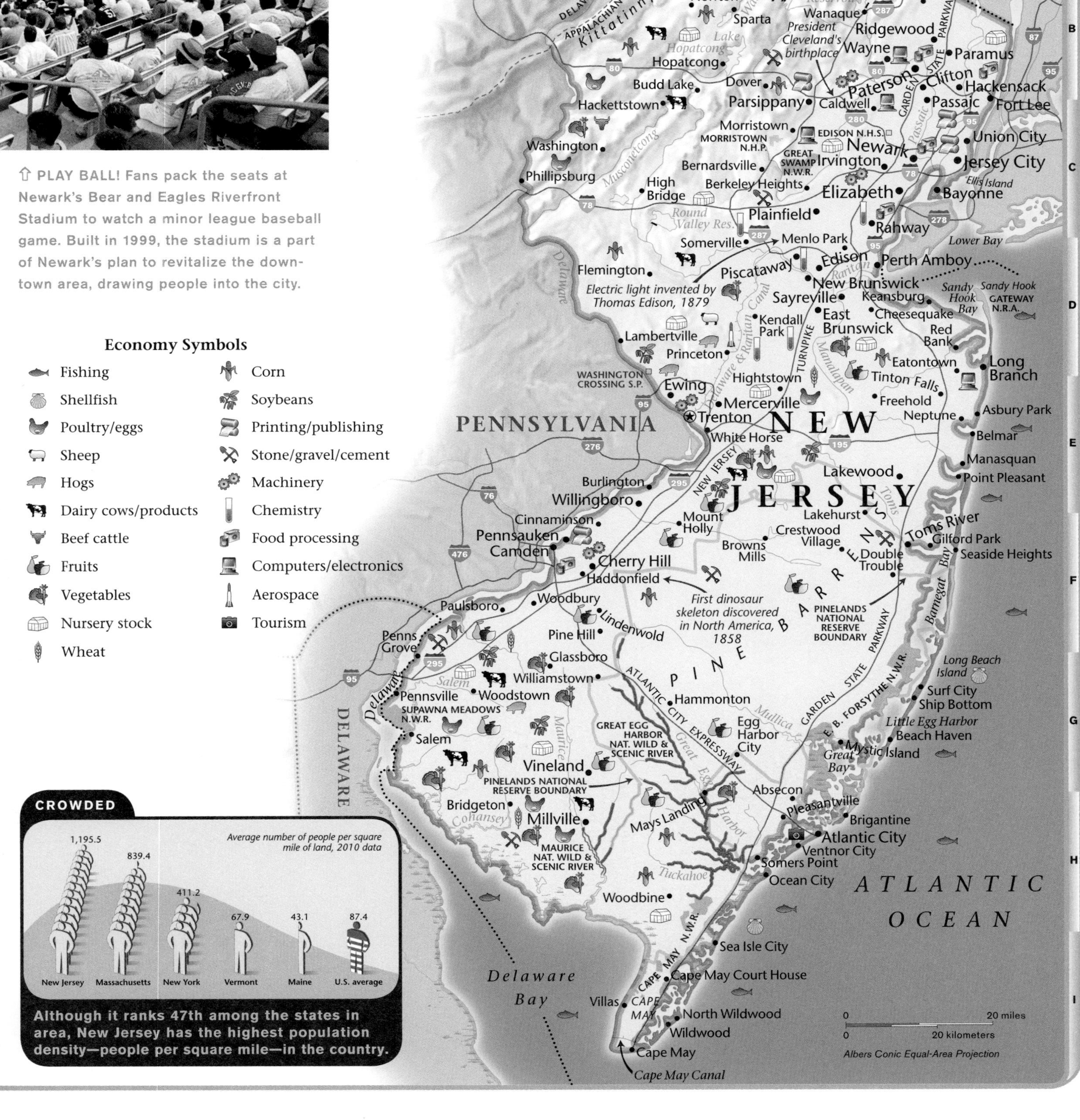

THE EMPIRE STATE:
NEW YORK

NEW YORK

When Englishman Henry Hudson explored New York's Hudson River Valley in 1609, the territory was already inhabited by large tribes of Native Americans, including the powerful Iroquois. In 1624 a Dutch trading company established the New Netherland colony, but after just 40 years the colony was taken over by the English and renamed for England's Duke of York. In 1788 New York became the 11th state. The state can be divided into two parts. The powerful port city of New York, center of trade and commerce and gateway to immigrants, is the largest city in the U.S. Its metropolitan area has more than 18 million people. Everything north of the city is simply referred to as "Upstate." Cities such as Buffalo and Rochester are industrial centers, while Ithaca and Syracuse boast major universities. Agriculture is also important in New York. With almost 5 million acres in cropland, the state is a major producer of dairy products, fruits, and vegetables.

THE BASICS

STATS

Area
54,556 sq mi (141,300 sq km)

Population
19,378,102

Capital
Albany
Population 97,856

Largest city
New York City
Population 8,175,133

Ethnic/racial groups
65.7% white; 15.9% African American; 7.3% Asian; .6% Native American. Hispanic (any race) 17.6%.

Industry
Printing and publishing, machinery, computer products, finance, tourism

Agriculture
Dairy products, cattle and other livestock, vegetables, nursery stock, apples

Statehood
July 26, 1788; 11th state

GEO WHIZ

Each year at Halloween the Headless Horseman rides again through the countryside of Sleepy Hollow as residents reenact Washington Irving's *The Legend of Sleepy Hollow*.

The Erie Canal, built in the 1820s between Albany and Buffalo, helped New York City become a worldwide trading center and opened the Midwest to development by linking the Hudson River and the Great Lakes.

Cooperstown, New York, home of the National Baseball Hall of Fame, takes its name from a town established in the late 1700s by the father of James Fenimore Cooper, author of such American classics as *The Last of the Mohicans* and *The Deerslayer*.

EASTERN BLUEBIRD
ROSE

⇧ LADY LIBERTY. Standing in New York Harbor, the Statue of Liberty, a gift from the people of France, is a symbol of freedom and democracy.

⇦ NATURAL WONDER. As many as 12 million tourists annually visit Niagara Falls on the U.S.-Canada border. Visitors in rain slickers trek through the mists below Bridal Veil Falls on the American side.

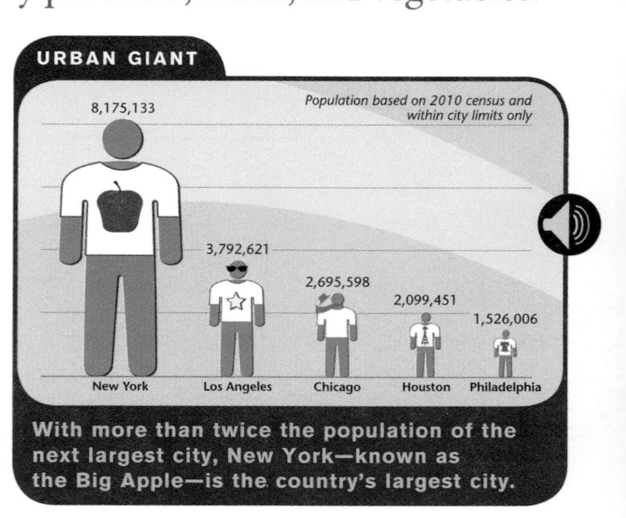

With more than twice the population of the next largest city, New York—known as the Big Apple—is the country's largest city.

THE EMPIRE STATE:
NEW YORK

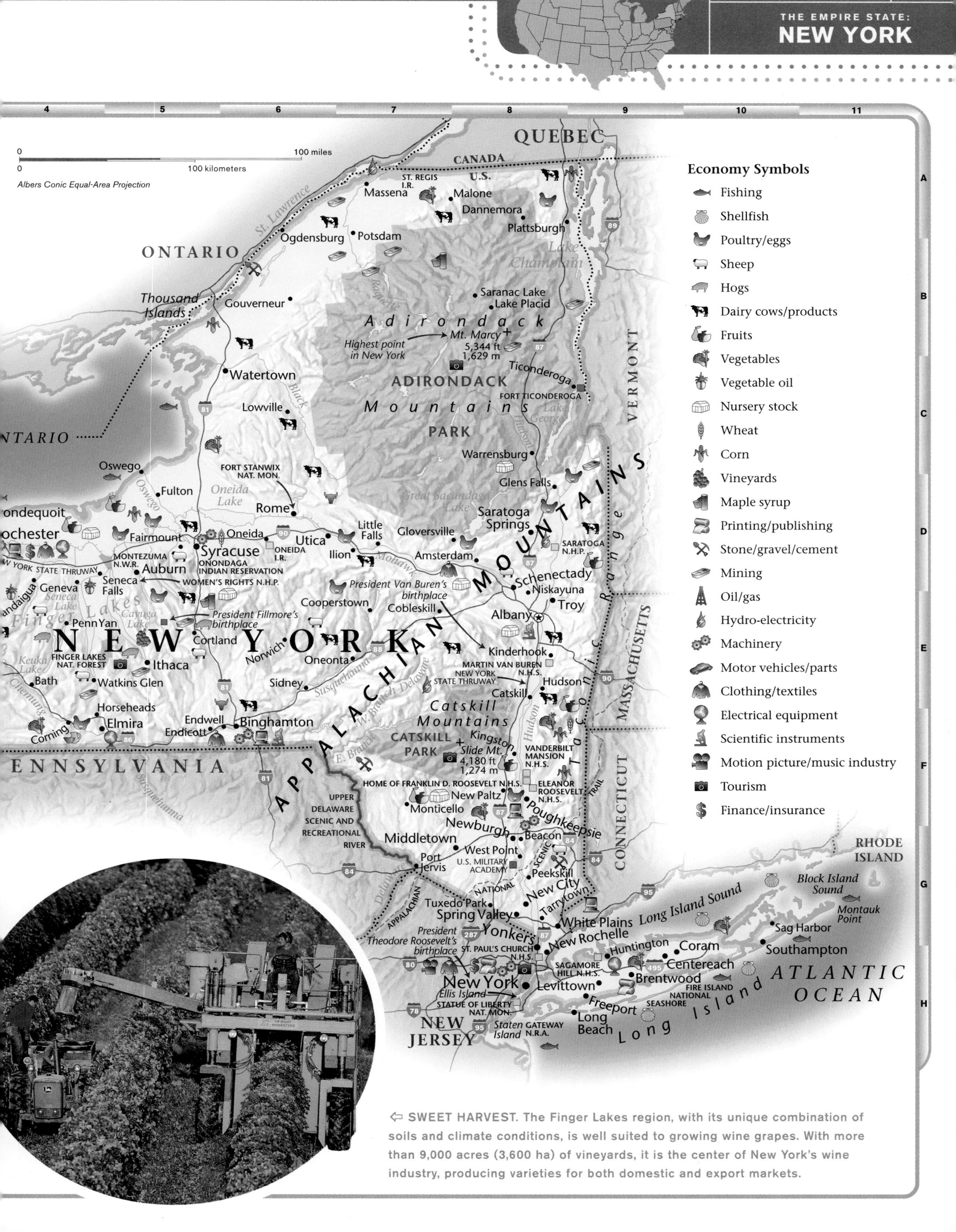

⇦ SWEET HARVEST. The Finger Lakes region, with its unique combination of soils and climate conditions, is well suited to growing wine grapes. With more than 9,000 acres (3,600 ha) of vineyards, it is the center of New York's wine industry, producing varieties for both domestic and export markets.

THE KEYSTONE STATE:
PENNSYLVANIA

PENNSYLVANIA

Pennsylvania, the 12th of England's 13 American colonies, was established in 1682 by Quaker William Penn and 360 settlers seeking religious freedom and fair government. The colony enjoyed abundant natural resources—dense woodlands, fertile soils, industrial minerals, and water power—that soon attracted Germans, Scotch-Irish, and other immigrants. Pennsylvania played a central role in the move for independence from Britain, and Philadelphia served as the new country's capital from 1790 to 1800. In the 19th century Philadelphia, in the east, and Pittsburgh, in the west, became booming centers of industrial growth. Philadelphia produced ships, locomotives, and textiles, while the iron and steel industry fueled Pittsburgh's growth. Jobs in industry as well as agriculture attracted immigrants from around the world. Today, Pennsylvania's economy has shifted toward information technology, health care, financial services, and tourism, but the state remains a leader in coal and steel production.

THE BASICS

STATS

Area
46,055 sq mi (119,283 sq km)

Population
12,702,379

Capital
Harrisburg
Population 49,528

Largest city
Philadelphia
Population 1,526,006

Ethnic/racial groups
81.9% white; 10.8% African American; 2.7% Asian; .2% Native American. Hispanic (any race) 5.7%.

Industry
Machinery, printing and publishing, forest products, metal products

Agriculture
Dairy products, poultry and eggs, mushrooms, cattle, hogs, grains

Statehood
December 12, 1787; 2nd state

GEO WHIZ

If you are into guitars or other acoustic instruments, you will want to put the Martin Guitar Company, in Nazareth, on your list of places to visit. It has been handcrafting these instruments for musicians all over the world for more than 150 years.

For more than a century, the streets of Philadelphia have been transformed on New Year's Day as some 15,000 revelers dressed in sequined and feathered costumes "strut their stuff" to the sound of string-band music in the Mummers Parade past millions of onlookers.

RUFFED GROUSE
MOUNTAIN LAUREL

⇧ LET FREEDOM RING. The Liberty Bell, cast in 1753 by Pennsylvania craftsmen, hangs silent in Philadelphia. Because of a crack, it is no longer rung.

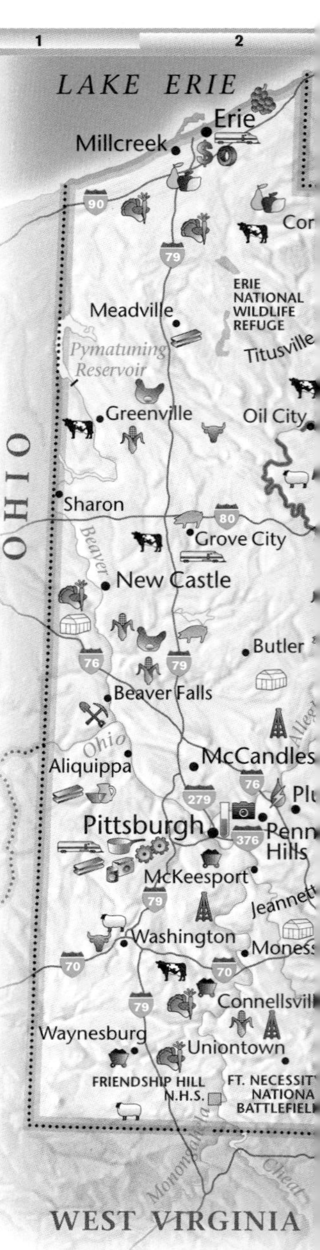

⇨ RIVER TOWN. Pittsburgh, one of the largest inland ports in the U.S., was established in 1758 where the Monongahela and Allegheny Rivers meet to form the Ohio River. Once a booming steel town, Pittsburgh is now a center of finance, medicine, and education.

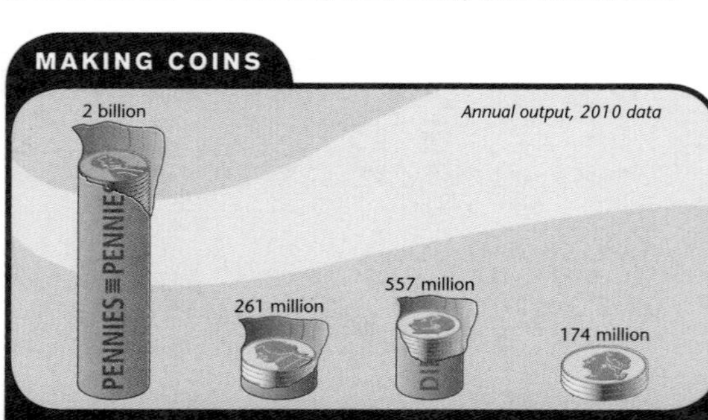

The 1792 Coinage Act established the first U.S. mint in Philadelphia. It is still one of the country's main coin-producing facilities.

THE KEYSTONE STATE:
PENNSYLVANIA

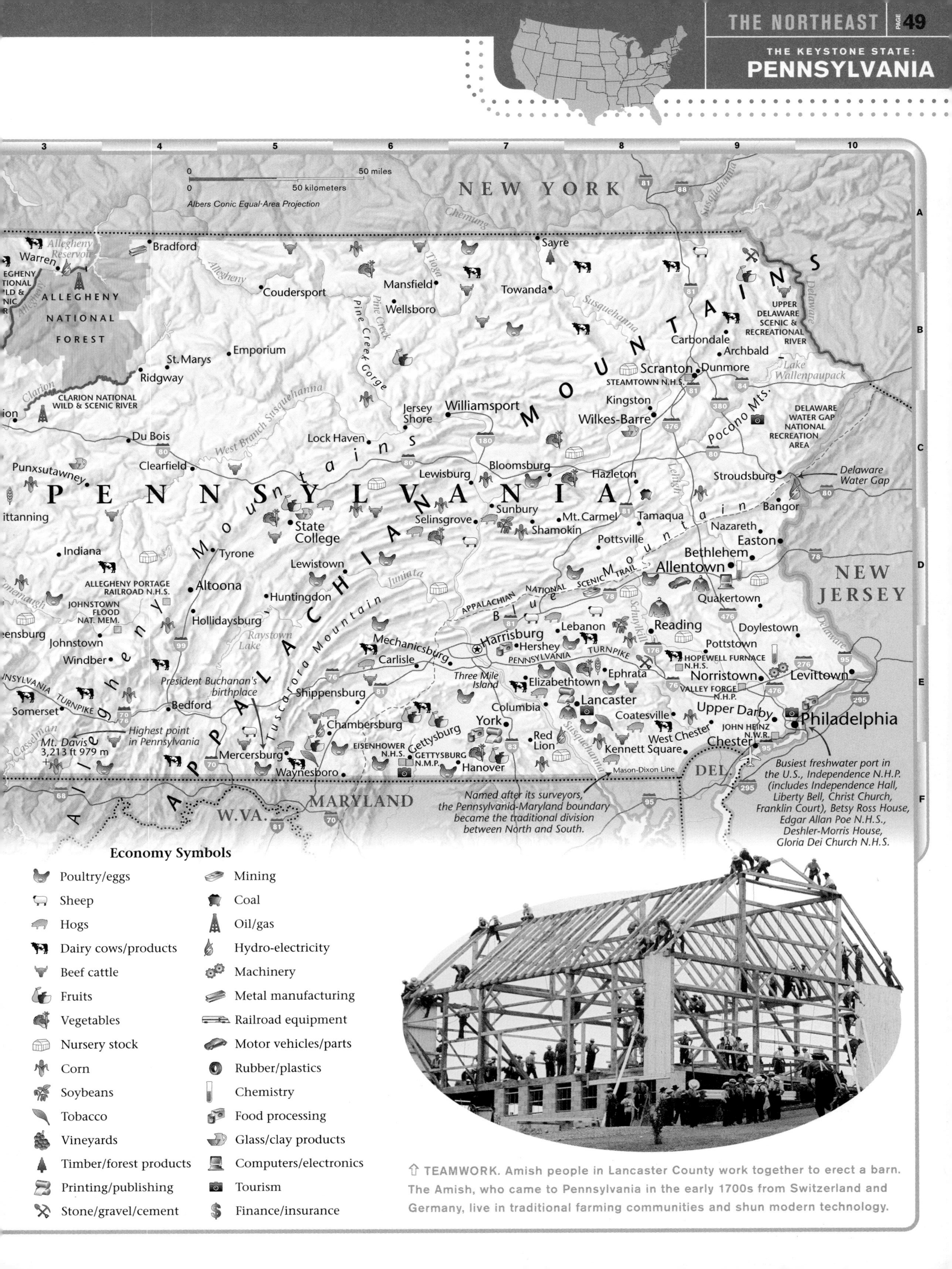

Economy Symbols

- Poultry/eggs
- Sheep
- Hogs
- Dairy cows/products
- Beef cattle
- Fruits
- Vegetables
- Nursery stock
- Corn
- Soybeans
- Tobacco
- Vineyards
- Timber/forest products
- Printing/publishing
- Stone/gravel/cement
- Mining
- Coal
- Oil/gas
- Hydro-electricity
- Machinery
- Metal manufacturing
- Railroad equipment
- Motor vehicles/parts
- Rubber/plastics
- Chemistry
- Food processing
- Glass/clay products
- Computers/electronics
- Tourism
- Finance/insurance

⇧ TEAMWORK. Amish people in Lancaster County work together to erect a barn. The Amish, who came to Pennsylvania in the early 1700s from Switzerland and Germany, live in traditional farming communities and shun modern technology.

THE OCEAN STATE:
RHODE ISLAND

RHODE ISLAND

THE BASICS

STATS

Area
1,545 sq mi (4,002 sq km)

Population
1,052,567

Capital
Providence
Population 178,042

Largest city
Providence
Population 178,042

Ethnic/racial groups
81.4% white; 5.7% African American; 2.9% Asian; .6% Native American. Hispanic (any race) 12.4%.

Industry
Health services, business services, silver and jewelry products, metal products

Agriculture
Nursery stock, vegetables, dairy products, eggs

Statehood
May 29, 1790; 13th state

GEO WHIZ

Pawtucket is one of several communities in Rhode Island that have become home to a growing number of people from Cape Verde. Drought has forced people from this African country to find a new place to live. Massachusetts and North Dakota are the only other states with measurable Cape Verdean populations.

Wild coyotes are living and thriving on islands in Narragansett Bay. Researchers have outfitted some of the animals with radio collars so that their numbers and whereabouts can be tracked online—even by schoolkids.

RHODE ISLAND RED
VIOLET

In 1524 Italian navigator Giovanni Verrazzano was the first European explorer to visit Rhode Island, but place-names such as Quonochontaug and Narragansett tell of an earlier Native American population. In 1636 Roger Williams, seeking greater religious freedom, left Massachusetts and established the first European settlement in what was to become the colony of Rhode Island. In the years following the Revolutionary War, Rhode Island pressed for fairness in trade, taxes, and representation in Congress, as well as greater freedom of worship, before becoming the 13th state. By the 19th century, Rhode Island had become an important center of trade and textile factories, attracting many immigrants from Europe. In addition to commercial activities, Rhode Island's coastline became a popular vacation retreat for the wealthy. Today, Rhode Island, like many other states, has seen its economy shift toward high-tech jobs and service industries. It is also promoting its coastline and bays, as well as its rich history, to attract tourists.

⇧ CLUES TO THE PAST. Fossils embedded in rocks left behind 10,000 years ago by retreating glaciers tell of Block Island's past.

⇦ SETTING SAIL. Newport Harbor invites sailors of all ages. From 1930 to 1983, the prestigious America's Cup Yacht Race took place in the waters off Newport. Today, the town provides 900 moorings for boats of all types.

THE OCEAN STATE: RHODE ISLAND

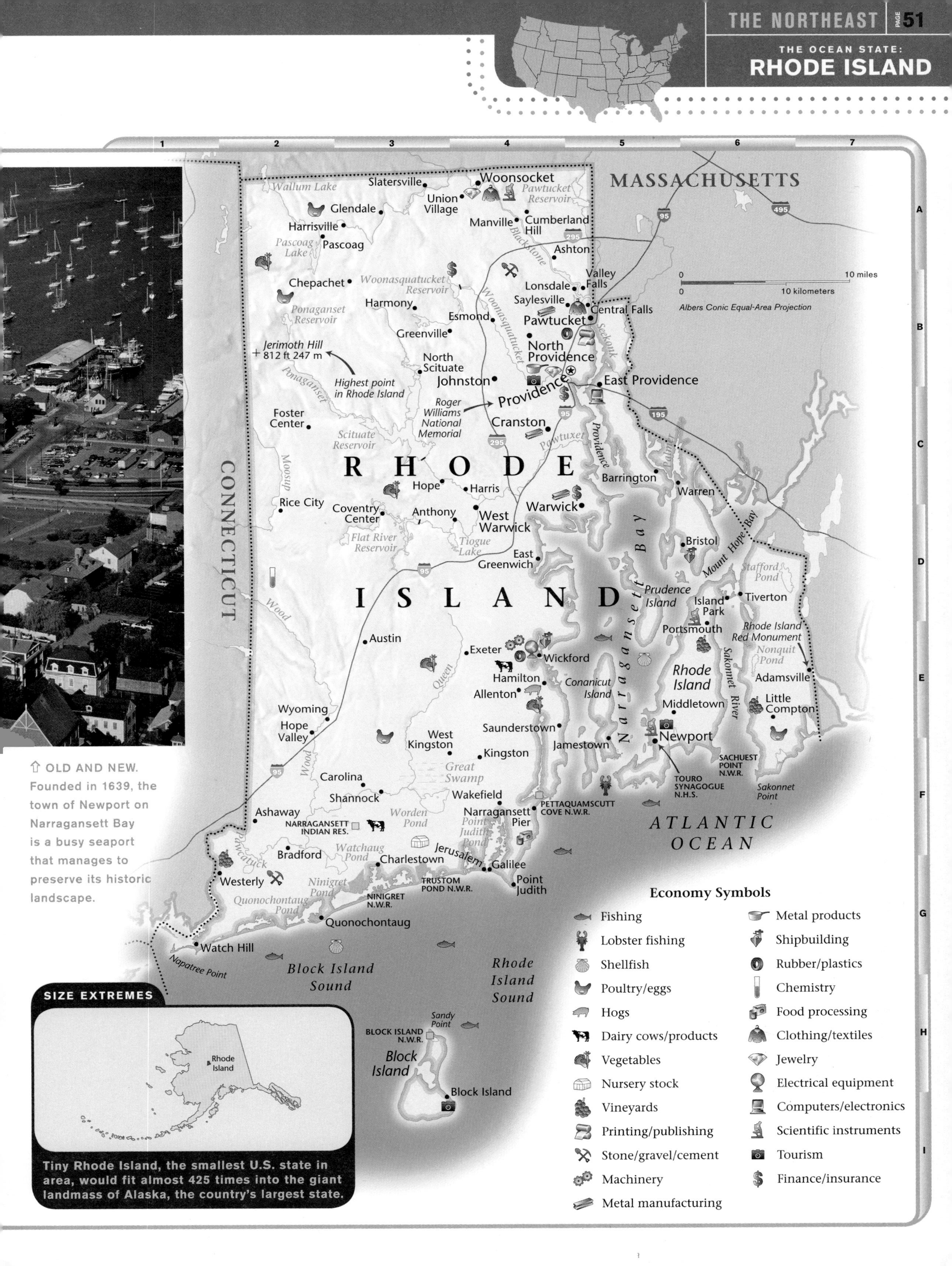

⇧ OLD AND NEW. Founded in 1639, the town of Newport on Narragansett Bay is a busy seaport that manages to preserve its historic landscape.

SIZE EXTREMES

Tiny Rhode Island, the smallest U.S. state in area, would fit almost 425 times into the giant landmass of Alaska, the country's largest state.

THE GREEN MOUNTAIN STATE:
VERMONT

THE BASICS

STATS

Area
9,614 sq mi (24,901 sq km)

Population
625,741

Capital
Montpelier
Population 7,855

Largest city
Burlington
Population 42,417

Ethnic/racial groups
95.3% white; 1.3% Asian; 1.0% African American; .4% Native American. Hispanic (any race) 1.5%.

Industry
Health services, tourism, finance, real estate, computer components, electrical parts, printing and publishing, machine tools

Agriculture
Dairy products, maple products, apples

Statehood
March 4, 1791; 14th state

GEO WHIZ

Barre is famous for producing granite gravestones. The tombstones of President Harry S. Truman, industrialist John D. Rockefeller, Sr., songwriter Stephen Foster, and fast-food-chain founder Col. Harland Sanders are all made of Barre Gray granite, as are the steps of the U.S. Capitol in Washington, D.C.

Burlington is the home of Ben & Jerry's ice cream. The company gives its leftovers to local farmers, who feed it to their hogs. The hogs seem to like every flavor except Mint Oreo.

From 1777 until it became a state in 1791, Vermont was an independent country. It had its own postal and monetary systems.

Vermont, the third-largest state in New England, is the only state in the region that does not border the Atlantic Ocean.

HERMIT THRUSH
RED CLOVER

VERMONT

When French explorer Jacques Cartier arrived in Vermont in 1535, Native Americans living in woodland villages had been there for hundreds of years. Settled first by the French in 1666 and then by the English in 1724, the territory of Vermont became an area of conflict between these colonial powers. The French finally withdrew, but conflict continued between New York and New Hampshire, both of which wanted to take over Vermont. The people of Vermont declared their independence in 1777, and Vermont became the 14th U.S. state in 1791. Vermont's name, which means "Green Mountain," comes from the extensive forests that cover much of the state and provide the basis for furniture and pulp industries. Vermont also boasts the world's largest granite quarry and the largest underground marble quarry, both of which produce valuable building materials. Tourism and recreation are also important in Vermont. Lakes, rivers, and mountain trails are popular summer attractions, while snow-covered mountains attract skiers throughout the winter.

⇧ LIQUID GOLD. In spring, sap from maple trees is collected in buckets by drilling a hole in the tree trunk—called "tapping." The sap is boiled to remove water, then filtered, and finally bottled.

⇧ WINTER WONDERLAND. One of the snowiest places in the Northeast, Jay Peak averages 355 inches (900 cm) of snow each year. With 76 trails, the mountain, near Vermont's border with Canada, attracts beginner and expert skiers from near and far.

SWEET DELIGHT

Thousands of gallons (liters), 2011 data

Vermont	New York	Maine	Wisconsin	Pennsylvania	Ohio	Michigan
1,140 (4,315)	564 (2,135)	360 (1,363)	155 (587)	128 (485)	125 (473)	123 (466)

Vermont is the country's leading producer of maple syrup. The syrup is all natural, with no added ingredients or preservatives, just boiled sap collected from maple trees.

THE GREEN MOUNTAIN STATE:
VERMONT

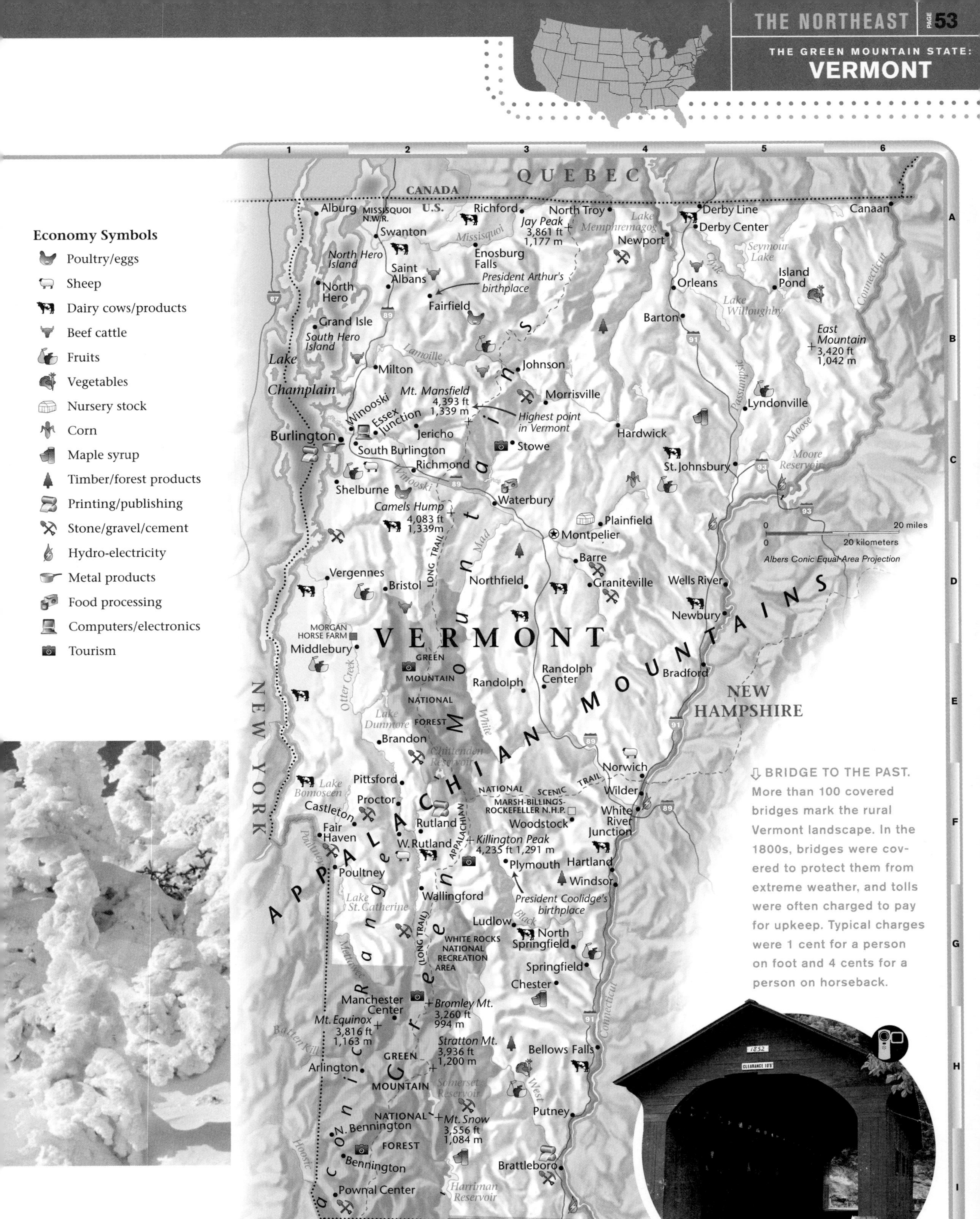

⇩ BRIDGE TO THE PAST. More than 100 covered bridges mark the rural Vermont landscape. In the 1800s, bridges were covered to protect them from extreme weather, and tolls were often charged to pay for upkeep. Typical charges were 1 cent for a person on foot and 4 cents for a person on horseback.

THE REGION

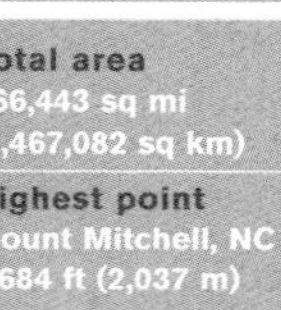

PHYSICAL

Total area
566,443 sq mi
(1,467,082 sq km)

Highest point
Mount Mitchell, NC
6,684 ft (2,037 m)

Lowest point
New Orleans, LA
8 ft (2 m) below sea level

Longest rivers
Mississippi, Arkansas,
Red, Ohio

Largest lakes
Okeechobee, Pontchartrain,
Kentucky (reservoir)

Vegetation
Needleleaf, broadleaf, and
mixed forest

Climate
Continental to mild, ranging
from cool summers in the
north to humid, subtropical
conditions in the south

POLITICAL

Total population
78,385,623

States (12):
Alabama, Arkansas, Florida, Georgia,
Kentucky, Louisiana, Mississippi, North
Carolina, South Carolina, Tennessee,
Virginia, West Virginia

Largest state
Florida: 65,755 sq mi (170,304 sq km)

Smallest state
West Virginia: 24,230 sq mi (62,755 sq km)

Most populous state
Florida: 18,801,310

Least populous state
West Virginia: 1,852,994

Largest city proper
Jacksonville, FL: 821,784

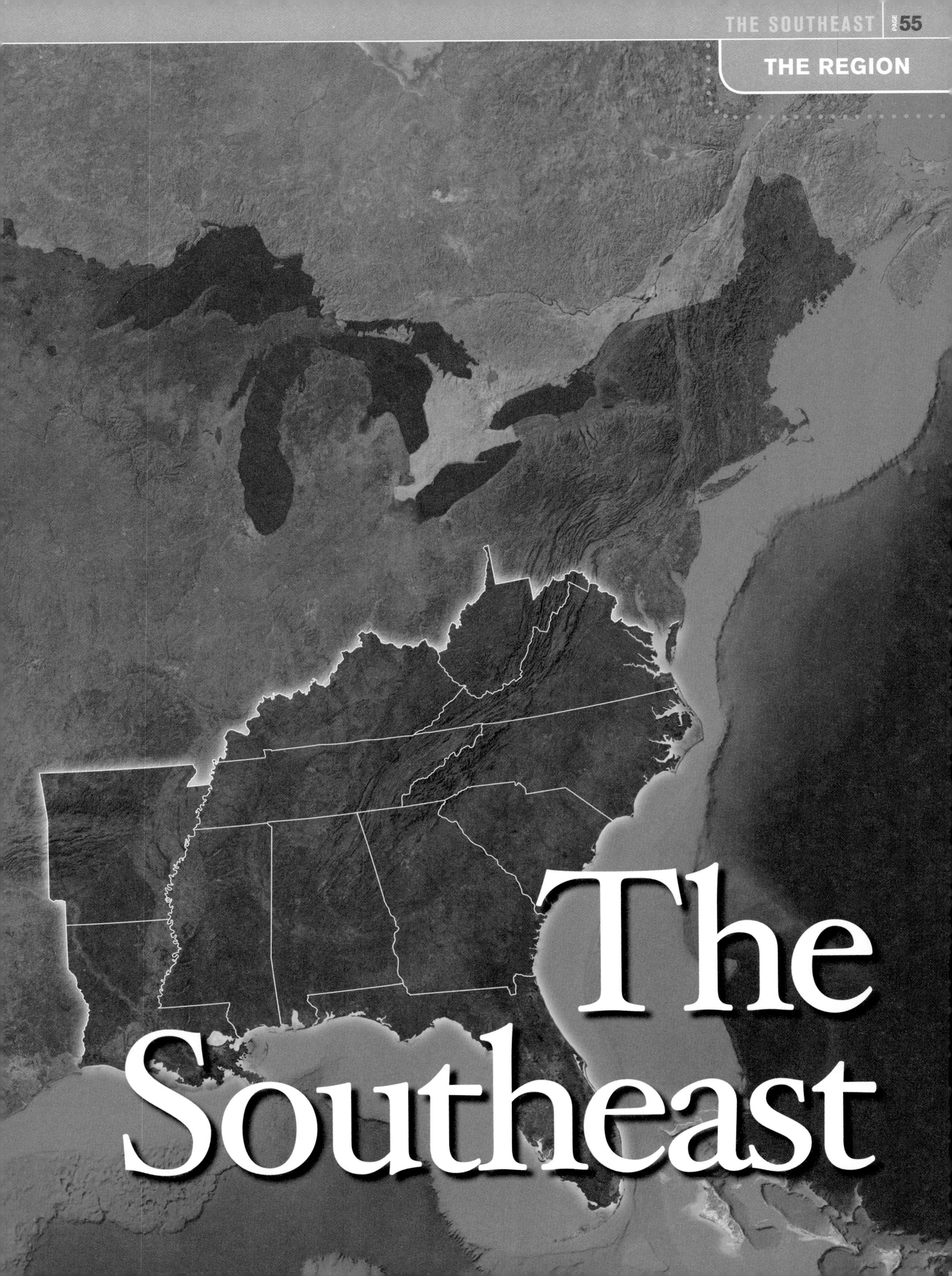
The Southeast

PHYSICAL MAP

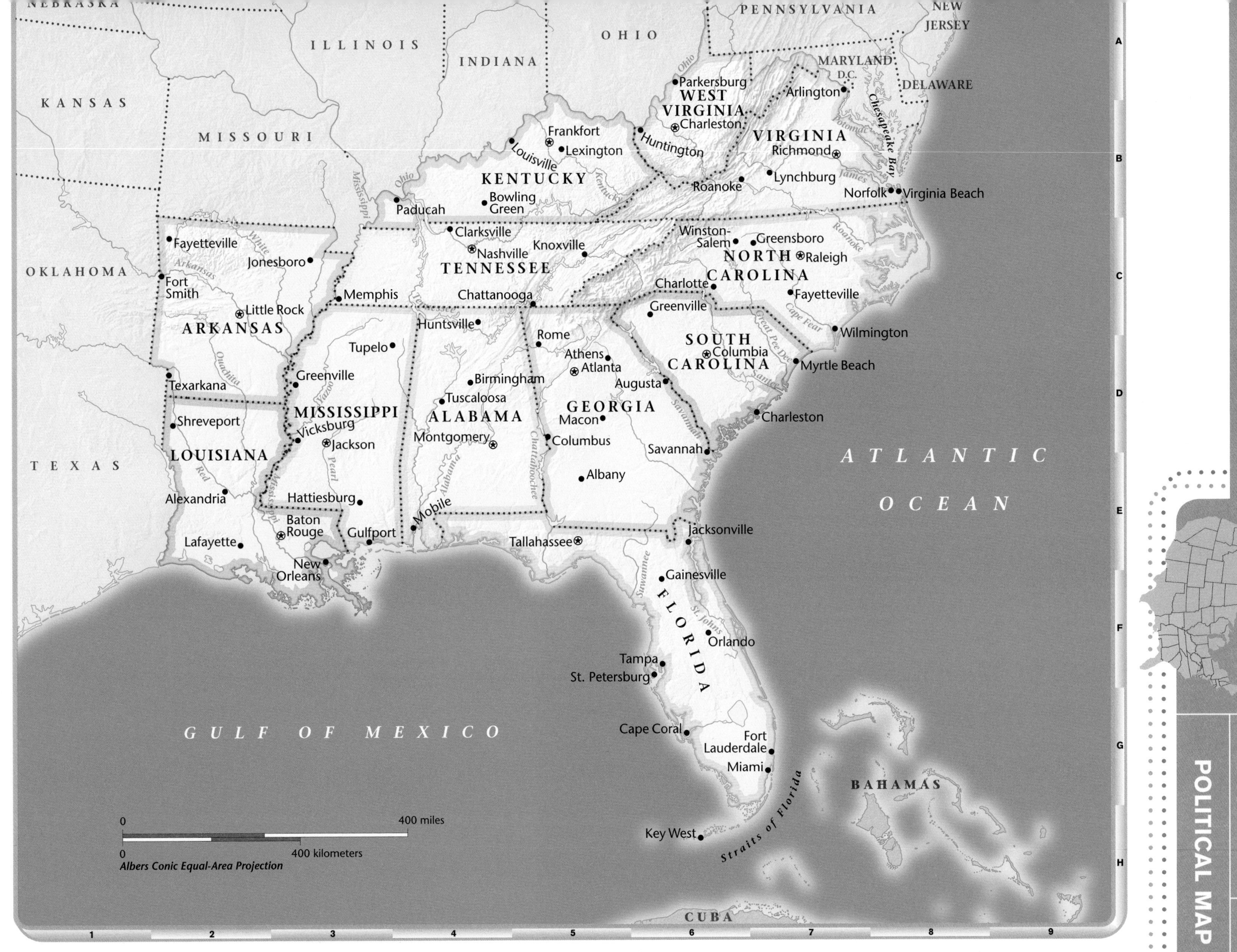

THE SOUTHEAST
POLITICAL MAP
PAGE 57

ABOUT THE **SOUTHEAST**

⇨ OPEN WIDE. An American alligator in Florida's Big Cypress Swamp shows off sharp teeth. These large reptiles live mainly in freshwater swamps and marshes in coastal areas of the Southeast. Adult males average 14 feet (4 m) in length.

The Southeast

TRADITION MEETS TECHNOLOGY

From deeply weathered mountains in West Virginia to warm, humid wetlands in south Florida and the Mississippi River's sprawling delta in southern Louisiana, the Southeast is marked by great physical diversity. The region's historical roots are in agriculture—especially cotton and tobacco. The Civil War brought economic and political upheaval in the mid-19th century, but today the Southeast is part of the Sunbelt, where 6 of the top 20 metropolitan areas of the U.S. are found and where high-tech industries are redefining the way people earn a living and the way the region is connected to the global economy.

⇨ ENCHANTED KINGDOM. Fireworks light up the night sky above Cinderella's Castle at Walt Disney World near Orlando, Florida. The park, which accounts for 6 percent of all jobs in central Florida, attracts millions of tourists from around the world each year.

⇧ SOCIAL CONSCIENCE. Members of the Big Nine Social Aid and Pleasure Club of New Orleans's Lower Ninth Ward march in a parade through a neighborhood devastated by Hurricane Katrina. Such clubs, which date back to late-19th-century benevolent societies, bring support and hope to communities in need.

⇧ VIEW FROM ABOVE. Cyclists look out from a rocky ledge across West Virginia's Germany Valley. The area took its name from German immigrants who moved there in the mid-1700s from North Carolina and Pennsylvania and established farming villages.

WHERE THE PICTURES ARE

Banjo playing p. 69
Horse race p. 68
Black bear family p. 78
Motorboats p. 79
Grand Ole Opry p. 79
Indian Woman p. 75
Space camp p. 60
Race car p. 59
Rockclimber p. 62
Bird-watchers p. 62
Diamond hunter p. 63
Paddleboat p. 72
Blues guitarist p. 72
Catfish p. 73
Oak Alley Plantation p. 70
Katrina parade p. 58
Shrimp fisherman p. 70
Atlanta p. 66
Oil rig p. 60
Peanuts p. 66
Manatee p. 64
Cinderella's Castle p. 58, Girl in parade p. 64
River rafting p. 83
Coal miner p. 82
Cyclists on outcrop pp. 58-59
Harpers Ferry p. 82
Luray Caverns p. 80
Cyclists pp. 80-81
Dice p. 80
Wright Brothers Memorial p. 74
Blackbeard's cannon p. 59
Boys playing basketball p. 74
Beach scene p. 76
Wild turkey p. 77
Historic Charleston pp. 76-77
Aerial of Sea Islands p. 66
Shuttle launch pp. 64-65
Alligator p. 58

⇨ CAR STARS. For more than 50 years, auto racing has been a leading sport in the U.S., especially in the Southeast. The International Motorsports Hall of Fame, located adjacent to the Talledega Superspeedway in Alabama, features racing cars, motorcycles, and vintage cars.

⇦ PIRATE'S DEFENSE. This 4.5-foot (1.4-m) cast-iron cannon was recovered from the wreck of the *Queen Anne's Revenge* off North Carolina's coast. The vessel, which probably belonged to the notorious pirate Blackbeard, grounded on a sandbar and sank in 1718 near Cape Lookout.

THE HEART OF DIXIE STATE:
ALABAMA

ALABAMA

Alabama has a colorful story. The French established the first permanent European settlement at Mobile Bay in 1702, but different groups—British, Native Americans, and U.S. settlers—struggled over control of the land for more than 100 years. In 1819 Alabama became the 22nd state, but in 1861 it joined the Confederacy. During the Civil War, Montgomery was the capital of the secessionist South for a time. After the war Alabama struggled to rebuild its agriculture-based economy. By 1900 the state was producing more than one million bales of cotton annually. In the mid-20th century, Alabama was at the center of the civil rights movement, which pressed for equal rights for all people regardless of race or social status. Key players included Martin Luther King, Jr., and Rosa Parks. Modern industries, including the NASA space program, have given the state's economy a big boost. In 2002 assembly plants built by automakers from Asia created thousands of new jobs.

⇧ UNDERWATER RESOURCE. A massive drill descends from an offshore oil rig to tap petroleum deposits beneath the water of the Gulf of Mexico off Alabama's shore.

THE BASICS

STATS

Area
52,419 sq mi (135,765 sq km)

Population
4,779,736

Capital
Montgomery
Population 205,764

Largest city
Birmingham
Population 212,237

Ethnic/racial groups
68.5% white; 26.2% African American; 1.1% Asian; .6% Native American. Hispanic (any race) 3.9%.

Industry
Retail and wholesale trade, services, government, finance, insurance, real estate, transportation, construction, communication

Agriculture
Fruits and vegetables, dairy products, cattle, forest products, commercial fishing

Statehood
December 14, 1819; 22nd state

GEO WHIZ

Condoleezza Rice, the first African-American woman to serve as U.S. Secretary of State, and Rosa Parks, whose refusal to give up her seat on a Montgomery bus earned her the title "mother of the modern-day civil rights movement," were both born in Alabama: Rice in Birmingham and Parks in Tuskegee.

Russell Cave, near Bridgeport, was home to prehistoric peoples for more than 10,000 years. In 1961 a national monument was established on land donated by the National Geographic Society. Today, visitors can take guided tours of the cave and see the kinds of tools and weapons its early inhabitants used.

In 2004 Hurricane Ivan, one of the worst storms to batter Alabama's gulf coast since 1900, struck Orange Beach.

NORTHERN FLICKER
CAMELLIA

ON THE ROAD

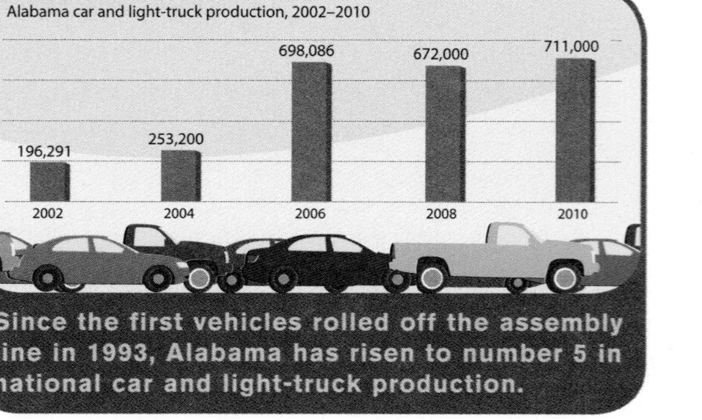

Since the first vehicles rolled off the assembly line in 1993, Alabama has risen to number 5 in national car and light-truck production.

⇧ ROCKET POWER. Students inspect giant booster rockets during Space Camp at Marshall Space Flight Center, in Huntsville, Alabama. The center is one of NASA's largest installations, providing support to space shuttle missions and the International Space Station.

THE HEART OF DIXIE STATE: ALABAMA

THE NATURAL STATE:
ARKANSAS

ARKANSAS

The land that is Arkansas was explored by the Spanish in 1541 and later by the French, but it came under U.S. control with the Louisiana Purchase in 1803. As settlers arrived, Native Americans were pushed out, and cotton fields spread across the fertile valleys of the Arkansas and Mississippi Rivers. Arkansas became the 25th state in 1836, but joined the Confederacy in 1861. Following the war, Arkansas faced hard times, and many people moved away in search of jobs. Today, agriculture remains an important part of the economy. Rice has replaced cotton as the state's main crop, and poultry and grain production are also important. Natural gas, in the northwestern part of the state, and petroleum, along the southern border with Louisiana, are key mining products in Arkansas. The state is headquarters for Wal-Mart, the world's largest retail chain, and tourism is growing as visitors are attracted to the natural beauty of the Ozark and Ouachita Mountains.

THE BASICS

STATS

Area
53,179 sq mi (137,732 sq km)

Population
2,915,918

Capital
Little Rock
Population 193,524

Largest city
Little Rock
Population 193,524

Ethnic/racial groups
77.0% white; 15.4% African American; 1.2% Asian; .8% Native American. Hispanic (any race) 6.4%.

Industry
Services, food processing, paper products, transportation, metal products, machinery, electronics

Agriculture
Poultry and eggs, rice, soybeans, cotton, wheat

Statehood
June 15, 1836; 25th state

GEO WHIZ

In 1924 Arkansas's Crater of Diamonds State Park yielded the largest natural diamond ever found in the United States—a 40.23-carat whopper named "Uncle Sam." A 13-year-old girl from Missouri found a 2.93-carat diamond there in 2007.

Since 1936 Stuttgart has been the site of the annual World Championship Duck Calling Contest. The first winner took home a grand total of $6.60. Today, the prize package is worth more than $15,000.

The city of Texarkana is divided by the Arkansas-Texas border. It has two governments, one for each state.

MOCKINGBIRD
APPLE BLOSSOM

⇧ HOLD ON! A rock climber clings to a sandstone cliff in northwest Arkansas, where the Ozark and Ouachita Mountains make up the Interior Highlands of the United States. The Ouachita are folded mountains, but the Ozarks are really a deeply eroded plateau.

SUPERSTORE

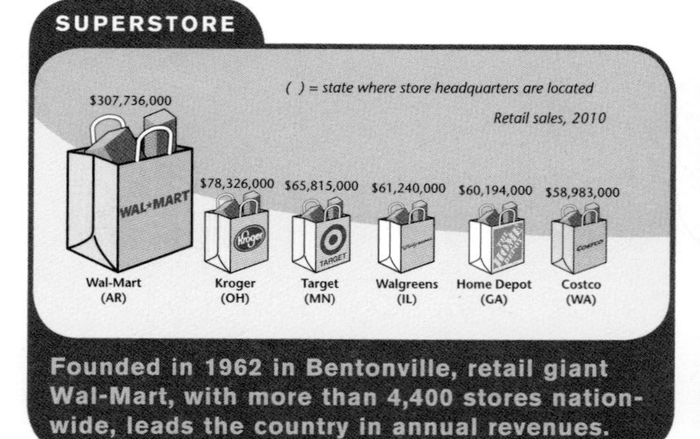

Founded in 1962 in Bentonville, retail giant Wal-Mart, with more than 4,400 stores nationwide, leads the country in annual revenues.

⇦ BIRDWATCHERS. Biologists and volunteers scan the treetops for a rare ivory-billed woodpecker in the White River National Wildlife Refuge. Established in 1935 along the White River near where it joins the Mississippi, the refuge provides a protected habitat for migratory birds.

THE NATURAL STATE:
ARKANSAS

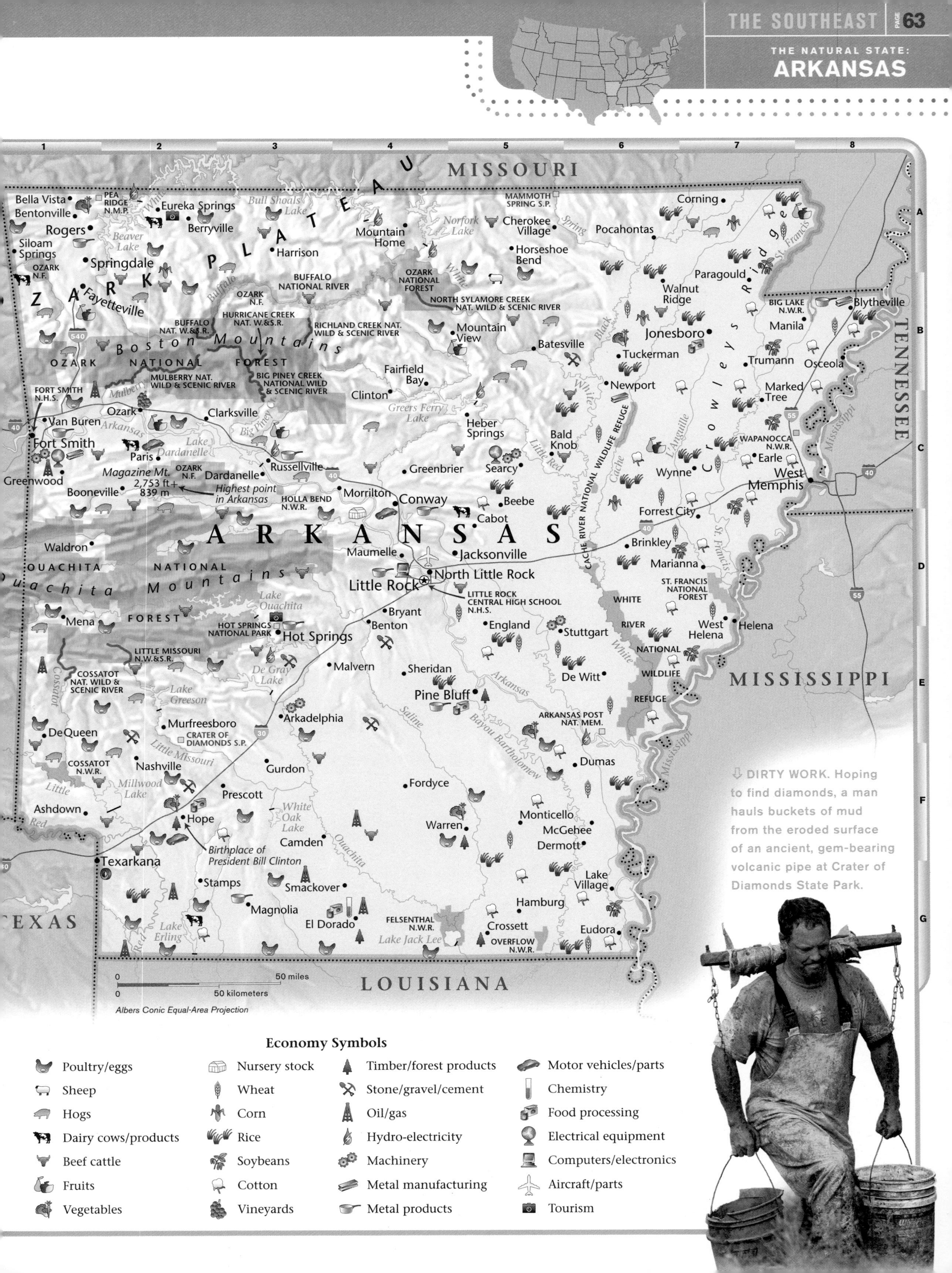

⇩ DIRTY WORK. Hoping to find diamonds, a man hauls buckets of mud from the eroded surface of an ancient, gem-bearing volcanic pipe at Crater of Diamonds State Park.

THE SUNSHINE STATE:
FLORIDA

THE BASICS

STATS

Area
65,755 sq mi (170,304 sq km)

Population
18,801,310

Capital
Tallahassee
Population 181,376

Largest city
Jacksonville
Population 821,784

Ethnic/racial groups
75.0% white; 16.0% African American; 2.4% Asian; .4% Native American. Hispanic (any race) 22.5%.

Industry
Tourism, health services, business services, communications, banking, electronic equipment, insurance

Agriculture
Citrus fruits, vegetables, field crops, nursery stock, cattle, dairy products

Statehood
March 3, 1845; 27th state

GEO WHIZ

Key West, the southernmost point in the continental U.S., is just 90 miles (145 km) from Cuba.

In 1937 Amelia Earhart and her navigator took off from Miami with the goal of making an around-the-world flight, but disappeared over the Pacific Ocean and were never seen again. You can read all about this famous flying ace in our children's book *Sky Pioneer*, by Corine Szabo.

Everglades National Park, the largest subtropical wilderness in the United States, is home to rare and endangered species such as the American crocodile, Florida panther, and West Indian manatee.

Britton Hill, Florida's highest point, is only 345 feet (105 m) above sea level.

Lightning strikes occur more often in Florida than in any other U.S. state.

MOCKINGBIRD
ORANGE BLOSSOM

FLORIDA

Florida is home to St. Augustine, the country's oldest permanent European settlement, established by the Spanish in 1565. But native peoples had called Florida home long before then. Florida became a U.S. territory in 1821 and a state in 1845. The state's turbulent early history included the Civil War and three wars with Native Americans over control of the land. Railroads opened Florida to migration from the northern states as early as the 1890s. The mild climate and sandy beaches attracted people seeking to escape cold winters in the north. This trend continues today and includes both tourists and retirees. South Florida has a large Hispanic population that has migrated from all over Latin America—especially from nearby Cuba. Florida is working to solve many challenges: competition between city-dwellers and farmers for limited water resources; the annual risk of tropical storms; and the need to preserve its natural environment, including the vast Everglades wetland.

⇧ CULTURAL PRIDE. A young girl marches in Orlando's Puerto Rican Parade, a celebration of the music, dance, and culture of this U.S. island territory.

ALABAMA
POARCH CREEK I.R.
Perdido
Highest point in Florida
Britton Hill 345 ft 105 m
Crestview
10
Pensacola
Niceville
Fort Walton Beach
FORT PICKENS
GULF ISLANDS NATIONAL SEASHORE
Intracoastal Waterway

⇨ LIFTOFF! A NASA rocket rises amid clouds of steam from Cape Canaveral Space Center on Florida's Atlantic coast. The center has been the launch site for many U.S. space exploration projects.

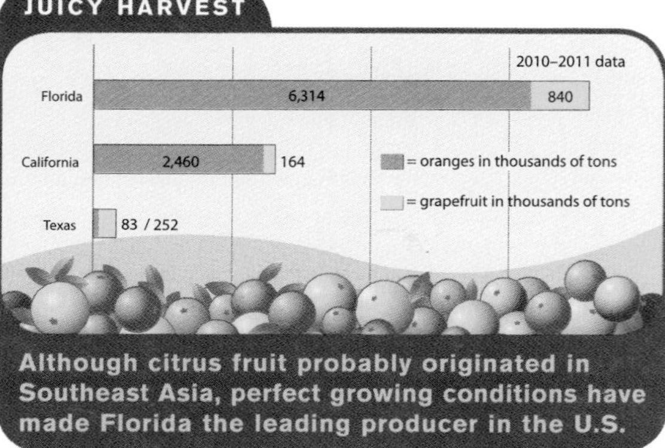

Although citrus fruit probably originated in Southeast Asia, perfect growing conditions have made Florida the leading producer in the U.S.

⇨ GENTLE GIANT. The manatee, which is closely related to the elephant, is Florida's state marine mammal. Averaging 10 feet (3 m) in length and 1,000 pounds (453 kg), these endangered animals live on a diet of sea grasses.

THE SUNSHINE STATE:
FLORIDA

THE EMPIRE STATE OF THE SOUTH:
GEORGIA

GEORGIA

When Spanish explorers arrived in the mid-1500s in what would become Georgia, they found the land already occupied by Cherokees, Creeks, and other native peoples. Georgia was the frontier separating Spanish Florida and English South Carolina, but in 1733 James Oglethorpe founded a new colony on the site of present-day Savannah. Georgia became the 4th state in 1788 and built an economy based on agriculture and slave labor. The state suffered widespread destruction during the Civil War and endured a long period of poverty in the years that followed. Modern-day Georgia is part of the fast-changing Sunbelt region. Agriculture—especially poultry, cotton, and forest products—remains important. Atlanta has emerged as a regional center of banking, telecommunications, and transportation, and Savannah is a major container port near the Atlantic coast, linking the state to the global economy. Historic sites, sports, and beaches draw thousands of tourists to the state every year.

THE BASICS

STATS

Area
59,425 sq mi (153,910 sq km)

Population
9,687,653

Capital
Atlanta
Population 420,003

Largest city
Atlanta
Population 420,003

Ethnic/racial groups
59.7% white; 30.5% African American; 3.2% Asian; .3% Native American. Hispanic (any race) 8.8%.

Industry
Textiles and clothing, transportation equipment, food processing, paper products, chemicals, electrical equipment, tourism

Agriculture
Poultry and eggs, cotton, peanuts, vegetables, sweet corn, melons, cattle

Statehood
January 2, 1788; 4th state

GEO WHIZ

The Okefenokee Swamp, the largest swamp in North America, is home to many meat-eating plants, which capture animals for food. The swamp was also the setting for the adventures of Pogo the Possum, Albert the Alligator, and other characters created by cartoonist Walt Kelly.

The Georgia Aquarium in Atlanta, the world's largest, features more than 100,000 animals in more than 8 million gallons (30.3 million liters) of water.

Stone Mountain near Atlanta is famous for its enormous carving of three historic figures from the Confederate States of America: Stonewall Jackson, Robert E. Lee, and Jefferson Davis. It is one of the largest single masses of exposed granite in the world.

BROWN THRASHER
CHEROKEE ROSE

⇧ CASH CROP. Peanuts are a big moneymaker in Georgia, where almost half the U.S. crop is grown—about half of which is used to make peanut butter.

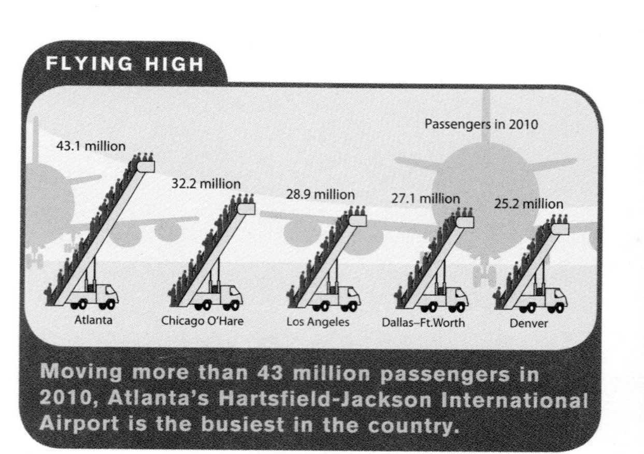

⇧ LIGHT SHOW. Busy Interstate traffic appears as ribbons of light below Atlanta's nighttime skyline. Atlanta is a center of economic growth, leading all cities in the region with 10 Fortune 500 companies. Its metropolitan area leads the country in population growth, adding almost one million people since 2000.

⇦ PAST MEETS PRESENT. Georgia's 100-mile (160-km) coastline is laced with barrier islands, wetlands, and winding streams. In the 19th century plantations grew Sea Island cotton here. Today, tourists are attracted to the area's natural beauty and beaches.

FLYING HIGH

Moving more than 43 million passengers in 2010, Atlanta's Hartsfield-Jackson International Airport is the busiest in the country.

THE EMPIRE STATE OF THE SOUTH: GEORGIA

THE BLUEGRASS STATE:
KENTUCKY

KENTUCKY

The original inhabitants of the area known today as Kentucky were Native Americans, but a treaty with the Cherokees, signed in 1775, opened the territory to settlers—including the legendary Daniel Boone—from the soon-to-be-independent eastern colonies. In 1776 Kentucky became a western county of the state of Virginia. In 1792 it became the 15th state of the young U.S. Eastern Kentucky is a part of Appalachia, a region rich in soft bituminous coal but burdened with environmental problems that often accompany the mining industry. The region is known for crafts and music that can be traced back to Scotch-Irish immigrants who settled there. In central Kentucky, the Bluegrass region produces some of the finest Thoroughbred horses in the world, and the Kentucky Derby, held in Louisville, is a part of racing's coveted Triple Crown. In western Kentucky, coal found near the surface is strip mined, leaving scars on the landscape, but federal laws now require that the land be restored.

THE BASICS

STATS

Area
40,409 sq mi (104,659 sq km)

Population
4,339,367

Capital
Frankfort
Population 25,527

Largest city
Louisville/Jefferson County
Population 597,337

Ethnic/racial groups
87.8% white; 7.8% African American; 1.1% Asian; .2% Native American. Hispanic (any race) 3.1%.

Industry
Manufacturing, services, government, finance, insurance, real estate, retail trade, transportation, wholesale trade, construction, mining

Agriculture
Horses, tobacco, cattle, corn, dairy products

Statehood
June 1, 1792; 15th state

GEO WHIZ

A favorite Kentucky dessert is Derby Pie, a rich chocolate-and-walnut pastry that was first created by George Kern, manager of the Melrose Inn, in Prospect, in the 1950s. It became so popular that the name was registered with the U.S. Patent Office and the Commonwealth of Kentucky.

Pleasant Hill, near Lexington, was the site of a Shaker religious community. It is now a National Historic Site where visitors can tour the living history museum.

The song "Happy Birthday to You," one of the most popular songs in the English language, was the creation of two Louisville sisters in 1893.

Post-it notes are manufactured exclusively in Cynthiana. Millions of self-stick notes in 27 sizes and 57 colors are produced each year.

CARDINAL
GOLDENROD

BENEATH THE SURFACE

Cave	Length
Mammoth Cave System, KY	367 miles/591 km
Jewel Cave, SD	140 miles/225 km
Wind Cave, SD	125 miles/201 km
Lechuguilla Cave, NM	121 miles/195 km
Fisher Ridge Cave System, KY	110 miles/177 km

Caves, natural openings in Earth's surface extending beyond the reach of sunlight, are often created by water dissolving limestone.

⇧ THEY'RE OFF! Riders and horses press for the finish line at Churchill Downs, in Louisville. Kentucky is a major breeder of Thoroughbred race horses, and horses are the leading source of farm income in the state.

KENTUCKY

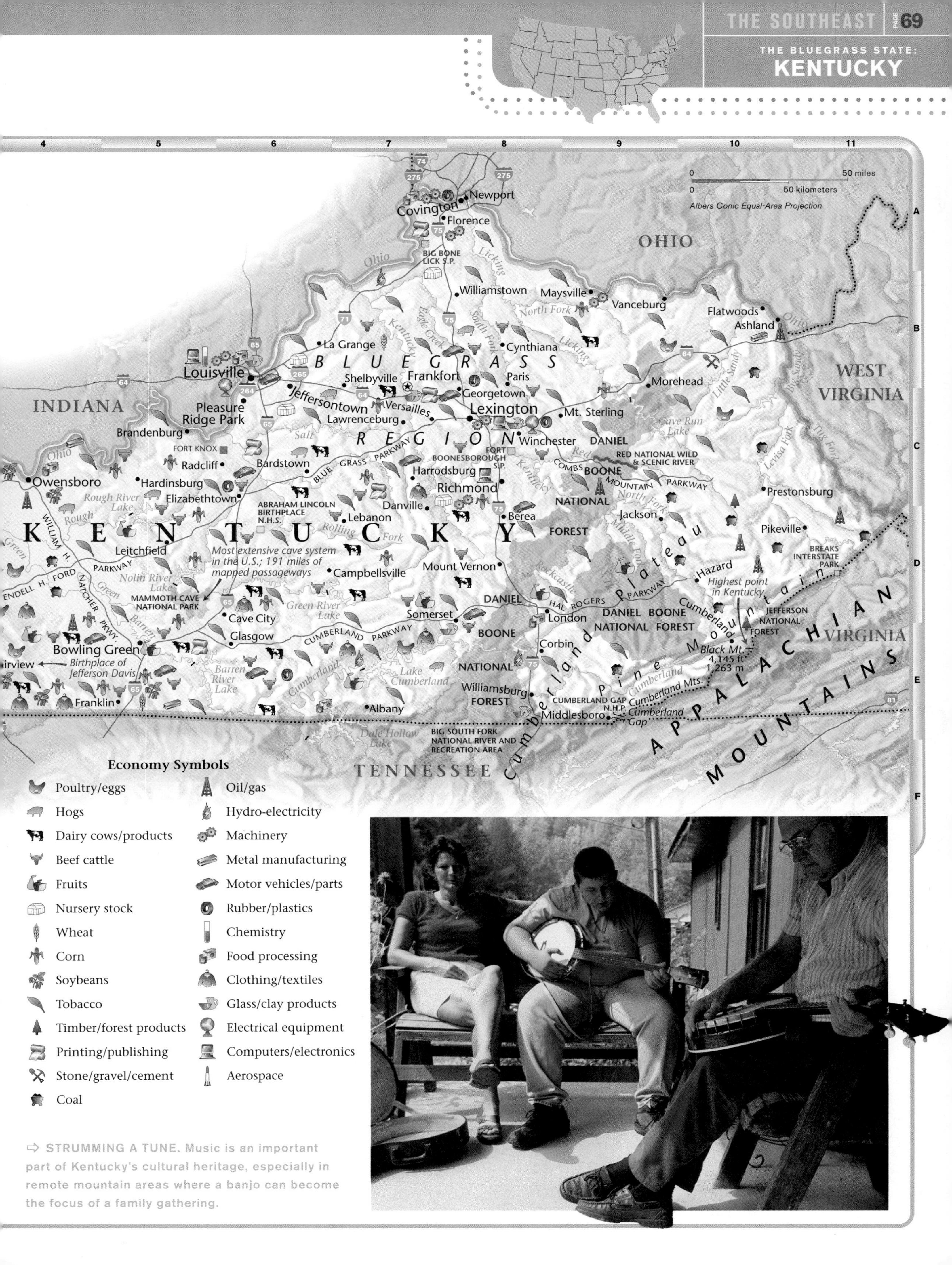

⇨ STRUMMING A TUNE. Music is an important part of Kentucky's cultural heritage, especially in remote mountain areas where a banjo can become the focus of a family gathering.

THE PELICAN STATE:
LOUISIANA

LOUISIANA

Louisiana's Native American heritage is evident in place-names such as Natchitoches and Opelousas. Spanish sailors explored the area in 1528, but the French, traveling down the Mississippi River, established permanent settlements in the mid-17th century and named the region for King Louis XIV. The U.S. gained possession of the territory as part of the Louisiana Purchase in 1803, and Louisiana became the 18th state in 1812. New Orleans and the Port of South Louisiana, located near the delta of the Mississippi River, are Louisiana's main ports. Trade from the interior of the U.S. moves through these ports and out to world markets. Oil and gas are drilled in the Mississippi Delta area, and coastal waters are an important source of seafood. Louisiana is vulnerable to tropical storms. In late August 2005 Hurricane Katrina roared in off the Gulf of Mexico, flooding towns, breaking through levees, and changing forever the lives of everyone in southern Louisiana.

THE BASICS

STATS

Area
51,840 sq mi (134,265 sq km)

Population
4,533,372

Capital
Baton Rouge
Population 229,493

Largest city
New Orleans
Population 343,829

Ethnic/racial groups
62.6% white; 32.0% African American; 1.5% Asian; .7% Native American. Hispanic (any race) 4.2%.

Industry
Chemicals, petroleum products, food processing, health services, tourism, oil and natural gas extraction, paper products

Agriculture
Forest products, poultry, marine fisheries, sugarcane, rice, dairy products, cotton, cattle, aquaculture

Statehood
April 30, 1812; 18th state

GEO WHIZ

The brown pelican, the state bird of Louisiana, was placed on the endangered species list in 1970. The species has made a remarkable recovery in the Atlantic coastal states, but it is still considered endangered in the Gulf Coast area.

The magnolia, Louisiana's state flower, is the oldest flowering plant in the world. Some species are believed to be 100 million years old.

Cajuns, people whose French-speaking ancestors were exiled by the British from Acadia, in what is now Canada, live primarily in the bayou region of Louisiana. Their distinctive music and spicy food have become popular throughout the country.

BROWN PELICAN
MAGNOLIA

⇧ TASTY HARVEST. Louisiana produces more than half of all shrimp caught in the U.S. Most of this harvest comes from the Barataria-Terrebonne region, an estuary at the mouth of the Mississippi River that supports shrimp, oysters, crabs, and fish.

⇦ AVENUE TO THE PAST. Stately live oaks, believed to be 300 years old, frame Oak Alley Plantation on the banks of the Mississippi River west of New Orleans. Built in 1839, the house has been restored to its former grandeur and is open to the public for tours and private events.

Springhill
Vivian
Caddo Lake
Red
Shreveport
Bossier City
Lake Bistineau
Mansfield
Natchitoc
CANE RIVER CREOLE N
AND HERITAGE A
Many
Toledo Bend Reservoir
Leesville
TEXAS
Rosepine
De Ridder
Sabine
De Quincy
Sulphur
Intracoastal
Calcasieu Lake
Sabine Lake
SABINE NAT. WILDLIFE REFUGE

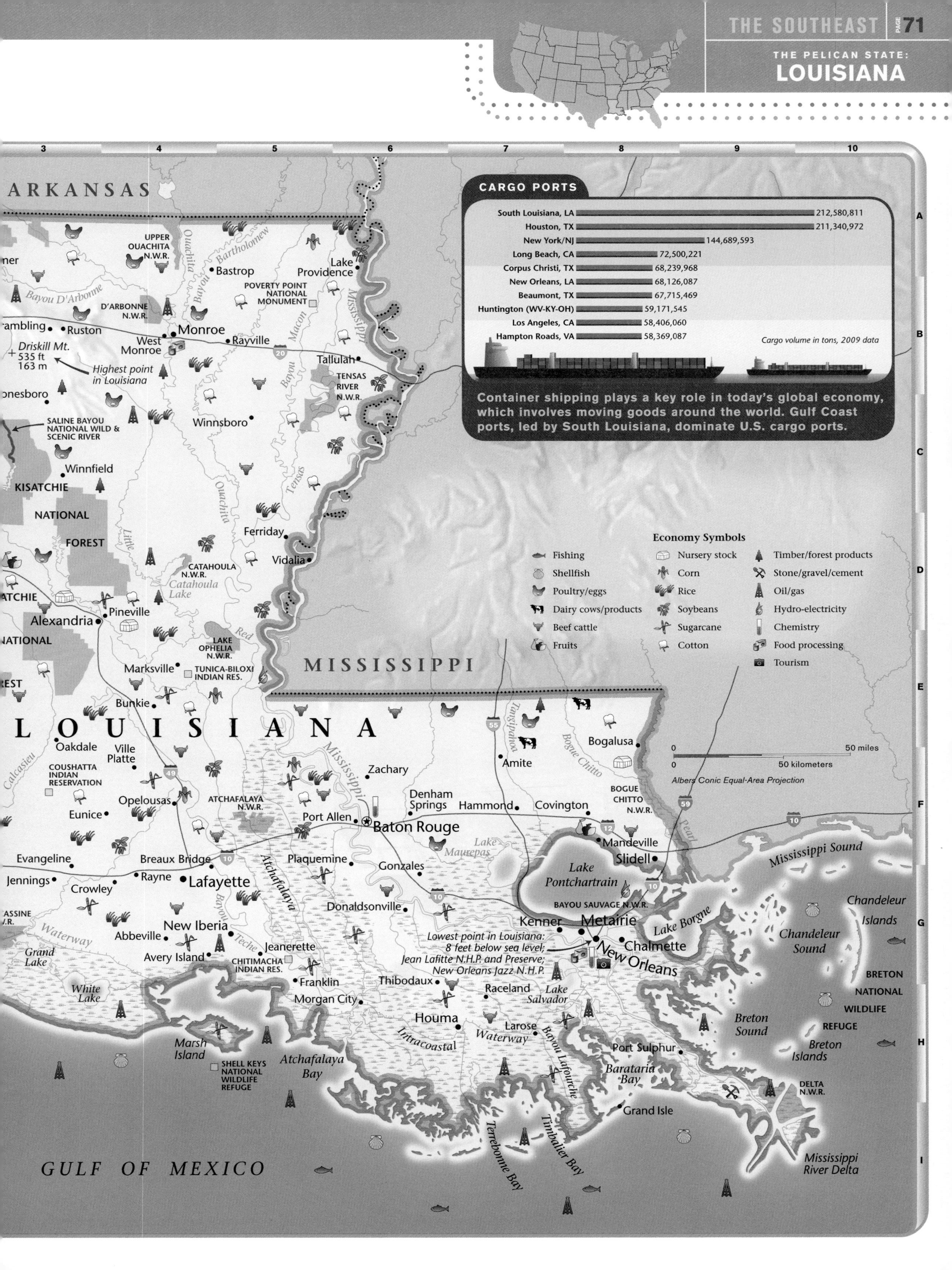
CARGO PORTS
South Louisiana, LA 212,580,811
Houston, TX 211,340,972
New York/NJ 144,689,593
Long Beach, CA 72,500,221
Corpus Christi, TX 68,239,968
New Orleans, LA 68,126,087
Beaumont, TX 67,715,469
Huntington (WV-KY-OH) 59,171,545
Los Angeles, CA 58,406,060
Hampton Roads, VA 58,369,087
Cargo volume in tons, 2009 data
Container shipping plays a key role in today's global economy, which involves moving goods around the world. Gulf Coast ports, led by South Louisiana, dominate U.S. cargo ports.
Economy Symbols
Fishing
Shellfish
Poultry/eggs
Dairy cows/products
Beef cattle
Fruits
Nursery stock
Corn
Rice
Soybeans
Sugarcane
Cotton
Timber/forest products
Stone/gravel/cement
Oil/gas
Hydro-electricity
Chemistry
Food processing
Tourism
0 50 miles
0 50 kilometers
Albers Conic Equal-Area Projection
ARKANSAS
MISSISSIPPI
LOUISIANA
GULF OF MEXICO
UPPER OUACHITA N.W.R.
D'ARBONNE N.W.R.
Bayou D'Arbonne
Bastrop
Lake Providence
POVERTY POINT NATIONAL MONUMENT
Ruston
West Monroe
Monroe
Rayville
Tallulah
Driskill Mt. 535 ft 163 m
Highest point in Louisiana
TENSAS RIVER N.W.R.
SALINE BAYOU NATIONAL WILD & SCENIC RIVER
Winnsboro
Winnfield
KISATCHIE NATIONAL FOREST
Ferriday
Vidalia
CATAHOULA N.W.R.
Catahoula Lake
Pineville
Alexandria
LAKE OPHELIA N.W.R.
Marksville
TUNICA-BILOXI INDIAN RES.
Bunkie
Oakdale
Ville Platte
COUSHATTA INDIAN RESERVATION
Opelousas
Eunice
ATCHAFALAYA N.W.R.
Zachary
Denham Springs
Hammond
Covington
Amite
Bogalusa
BOGUE CHITTO N.W.R.
Port Allen
Baton Rouge
Mandeville
Slidell
Evangeline
Breaux Bridge
Plaquemine
Gonzales
Lake Maurepas
Lake Pontchartrain
Jennings
Rayne
Lafayette
Crowley
Donaldsonville
BAYOU SAUVAGE N.W.R.
Kenner
Metairie
Lake Borgne
New Iberia
Abbeville
Jeanerette
Lowest point in Louisiana: 8 feet below sea level; Jean Lafitte N.H.P. and Preserve; New Orleans Jazz N.H.P.
Chalmette
New Orleans
Avery Island
CHITIMACHA INDIAN RES.
Franklin
Thibodaux
Raceland
Lake Salvador
Grand Lake
White Lake
Morgan City
Houma
Larose
Intracoastal Waterway
Bayou Lafourche
Marsh Island
SHELL KEYS NATIONAL WILDLIFE REFUGE
Atchafalaya Bay
Port Sulphur
Barataria Bay
Grand Isle
Terrebonne Bay
Timbalier Bay
Mississippi Sound
Chandeleur Islands
Chandeleur Sound
BRETON NATIONAL WILDLIFE REFUGE
Breton Sound
Breton Islands
DELTA N.W.R.
Mississippi River Delta

THE MAGNOLIA STATE:
MISSISSIPPI

MISSISSIPPI

Mississippi is named for the river that forms its western boundary. The name comes from the Chippewa words *mici zibi,* meaning "great river." Indeed it is a great river, draining much of the interior U.S. and providing a trade artery to the world. Explored by the Spanish in 1540 and claimed by the French in 1699, the territory of Mississippi passed to the U.S. in 1783 and became the 20th state in 1817. For more than a hundred years following statehood, Mississippi was the center of U.S. cotton production and trade. The fertile soils and mild climate of the delta region in northwestern Mississippi provided a perfect environment for cotton, a crop that depended on slave labor. When the Civil War broke out, it took a heavy toll on the state. Today, poverty, especially in rural areas, is a major challenge for the state where agriculture—poultry, cotton, soybeans, and rice—is still the base of the economy.

⇧ SINGING THE BLUES. B.B. King sings the soulful sounds of the blues, a music form that traces its roots to Mississippi's cotton fields and the sorrows of West Africans traveling on slave ships to the Americas.

THE BASICS

STATS

Area
48,430 sq mi (125,434 sq km)

Population
2,967,297

Capital
Jackson
Population 173,514

Largest city
Jackson
Population 173,514

Ethnic/racial groups
59.1% white; 37.0% African American; .9% Asian; .5% Native American. Hispanic (any race) 2.7%.

Industry
Petroleum products, health services, electronic equipment, transportation, banking, forest products, communications

Agriculture
Poultry and eggs, cotton, catfish, soybeans, cattle, rice, dairy products

Statehood
December 10, 1817; 20th state

GEO WHIZ

The Windsor Ruins, located near Port Gibson, are 23 monolithic columns that once made up the largest antebellum mansion in the state. The mansion survived the Civil War but was destroyed by a fire in 1890.

The Marine Life Oceanarium in Gulfport was almost completely destroyed by Hurricane Katrina in 2005. Eight of its 14 bottlenose dolphins were swept into the Gulf of Mexico by a 40-foot (12-m) wave. These animals and two sea lions named Splash and Elliot were eventually rescued. Others were not so lucky.

Greenville is the birthplace of Jim Henson, creator of Kermit the Frog, Miss Piggy, Big Bird, and other famous Muppets.

MOCKINGBIRD
MAGNOLIA

GONE FISHIN'

2011 data

State	Catfish sales
Mississippi	147 million
Alabama	97 million
Arkansas	35 million

The Southeast, especially Mississippi, is the leading producer of pond-raised catfish. Mississippi also tops all other states in revenue for catfish sales.

⇨ BIG WHEEL TURNING. Now popular with tourists, paddlewheel boats made the Mississippi River a major artery for trade and travel in the 19th century.

THE MAGNOLIA STATE: MISSISSIPPI

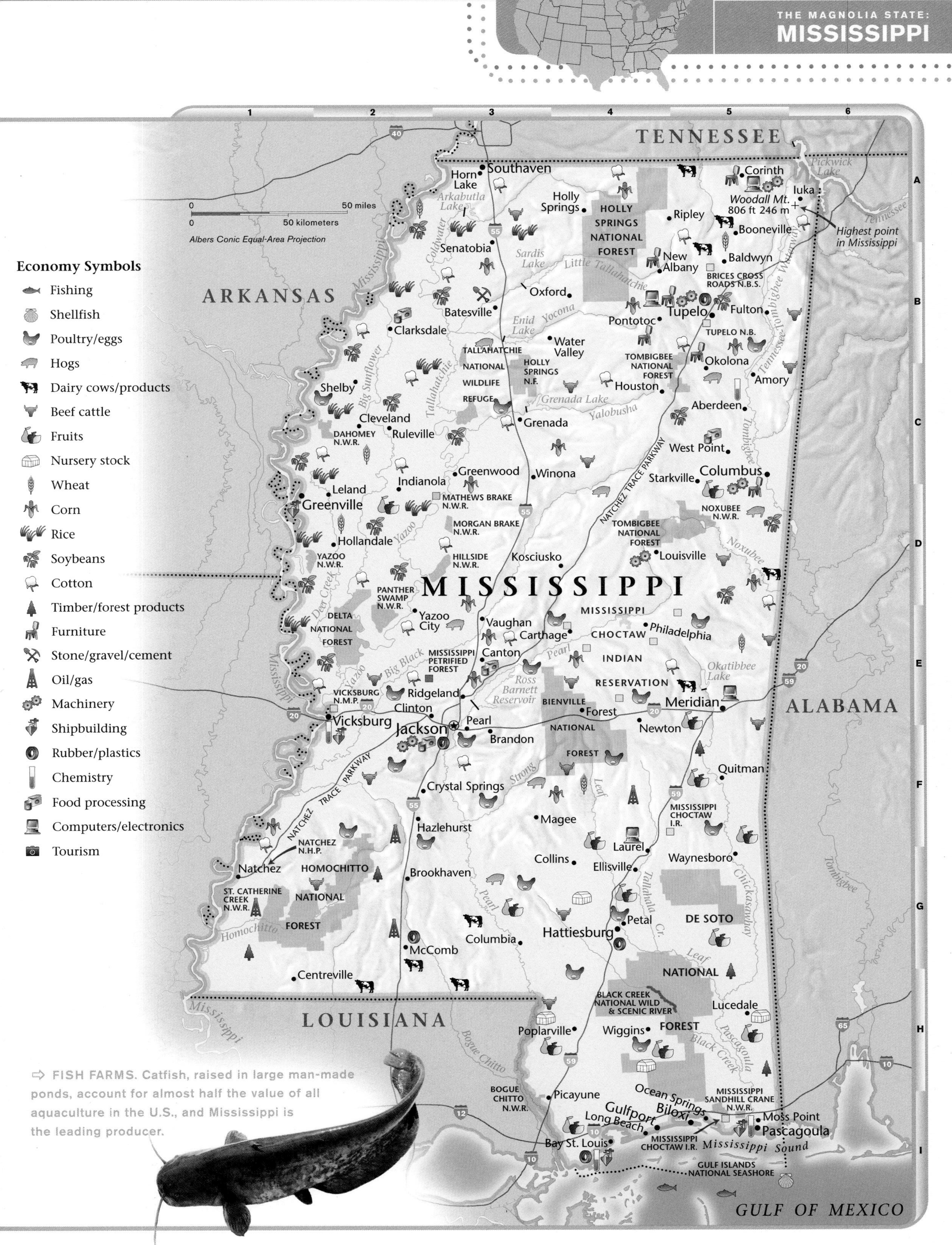

⇨ FISH FARMS. Catfish, raised in large man-made ponds, account for almost half the value of all aquaculture in the U.S., and Mississippi is the leading producer.

THE TAR HEEL STATE:
NORTH CAROLINA

NORTH CAROLINA

THE BASICS

STATS

Area
53,819 sq mi (139,390 sq km)

Population
9,535,483

Capital
Raleigh
Population 403,892

Largest city
Charlotte
Population 731,424

Ethnic/racial groups
68.5% white; 21.5% African American; 2.2% Asian; 1.3% Native American. Hispanic (any race) 8.4%.

Industry
Real estate, health services, chemicals, tobacco products, finance, textiles

Agriculture
Poultry, hogs, tobacco, nursery stock, cotton, soybeans

Statehood
November 21, 1789; 12th state

GEO WHIZ

The University of North Carolina at Chapel Hill, which opened its doors in 1795, is the oldest state university in the United States.

The Biltmore estate in Asheville is the largest private residence in the United States. Built to resemble a French chateau, the mansion is still owned by descendants of Cornelius Vanderbilt, who made the family's original fortune in the late 1800s.

Standing 208 feet (63 m) high, Cape Hatteras Light is the tallest lighthouse in the U.S. Its beacon can be seen some 20 miles (32 km) out to sea and has warned sailors for more than a century about the shallow waters around a group of treacherous sandbars called Diamond Shoals.

CARDINAL
FLOWERING DOGWOOD

Before European contact, the land that became North Carolina was inhabited by numerous Native American groups. Early attempts to settle the area met with strong resistance, and one early colony established in 1587 on Roanoke Island disappeared without a trace. More attempts at settlement came in 1650, and in 1663 King Charles granted a charter for the Carolina colony, which included present-day North Carolina, South Carolina, and part of Georgia. In 1789 North Carolina became the 12th state, but in 1861 it joined the Confederacy, supplying more men and equipment to the Southern cause than any other state. In 1903 the Wright brothers piloted the first successful airplane near Kitty Hawk, foreshadowing the change and growth coming to the Tar Heel State. Traditional industries included agriculture, textiles, and furniture making. Today, these, plus high-tech industries and education in the Raleigh-Durham Research Triangle area, as well as banking and finance in Charlotte, are important to the economy.

⇨ FAVORITE PASTIME. With four of the state's major schools represented in the powerful Atlantic Coast Conference, it is not surprising that basketball is a popular sport among all ages, whether on the court or in the backyard.

⇦ TAKING FLIGHT. The Wright Brothers Memorial on Kill Devil Hill, near Kitty Hawk on North Carolina's Outer Banks, marks the site of the first successful airplane flight in 1903.

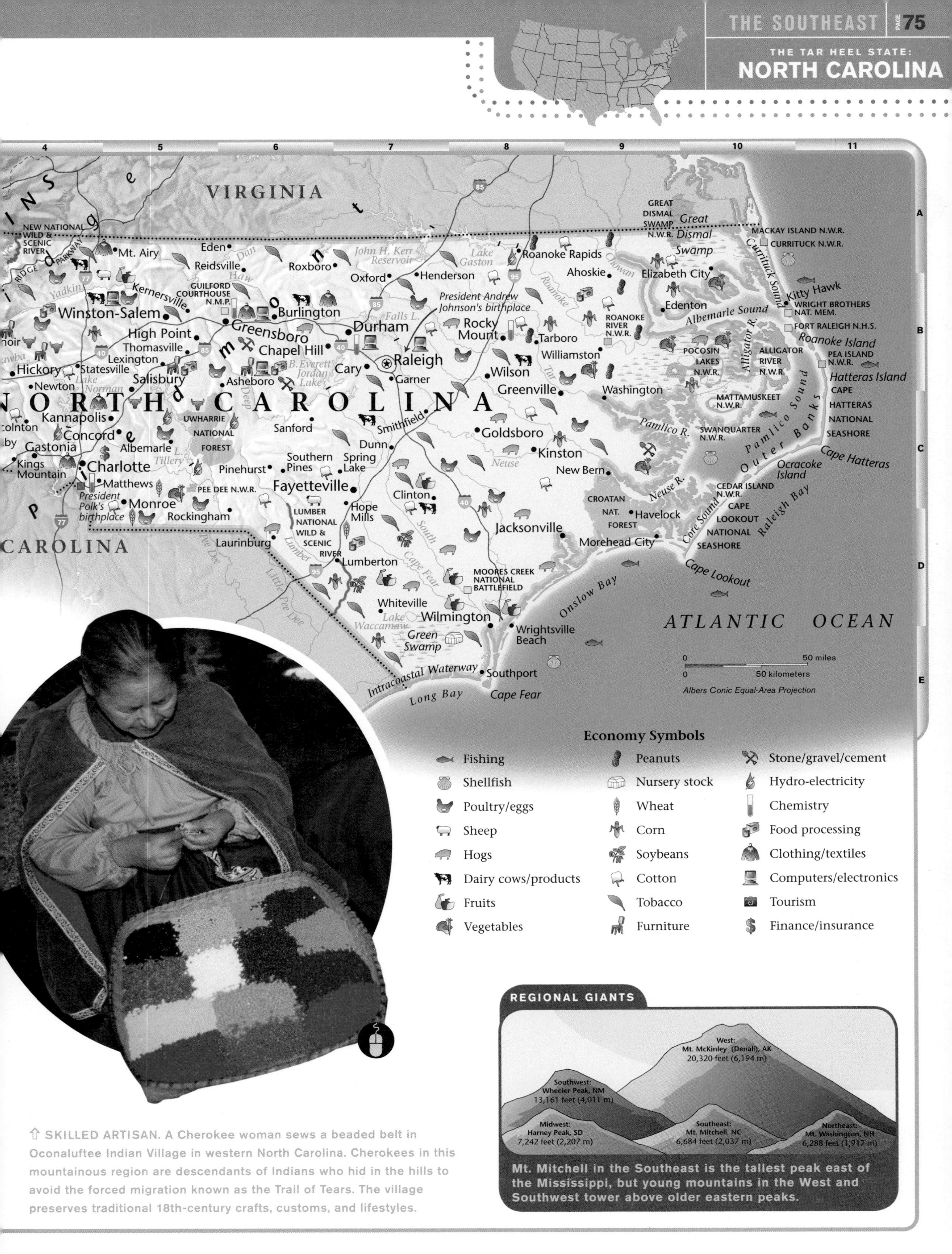

⇧ SKILLED ARTISAN. A Cherokee woman sews a beaded belt in Oconaluftee Indian Village in western North Carolina. Cherokees in this mountainous region are descendants of Indians who hid in the hills to avoid the forced migration known as the Trail of Tears. The village preserves traditional 18th-century crafts, customs, and lifestyles.

THE PALMETTO STATE:
SOUTH CAROLINA

SOUTH CAROLINA

THE BASICS

STATS

Area
32,020 sq mi (82,932 sq km)

Population
4,625,364

Capital
Columbia
Population 129,272

Largest city
Columbia
Population 129,272

Ethnic/racial groups
66.2% white; 27.9% African American; 1.3% Asian; .4% Native American. Hispanic (any race) 5.1%.

Industry
Service industries, tourism, chemicals, textiles, machinery, forest products

Agriculture
Chickens, tobacco, nursery stock, beef cattle, dairy products, cotton

Statehood
May 23, 1788; 8th state

GEO WHIZ

The loggerhead sea turtle, South Carolina's state reptile, is threatened throughout its range. These turtles weigh between 200–450 pounds (90–204 kg).

North America's largest remnant of old-growth bottomland hardwood forest towers above the Congaree River and is protected as a 22,000-acre (8,903-ha) refuge called Congaree National Park.

Sweetgrass basketmaking, a traditional art form of African origin, has been a part of the Mount Pleasant community for more than 300 years. The baskets were originally used by slaves in the planting and processing of rice in coastal lowland regions.

Bobcats are thriving on Kiawah Island, a resort community southeast of Charleston. The elusive, nocturnal cats, which are about twice the size of an average house cat, play an important role in controlling the island's deer population.

CAROLINA WREN
YELLOW JESSAMINE

Attempts in the 16th century by the Spanish and the French to colonize the area that would become South Carolina met fierce resistance from local Native American groups, but in 1670 the English were the first to establish a permanent European settlement at present-day Charleston. The colony prospered by relying on slave labor to produce first cotton, then rice and indigo. South Carolina became the 8th state in 1788 and the first to leave the Union just months before the first shots of the Civil War were fired on Fort Sumter in 1861. After the war, South Carolina struggled to rebuild its economy. Early in the 20th century, textile mills introduced new jobs. Today, agriculture remains important, manufacturing and high-tech industries are expanding along interstate highway corridors, and tourists and retirees are drawn to the state's Atlantic coastline. But these coastal areas are not without risk. In 1989 Hurricane Hugo's 135-mile-per-hour (217-kmph) winds left a trail of destruction.

⇧ GLOW OF DAWN. The rising sun reflects off the water along the Atlantic coast. Beaches attract visitors year-round, contributing to tourism, the state's largest industry.

TRADE PARTNERS

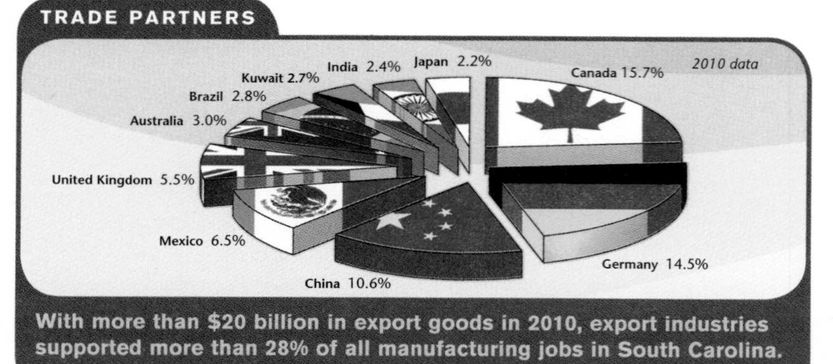

With more than $20 billion in export goods in 2010, export industries supported more than 28% of all manufacturing jobs in South Carolina. Transportation equipment is the leading manufactured export.

⇩ SOUTHERN CHARM. Twilight settles over antebellum homes in the historic district of Charleston. The city, established in 1670, is an important port located where the Ashley and Cooper Rivers merge before flowing to the Atlantic Ocean.

THE PALMETTO STATE: SOUTH CAROLINA

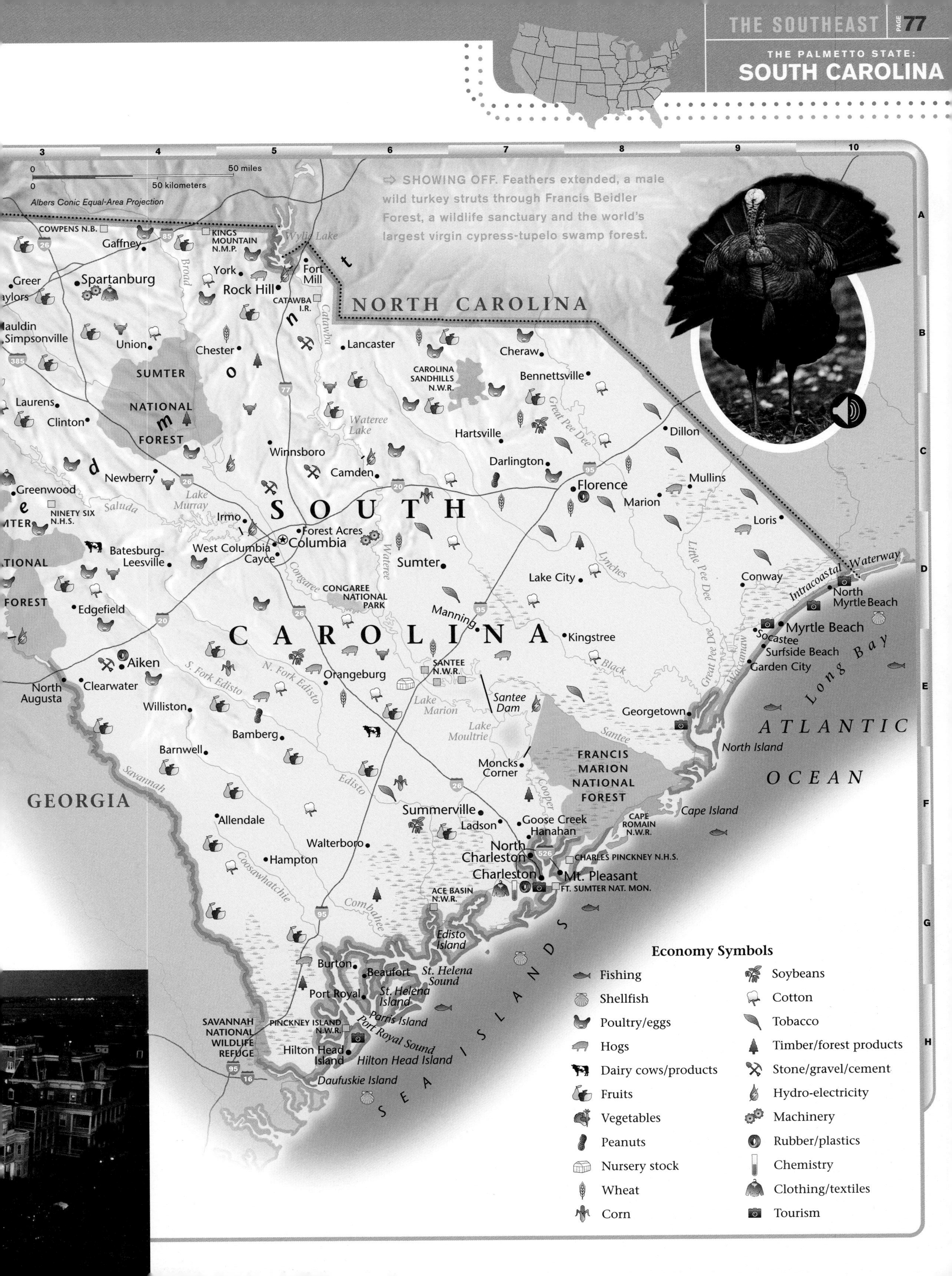

⇨ SHOWING OFF. Feathers extended, a male wild turkey struts through Francis Beidler Forest, a wildlife sanctuary and the world's largest virgin cypress-tupelo swamp forest.

THE VOLUNTEER STATE:
TENNESSEE

TENNESSEE

THE BASICS

STATS

Area
42,143 sq mi (109,151 sq km)

Population
6,346,105

Capital
Nashville-Davidson
Population 601,222

Largest city
Memphis
Population 646,889

Ethnic/racial groups
77.6% white; 16.7% African American; 1.4% Asian; .3% Native American. Hispanic (any race) 4.6%.

Industry
Service industries, chemicals, transportation equipment, processed foods, machinery

Agriculture
Cattle, cotton, dairy products, hogs, poultry, nursery stock

Statehood
June 1, 1796; 16th state

GEO WHIZ

Twenty-seven species of salamanders live in Great Smoky Mountains National Park, earning it the nickname Salamander Capital of the World. Among the species are the spotted; the Jordans, which is found nowhere else; and the five-foot-long hellbender (1.5 m).

The New Madrid Earthquakes of 1811–1812, some of the largest earthquakes in the history of the U.S., created Reelfoot Lake in northwestern Tennessee. It is the state's only large, natural lake; others were created by damming waterways.

The Tennessee-Tombigbee Waterway is a 234-mile (376-km) artificial waterway that connects the Tennessee and Tombigbee Rivers. This water transportation route provides inland ports with an outlet to the Gulf of Mexico.

MOCKINGBIRD
IRIS

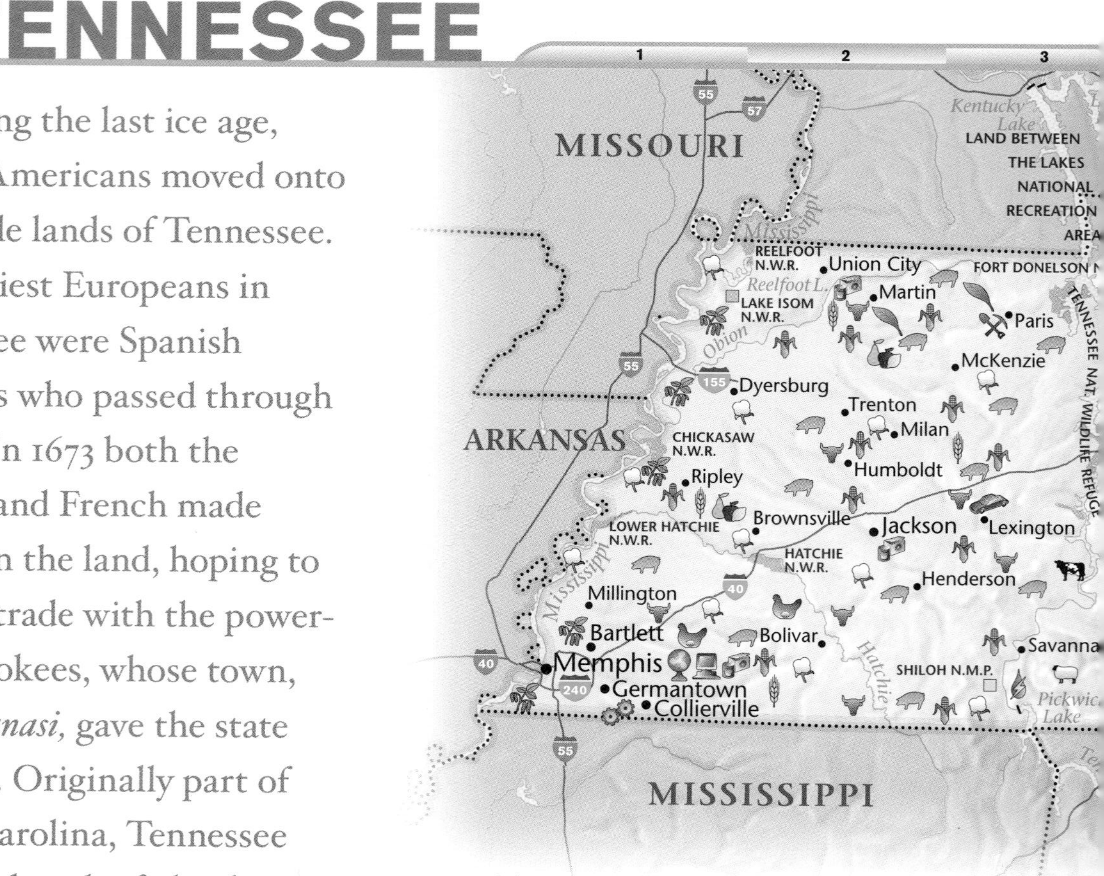

Following the last ice age, Native Americans moved onto the fertile lands of Tennessee. The earliest Europeans in Tennessee were Spanish explorers who passed through in 1541. In 1673 both the English and French made claims on the land, hoping to develop trade with the powerful Cherokees, whose town, called *Tanasi,* gave the state its name. Originally part of North Carolina, Tennessee was ceded to the federal government and became the 16th state in 1796. Tennessee was the last state to join the Confederacy and endured years of hardship after the war. Beginning in the 1930s, the federally funded Tennessee Valley Authority (TVA) set a high standard in water management in the state, and the hydropower it generated supported major industrial development. Tennessee played a key role in the civil rights movement of the 1960s. Today, visitors to Tennessee are drawn to national parks, Nashville's country music, and the mournful sound of the blues in Memphis.

⇦ OUT FOR A STROLL. Black bear cubs are usually born in January and remain with their mother for about 18 months. The Great Smoky Mountains National Park is one of the few remaining natural habitats for black bears in the eastern U.S.

NATURE'S PLAYGROUND

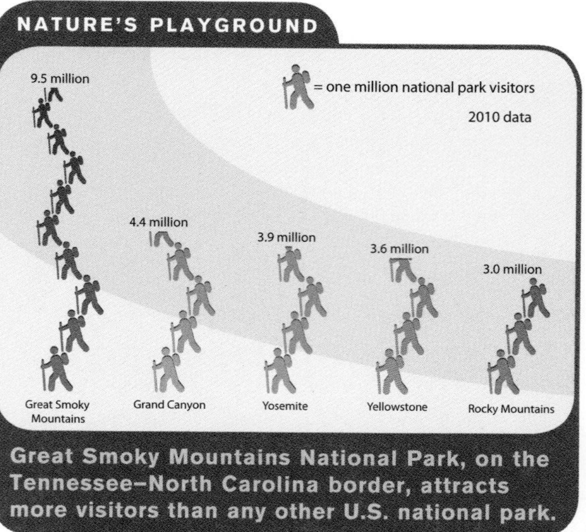

Great Smoky Mountains National Park, on the Tennessee–North Carolina border, attracts more visitors than any other U.S. national park.

THE VOLUNTEER STATE: TENNESSEE

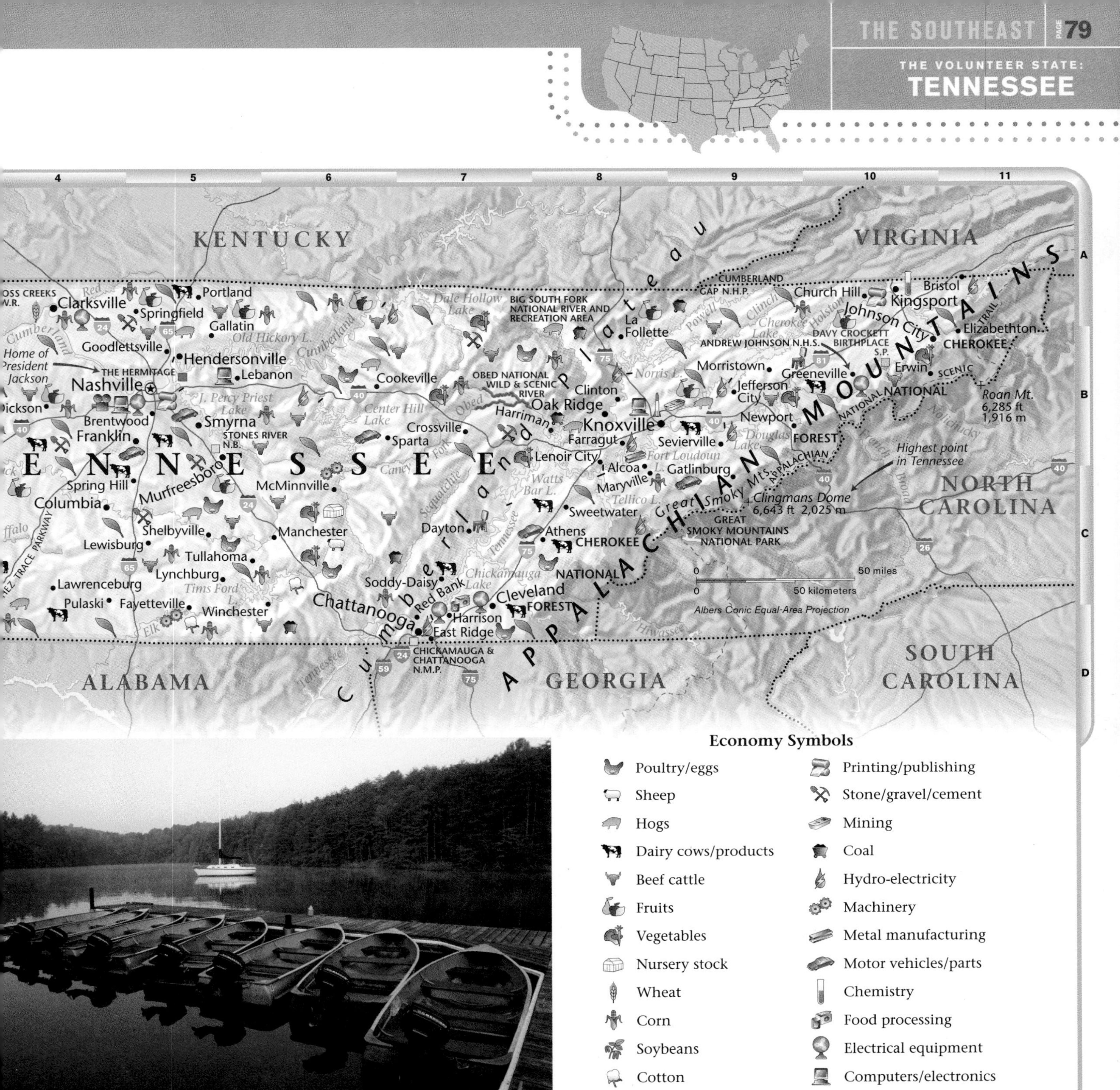

⇧ WATTS BAR DAM is one of nine TVA dams built on the Tennessee River to aid navigation and flood control and to supply power. The large reservoir behind the dam provides a recreation area that attracts millions of vacationers each year. Without the dam, cities such as Chattanooga would face devastating floods.

⇨ SOUTHERN TRADITION. Nashville's Grand Ole Opry is the home of country music. Originally a 1925 radio show called "Barn Dance," the Opry now occupies a theater with a seating capacity of 4,400 and the largest broadcasting studio in the world. Country music, using mainly stringed instruments, evolved from traditional folk tunes of the Appalachians.

THE OLD DOMINION STATE:
VIRGINIA

VIRGINIA

THE BASICS

STATS

Area
42,774 sq mi (110,785 sq km)

Population
8,001,024

Capital
Richmond
Population 204,214

Largest city
Virginia Beach
Population 437,994

Ethnic/racial groups
68.6% white; 19.4% African American; 5.5% Asian; .4% Native American. Hispanic (any race) 7.9%.

Industry
Food processing, communication and electronic equipment, transportation equipment, printing, shipbuilding, textiles

Agriculture
Tobacco, poultry, dairy products, beef cattle, soybeans, hogs

Statehood
June 25, 1788; 10th state

GEO WHIZ

In the early 1700s the bustling port of Hampton was a major target for pirates, including the notorious Blackbeard. Today, each spring the city hosts the Blackbeard Festival, complete with pirate re-enactors, live music, games, and fireworks.

Virginia is the birthplace of eight U.S. presidents—more than any other state. They are: George Washington, Thomas Jefferson, James Madison, James Monroe, William Harrison, John Tyler, Zachary Taylor, and Woodrow Wilson. Learn about them and more in our book *Our Country's Presidents*.

During the Battle of Hampton Roads in 1862, the USS *Monitor* and the CSS *Virginia* (a rebuilt version of the USS *Merrimac*) met in one of the most famous naval engagements in U.S. history. It marked the dawn of a new era of naval warfare.

More than 200,000 telephone calls are made each day at the Pentagon, the headquarters for the U.S. Department of Defense, through phones connected by 100,000 miles (160,000 km) of telephone cable. It is one of the largest office buildings in the world.

CARDINAL
FLOWERING DOGWOOD

Long before Europeans arrived in present-day Virginia, Native Americans populated the area. Early Spanish attempts to establish a colony failed, but in 1607 merchants established the first permanent English settlement in North America at Jamestown. Virginia became a prosperous colony, growing tobacco using slave labor. Virginia played a key role in the drive for independence, and the final battle of the Revolutionary War was at Yorktown, near Jamestown. In 1861 Virginia joined the Confederacy and became a major battleground of the Civil War, which left the state in financial ruin. Today, Virginia has a diversified economy. Farmers still grow tobacco, along with other crops. The Hampton Roads area, near the mouth of Chesapeake Bay, is a center for shipbuilding and home to major naval bases. Northern Virginia, across the Potomac River from Washington, D.C., boasts federal government offices and high-tech businesses. And the state's natural beauty and many historic sites attract tourists from around the world.

⇧ EARLY ENTERTAINMENT. Dating back to ancient Greece and Rome, dice made of bone, ivory, or lead were popular during colonial times.

⇨ NATURAL WONDER. Winding under the Appalachian Mountains, Luray Caverns formed as water dissolved limestone rocks and precipitated calcium deposits to form stalactites and stalagmites.

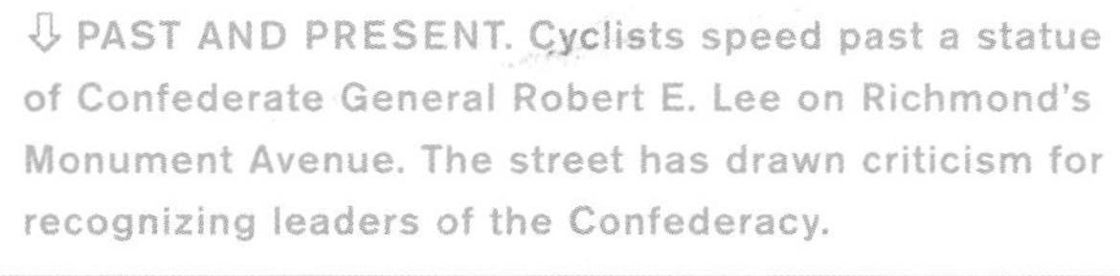

THE OLD DOMINION STATE: VIRGINIA

⇩ PAST AND PRESENT. Cyclists speed past a statue of Confederate General Robert E. Lee on Richmond's Monument Avenue. The street has drawn criticism for recognizing leaders of the Confederacy.

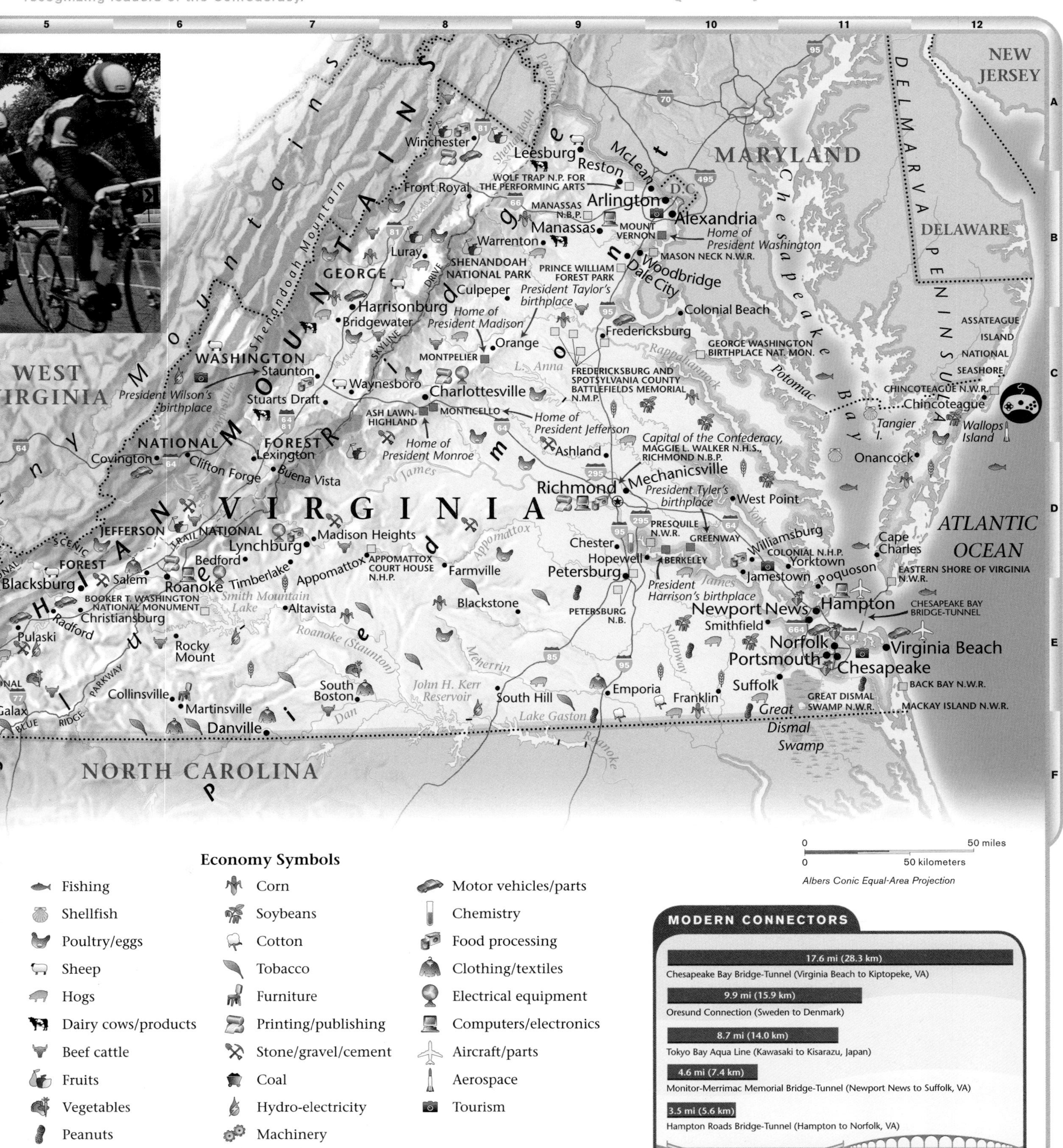

Economy Symbols

Fishing
Shellfish
Poultry/eggs
Sheep
Hogs
Dairy cows/products
Beef cattle
Fruits
Vegetables
Peanuts
Wheat
Corn
Soybeans
Cotton
Tobacco
Furniture
Printing/publishing
Stone/gravel/cement
Coal
Hydro-electricity
Machinery
Ship Building
Motor vehicles/parts
Chemistry
Food processing
Clothing/textiles
Electrical equipment
Computers/electronics
Aircraft/parts
Aerospace
Tourism

MODERN CONNECTORS

17.6 mi (28.3 km)
Chesapeake Bay Bridge-Tunnel (Virginia Beach to Kiptopeke, VA)

9.9 mi (15.9 km)
Oresund Connection (Sweden to Denmark)

8.7 mi (14.0 km)
Tokyo Bay Aqua Line (Kawasaki to Kisarazu, Japan)

4.6 mi (7.4 km)
Monitor-Merrimac Memorial Bridge-Tunnel (Newport News to Suffolk, VA)

3.5 mi (5.6 km)
Hampton Roads Bridge-Tunnel (Hampton to Norfolk, VA)

Advanced engineering has made it possible to span wide expanses of water. Three of the world's longest bridge-tunnels are in Virginia.

THE MOUNTAIN STATE:
WEST VIRGINIA

WEST VIRGINIA

Mountainous West Virginia was first settled by Native Americans who favored the wooded region for hunting. The first Europeans to settle in what originally was an extension of Virginia were Germans and Scotch-Irish, who came through mountain valleys of Pennsylvania in the early 1700s. Because farms in West Virginia did not depend upon slaves, residents opposed secession during the Civil War and broke away from Virginia, becoming the 35th state in 1863. In the early 1800s West Virginia harvested forest products and mined salt, but it was the exploitation of vast coal deposits that brought industrialization to the state. Coal fueled steel mills, steamboats, and trains, and jobs in the mines attracted immigrants from far and near. However, poor work conditions resulted in a legacy of poverty, illness, and environmental degradation—problems the state continues to face. Today, the state is working to build a tourist industry based on its natural beauty and mountain crafts and culture.

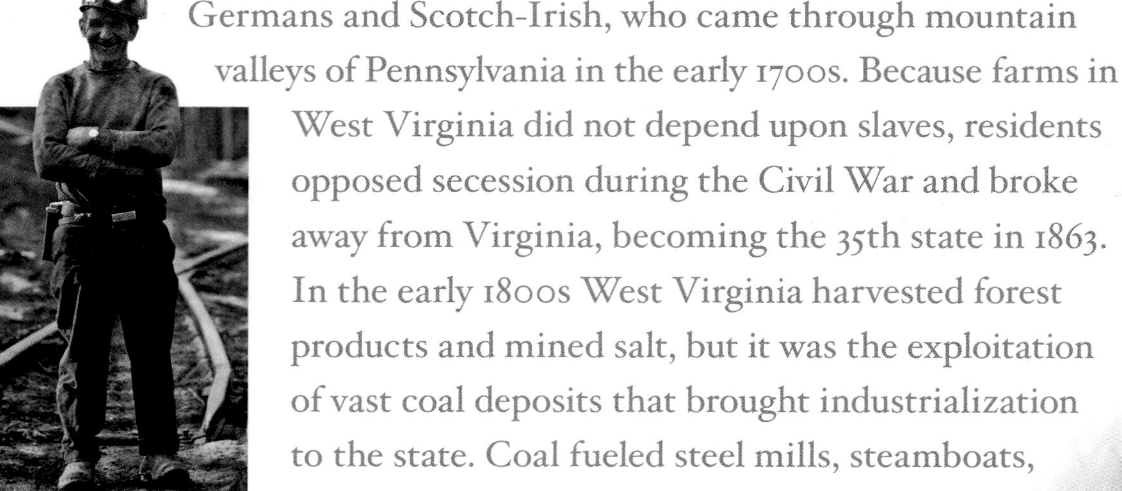

⇧ HARD LABOR. Coal miners work under difficult conditions. In 2010 West Virginia mined more than 178 million tons of coal, or 12.5 percent of U.S. production.

THE BASICS

STATS

Area
24,230 sq mi (62,755 sq km)

Population
1,852,994

Capital
Charleston
Population 51,400

Largest city
Charleston
Population 51,400

Ethnic/racial groups
93.9% white; 3.4% African American; .7% Asian; .2% Native American. Hispanic (any race) 1.2%.

Industry
Tourism, coal mining, chemicals, metal manufacturing, forest products, stone, clay, oil, glass products

Agriculture
Poultry and eggs, cattle, dairy products, apples

Statehood
June 20, 1863; 35th state

GEO WHIZ

The FBI crime data center in Clarksburg has the largest collection of fingerprints in the world. The center processes some 50,000 fingerprints each day.

The city of Weirton is nestled in the panhandle between Ohio and Pennsylvania. It is the only city in the U.S. that sits in one state and borders two others.

Bridge Day, held each October, is the only day of the year when it is legal to jump off the 876-foot- (267-m-) high New River Gorge Bridge using bungee cords, parachutes, or other equipment.

The first rural free mail delivery in the United States started in Charles Town on October 1, 1896.

CARDINAL
RHODODENDRON

⇦ STRATEGIC LOCATION. Founded in 1751 by Robert Harper, who built a ferry to cross the Shenandoah River, Harpers Ferry was a departure point for pioneers heading West as well as the site of many battles during the Civil War.

THE MOUNTAIN STATE:
WEST VIRGINIA

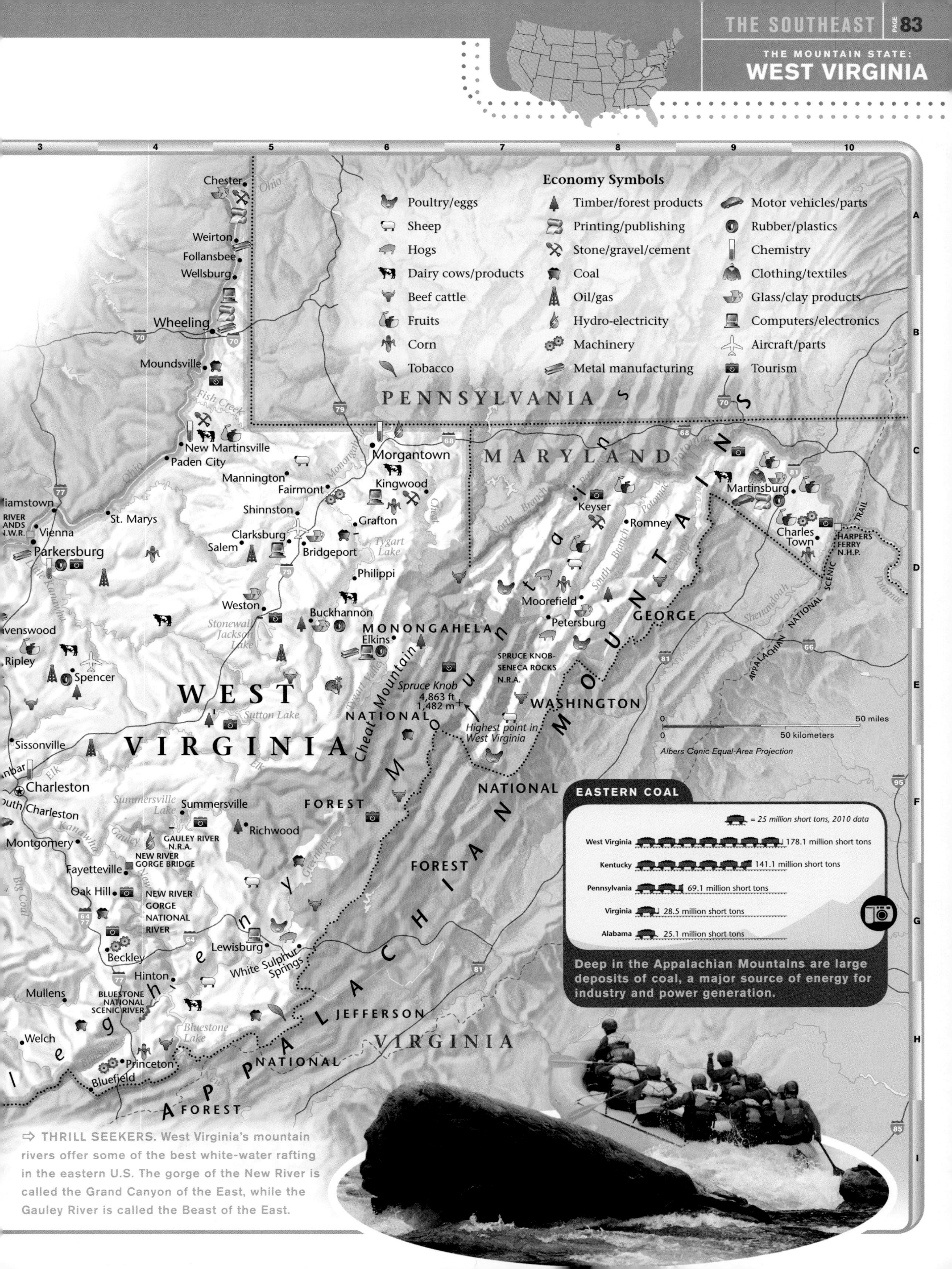

⇨ THRILL SEEKERS. West Virginia's mountain rivers offer some of the best white-water rafting in the eastern U.S. The gorge of the New River is called the Grand Canyon of the East, while the Gauley River is called the Beast of the East.

THE REGION

PHYSICAL

Total area
821,739 sq mi
(2,128,287 sq km)

Highest point
Harney Peak, SD
7,242 ft (2,207 m)

Lowest point
St. Francis River, MO
230 ft (70 m)

Longest rivers
Mississippi, Missouri, Arkansas, Ohio

Largest lakes
Superior, Michigan, Huron, Erie

Vegetation
Grassland; broadleaf, needleleaf, and mixed forest

Climate
Continental to mild, ranging from cold winters and cool summers in the north to mild winters and humid summers in the south

POLITICAL

Total population
66,927,001

States (12):
Illinois, Indiana, Iowa, Kansas, Michigan, Minnesota, Missouri, Nebraska, North Dakota, Ohio, South Dakota, Wisconsin

Largest state
Michigan: 96,716 sq mi (250,495 sq km)

Smallest state
Indiana: 36,418 sq mi (94,322 sq km)

Most populous state
Illinois: 12,830,632

Least populous state
North Dakota: 672,591

Largest city proper
Chicago, IL: 2,695,598

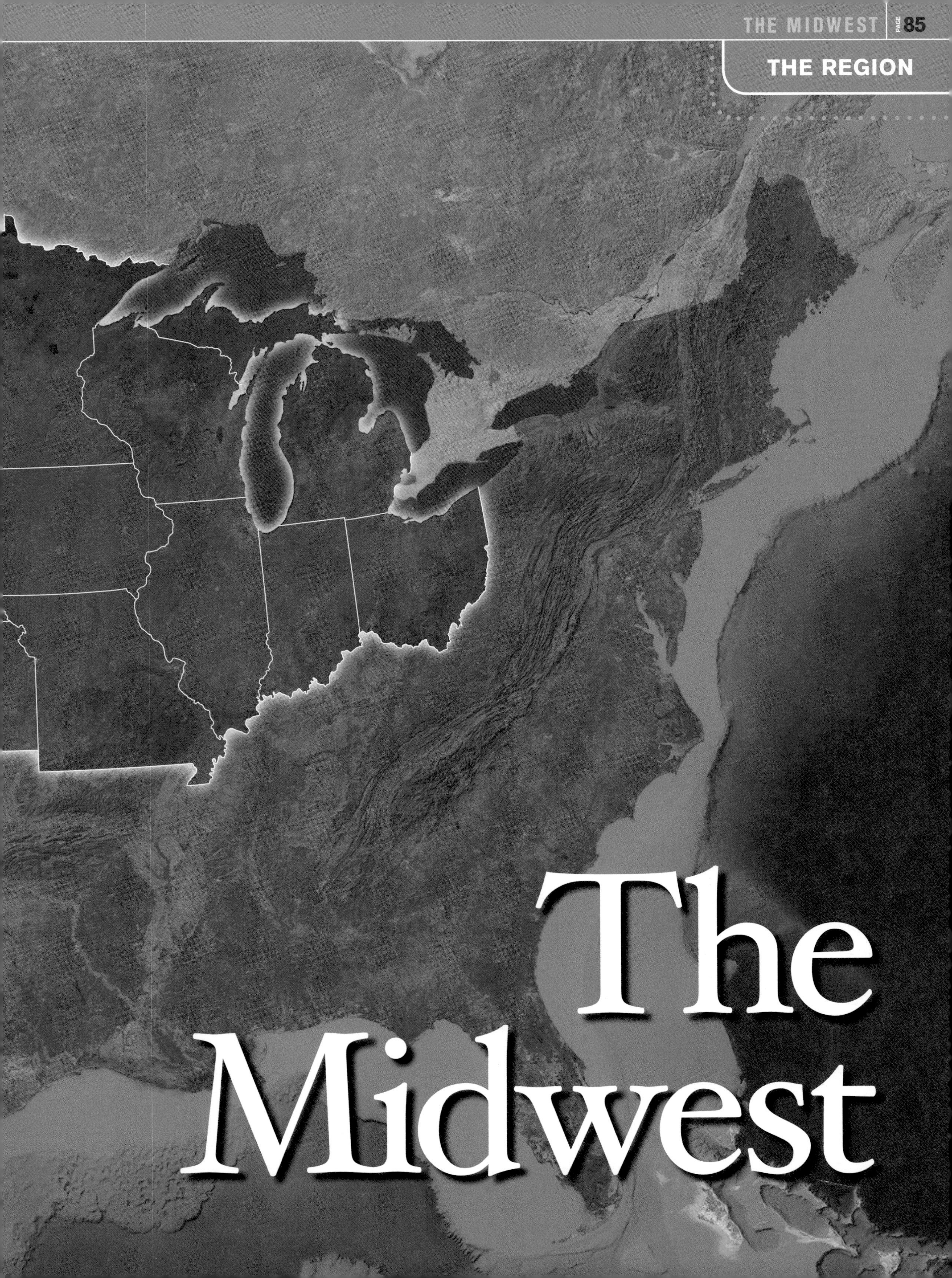

The Midwest

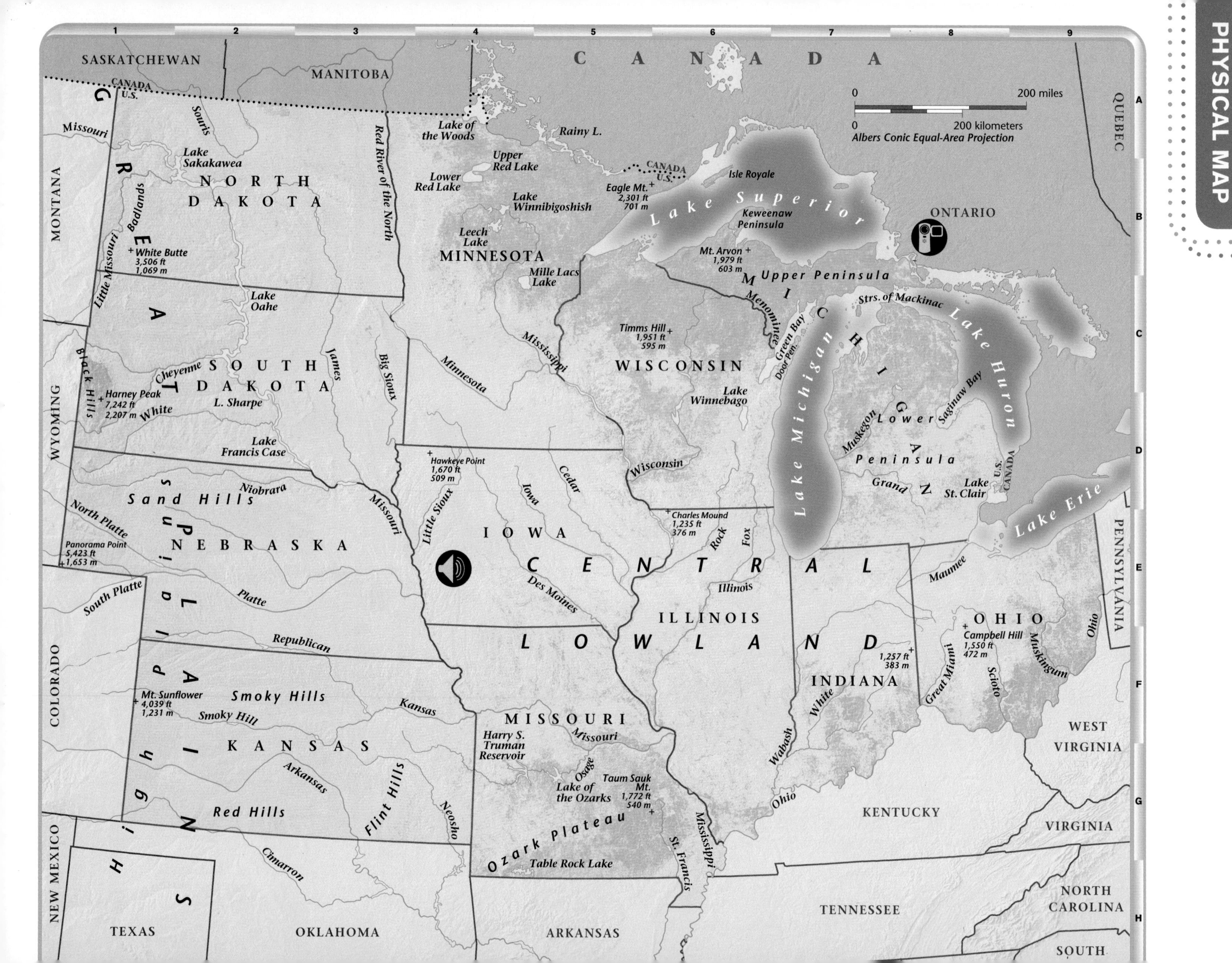
CANADA
SASKATCHEWAN
MANITOBA
ONTARIO
QUEBEC
0 200 miles
0 200 kilometers
Albers Conic Equal-Area Projection
Lake of the Woods
Rainy L.
Upper Red Lake
Lower Red Lake
Lake Winnibigoshish
Leech Lake
MINNESOTA
Mille Lacs Lake
Eagle Mt. 2,301 ft 701 m
Isle Royale
Lake Superior
Keweenaw Peninsula
Mt. Arvon 1,979 ft 603 m
Upper Peninsula
MICHIGAN
Strs. of Mackinac
Lake Huron
Lake Michigan
Green Bay
Door Pen.
Menominee
Saginaw Bay
Lower Peninsula
Muskegon
Grand
Lake St. Clair
U.S.
CANADA
Lake Erie
Timms Hill 1,951 ft 595 m
WISCONSIN
Lake Winnebago
Wisconsin
Mississippi
Minnesota
Missouri
Souris
Lake Sakakawea
NORTH DAKOTA
Badlands
White Butte 3,506 ft 1,069 m
Little Missouri
Red River of the North
MONTANA
WYOMING
Lake Oahe
SOUTH DAKOTA
Cheyenne
Black Hills
Harney Peak 7,242 ft 2,207 m
White
L. Sharpe
James
Big Sioux
Lake Francis Case
Niobrara
Sand Hills
North Platte
Panorama Point 5,423 ft 1,653 m
NEBRASKA
South Platte
Platte
Republican
COLORADO
Mt. Sunflower 4,039 ft 1,231 m
Smoky Hills
Smoky Hill
Kansas
KANSAS
Arkansas
Flint Hills
Neosho
Red Hills
Cimarron
NEW MEXICO
TEXAS
OKLAHOMA
GREAT PLAINS
High Plains
Hawkeye Point 1,670 ft 509 m
Little Sioux
IOWA
Iowa
Cedar
Des Moines
CENTRAL LOWLAND
Charles Mound 1,235 ft 376 m
Rock
Fox
Illinois
ILLINOIS
MISSOURI
Harry S. Truman Reservoir
Osage
Taum Sauk Mt. 1,772 ft 540 m
Lake of the Ozarks
Ozark Plateau
Table Rock Lake
St. Francis
ARKANSAS
INDIANA
1,257 ft 383 m
White
Wabash
Ohio
Maumee
OHIO
Campbell Hill 1,550 ft 472 m
Great Miami
Scioto
Muskingum
PENNSYLVANIA
WEST VIRGINIA
KENTUCKY
VIRGINIA
TENNESSEE
NORTH CAROLINA
SOUTH
1
2
3
4
5
6
7
8
9
A
B
C
D
E
F
G
H

SASKATCHEWAN
MANITOBA
CANADA
U.S.
0 200 miles
0 200 kilometers
Albers Conic Equal-Area Projection
QUEBEC
ONTARIO
MONTANA
WYOMING
COLORADO
NEW MEXICO
NORTH DAKOTA
SOUTH DAKOTA
NEBRASKA
KANSAS
MINNESOTA
IOWA
MISSOURI
WISCONSIN
ILLINOIS
MICHIGAN
INDIANA
OHIO
PENNSYLVANIA
WEST VIRGINIA
VIRGINIA
KENTUCKY
TENNESSEE
NORTH CAROLINA
SOUTH CAROLINA
GEORGIA
ALABAMA
MISSISSIPPI
ARKANSAS
OKLAHOMA
TEXAS
Lake Superior
Lake Michigan
Lake Huron
Lake Erie
Minot
Grand Forks
Bismarck
Fargo
International Falls
Duluth
Superior
Marquette
Sault Ste. Marie
Aberdeen
St. Cloud
St. Paul
Minneapolis
Eau Claire
Green Bay
Traverse City
Pierre
Rapid City
Rochester
La Crosse
Sioux Falls
Saginaw
Flint
Lansing
Milwaukee
Madison
Kenosha
Grand Rapids
Detroit
Ann Arbor
Sioux City
Rockford
Cedar Rapids
Chicago
Gary
South Bend
Toledo
Cleveland
Akron
Des Moines
Davenport
North Platte
Grand Island
Kearney
Omaha
Council Bluffs
Lincoln
Fort Wayne
Peoria
Bloomington
Quincy
Decatur
Springfield
Indianapolis
Columbus
Dayton
Cincinnati
Bloomington
St. Joseph
Manhattan
Kansas City
Salina
Topeka
Overland Park
Columbia
St. Louis
Jefferson City
Evansville
Dodge City
Witchita
Cape Girardeau
Springfield
Missouri
Souris
Red River of the North
Little Missouri
Mississippi
Menominee
Cheyenne
James
Big Sioux
Minnesota
White
Muskegon
Grand
Wisconsin
Iowa
Cedar
Niobrara
North Platte
Missouri
Little Sioux
Fox
Rock
Maumee
Platte
South Platte
Des Moines
Illinois
Muskingum
Ohio
Republican
Great Miami
Scioto
Kansas
Smoky Hill
White
Wabash
Arkansas
Osage
Neosho
Ohio
Cimarron
St. Francis
A
B
C
D
E
F
G
H
1
2
3
4
5
6
7
8
9

ABOUT THE
MIDWEST

⇨ FIERCE GIANT. Students in Chicago's Field Museum eye the skeleton of *Tyrannosaurus rex*, a dinosaur that roamed North America's plains 65 million years ago.

The Midwest

GREAT LAKES, GREAT RIVERS

The Midwest's early white settlers emigrated from eastern states or Europe, but recent immigrants come from all parts of the world. Hispanics, for example, are settling in communities large and small throughout the region, while many Arabs reside in Dearborn, Michigan. Drained by three mighty rivers—the Mississippi, Missouri, and Ohio—the Midwestern lowlands and plains are one of the world's most bountiful farmlands. Though the number of farmers has declined, new technologies and equipment have made farms larger and more productive. Meanwhile, industrial cities of the Rust Belt are adjusting to an economy focused more on information and services than on manufacturing.

⇩ CROP CIRCLES. Much of the western part of the region receives less than 20 inches (50 cm) of rain yearly—not enough to support agriculture. Large, circular center-pivot irrigation systems draw water from underground reserves called aquifers to provide life-giving water to crops.

⇩ DAIRY HEARTLAND. Dairy cows, such as these in Wisconsin, are sometimes treated with growth hormones to increase milk production. These animals play an important role in the economy of the Midwest, which supplies much of the country's milk, butter, and cheese.

ABOUT THE
MIDWEST

⇩ MIDWEST URBAN HUB. Chicago, the third largest urban area in the U.S., with almost 10 million people, is the economic and cultural core of the Midwest and a major transportation hub.

⇨ PRESERVING THE PAST. A young Cherokee man, dressed in beaded costume and feathered headband, dances at a powwow in Milwaukee. Such gatherings provide Indians from across the country with a chance to share their traditions.

⇧ NATURE'S MOST VIOLENT STORMS. Parts of the midwestern U.S. have earned the nickname Tornado Alley because these destructive, swirling storms, which develop in association with thunderstorms along eastward-moving cold fronts, occur here more than any other place on Earth.

WHERE THE PICTURES ARE

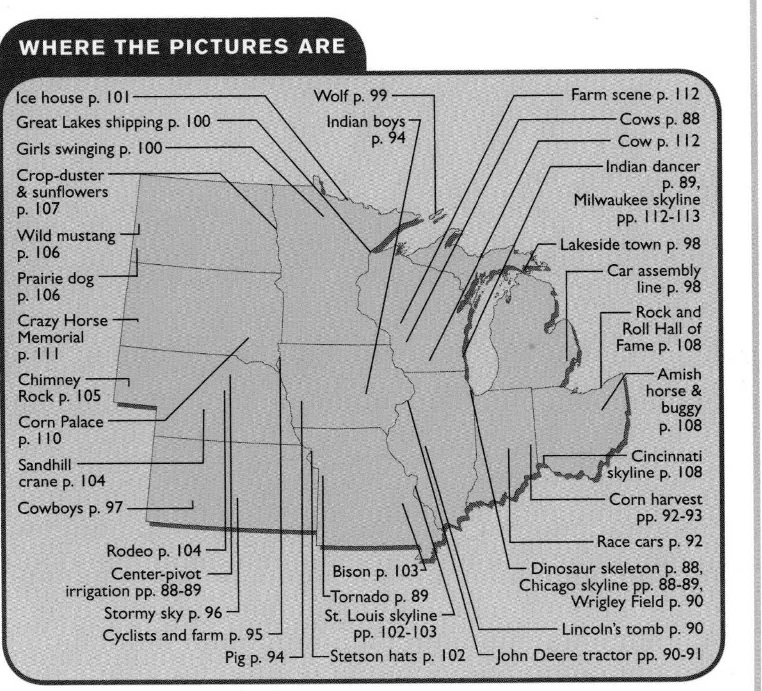

THE LAND OF LINCOLN STATE:
ILLINOIS

THE BASICS

STATS

Area
57,914 sq mi (149,998 sq km)

Population
12,830,632

Capital
Springfield
Population 116,250

Largest city
Chicago
Population 2,695,598

Ethnic/racial groups
71.5% white; 14.5% African American; 4.6% Asian; .3% Native American. Hispanic (any race) 15.8%.

Industry
Industrial machinery, electronic equipment, food processing, chemicals, metals, printing and publishing, rubber and plastics, motor vehicles

Agriculture
Corn, soybeans, hogs, cattle, dairy products, nursery stock

Statehood
December 3, 1818; 21st state

GEO WHIZ

A giant fossilized rain forest has been unearthed in an eastern Illinois coal mine near the town of Danville. Scientists believe an earthquake buried the entire forest 300 million years ago.

The Great Chicago fire of 1871 destroyed the city's waterworks, so firemen had to drag water in buckets from Lake Michigan and the Chicago River. The fire burned out of control for two days until rain finally put it out.

CARDINAL
VIOLET

ILLINOIS

Two rivers that now form the borders of Illinois aided the state's early white settlement. Frenchmen first explored the area in 1673 by traveling down the Mississippi, and the Ohio brought many 19th-century settlers to southern Illinois. Most Indians were forced out by the 1830s, more than a decade after Illinois became the 21st state. Ethnically diverse Chicago, the most populous city in the Midwest, is an economic giant and one of the country's busiest rail, highway, and air transit hubs. Barges from its port reach the Gulf of Mexico via rivers and canals, while ships reach the Atlantic Ocean via the Great Lakes and St. Lawrence Seaway. Flat terrain and fertile prairie soils in the northern and central regions help make the state a top producer of corn and soybeans. The more rugged, forested south has deposits of bituminous coal. Springfield, capital of the Land of Lincoln, welcomes tourists visiting the home and tomb of the country's 16th president.

⇧ REMEMBERING A PRESIDENT. Dedicated in 1874, the National Lincoln Monument in Springfield honors Abraham Lincoln, who was assassinated in 1865. A special vault holds the remains of the slain president, who led the country during the Civil War.

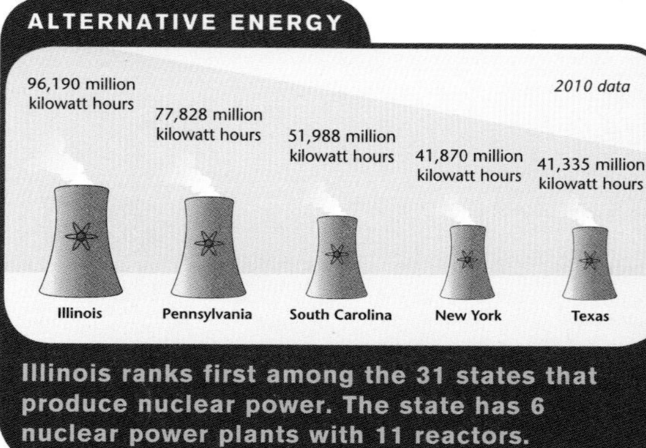

⇧ PLAY BALL! Wrigley Field, home to the Chicago Cubs baseball team, is affected by wind conditions more than any other major league park due to its location near Lake Michigan.

⇧ FIELDS OF GRAIN. Illinois has long been a major grain producer, but farming today is highly mechanized. Above, a tractor moves bales of rolled hay.

THE LAND OF LINCOLN STATE:
ILLINOIS

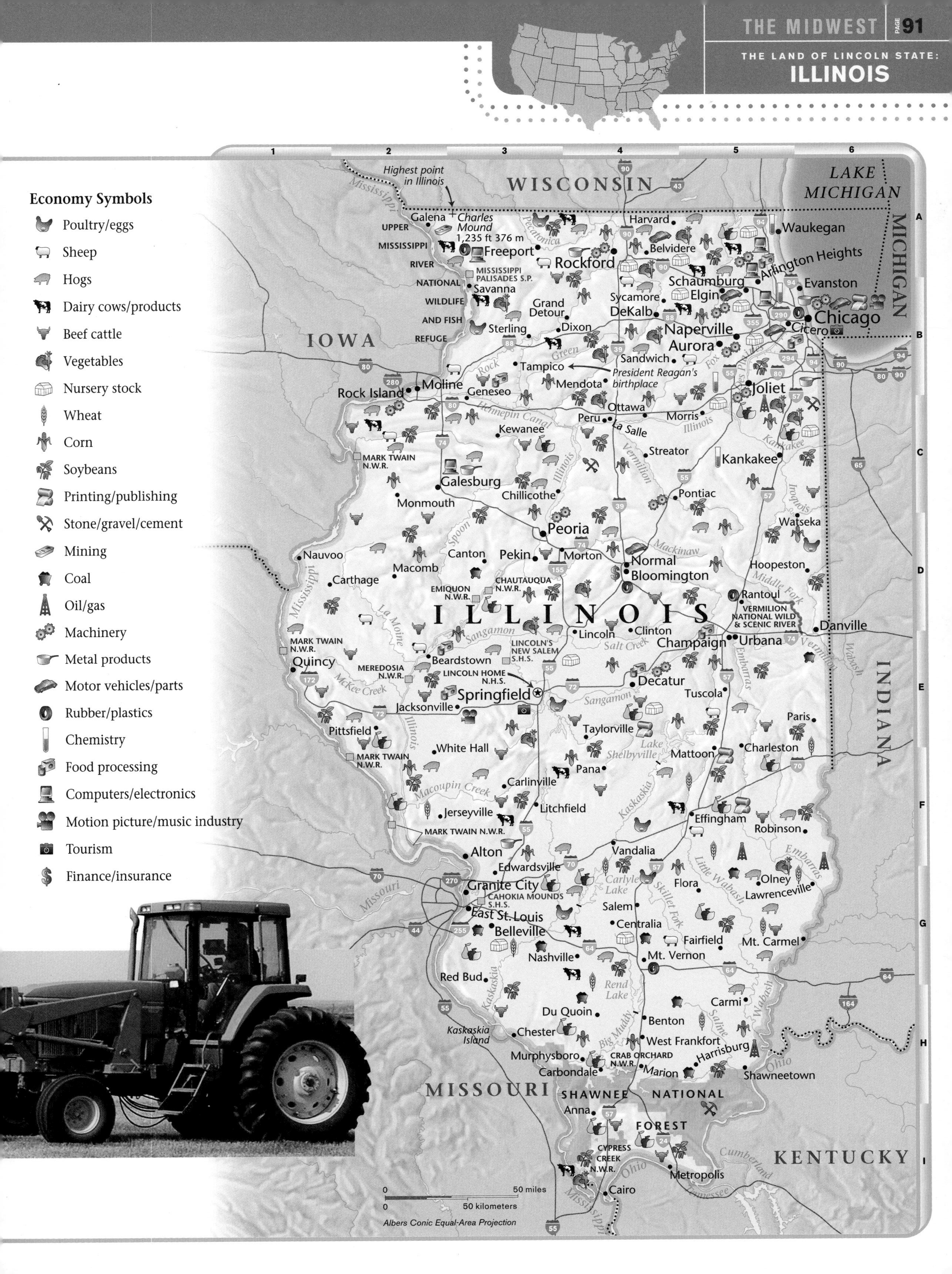

THE HOOSIER STATE:
INDIANA

INDIANA

⇧ START YOUR ENGINES. The Indianapolis Motor Speedway seats 250,000 sports fans. Nicknamed the Brickyard, its track was once paved with 3.2 million bricks.

Indiana's name, meaning "Land of the Indians," honors the tribes who lived in the region before the arrival of Europeans. The first permanent white settlement was Vincennes, established by the French in the early 1700s. Following statehood in 1816, most Indians were forced out to make way for white settlement. Lake Michigan, in the state's northwest corner, brings economic and recreational opportunities. The lakefront city of Gary anchors a major industrial region. Nearby, the natural beauty and shifting sands of the Indiana Dunes National Lakeshore attract many visitors. Corn, soybeans, and hogs are the most important products from Indiana's many farms. True to the state motto, "The Crossroads of America," highways from all directions converge at Indianapolis. Traveling at a much higher speed are cars on that city's famed Motor Speedway, home to the Indy 500 auto race since 1911. Cheering for a favorite high school or college team is a favorite pastime for many Hoosiers who catch basketball fever.

THE BASICS

STATS

Area
36,418 sq mi (94,322 sq km)

Population
6,483,802

Capital
Indianapolis
Population 820,445

Largest city
Indianapolis
Population 820,445

Ethnic/racial groups
84.3% white; 9.1% African American; 1.6% Asian; .3% Native American. Hispanic (any race) 6.0%.

Industry
Transportation equipment, steel, pharmaceutical and chemical products, machinery, petroleum, coal

Agriculture
Corn, soybeans, hogs, poultry and eggs, cattle, dairy products

Statehood
December 11, 1816; 19th state

GEO WHIZ

Every July during Circus Festival, in Peru, a couple hundred local kids and a couple thousand volunteers put on a three-ring circus complete with clowns, snow cones, and standing ovations from sellout crowds. The city is home to the International Circus Hall of Fame.

Every year Fort Wayne hosts the Johnny Appleseed Festival to honor John Chapman, the man who planted apple orchards from Pennsylvania to Illinois.

The Indianapolis Children's Museum, in partnership with National Geographic and the Environmental Research Systems Institute, has created an international traveling exhibit to teach children and parents that maps are tools of adventure.

CARDINAL
PEONY

⇨ FUEL FARMING. Indiana farming is undergoing dramatic changes as corn is used in the production of ethanol, a non-fossil fuel energy source that is increasingly popular.

HEAVY INDUSTRY

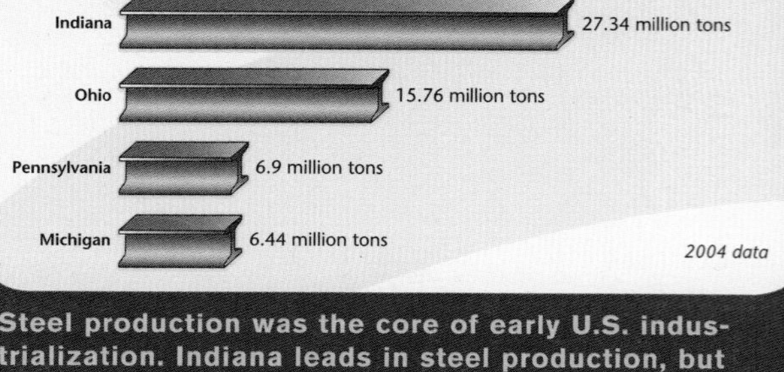

Steel production was the core of early U.S. industrialization. Indiana leads in steel production, but the U.S. also imports steel from other countries.

THE HOOSIER STATE:
INDIANA

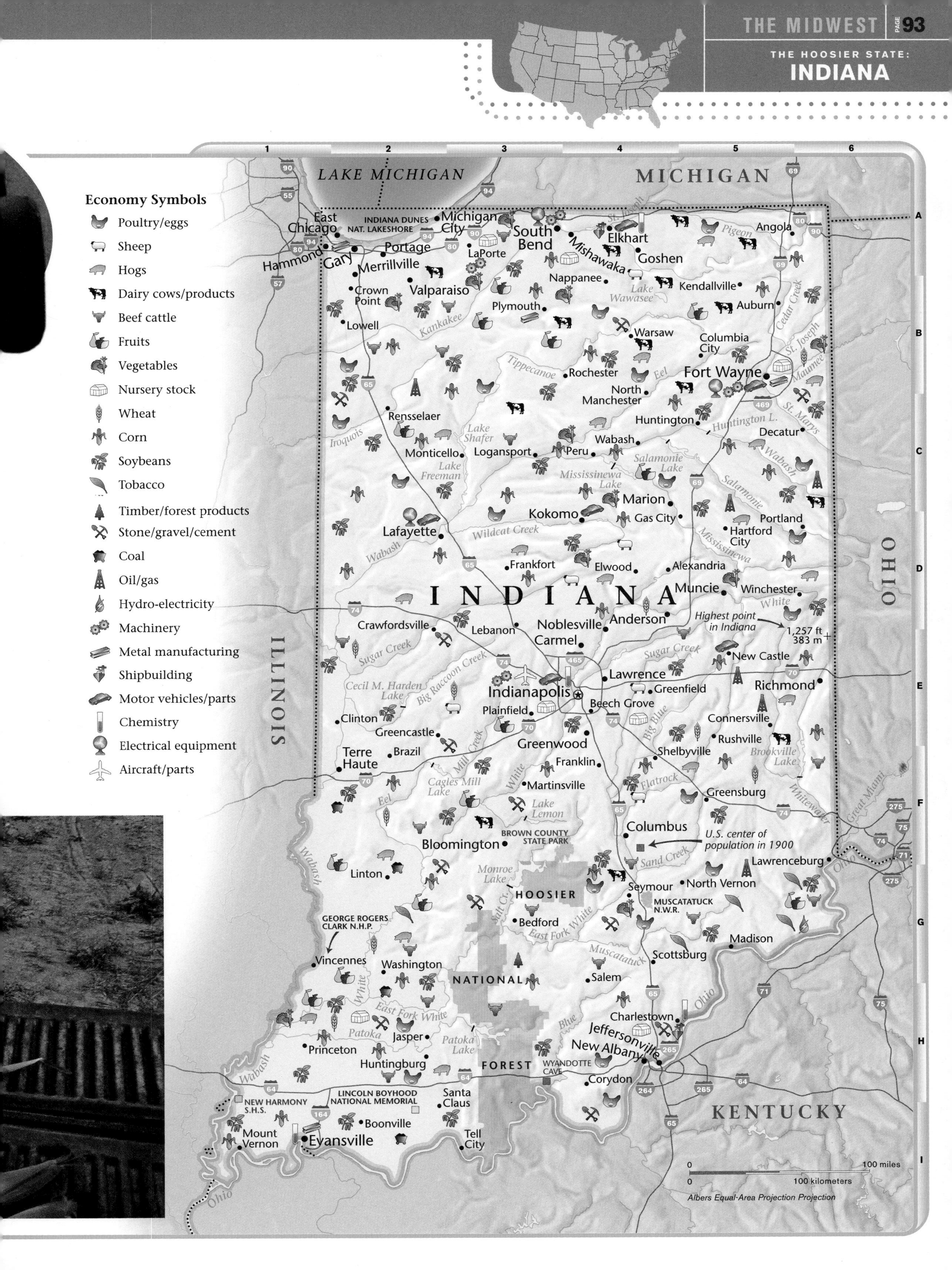

THE HAWKEYE STATE: IOWA

IOWA

IOWA

Iowa's prehistoric inhabitants built earthen mounds—some shaped like birds and bears—that are visible in the state's northeast. Nineteenth-century white settlers found rolling prairies covered by a sea of tall grasses that soon yielded to the plow. A decade after statehood in 1846, a group of religious German immigrants established the Amana Colonies, a communal society that still draws visitors. Blessed with ample precipitation and rich soils, Iowa is the heart of one of the world's most productive farming regions. The state is the country's top producer of corn, soybeans, hogs, and eggs. Food processing and manufacturing machinery are two of the biggest industries. Much of the grain crop feeds livestock destined to reach dinner plates in the U.S. and around the world. An increasing amount of corn is used to make ethanol, which is mixed with gasoline to fuel cars and trucks. Des Moines, the capital and largest city, is a center of insurance and publishing.

⇧ PIG BUSINESS. Hogs outnumber people more than six to one in Iowa. The state raises 30 percent of the nation's hogs, making it the leading producer.

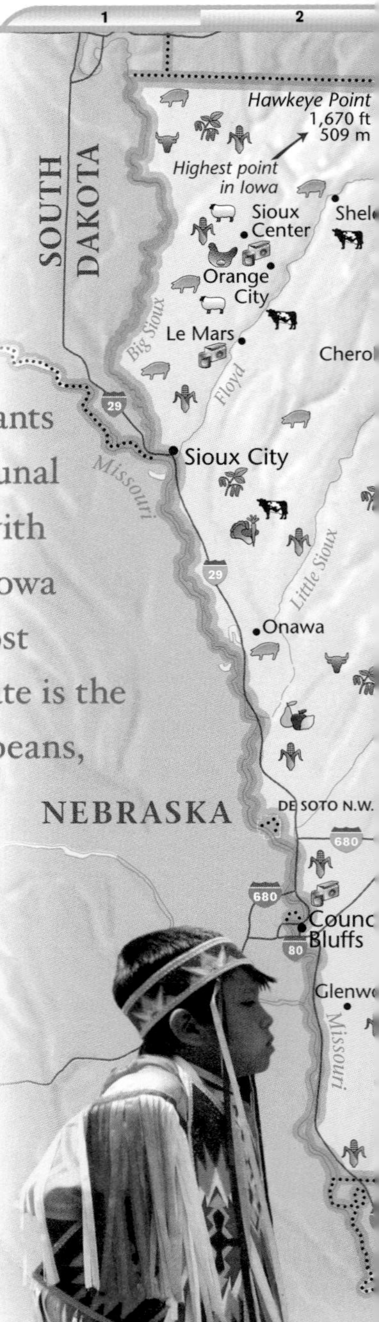

THE BASICS

STATS

Area
56,272 sq mi (145,743 sq km)

Population
3,046,355

Capital
Des Moines
Population 203,433

Largest city
Des Moines
Population 203,433

Ethnic/racial groups
91.3% white; 2.9% African American; 1.7% Asian; .4% Native American. Hispanic (any race) 5.0%.

Industry
Real estate, health services, industrial machinery, food processing, construction

Agriculture
Hogs, corn, soybeans, oats, cattle, dairy products

Statehood
December 28, 1846; 29th state

GEO WHIZ

The most famous house in Iowa and one of the most famous houses in America is in Eldon. It was immortalized in Grant Wood's famous painting "American Gothic." The stern-faced, pitchfork-holding farmer and his wife shown in the art were not farmers at all. Wood's sister and his dentist posed for the painting.

Effigy Mounds National Monument, in the northeast corner of Iowa, is the only place in the country with such a large collection of mounds in the shapes of mammals, birds, and reptiles. Of the 191 mounds, 29 are shaped like animals. Eastern Woodland Indians built these mounds from about 500 B.C. to 1300 A.D.

Iowa ranks number 7 among leading U.S. wind energy producers, which are led by Texas and Kansas.

AMERICAN GOLDFINCH
WILD ROSE

GREEN ENERGY

2010 production capacity in millions of gallons (liters)

Iowa	Nebraska	Illinois	Minnesota	South Dakota
3,595 (13,609)	1,839 (6,961)	1,480 (5,602)	1,119 (4,234)	1,016 (3,846)

Iowa is the leading producer of ethanol fuel, a clean-burning, renewable, non-fossil fuel energy source made mainly from corn.

⇨ LEGACY OF THE PAST. Young boys dressed in colorful outfits participate in a traditional dance ceremony, calling to mind Iowa's rich Native American heritage.

1 2
SOUTH DAKOTA
Hawkeye Point 1,670 ft 509 m
Highest point in Iowa
Sioux Center
Orange City
Le Mars
Big Sioux
Floyd
Sioux City
Missouri
Little Sioux
Onawa
NEBRASKA
DE SOTO N.W.
Council Bluffs
Glenwood
29
680
80

THE HAWKEYE STATE: IOWA

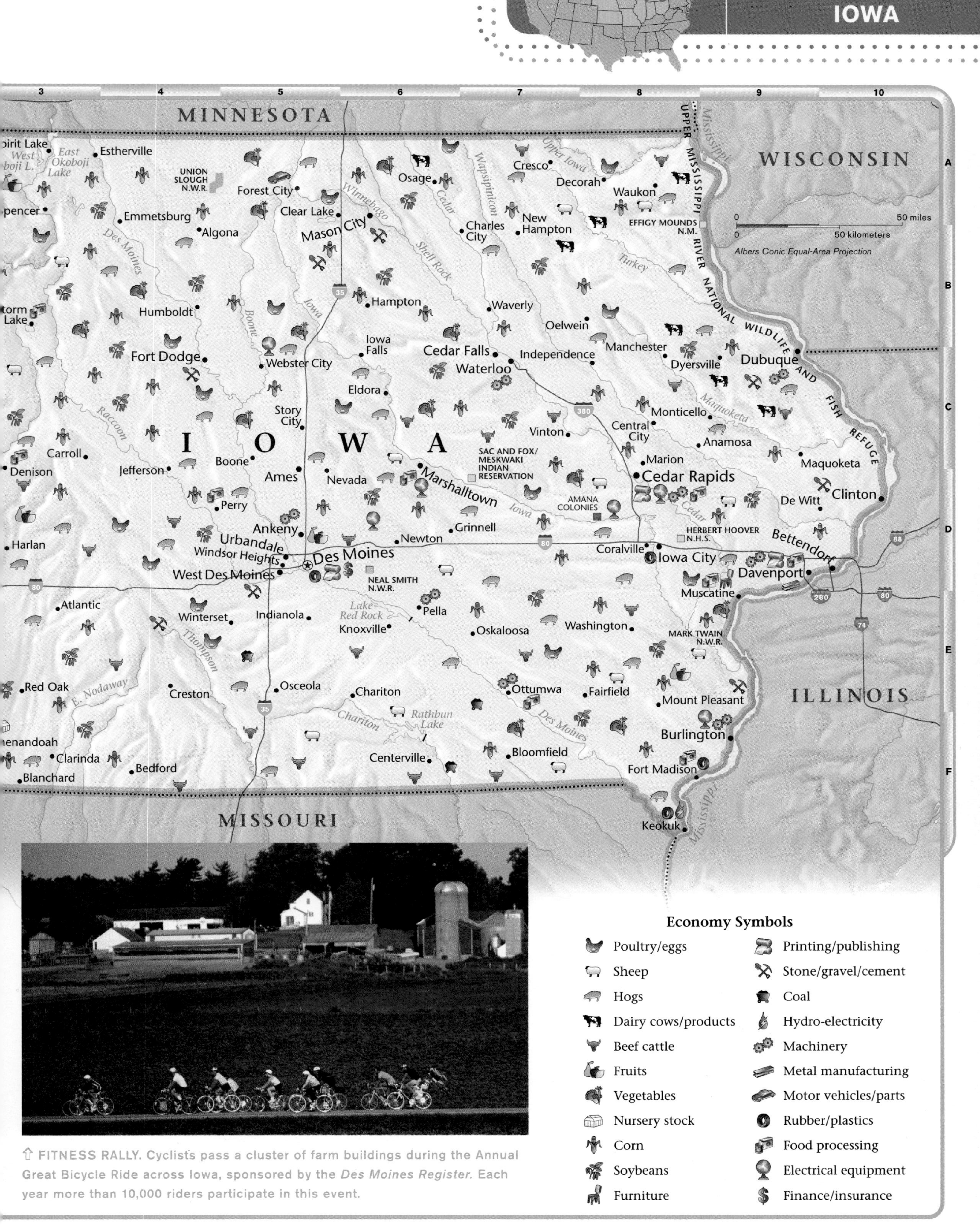

⇧ FITNESS RALLY. Cyclists pass a cluster of farm buildings during the Annual Great Bicycle Ride across Iowa, sponsored by the *Des Moines Register*. Each year more than 10,000 riders participate in this event.

THE SUNFLOWER STATE:
KANSAS

KANSAS

THE BASICS

STATS

Area
82,277 sq mi (213,097 sq km)

Population
2,853,118

Capital
Topeka
Population 127,473

Largest city
Wichita
Population 382,368

Ethnic/racial groups
83.8% white; 5.9% African American; 4.8% Asian; 1.0% Native American. Hispanic (any race) 10.5%.

Industry
Aircraft manufacturing, transportation equipment, construction, food processing, printing and publishing, health care

Agriculture
Cattle, wheat, sorghum, soybeans, hogs, corn

Statehood
January 29, 1861; 34th state

GEO WHIZ

Plesiosaur skeletons and many other marine reptile fossils have been unearthed in Kansas. In 2007 National Geographic released the IMAX film *Sea Monsters*, which explores the kinds of animals that lived in the prehistoric sea that covered Kansas and much of North America 82 million years ago.

The Tallgrass Prairie National Preserve, the nation's last great expanse of tallgrass prairie, anchors a world renewed by fire. It is in the Flint Hills of Kansas.

Lindsborg is proud of its Swedish heritage and the fact that it is home to the Anatoly Karpov International School of Chess. The school is named for the Russian player who succeeded American Bobby Fischer as world champion in 1975.

WESTERN MEADOWLARK
SUNFLOWER

KANSAS

Considered by whites to be unsuitable for settlement, Kansas was made part of Indian Territory—a vast tract of land between Missouri and the Rockies—in the 1830s. By the 1850s whites were fighting Indians for more land and among themselves over the issue of slavery. In 1861 Kansas entered the Union as a free state. After the Civil War, cowboys drove Texas cattle to railheads in the Wild West towns of Abilene and Dodge City, where waiting trains hauled cattle to slaughterhouses in the East. Today, the state remains a major beef producer and the country's top wheat grower. Oil and natural gas wells dot the landscape, while factories in Wichita, the largest city, make aircraft equipment. A preserve in the Flint Hills boasts one of the few tallgrass prairies to escape farmers' plows. Heading west toward the Rockies, elevations climb slowly, and the climate gets drier. Threats of fierce thunderstorms accompanied by tornados have many Kansans keeping an eye on the sky.

⇧ OMINOUS SKY. Lightning splits the sky as black clouds of a thunderstorm roll across a field of wheat. Such storms bring heavy rain and often spawn dangerous tornadoes.

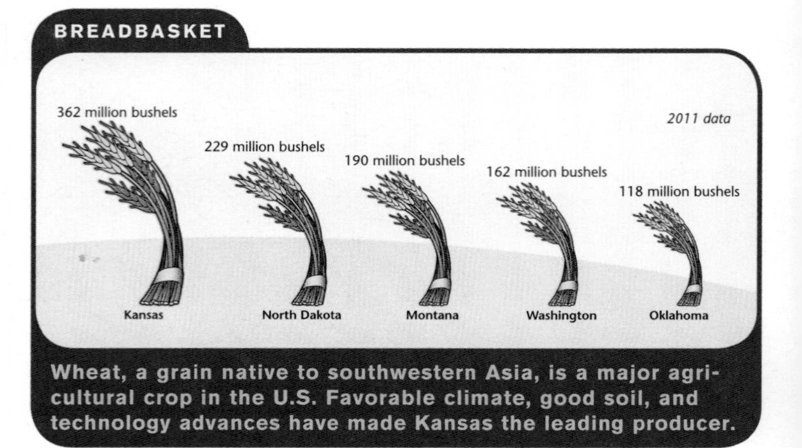

Wheat, a grain native to southwestern Asia, is a major agricultural crop in the U.S. Favorable climate, good soil, and technology advances have made Kansas the leading producer.

THE SUNFLOWER STATE: KANSAS

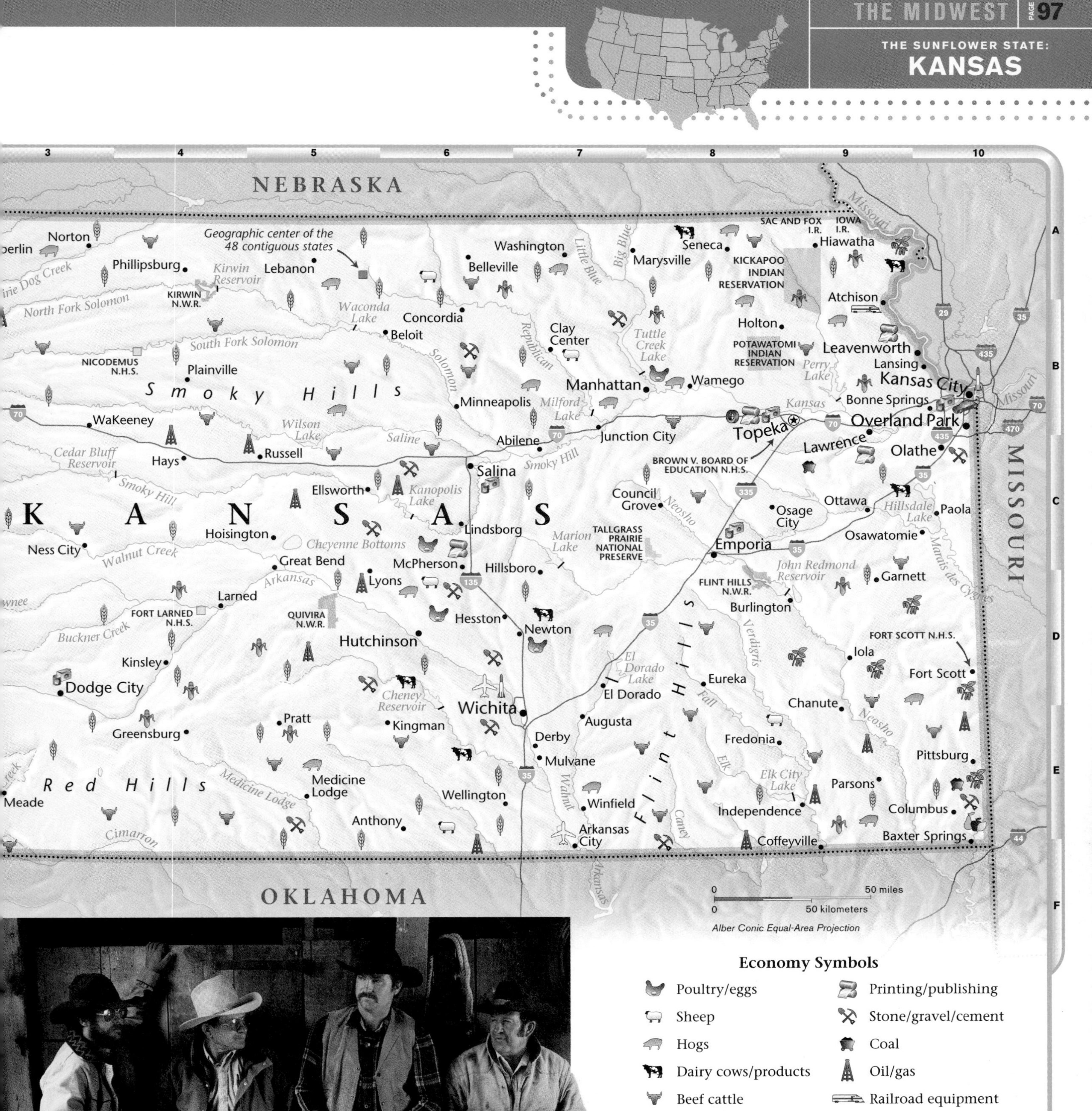

⇦ MODERN-DAY COWBOYS. Dodge City traces its history to Fort Dodge, built on the Santa Fe Trail in 1865 to protect pioneer wagon trains and the mail service from Indian attacks. Frequented by cattle herders and buffalo hunters, the town was known for its lawlessness.

THE GREAT LAKE STATE:
MICHIGAN

MICHIGAN

Indians had friendly relations with early French fur traders who came to what is now Michigan, but they waged battles with the British who later assumed control. Completion of New York's Erie Canal in 1825 made it easier for settlers to reach the area, and statehood came in 1837. Michigan consists of two large peninsulas that border four of the five Great Lakes—Erie, Huron, Michigan, and Superior. Most of the population is on the state's Lower Peninsula, while the Upper Peninsula, once a productive mining area, now is popular among vacationing nature lovers. The five-mile-long Mackinac Bridge (8 km) has linked the peninsulas since 1957. In the 20th century, Michigan became the center of the American auto industry, and the state's fortunes have risen and fallen with those of the Big Three car companies. Though it remains a big producer of cars and trucks, the state is working to diversify its economy. Michigan's farms grow crops ranging from grains to fruits and vegetables.

⇧ ROLLING OFF THE ASSEMBLY LINE. Motor vehicle production is one of the largest manufacturing sectors in the U.S., and Michigan is the center of the industry. At Chrysler's Sterling Heights assembly plant, almost 800 robots speed production by making it possible to build different car models on the same assembly line.

THE BASICS

STATS

Area
96,716 sq mi (250,495 sq km)

Population
9,883,640

Capital
Lansing
Population 114,297

Largest city
Detroit
Population 713,777

Ethnic/racial groups
78.9% white; 14.2% African American; 2.4% Asian; .6% Native American. Hispanic (any race) 4.4%.

Industry
Motor vehicles and parts, machinery, metal products, office furniture, tourism, chemicals

Agriculture
Dairy products, cattle, vegetables, hogs, corn, nursery stock, soybeans, hay, fruit

Statehood
January 26, 1837; 26th state

GEO WHIZ

Researchers at the Seney National Wildlife Refuge near Seney, Michigan, have discovered that male loons change the sound of their call when they move to a new territory. The reason is still a mystery, but it does explain why people say that loons sound different on different lakes.

The Keweenaw Peninsula is an adventurer's paradise. There's a 100-mile (161-km) water trail for canoers, scores of wrecks for divers, 14 miles (23 km) of forested bike paths, and more than 150 miles (240 km) of hiking trails on nearby Isle Royale National Park.

Climate change is causing Lake Michigan and the other Great Lakes to shrink, a fact that is very costly to shipping. For every inch (2.5 cm) of draft that a ship loses, a freighter must lighten its cargo by as much as 270 tons to keep from running aground. The collective annual cost can be in the billions of dollars.

ROBIN
APPLE BLOSSOM

WINTER SPORT

Registered snowmobiles
2010, 2011 data

Michigan	Minnesota	Wisconsin	New York	Maine
301,805	277,290	232,320	146,662	96,600

Snowmobiling has become a popular winter sport. Michigan and other states of the upper Midwest lead in number of registered snowmobiles.

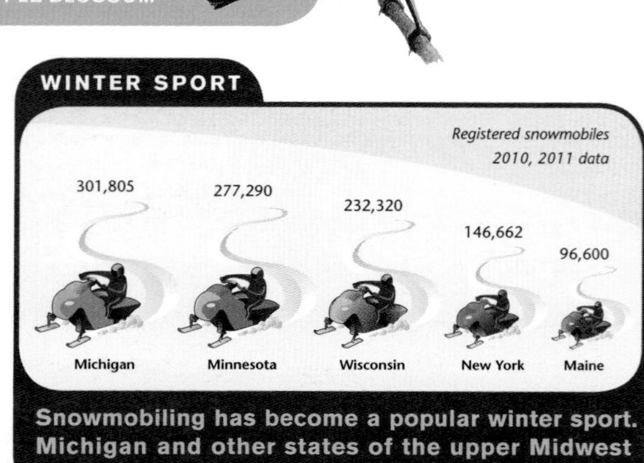

⇧ REFLECTION OF THE PAST. Victorian-style summer homes, built on Mackinac Island in the late 19th century by wealthy railroad families, now welcome vacationers to the island. To protect the environment, cars are not allowed.

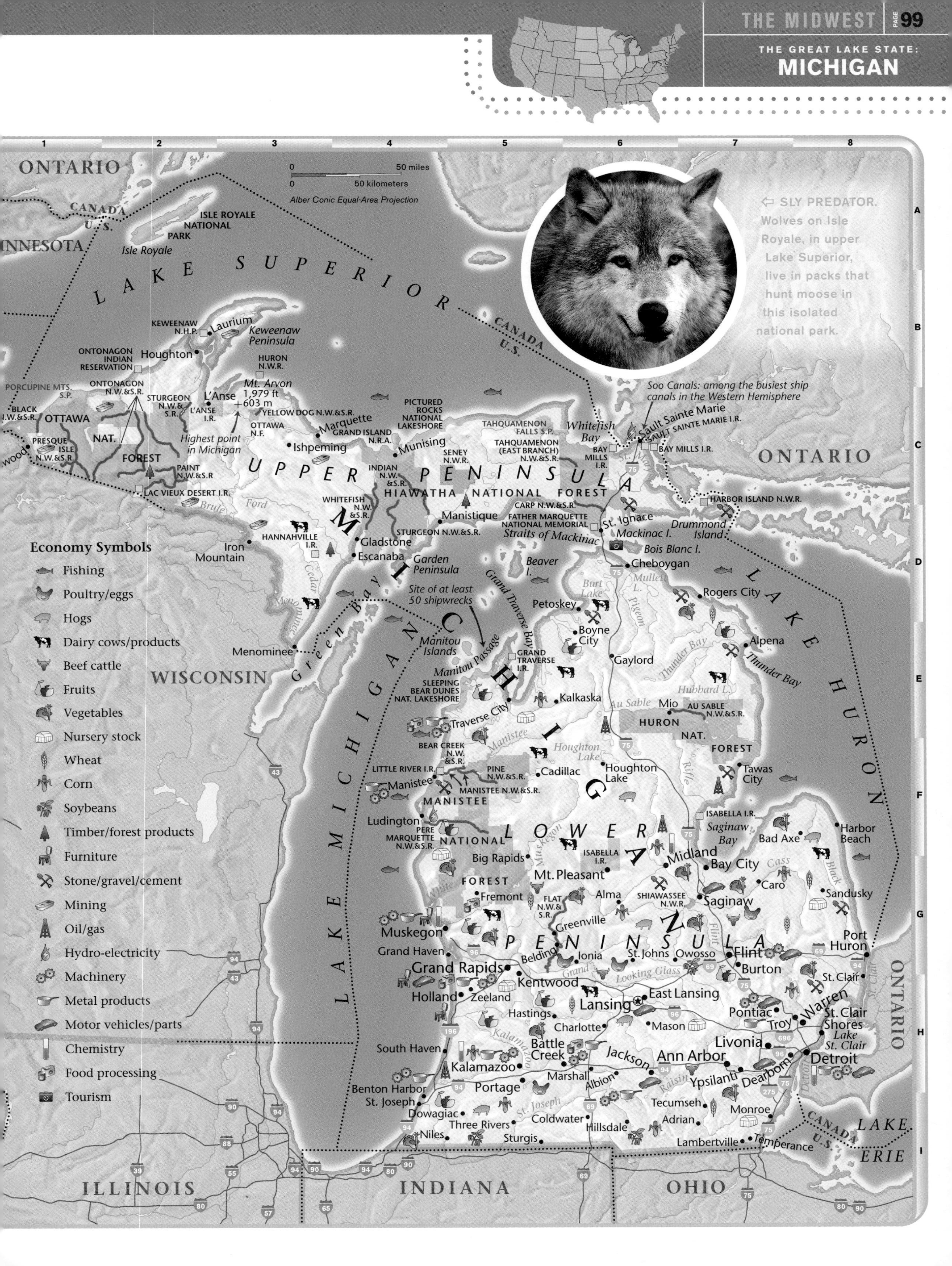
THE MIDWEST
PAGE 99
THE GREAT LAKE STATE:
MICHIGAN
SLY PREDATOR. Wolves on Isle Royale, in upper Lake Superior, live in packs that hunt moose in this isolated national park.
Soo Canals: among the busiest ship canals in the Western Hemisphere
Site of at least 50 shipwrecks
Highest point in Michigan
Mt. Arvon 1,979 ft +603 m
50 miles
50 kilometers
Alber Conic Equal-Area Projection
Economy Symbols
Fishing
Poultry/eggs
Hogs
Dairy cows/products
Beef cattle
Fruits
Vegetables
Nursery stock
Wheat
Corn
Soybeans
Timber/forest products
Furniture
Stone/gravel/cement
Mining
Oil/gas
Hydro-electricity
Machinery
Metal products
Motor vehicles/parts
Chemistry
Food processing
Tourism
LAKE SUPERIOR
LAKE MICHIGAN
LAKE HURON
LAKE ERIE
UPPER PENINSULA
LOWER PENINSULA
MICHIGAN
ONTARIO
WISCONSIN
ILLINOIS
INDIANA
OHIO
CANADA
U.S.
ISLE ROYALE NATIONAL PARK
Isle Royale
Keweenaw Peninsula
HIAWATHA NATIONAL FOREST
OTTAWA NAT. FOREST
HURON NAT. FOREST
MANISTEE NATIONAL FOREST
PICTURED ROCKS NATIONAL LAKESHORE
SLEEPING BEAR DUNES NAT. LAKESHORE
Straits of Mackinac
Green Bay
Grand Traverse Bay
Saginaw Bay
Thunder Bay
Whitefish Bay
Manitou Passage
Manitou Islands
Garden Peninsula
Beaver I.
Drummond Island
Bois Blanc I.
Mackinac I.
Houghton
Marquette
Ishpeming
Munising
Escanaba
Gladstone
Iron Mountain
Menominee
Manistique
Sault Sainte Marie
St. Ignace
Cheboygan
Petoskey
Traverse City
Gaylord
Alpena
Cadillac
Ludington
Muskegon
Grand Rapids
Holland
Kalamazoo
Battle Creek
Lansing
East Lansing
Jackson
Ann Arbor
Flint
Saginaw
Midland
Bay City
Pontiac
Troy
Warren
Livonia
Dearborn
Detroit
Ypsilanti
Monroe
Port Huron
St. Clair Shores
Mt. Pleasant
Big Rapids
Fremont
Greenville
Ionia
Owosso
Burton
Alma
St. Johns
Charlotte
Hastings
Kentwood
Zeeland
Grand Haven
South Haven
Benton Harbor
St. Joseph
Portage
Niles
Dowagiac
Three Rivers
Sturgis
Coldwater
Hillsdale
Adrian
Tecumseh
Lambertville
Temperance
Marshall
Albion
Mason
Caro
Sandusky
Bad Axe
Harbor Beach
Tawas City
Houghton Lake
Mio
Kalkaska
Boyne City
Rogers City
Laurium
L'Anse

THE GOPHER STATE:
MINNESOTA

THE BASICS

STATS

Area
86,939 sq mi (225,172 sq km)

Population
5,303,925

Capital
St. Paul
Population 285,068

Largest city
Minneapolis
Population 382,578

Ethnic/racial groups
85.3% white; 5.2% African American; 4.0% Asian; 1.1% Native American. Hispanic (any race) 4.7%.

Industry
Health services, tourism, real estate, banking and insurance, industrial machinery, printing and publishing, food processing, scientific equipment

Agriculture
Corn, soybeans, dairy products, hogs, cattle, turkeys, wheat

Statehood
May 11, 1858; 32nd state

GEO WHIZ

Nett Lake on the Bois Forte Chippewa reservation, in northern Minnesota, is the largest contiguous wild rice lake in the world. Native people have been gathering what the Indians call *manoomin* for thousands of years.

The Mayo Clinic, a world-famous medical research center founded in 1889 by Dr. William W. Mayo, is in Rochester.

The Boundary Waters Canoe Area Wilderness, along the Minnesota-Ontario border, was the first wilderness area in the U.S. to be set aside for canoeing.

COMMON LOON
SHOWY LADY'S SLIPPER

MINNESOTA

French fur traders began arriving in present-day Minnesota in the mid-17th century. Statehood was established in 1858, and most remaining Indians were forced from the state after a decisive battle in 1862. During the late 1800s large numbers of Germans, Scandinavians, and other immigrants settled a land rich in wildlife, timber, minerals, and fertile soils. Today, farming is concentrated in the south and west. In the northeast, the Mesabi Range's open-pit mines make the state the country's source of iron ore. Most of the ore is shipped from Duluth. It, along with Superior, in nearby Wisconsin (see p. 113), is the leading Great Lakes port. Ships from the port reach the Atlantic Ocean via the St. Lawrence Seaway. Scattered across the state's landscape are thousands of lakes—ancient footprints of retreating glaciers—that draw anglers and canoeists. One of those lakes, Lake Itasca, is the source of the mighty Mississippi River, which flows through the Twin Cities of Minneapolis and St. Paul.

⇧ SUMMER FUN. Young girls play on a rope swing near Leech Lake in northern Minnesota. The state's many lakes are remnants of the last ice age, when glaciers gouged depressions that filled with water as the ice sheets retreated.

SHOPPER'S PARADISE

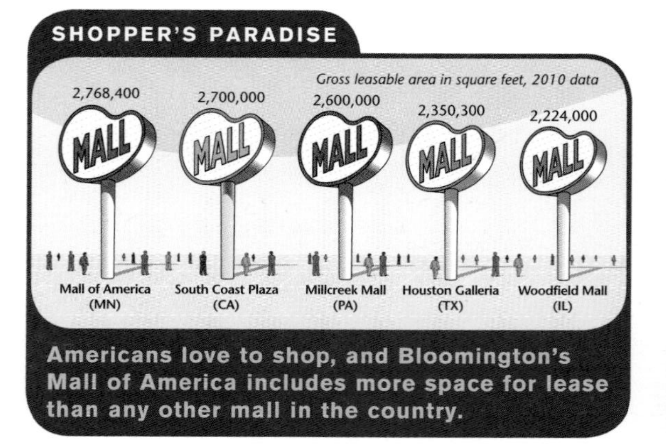

Americans love to shop, and Bloomington's Mall of America includes more space for lease than any other mall in the country.

⇦ INLAND PORT. Duluth, on the northern shore of Lake Superior, is the westernmost deep-water port on the St. Lawrence Seaway. Barges and container ships move products such as iron ore and grain along the Great Lakes to the Atlantic Ocean and to markets around the world.

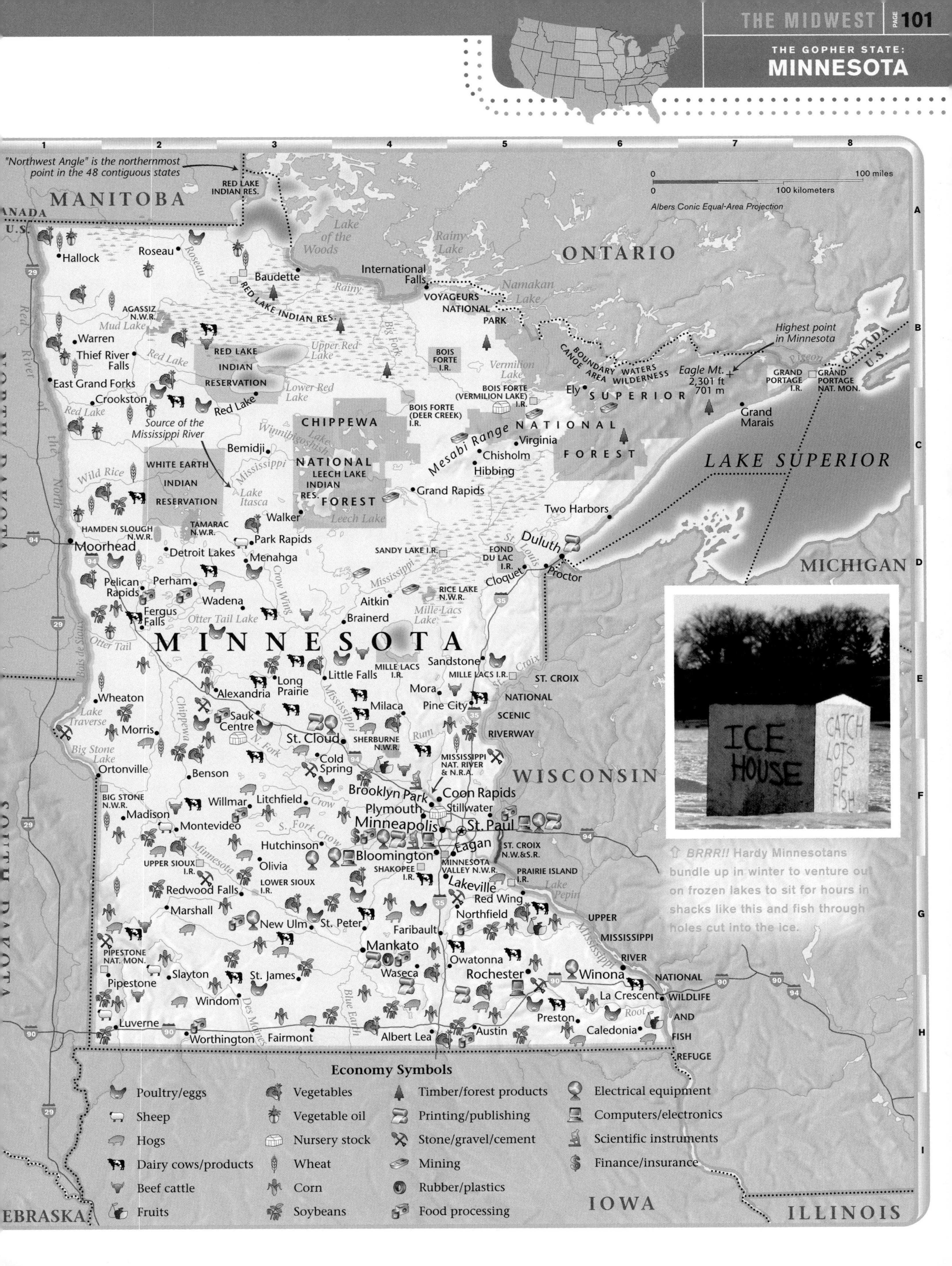

⇧ *BRRR!!* Hardy Minnesotans bundle up in winter to venture out on frozen lakes to sit for hours in shacks like this and fish through holes cut into the ice.

THE SHOW-ME STATE:
MISSOURI

MISSOURI

The Osage people were among the largest tribes in present-day Missouri when the French began establishing permanent settlements in the 1700s. The U.S. obtained the territory in the 1803 Louisiana Purchase, and Lewis and Clark began exploring the vast wilderness by paddling up the Missouri River from the St. Louis area. Missouri entered the Union as a slave state in 1821. Though it remained in the Union during the Civil War, sympathies were split between the North and South. For much of the 1800s the state was the staging ground for pioneers traveling to western frontiers on the Santa Fe and Oregon Trails. Today, Missouri leads the country in lead mining. Farmers raise cattle, hogs, poultry, corn, and soybeans. Cotton and rice are grown in the southeastern Bootheel region. Cross-state river-port rivals St. Louis and Kansas City are centers of transportation, manufacturing, and finance. Lakes, caves, scenic views, and Branson's country music shows bring many tourists to the Ozarks.

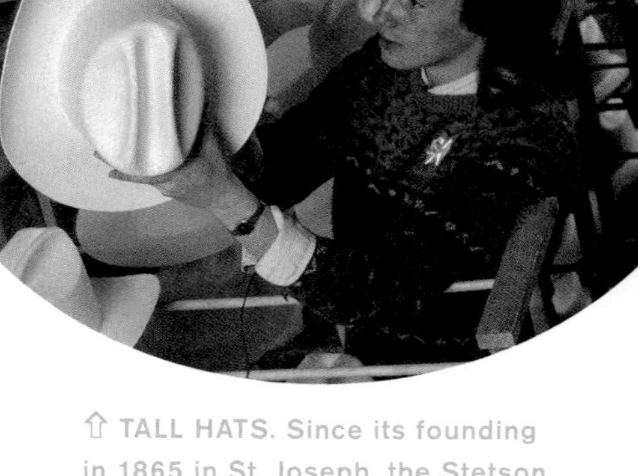

⇧ TALL HATS. Since its founding in 1865 in St. Joseph, the Stetson Company has been associated with western hats worn by men and women around the world.

THE BASICS

STATS

Area
69,704 sq mi (180,534 sq mi)

Population
5,988,927

Capital
Jefferson City
Population 43,079

Largest city
Kansas City
Population 459,787

Ethnic/racial groups
82.8% white; 11.6% African American; 1.6% Asian; .5% Native American. Hispanic (any race) 3.5%.

Industry
Transportation equipment, food processing, chemicals, electrical equipment, metal products

Agriculture
Cattle, soybeans, hogs, corn, poultry and eggs, dairy products

Statehood
August 10, 1821; 24th state

GEO WHIZ

Camp Wood, near St. Louis, was the starting point for Lewis and Clark's Corps of Discovery, commissioned by President Thomas Jefferson to seek a water route to the Pacific. Along the way their encounters included hundreds of new species of plants and animals, nearly 50 Indian tribes, and the Rocky Mountains.

In Ash Grove, near Springfield, Father Moses Berry has turned his family history into a museum for slavery education. His family was one of the few who didn't flee the area after three falsely accused black men were lynched in 1906. The museum is the only one of its kind in the Ozark region.

EASTERN BLUEBIRD
HAWTHORN

HISTORICAL MARKERS

Monument	Height
Gateway Arch (MO)	630 feet (192 m)
San Jacinto Monument (TX)	570 feet (174 m)
Washington Monument (DC)	555 feet (169 m)
Perry's Victory and International Peace Memorial (OH)	352 feet (107 m)
Jefferson Davis Monument (KY)	351 feet (107 m)

The tallest of all monuments in the U.S. is Gateway Arch in St. Louis, which marks the departure point for westward-bound pioneers during the 19th century.

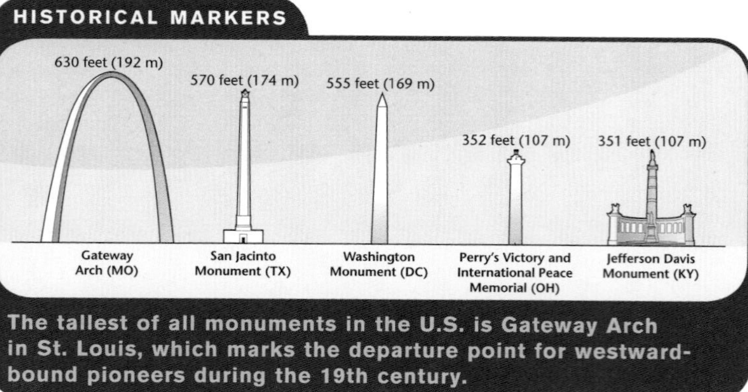

⇨ HEADING WEST. The 630-foot (192-m) Gateway Arch honors the role St. Louis played in U.S. westward expansion. Trams carry one million tourists to the top of the arch each year.

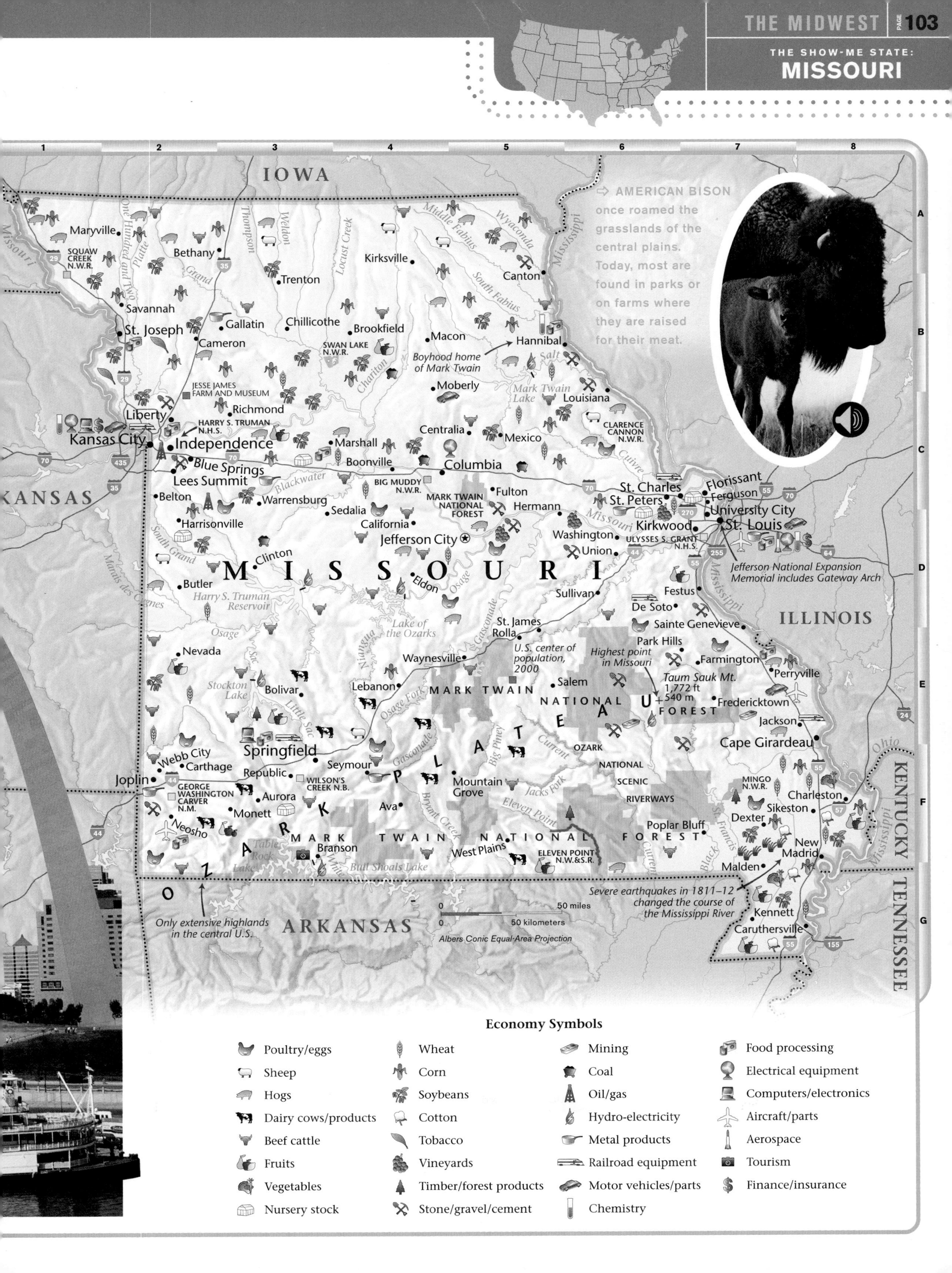

Economy Symbols

Poultry/eggs	Wheat	Mining	Food processing
Sheep	Corn	Coal	Electrical equipment
Hogs	Soybeans	Oil/gas	Computers/electronics
Dairy cows/products	Cotton	Hydro-electricity	Aircraft/parts
Beef cattle	Tobacco	Metal products	Aerospace
Fruits	Vineyards	Railroad equipment	Tourism
Vegetables	Timber/forest products	Motor vehicles/parts	Finance/insurance
Nursery stock	Stone/gravel/cement	Chemistry	

THE CORNHUSKER STATE:
NEBRASKA

THE BASICS

STATS

Area
77,354 sq mi (200,346 sq km)

Population
1,826,341

Capital
Lincoln
Population 258,379

Largest city
Omaha
Population 408,958

Ethnic/racial groups
86.1% white; 4.5% African American; 1.8% Asian; 1.0% Native American. Hispanic (any race) 9.2%.

Industry
Food processing, machinery, electrical equipment, printing and publishing

Agriculture
Cattle, corn, hogs, soybeans, wheat, sorghum

Statehood
March 1, 1867; 37th state

GEO WHIZ

Many of Nebraska's early settlers were called sodbusters because they cut chunks of the grassy prairie (sod) to build their houses. These building blocks became known as "Nebraska marble."

Nebraska's state fossil is the mammoth. Fossils of these prehistoric elephants have been found in all 93 counties. The state estimates that as many as ten mammoths are buried beneath an average square mile of territory.

Boys Town, founded in 1917 as a home for troubled boys, has provided a haven for girls since 1979. They now make up about half the population of 500 kids in this village-style community near Omaha.

WESTERN MEADOWLARK
GOLDENROD

NEBRASKA

For thousands of westbound pioneers on the Oregon and California Trails, Scotts Bluff and Chimney Rock were unforgettable landmarks, towering above the North Platte River. Once reserved for Indians by the government, Nebraska was opened for white settlement in 1854. Following statehood in 1867, ranchers clashed with farmers in an unsuccessful bid to preserve open rangelands. Before white settlers arrived, Indians hunted bison and grew corn, pumpkins, beans, and squash. Today, farms and ranches cover nearly all of the state. Ranchers graze beef cattle on the grass-covered Sand Hills, while farmers grow corn, soybeans, and wheat elsewhere. The vast underground Ogallala Aquifer feeds center-pivot irrigation systems needed to water crops in areas that do not receive enough rain. Processing the state's farm products, especially meatpacking, is a big part of the economy. Omaha, which sits along the Missouri River, is a center of finance, insurance, and agribusiness. Lincoln, the state capital, has the only unicameral, or one-house, legislature in the United States.

⇧ TAKING FLIGHT. Migratory Sandhill cranes pass through Nebraska in late winter, stopping in the Platte River Valley to feed and rest.

OGLALA NATIONAL GRASSLAND
Chadron
Crawford
Pine Ridge
NEBRASKA NATIONAL FOREST
White
AGATE FOSSIL BEDS NAT. MON.
Fossils of extinct mammals that lived here about 20 million years ago
NORTH PLATTE N.W.R.
Alliance
Scottsbluff
Gering
SCOTTS BLUFF N.M.
CHIMNEY ROCK N.H.S.
Bridgeport
Pumpkin Creek
North Platte
Highest point in Nebraska
Kimball
Lodgepole Cr.
Panorama Point +5,423 ft, 1,653 m
Sidney
80
WYOMING
COLORADO

⇩ RIDER DOWN. The Big Rodeo is an annual event in tiny Burwell (population 1,130) in Nebraska's Sand Hills. The town, sometimes called "the place where the Wild West meets the 21st century," has hosted the rodeo for more than 80 years.

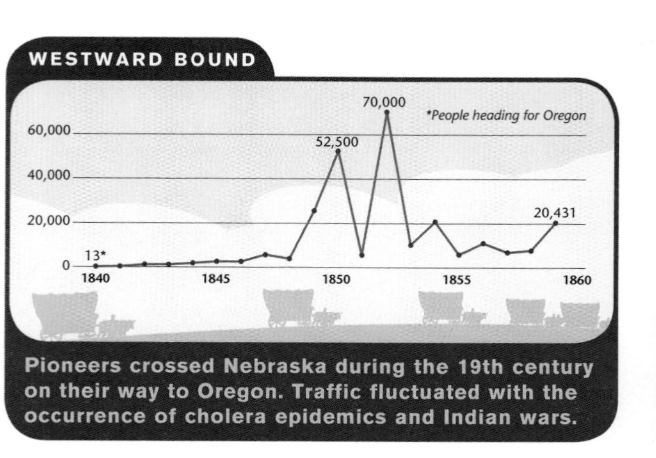

Pioneers crossed Nebraska during the 19th century on their way to Oregon. Traffic fluctuated with the occurrence of cholera epidemics and Indian wars.

THE CORNHUSKER STATE: NEBRASKA

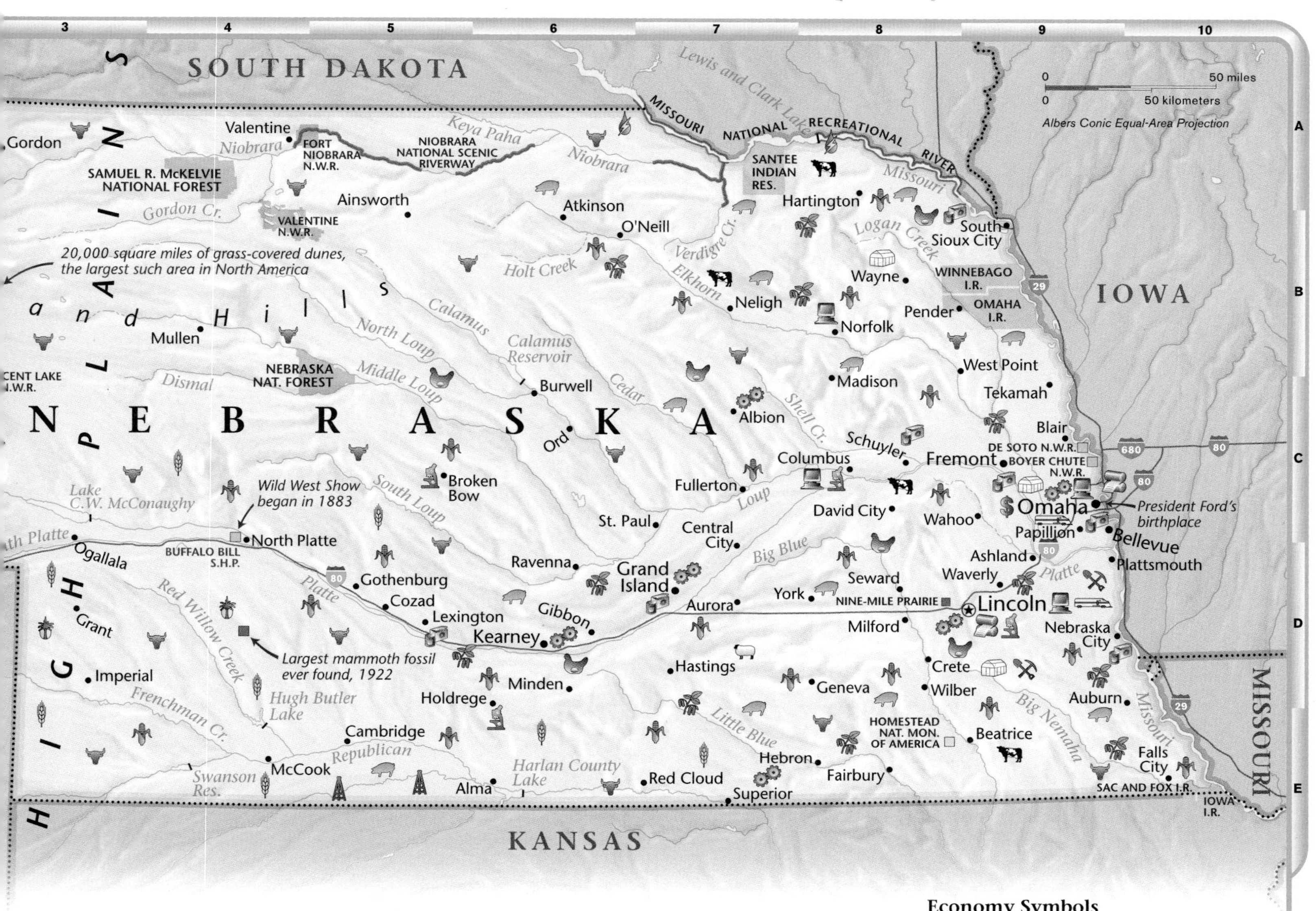

Economy Symbols

- Poultry/eggs
- Sheep
- Hogs
- Dairy cows/products
- Beef cattle
- Vegetables
- Vegetable oil
- Nursery stock
- Wheat
- Corn
- Soybeans
- Printing/publishing
- Stone/gravel/cement
- Oil/gas
- Hydro-electricity
- Machinery
- Railroad equipment
- Food processing
- Computers/electronics
- Scientific instruments
- Finance/insurance

⇦ THE WAY WEST. Longhorn cattle and a bison stand knee-deep in grass below Chimney Rock, which rises more than 300 feet (91 m) above western Nebraska's rolling landscape. An important landmark on the Oregon Trail for 19th-century westbound pioneers and now a national historic site, the formation is being worn away by forces of erosion.

THE FLICKERTAIL STATE:
NORTH DAKOTA

NORTH DAKOTA

THE BASICS

STATS

Area
70,700 sq mi (183,113 sq km)

Population
672,591

Capital
Bismarck
Population 61,272

Largest city
Fargo
Population 105,549

Ethnic/racial groups
90.0% white; 5.4% Native American; 1.2% African American; 1.0% Asian. Hispanic (any race) 2.0%.

Industry
Services, government, finance, construction, transportation, oil and gas

Agriculture
Wheat, cattle, sunflowers, barley, soybeans

Statehood
November 2, 1889; 39th state

GEO WHIZ

Teenage Indian guide Sacagawea (also known as Sakakawea) joined the Lewis and Clark expedition in the spring of 1805 after the explorers spent the winter in the Mandan-Hidatsa villages near present-day Washburn. Today, the state's largest reservoir is named in her honor.

Devils Lake has earned the title Perch Capital of the World for the large number of walleye—a kind of perch—that anglers catch there.

North Dakota's landscape boasts some of the world's largest outdoor animal sculptures, including Salem Sue, the world's largest Holstein cow; a 60-ton buffalo; a 40-by-60-foot (12-by-18-m) grasshopper; a giant snowmobiling turtle; and Wally the Giant Walleye.

WESTERN MEADOWLARK
WILD PRAIRIE ROSE

During the winter of 1804–05, Lewis and Clark camped at a Mandan village where they met Sacagawea, the Shoshone woman who helped guide them through the Rockies and onto the Pacific Ocean. White settlement of the vast grassy plains coincided with the growth of railroads, and statehood was gained in 1889. The geographic center of North America is southwest of Rugby. The state's interior location helps give it a huge annual temperature range. A record low temperature of -60°F (-51°C) and record high of 121°F (49°C) were recorded in 1936. Fargo, located on the northward flowing Red River of the North, is the state's largest city. Garrison Dam, on the Missouri River, generates electricity and provides water for irrigation. The state leads the country in the production of flaxseed, canola, sunflowers, and barley, but it is wheat, cattle, and soybeans that provide the greatest income. Oil and lignite coal are important in the western part of the state.

⇧ VIGILANT LOOKOUT. A black-tailed prairie dog watches for signs of danger. This member of the squirrel family lives in burrows in the Great Plains.

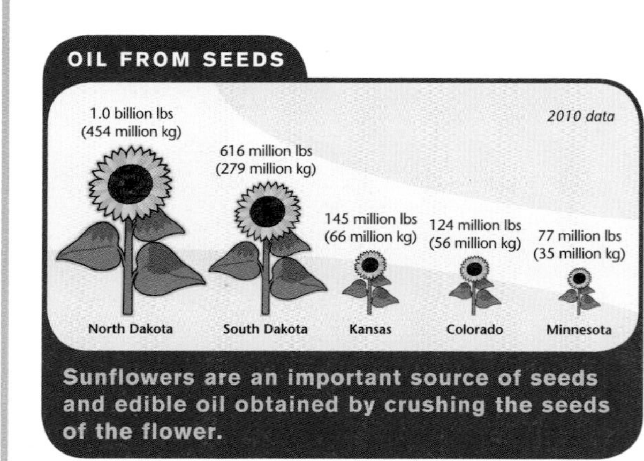

Sunflowers are an important source of seeds and edible oil obtained by crushing the seeds of the flower.

⇨ RUNNING FREE. A wild horse runs through a landscape dramatically eroded by the Little Missouri River in Theodore Roosevelt National Park in North Dakota's Badlands region.

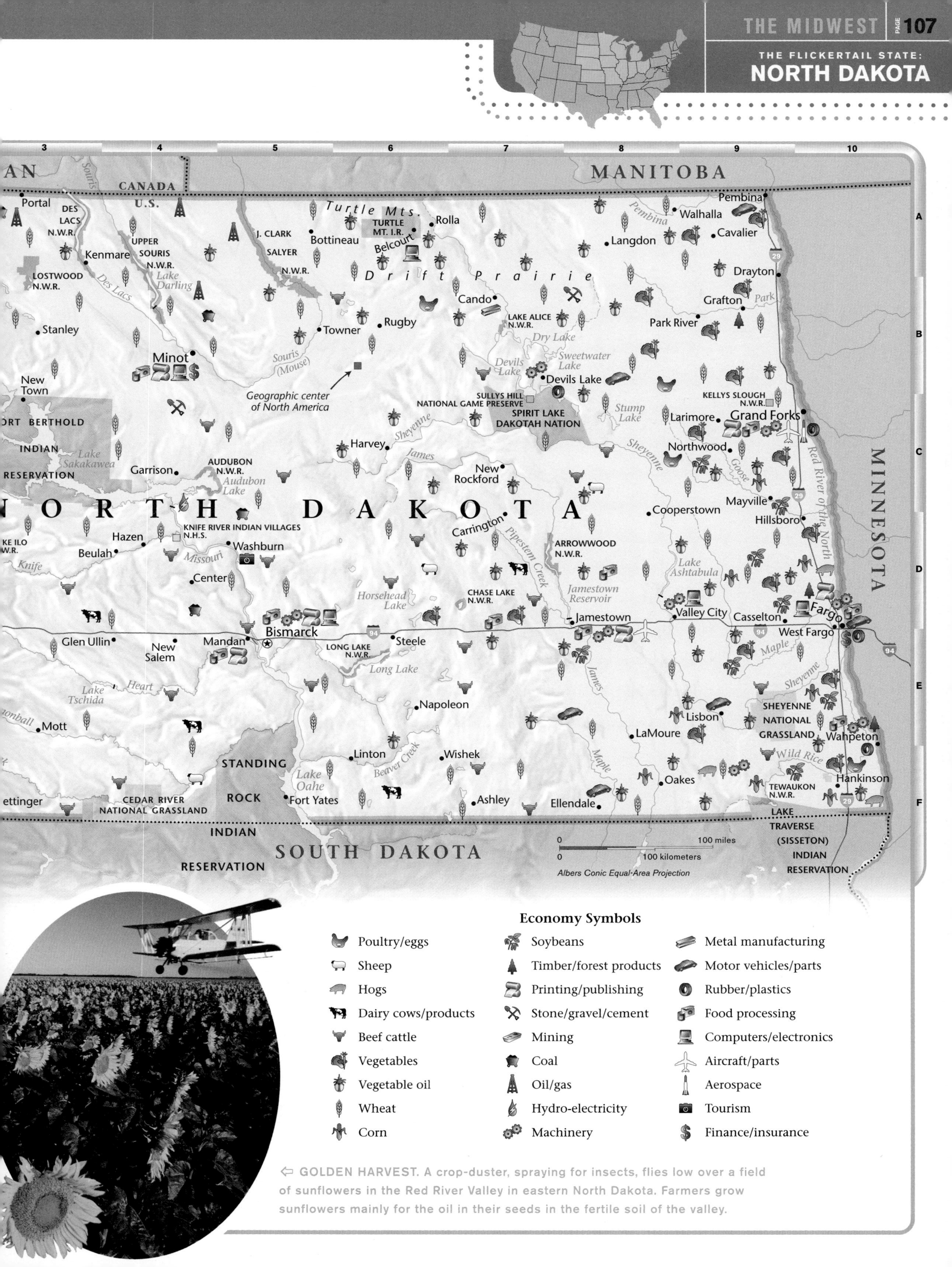

⇦ GOLDEN HARVEST. A crop-duster, spraying for insects, flies low over a field of sunflowers in the Red River Valley in eastern North Dakota. Farmers grow sunflowers mainly for the oil in their seeds in the fertile soil of the valley.

THE BUCKEYE STATE:
OHIO

OHIO

Ohio and the rest of the Northwest Territory became part of the United States after the Revolutionary War. The movement of white settlers into the region led to conflicts with the native inhabitants until 1794 when Indian resistance was defeated at Fallen Timbers. Ohio entered the Union nine years later. Lake Erie in the north and the Ohio River in the south, along with canals and railroads, provided transportation links that spurred early immigration and commerce. The state became an industrial giant, producing steel, machinery, rubber, and glass. From 1869 to 1923, 7 of 12 U.S. presidents were Ohioans. With 18 electoral votes, seventh highest in the country, Ohio is still a big player in presidential elections. Education, government, and finance employ many people in Columbus, the capital and largest city. Manufacturing in Cleveland, Toledo, Cincinnati, and other cities remains a vital segment of the state's economy. Farmers on Ohio's western, glaciated plains grow soybeans and corn, the two largest cash crops.

⇧ INLAND URBAN CENTER. Cincinnati's skyline sparkles in the red glow of twilight. Founded in 1788, the modern city boasts education and medical centers as well as headquarters for companies such as Procter & Gamble.

THE BASICS

STATS

Area
44,825 sq mi (116,097 sq km)

Population
11,536,504

Capital
Columbus
Population 787,033

Largest city
Columbus
Population 787,033

Ethnic/racial groups
82.7% white; 12.2% African American; 1.7% Asian; .2% Native American. Hispanic (any race) 3.1%.

Industry
Transportation equipment, metal products, machinery, food processing, electrical equipment

Agriculture
Soybeans, dairy products, corn, hogs, cattle, poultry and eggs

Statehood
March 1, 1803; 17th state

GEO WHIZ

Cedar Point Amusement Park, in Sandusky, is known as the Roller Coaster Capital of the World. Top Thrill Dragster, the tallest and fastest roller coaster on Earth when it was built in 2003, is 420 feet (128 m) high with a top speed of 120 miles per hour (193 kmph)!

Ohio's state tree is the buckeye, so-called because the nut it produces resembles the eye of a buck. A buck is a male deer.

Ohio's state insect is the ladybird beetle, more commonly known as the ladybug. Use of these beetles to control plant-eating pests greatly reduces the need for chemical pesticides.

CARDINAL
SCARLET CARNATION

⇩ TRADITIONAL TRAVEL. Horse and buggy are a familiar sight in central Ohio, location of the world's largest Amish population.

⇧ SOUND OF MUSIC. Colorful guitars mark the entrance to the Rock and Roll Hall of Fame in downtown Cleveland. The museum, through its Rockin' the Schools program, attracts more than 50,000 students annually to experience the sounds of rock and roll music and learn about its history.

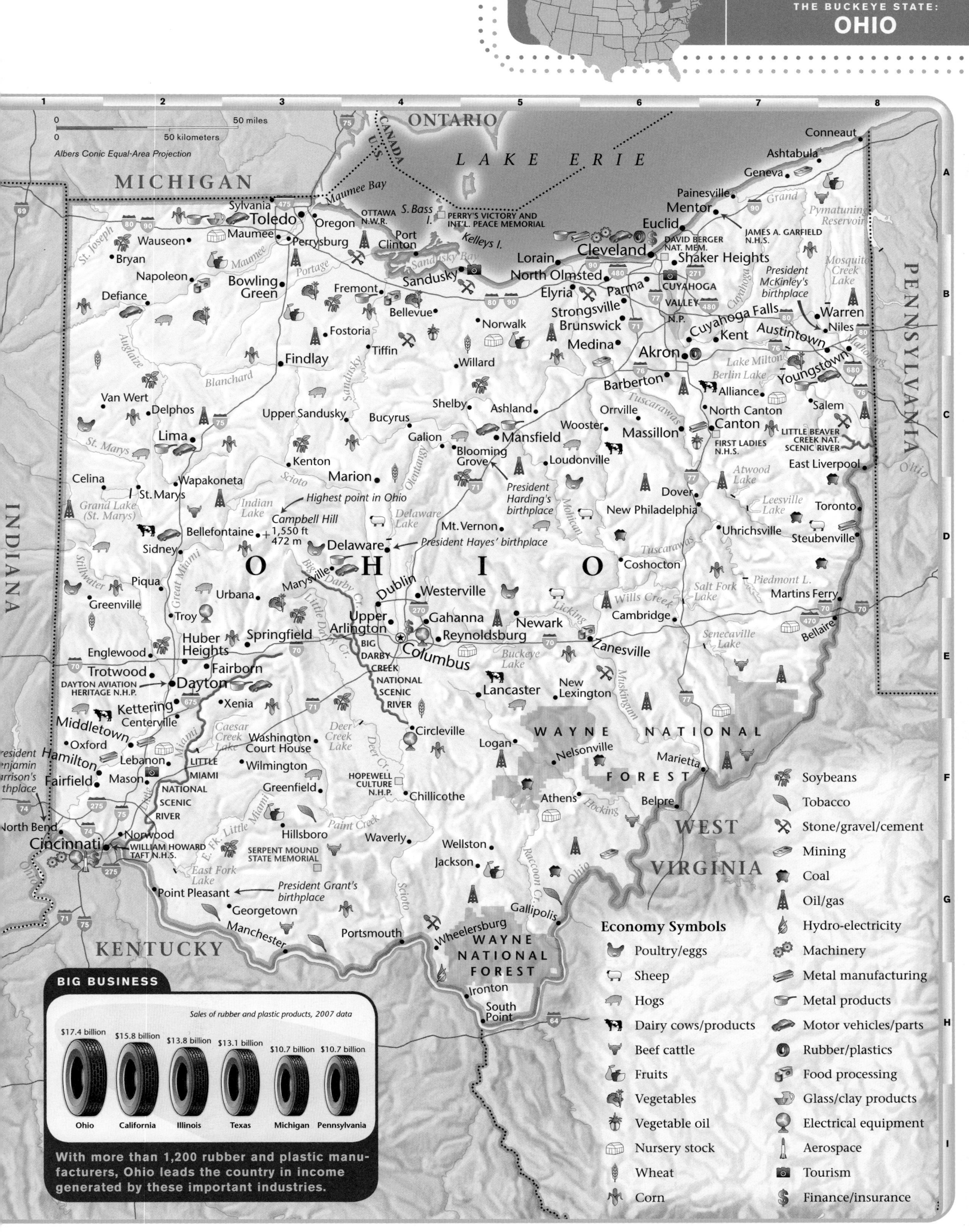
MICHIGAN
INDIANA
KENTUCKY
WEST VIRGINIA
PENNSYLVANIA
ONTARIO
LAKE ERIE
CANADA
U.S.
O H I O
0 50 miles
0 50 kilometers
Albers Conic Equal-Area Projection
Toledo
Cleveland
Columbus
Cincinnati
Dayton
Akron
Youngstown
Canton
Highest point in Ohio
Campbell Hill
1,550 ft
472 m
President Hayes' birthplace
President Harding's birthplace
President McKinley's birthplace
President Grant's birthplace
WAYNE NATIONAL FOREST
Economy Symbols
Poultry/eggs
Sheep
Hogs
Dairy cows/products
Beef cattle
Fruits
Vegetables
Vegetable oil
Nursery stock
Wheat
Corn
Soybeans
Tobacco
Stone/gravel/cement
Mining
Coal
Oil/gas
Hydro-electricity
Machinery
Metal manufacturing
Metal products
Motor vehicles/parts
Rubber/plastics
Food processing
Glass/clay products
Electrical equipment
Aerospace
Tourism
Finance/insurance
BIG BUSINESS
Sales of rubber and plastic products, 2007 data
$17.4 billion
$15.8 billion
$13.8 billion
$13.1 billion
$10.7 billion
$10.7 billion
Ohio
California
Illinois
Texas
Michigan
Pennsylvania
With more than 1,200 rubber and plastic manufacturers, Ohio leads the country in income generated by these important industries.

THE MOUNT RUSHMORE STATE:
SOUTH DAKOTA

SOUTH DAKOTA

After the discovery of Black Hills gold in 1874, prospectors poured in and established lawless mining towns such as Deadwood. Indians fought this invasion but were defeated, and statehood came in 1889. Today, South Dakota has several reservations, and nearly 9 percent of the state's people are Native Americans. The Missouri River flows through the center of the state, creating two distinct regions. To the east, farmers grow corn and soybeans on the fertile, rolling prairie. To the west, where it is too dry for most crops, farmers grow wheat and graze cattle and sheep on the vast plains. In the southwest, the Black Hills, named for the dark coniferous trees blanketing their slopes, are still a rich source of gold. Millions of tourists visit the area to see Mount Rushmore and a giant sculpture of Crazy Horse that has been in the works since 1948. Nearby, the fossil-rich Badlands, a region of eroded buttes and pinnacles, dominate the landscape.

THE BASICS

STATS

Area
77,117 sq mi (199,732 sq km)

Population
814,180

Capital
Pierre
Population 13,646

Largest city
Sioux Falls
Population 153,888

Ethnic/racial groups
85.9% white; 8.8% Native American; 1.3% African American; .9% Asian. Hispanic (any race) 2.7%.

Industry
Finance, services, manufacturing, government, retail trade, transportation and utilities, wholesale trade, construction, mining

Agriculture
Cattle, corn, soybeans, wheat, hogs, hay, dairy products

Statehood
November 2, 1889; 40th state

GEO WHIZ

Thirty years ago, black-footed ferrets were on the brink of extinction. Now, thanks to captive breeding programs, the world's largest wild black-footed ferret population is thriving in a black-tailed prairie dog colony in south-central South Dakota.

Called Shrine of Democracy by its creator Gutzon Borglum, Mount Rushmore National Monument features the faces of George Washington, Thomas Jefferson, Abraham Lincoln, and Theodore Roosevelt. Each is 60 feet (18 m) tall.

The Black Hills Institute of Geological Research in Hill City has been involved in digging up eight *Tyrannosaurus rex* skeletons, including Sue, Stan, Bucky, and WREX. In addition to research work, the institute prepares museum-quality reproductions.

RING-NECKED PHEASANT
PASQUEFLOWER

⇨ HONORING AGRICULTURE. The face of the Corn Palace in Mitchell is renewed each year using thousands of bushels of grain to create pictures depicting the role of agriculture in the state's history.

ALTERNATIVE BEEF

Bison sold, 2007 data

South Dakota	Nebraska	North Dakota	Colorado	Montana	Wyoming
10,862	7,266	6,042	5,456	5,270	4,668

Bison meat is popular among health-conscious consumers because it is lower in calories, fat, and cholesterol than other meats.

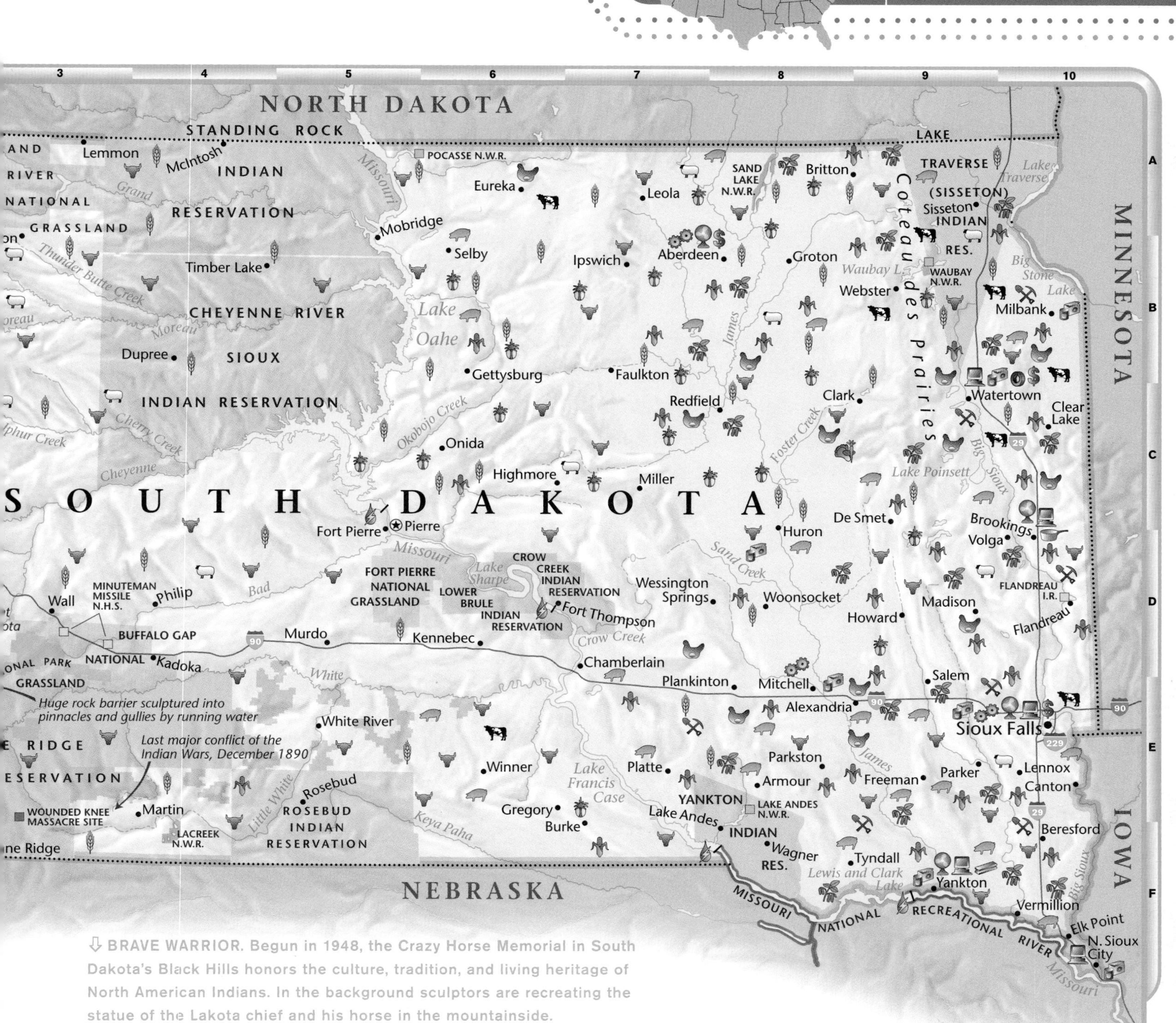

⇩ BRAVE WARRIOR. Begun in 1948, the Crazy Horse Memorial in South Dakota's Black Hills honors the culture, tradition, and living heritage of North American Indians. In the background sculptors are recreating the statue of the Lakota chief and his horse in the mountainside.

Economy Symbols

- Poultry/eggs
- Sheep
- Hogs
- Dairy cows/products
- Beef cattle
- Vegetable oil
- Wheat
- Corn
- Soybeans
- Stone/gravel/cement
- Mining
- Oil/gas
- Hydro-electricity
- Machinery
- Metal manufacturing
- Metal products
- Rubber/plastics
- Food processing
- Jewelry
- Electrical equipment
- Computers/electronics
- Tourism
- Finance/insurance

THE BADGER STATE:
WISCONSIN

WISCONSIN
1848

WISCONSIN

Frenchman Jean Nicolet was the first European to reach present-day Wisconsin when he stepped ashore from Green Bay in 1634. After decades of getting along, relations with the region's Indians soured as the number of settlers increased. The Black Hawk War in 1832 ended the last major Indian resistance, and statehood came in 1848. Many Milwaukee residents are descendants of German immigrants who labored in the city's breweries and meatpacking plants. Even as the economic importance of health care and other services has increased, food processing and the manufacture of machinery and metal products remains significant for the state.

More than one million dairy cows graze in America's Dairyland, as the state is often called. It leads the country in cheese production, and is the second-largest producer of milk and butter. Other farmers grow crops ranging from corn and soybeans to potatoes and cranberries. Northern Wisconsin is sparsely populated but heavily forested, and is the source of paper and paper products produced by the state.

⇧ CITY BY THE LAKE. Milwaukee, on the shore of Lake Michigan, derives its name from the Algonquian word for "beautiful land." The city, known for brewing and manufacturing, also has a growing service sector.

⇧ TASTY GRAZING. The largest concentration of Brown Swiss cows in the U.S. is in Wisconsin, where the milk of this breed is prized by cheese manufacturers.

THE BASICS

STATS

Area
65,498 sq mi (169,639 sq km)

Population
5,686,986

Capital
Madison
Population 233,209

Largest city
Milwaukee
Population 594,833

Ethnic/racial groups
86.2% white; 6.3% African American; 2.3% Asian; 1.0% Native American. Hispanic (any race) 5.9%.

Industry
Industrial machinery, paper products, food processing, metal products, electronic equipment, transportation

Agriculture
Dairy products, cattle, corn, poultry and eggs, soybeans

Statehood
May 29, 1848; 30th state

GEO WHIZ

The Indian Community School in Milwaukee offers courses in native languages, history, and rituals. In all of its programs—from math to tribal creation stories—seven core values are stressed: bravery, love, truth, wisdom, humility, loyalty, and respect.

Bogs left by retreating ice-age glaciers provide excellent conditions for raising cranberries. Wisconsin leads the nation in cranberry farming, producing more than half of the estimated 575 million pounds (261 million kg) consumed by Americans annually.

Wisconsin is nicknamed the Badger State, not for the animal but for the men who mined lead in the state during the 1820s. They dug living spaces by burrowing like badgers into the hillside.

ROBIN
WOOD VIOLET

⇦ RURAL ECONOMY. The dairy industry is an important part of Wisconsin's rural economy, and dairy farmers control most of the state's farmland.

DAIRY HEARTLAND

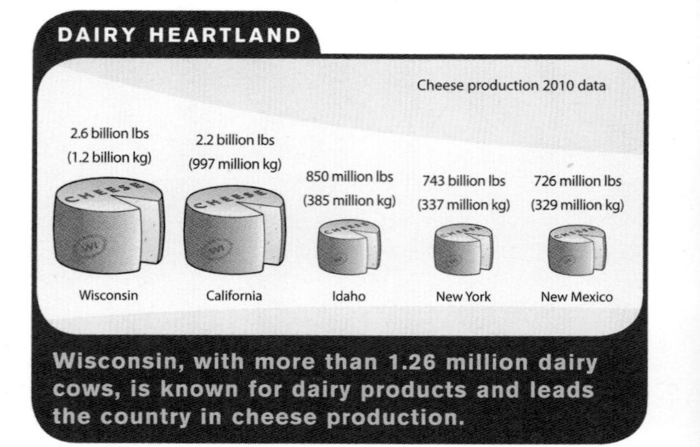

Wisconsin, with more than 1.26 million dairy cows, is known for dairy products and leads the country in cheese production.

THE BADGER STATE:
WISCONSIN

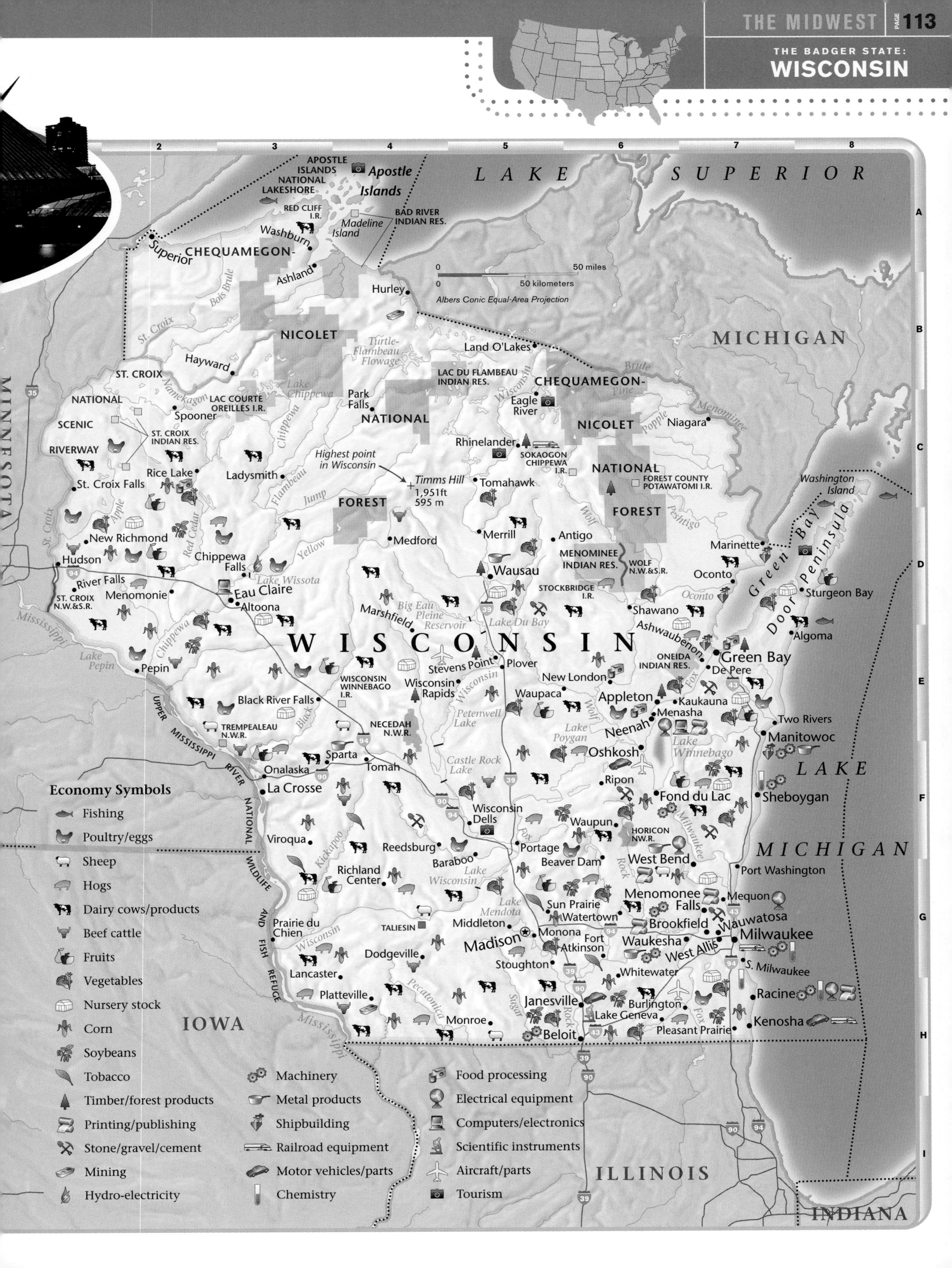

THE REGION

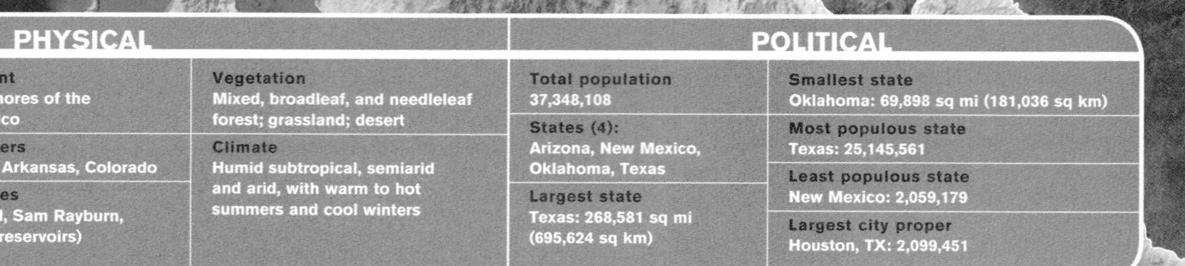

PHYSICAL

Total area
574,067 sq mi (1,486,833 sq km)

Highest point
Wheeler Peak, NM 13,161 ft (4,011 m)

Lowest point
Sea level, shores of the Gulf of Mexico

Longest rivers
Rio Grande, Arkansas, Colorado

Largest lakes
Toledo Bend, Sam Rayburn, Eufaula (all reservoirs)

Vegetation
Mixed, broadleaf, and needleleaf forest; grassland; desert

Climate
Humid subtropical, semiarid and arid, with warm to hot summers and cool winters

POLITICAL

Total population
37,348,108

States (4):
Arizona, New Mexico, Oklahoma, Texas

Largest state
Texas: 268,581 sq mi (695,624 sq km)

Smallest state
Oklahoma: 69,898 sq mi (181,036 sq km)

Most populous state
Texas: 25,145,561

Least populous state
New Mexico: 2,059,179

Largest city proper
Houston, TX: 2,099,451

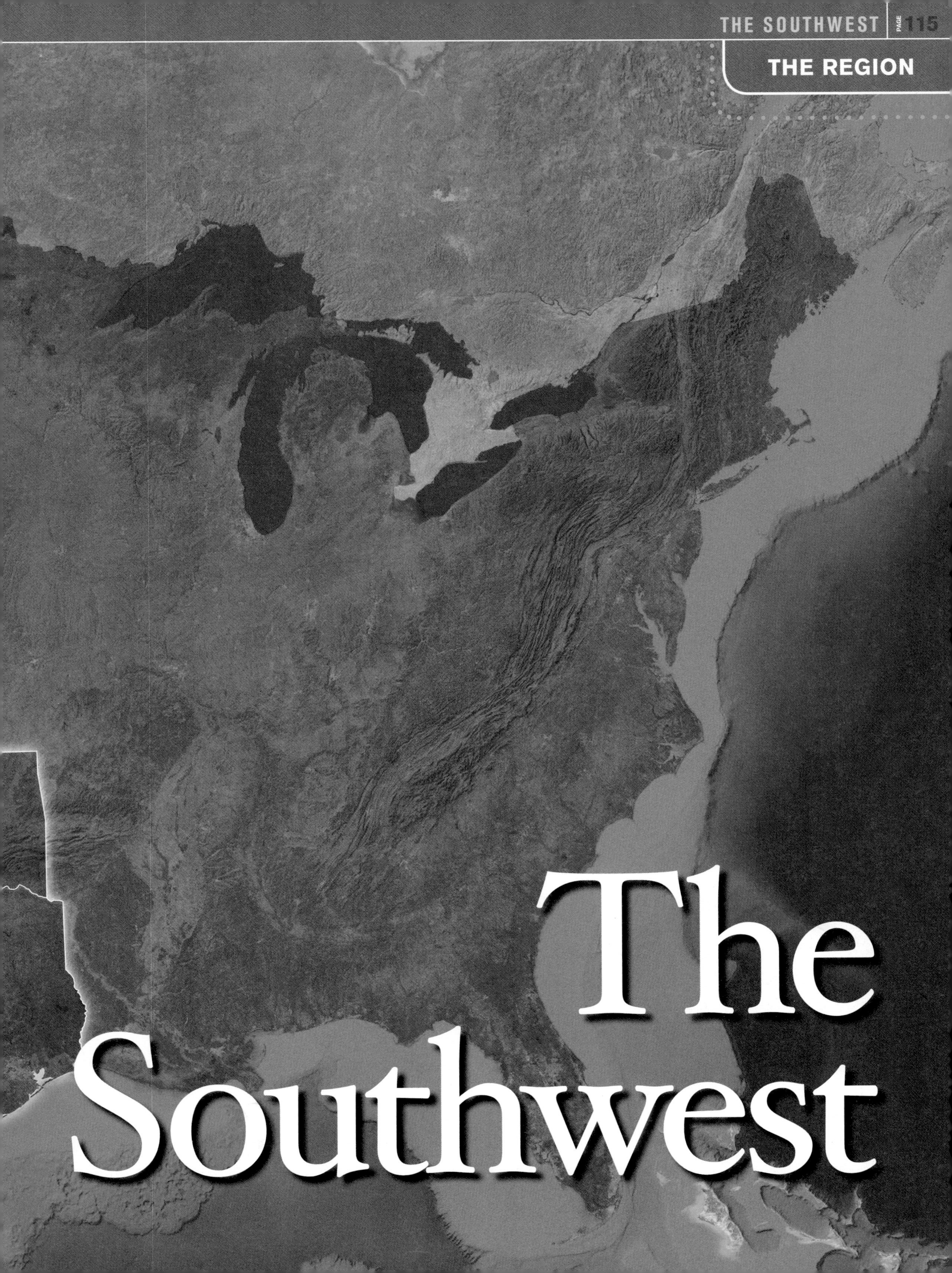

The Southwest

PHYSICAL MAP

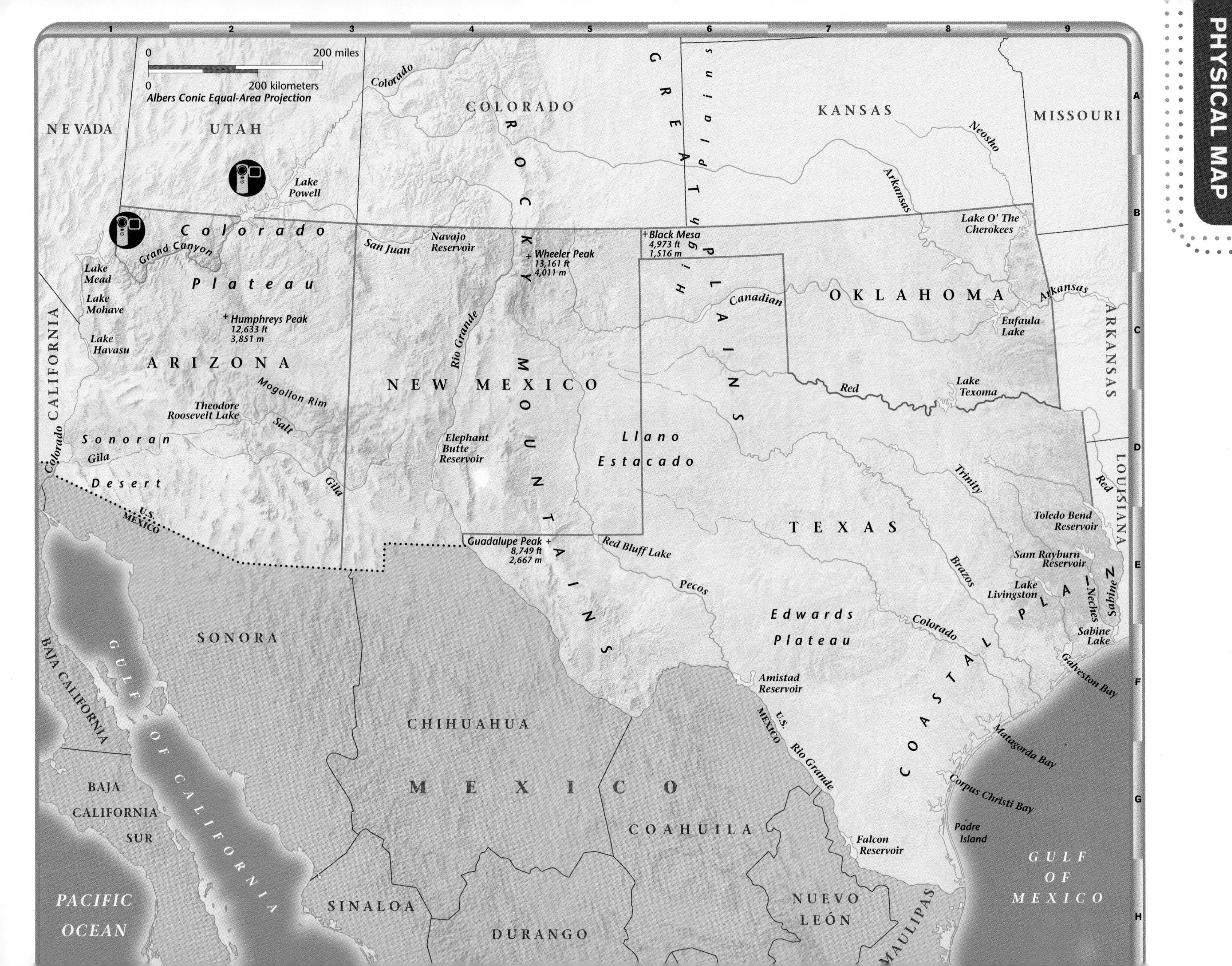

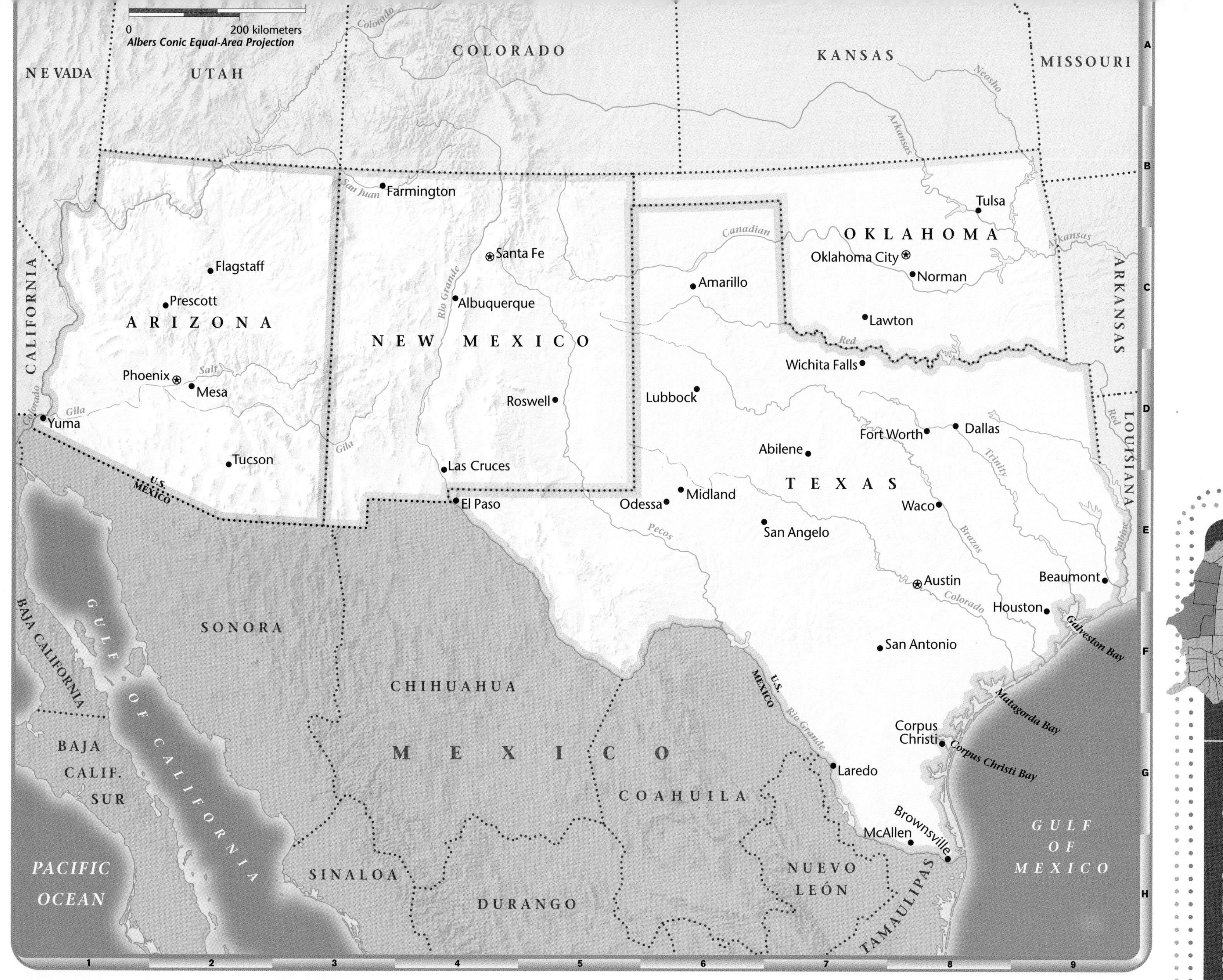
0
200 kilometers
Albers Conic Equal-Area Projection
NEVADA
UTAH
COLORADO
KANSAS
MISSOURI
CALIFORNIA
ARIZONA
NEW MEXICO
OKLAHOMA
ARKANSAS
LOUISIANA
TEXAS
Flagstaff
Prescott
Phoenix
Mesa
Yuma
Tucson
Farmington
Santa Fe
Albuquerque
Roswell
Las Cruces
El Paso
Tulsa
Oklahoma City
Norman
Lawton
Amarillo
Wichita Falls
Lubbock
Fort Worth
Dallas
Abilene
Midland
Odessa
Waco
San Angelo
Austin
Beaumont
Houston
San Antonio
Corpus Christi
Laredo
McAllen
Brownsville
Colorado
San Juan
Rio Grande
Salt
Gila
Canadian
Arkansas
Neosho
Red
Trinity
Brazos
Pecos
Sabine
U.S.
MEXICO
Galveston Bay
Matagorda Bay
Corpus Christi Bay
GULF OF MEXICO
SONORA
CHIHUAHUA
MEXICO
COAHUILA
NUEVO LEÓN
TAMAULIPAS
SINALOA
DURANGO
BAJA CALIFORNIA
BAJA CALIF. SUR
GULF OF CALIFORNIA
PACIFIC OCEAN
A
B
C
D
E
F
G
H
1
2
3
4
5
6
7
8
9

ABOUT THE **SOUTHWEST**

⇨ SKY STONE. According to Indian legend, turquoise stole its color from the sky. This Zuni woman is wearing turquoise jewelry for a festival in Phoenix. Zuni Indians, whose reservation is in western New Mexico, have made jewelry for more than one thousand years.

The Southwest

FROM CANYONS TO GRASSLANDS

Legendary cities of gold lured Spanish conquistadors to the Southwest in the 1500s. Today, the promise of economic opportunities brings people from other states as well as immigrants, both legal and illegal, from countries south of the border. This part of the Sunbelt region boasts future-oriented cities while preserving Wild West tales and Native American traditions. Stretching from the humid Gulf Coast to Arizona's deserts, the landscape is as diverse as its climate, ranging from sprawling plains in the east to plateaus cut by dramatic canyons in the west. Water is a major concern in the Southwest, one of the country's fastest-growing regions.

⇩ HIGH SOCIETY. Dressed in an elegant ball gown, a young woman participates in the Society of Martha Washington Pageant in Laredo, Texas. This event presents daughters of wealthy and long-established Hispanic families to the local community.

ABOUT THE SOUTHWEST

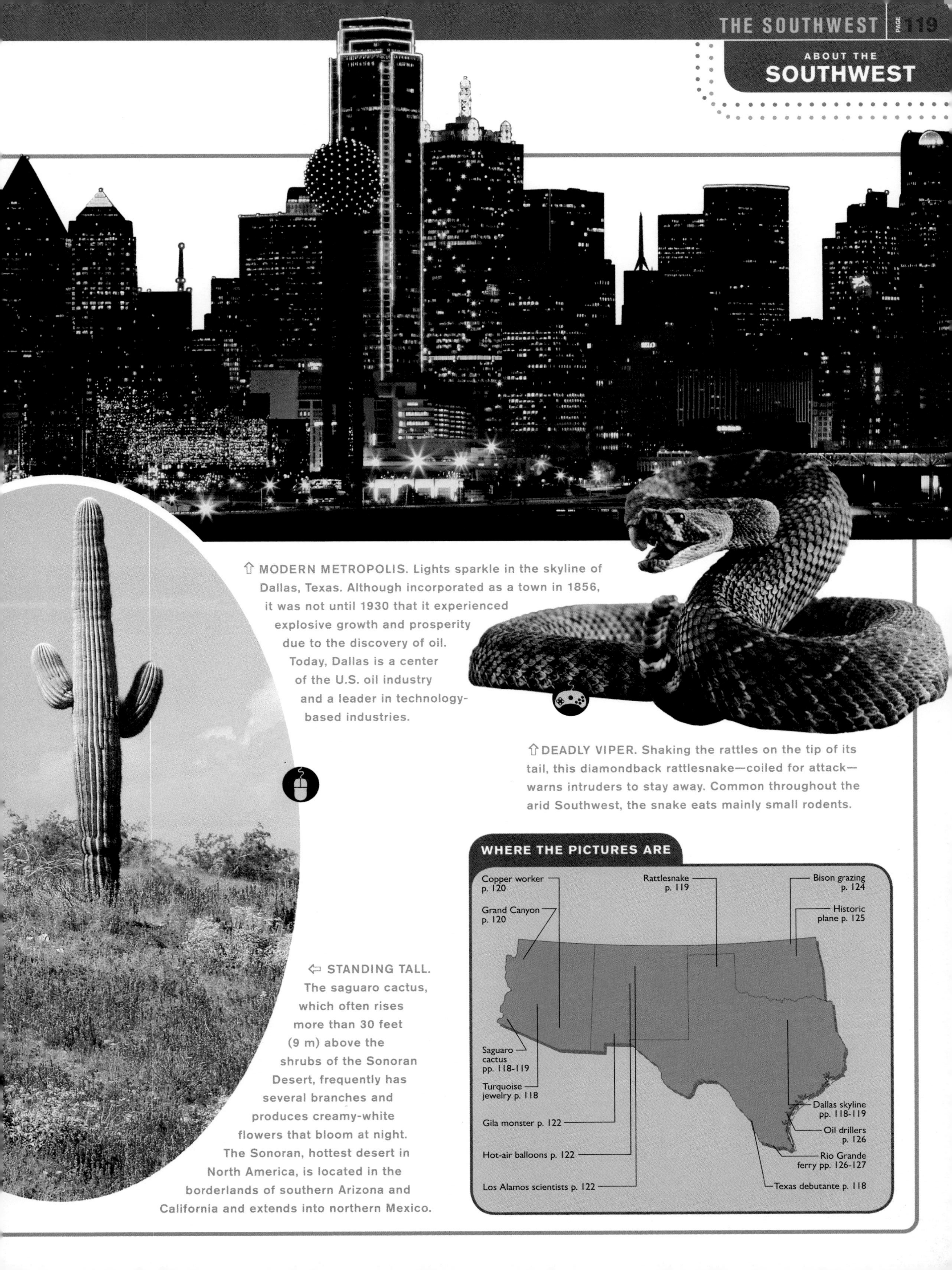

⇧ MODERN METROPOLIS. Lights sparkle in the skyline of Dallas, Texas. Although incorporated as a town in 1856, it was not until 1930 that it experienced explosive growth and prosperity due to the discovery of oil. Today, Dallas is a center of the U.S. oil industry and a leader in technology-based industries.

⇧ DEADLY VIPER. Shaking the rattles on the tip of its tail, this diamondback rattlesnake—coiled for attack—warns intruders to stay away. Common throughout the arid Southwest, the snake eats mainly small rodents.

⇦ STANDING TALL. The saguaro cactus, which often rises more than 30 feet (9 m) above the shrubs of the Sonoran Desert, frequently has several branches and produces creamy-white flowers that bloom at night. The Sonoran, hottest desert in North America, is located in the borderlands of southern Arizona and California and extends into northern Mexico.

WHERE THE PICTURES ARE

Copper worker p. 120
Grand Canyon p. 120
Saguaro cactus pp. 118-119
Turquoise jewelry p. 118
Gila monster p. 122
Hot-air balloons p. 122
Los Alamos scientists p. 122
Rattlesnake p. 119
Bison grazing p. 124
Historic plane p. 125
Dallas skyline pp. 118-119
Oil drillers p. 126
Rio Grande ferry pp. 126-127
Texas debutante p. 118

THE GRAND CANYON STATE:
ARIZONA

ARIZONA

The Europeans to first visit what is now Arizona were the Spanish in the 1500s. The territory passed from Spain to Mexico and then to the United States over the next three centuries. In the 1800s settlers clashed with the Apache warriors Cochise and Geronimo—and with one another in lawless towns like Tombstone. Youngest of the 48 contiguous states, statehood arrived in 1912. Arizona's economy was long based on the Five C's—copper, cattle, cotton, citrus, and climate—but manufacturing and service industries have gained prominence. A fast-growing population, sprawling cities, and agricultural irrigation strain limited water supplies in this dry state, which depends on water from the Colorado River and underground aquifers. Tourists flock to the Colorado Plateau in the north to see stunning vistas of the Grand Canyon, Painted Desert, and Monument Valley. To the south, the Sonoran Desert's unique ecosystem includes the giant saguaro cactus. Indian reservations scattered around the state offer outsiders the chance to learn about tribal history and culture.

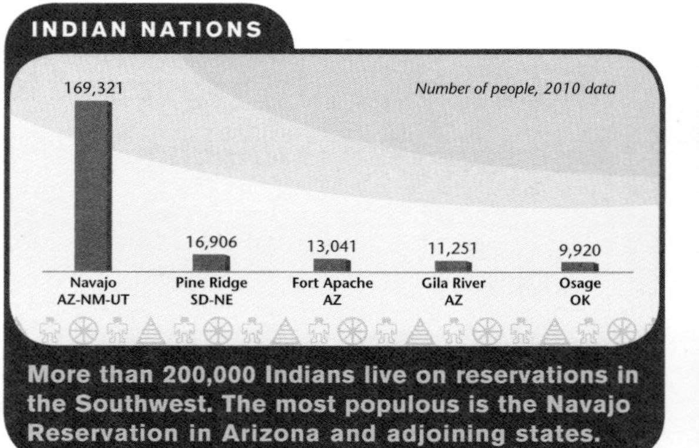

⇧ HOT WORK. A man in protective clothing works near a furnace that melts and refines copper ore at Magma Copper Company near Tucson. Arizona is one of the largest copper-producing regions in the world.

THE BASICS

STATS

Area
113,998 sq mi (295,256 sq km)

Population
6,392,017

Capital
Phoenix
Population 1,445,632

Largest city
Phoenix
Population 1,445,632

Ethnic/racial groups
73.0% white; 4.6% Native American; 4.1% African American; 2.8% Asian. Hispanic (any race) 29.6%.

Industry
Real estate, manufactured goods, retail, state and local government, transportation and public utilities, wholesale trade, health services, tourism, electronics

Agriculture
Vegetables, cattle, dairy products, cotton, fruit, nursery stock, nuts

Statehood
February 14, 1912; 48th state

GEO WHIZ

The California condor, once common throughout the Southwest, nearly became extinct in 1987. Through captive breeding and other conservation measures, the species has been reintroduced to the wild in areas such as the Grand Canyon.

People have been carving pictures called petroglyphs into rock cliffs in Verde Valley near Flagstaff for thousands of years. The meanings of most are a mystery, but others reveal the plants and animals of bygone eras.

Introduced as wild game for sportsmen, bullfrogs have made Arizona their new home on the range. With no natural predators and plenty to eat, bullfrogs are taking over.

CACTUS WREN
SAGUARO

INDIAN NATIONS

Number of people, 2010 data

Reservation	Number of people
Navajo AZ-NM-UT	169,321
Pine Ridge SD-NE	16,906
Fort Apache AZ	13,041
Gila River AZ	11,251
Osage OK	9,920

More than 200,000 Indians live on reservations in the Southwest. The most populous is the Navajo Reservation in Arizona and adjoining states.

⇩ NATURAL WONDER. Carved by the rushing waters of the Colorado River, the Grand Canyon's geologic features and fossil record reveal almost two billion years of Earth's history. Archaeological evidence indicates human habitation dating back 12,000 years.

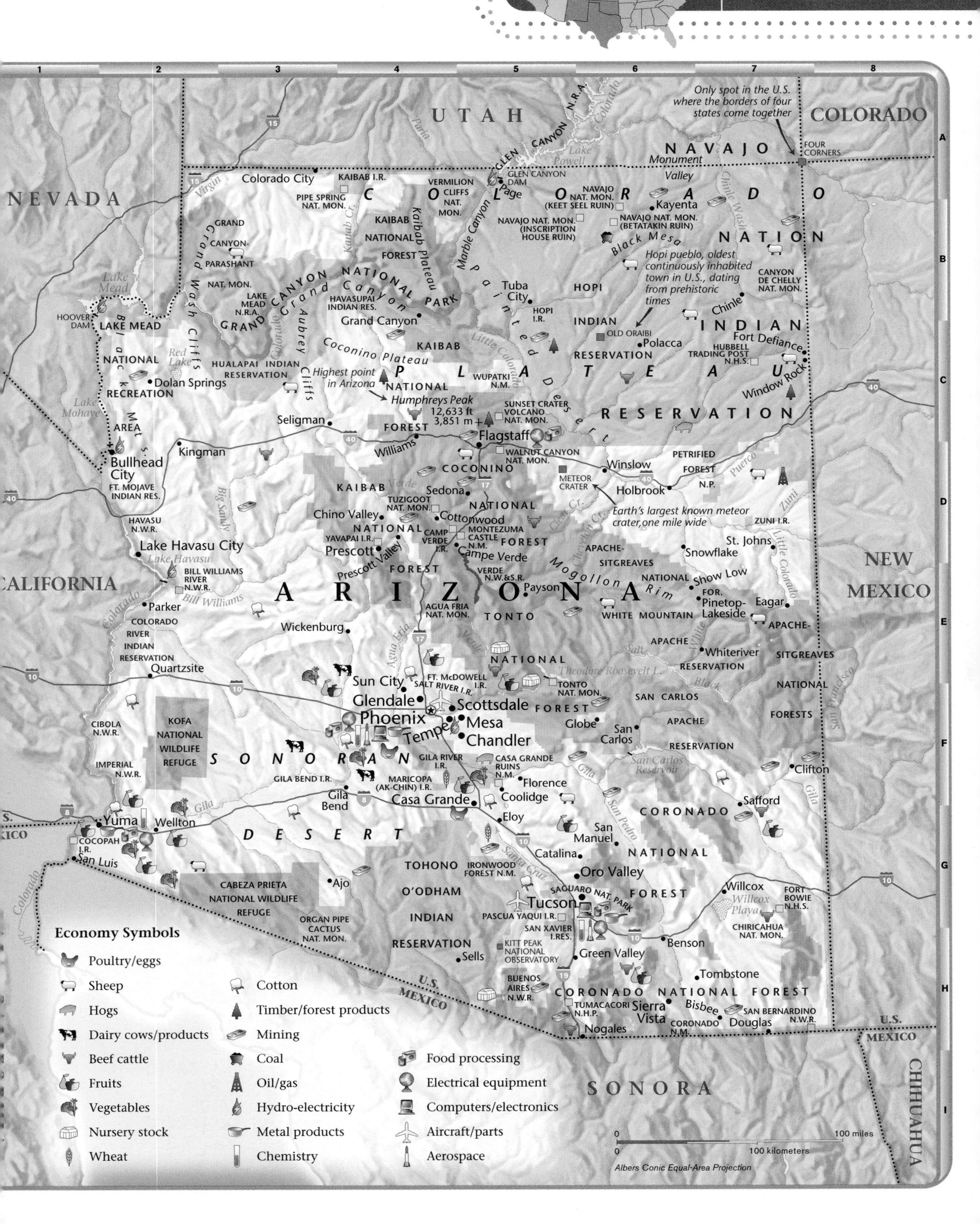
UTAH
COLORADO
NEVADA
CALIFORNIA
NEW MEXICO
SONORA
CHIHUAHUA
U.S.
MEXICO
ARIZONA
Only spot in the U.S. where the borders of four states come together
FOUR CORNERS
NAVAJO
Monument
Valley
COLORADO
PLATEAU
NAVAJO NATION
HOPI INDIAN RESERVATION
Hopi pueblo, oldest continuously inhabited town in U.S., dating from prehistoric times
OLD ORAIBI
Polacca
Kayenta
Chinle
Fort Defiance
Window Rock
HUBBELL TRADING POST N.H.S.
CANYON DE CHELLY NAT. MON.
NAVAJO NAT. MON. (KEET SEEL RUIN)
NAVAJO NAT. MON. (BETATAKIN RUIN)
NAVAJO NAT. MON. (INSCRIPTION HOUSE RUIN)
Black Mesa
GLEN CANYON N.R.A.
GLEN CANYON DAM
Lake Powell
Page
Marble Canyon
VERMILION CLIFFS NAT. MON.
KAIBAB I.R.
PIPE SPRING NAT. MON.
Colorado City
KAIBAB NATIONAL FOREST
Kaibab Plateau
GRAND CANYON NATIONAL PARK
Grand Canyon
HAVASUPAI INDIAN RES.
GRAND CANYON-PARASHANT NAT. MON.
LAKE MEAD N.R.A.
Grand Wash Cliffs
Aubrey Cliffs
HUALAPAI INDIAN RESERVATION
LAKE MEAD NATIONAL RECREATION AREA
HOOVER DAM
Lake Mead
Lake Mohave
Dolan Springs
Bullhead City
FT. MOJAVE INDIAN RES.
Kingman
Seligman
Coconino Plateau
Highest point in Arizona
Humphreys Peak 12,633 ft 3,851 m
SUNSET CRATER VOLCANO NAT. MON.
WUPATKI N.M.
Tuba City
HOPI I.R.
Painted Desert
Flagstaff
WALNUT CANYON NAT. MON.
Williams
COCONINO NATIONAL FOREST
METEOR CRATER
Earth's largest known meteor crater, one mile wide
Winslow
Holbrook
PETRIFIED FOREST N.P.
ZUNI I.R.
St. Johns
Snowflake
Show Low
Pinetop-Lakeside
Eagar
KAIBAB
Sedona
TUZIGOOT NAT. MON.
Cottonwood
Chino Valley
YAVAPAI I.R.
Prescott
Prescott Valley
PRESCOTT NATIONAL FOREST
CAMP VERDE I.R.
MONTEZUMA CASTLE N.M.
Camp Verde
VERDE N.W.&S.R.
Mogollon Rim
Payson
APACHE-SITGREAVES NATIONAL FOR.
WHITE MOUNTAIN APACHE RESERVATION
Whiteriver
AGUA FRIA NAT. MON.
TONTO NATIONAL FOREST
Theodore Roosevelt L.
TONTO NAT. MON.
SAN CARLOS APACHE RESERVATION
San Carlos
San Carlos Reservoir
Globe
APACHE-SITGREAVES NATIONAL FORESTS
Clifton
Safford
HAVASU N.W.R.
Lake Havasu City
Lake Havasu
BILL WILLIAMS RIVER N.W.R.
Bill Williams
Big Sandy
Parker
COLORADO RIVER INDIAN RESERVATION
Quartzsite
Wickenburg
Sun City
FT. McDOWELL I.R.
SALT RIVER I.R.
Glendale
Scottsdale
Phoenix
Mesa
Tempe
Chandler
Agua Fria
CIBOLA N.W.R.
KOFA NATIONAL WILDLIFE REFUGE
IMPERIAL N.W.R.
SONORAN DESERT
GILA BEND I.R.
Gila Bend
GILA RIVER I.R.
MARICOPA (AK-CHIN) I.R.
CASA GRANDE RUINS N.M.
Florence
Coolidge
Casa Grande
Eloy
Yuma
Wellton
COCOPAH I.R.
San Luis
CABEZA PRIETA NATIONAL WILDLIFE REFUGE
Ajo
ORGAN PIPE CACTUS NAT. MON.
TOHONO O'ODHAM INDIAN RESERVATION
IRONWOOD FOREST N.M.
Sells
KITT PEAK NATIONAL OBSERVATORY
Catalina
San Manuel
Oro Valley
SAGUARO NAT. PARK
Tucson
PASCUA YAQUI I.R.
SAN XAVIER I.RES.
Green Valley
BUENOS AIRES N.W.R.
TUMACACORI N.H.P.
Nogales
Sierra Vista
CORONADO N.M.
Bisbee
Douglas
Tombstone
Benson
Willcox
Willcox Playa
FORT BOWIE N.H.S.
CHIRICAHUA NAT. MON.
SAN BERNARDINO N.W.R.
CORONADO NATIONAL FOREST
Colorado
Little Colorado
Gila
Salt
Verde
San Pedro
Santa Cruz
San Francisco
Puerco
Zuni
Paria
Virgin
Kanab Cr.
Clear Cr.
Chevelon Cr.
White
Black
Chinle Wash
Economy Symbols
Poultry/eggs
Sheep
Hogs
Dairy cows/products
Beef cattle
Fruits
Vegetables
Nursery stock
Wheat
Cotton
Timber/forest products
Mining
Coal
Oil/gas
Hydro-electricity
Metal products
Chemistry
Food processing
Electrical equipment
Computers/electronics
Aircraft/parts
Aerospace
0 100 miles
0 100 kilometers
Albers Conic Equal-Area Projection

THE LAND OF ENCHANTMENT STATE:
NEW MEXICO

NEW MEXICO

THE BASICS

STATS

Area
121,590 sq mi (314,917 sq km)

Population
2,059,179

Capital
Santa Fe
Population 67,947

Largest city
Albuquerque
Population 545,852

Ethnic/racial groups
68.4% white; 9.4% Native American; 2.1% African American; 1.4% Asian. Hispanic (any race) 46.3%.

Industry
Electronic equipment, state and local government, real estate, business services, federal government, oil and gas extraction, health services

Agriculture
Cattle, dairy products, hay, chili peppers, onions

Statehood
January 6, 1912; 47th state

GEO WHIZ

Carlsbad Caverns National Park has more than a hundred caves, including the deepest limestone cavern in the U.S. From May through October, visitors can watch hundreds of thousands of Mexican free-tailed bats emerge from the cavern on their nightly search for food.

Taos Pueblo, in north-central New Mexico, has been continuously inhabited by Pueblo people for more than 1,000 years. When Spanish explorers reached it in 1540, they thought they had found one of the fabled golden cities of Cibola.

In 2007 voters in a county in south-central New Mexico approved a tax to help fund construction of a spaceport where rockets will launch tourists into space.

ROADRUNNER
YUCCA

New Mexico is among the youngest states—statehood was established in 1912—but its capital city is the country's oldest. The Spanish founded Santa Fe in 1610, a decade before the *Mayflower* reached America. Beginning in the 1820s, the Santa Fe Trail brought trade and settlers, and the United States acquired all the territory from Mexico by 1853. Most large cities are in the center of the state, along the Rio Grande. The Rocky Mountains divide the plains in the east from eroded mesas and canyons in the west. Cattle and sheep ranching on the plains is the chief agricultural activity, but hay, onions, and chili peppers are also important. Copper, potash, and natural gas produce mineral wealth. Cultural richness created by the historic interaction of Indian, Hispanic, and Anglo peoples abounds. Visitors experience this unique culture in the state's spicy cuisine, the famous art galleries of Taos, and the crafts made by Indians on the state's many reservations.

⇧ PAINFUL BITE. The strikingly patterned gila monster, the most poisonous lizard native to the United States, lives in desert areas of the Southwest.

⇧ FLYING HIGH. Brightly colored balloons rise into a brilliant blue October sky during Albuquerque's annual International Balloon Fiesta, the largest such event in the world. During the 9-day festival more than 700 hot-air balloons drift on variable air currents created by surrounding mountains.

SPICY HOT!

Chili peppers help give southwestern food its distinctive taste. New Mexico leads the country in acres planted of this fiery flavor enhancer.

⇦ NUCLEAR MYSTERIES. Scientists at Los Alamos National Laboratory, a leading scientific and engineering research institution responsible for national security, use 3-D simulations to study nuclear explosions.

NEW MEXICO

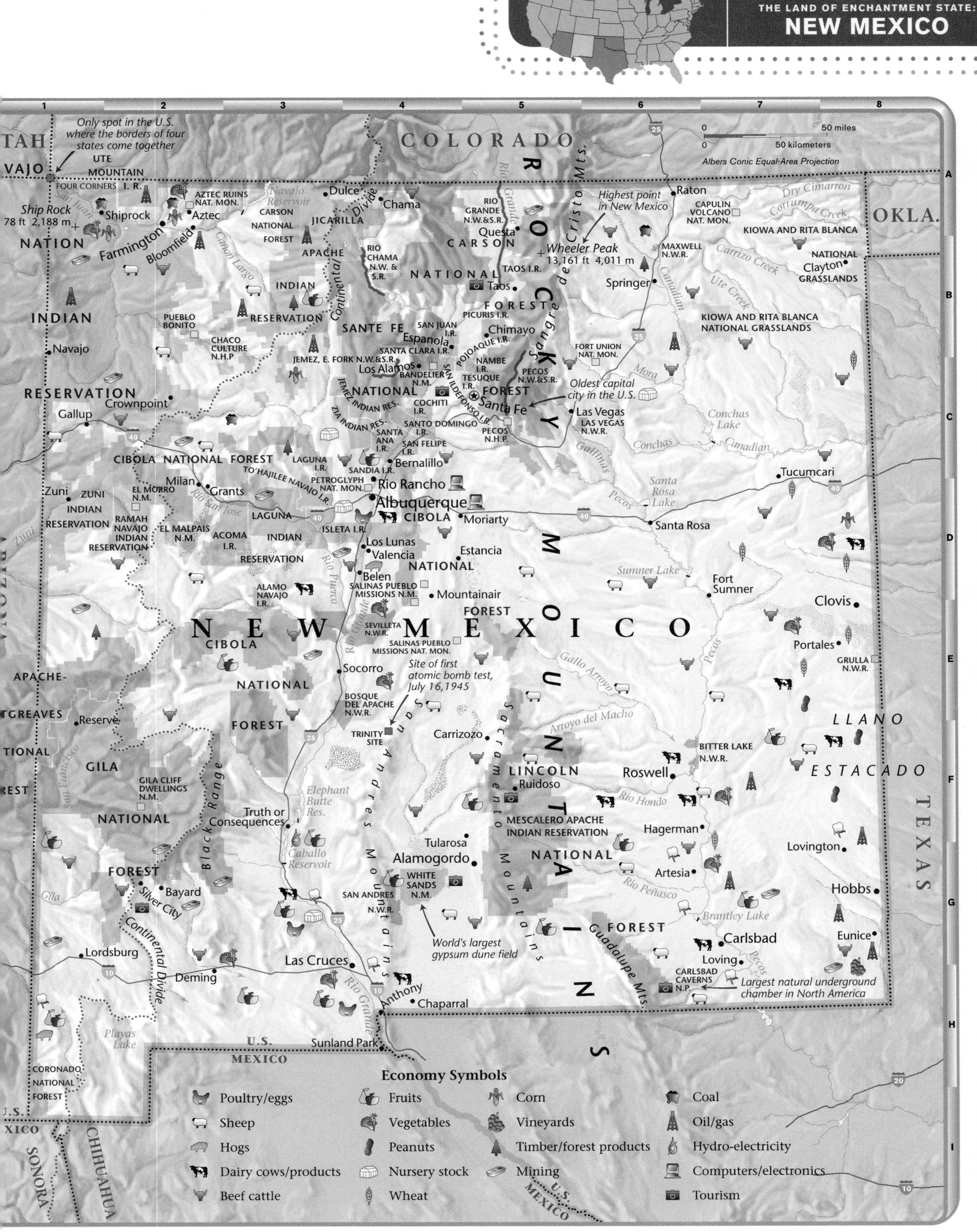
Only spot in the U.S. where the borders of four states come together
FOUR CORNERS
UTE MOUNTAIN I. R.
Ship Rock 78 ft 2,188 m
NAVAJO INDIAN RESERVATION
NATION
Shiprock
Farmington
Bloomfield
Aztec
AZTEC RUINS NAT. MON.
CARSON NATIONAL FOREST
JICARILLA APACHE INDIAN RESERVATION
Dulce
Chama
Continental Divide
RIO CHAMA N.W. & S.R.
RIO GRANDE N.W.&S.R.
Questa
CARSON NATIONAL FOREST
TAOS I.R.
Taos
Wheeler Peak 13,161 ft 4,011 m
Highest point in New Mexico
ROCKY MOUNTAINS
Sangre de Cristo Mts.
COLORADO
Raton
CAPULIN VOLCANO NAT. MON.
MAXWELL N.W.R.
Springer
KIOWA AND RITA BLANCA NATIONAL GRASSLANDS
Clayton
OKLA.
Dry Cimarron
Corrumpa Creek
Carrizo Creek
Ute Creek
Canadian
50 miles
50 kilometers
Albers Conic Equal-Area Projection
PUEBLO BONITO
CHACO CULTURE N.H.P
Navajo
Crownpoint
Gallup
SANTE FE NATIONAL FOREST
SAN JUAN I.R.
PICURIS I.R.
Chimayo
Espanola
SANTA CLARA I.R.
POJOAQUE I.R.
NAMBE I.R.
TESUQUE I.R.
JEMEZ, E. FORK N.W.&S.R.
Los Alamos
BANDELIER N.M.
JEMEZ INDIAN RES.
ZIA INDIAN RES.
COCHITI I.R.
SAN ILDEFONSO I.R.
SANTO DOMINGO I.R.
SANTA ANA I.R.
SAN FELIPE I.R.
PECOS N.H.P.
PECOS N.W.&S.R.
Santa Fe
Oldest capital city in the U.S.
FORT UNION NAT. MON.
Mora
Las Vegas
LAS VEGAS N.W.R.
Conchas Lake
Conchas
Gallinas
CIBOLA NATIONAL FOREST
LAGUNA I.R.
SANDIA I.R.
Bernalillo
TO'HAJILEE NAVAJO I.R.
PETROGLYPH NAT. MON.
Rio Rancho
Albuquerque
CIBOLA
Moriarty
Milan
Grants
Rio San Jose
EL MORRO N.M.
Zuni
ZUNI INDIAN RESERVATION
RAMAH NAVAJO INDIAN RESERVATION
EL MALPAIS N.M.
ACOMA I.R.
LAGUNA INDIAN RESERVATION
ISLETA I.R.
Los Lunas
Valencia
Belen
Estancia
NATIONAL FOREST
SALINAS PUEBLO MISSIONS N.M.
Mountainair
ALAMO NAVAJO I.R.
Rio Puerco
Santa Rosa Lake
Pecos
Santa Rosa
Tucumcari
Sumner Lake
Fort Sumner
Clovis
Portales
GRULLA N.W.R.
NEW MEXICO
CIBOLA NATIONAL FOREST
SEVILLETA N.W.R.
SALINAS PUEBLO MISSIONS NAT. MON.
Socorro
Site of first atomic bomb test, July 16, 1945
BOSQUE DEL APACHE N.W.R.
TRINITY SITE
San Andres Mountains
Rio Grande
Gallo Arroyo
Arroyo del Macho
Carrizozo
Sacramento Mountains
LINCOLN NATIONAL FOREST
Ruidoso
MESCALERO APACHE INDIAN RESERVATION
Roswell
BITTER LAKE N.W.R.
Rio Hondo
Hagerman
Artesia
Rio Penasco
LLANO ESTACADO
Lovington
Hobbs
APACHE-
GREAVES
Reserve
TIONAL
GILA
REST
San Francisco
GILA CLIFF DWELLINGS N.M.
GILA NATIONAL FOREST
Black Range
Truth or Consequences
Elephant Butte Res.
Caballo Reservoir
Tularosa
Alamogordo
WHITE SANDS N.M.
SAN ANDRES N.W.R.
World's largest gypsum dune field
Gila
Bayard
Silver City
Continental Divide
Lordsburg
Deming
Las Cruces
Anthony
Chaparral
Guadalupe Mts.
Brantley Lake
Carlsbad
Loving
CARLSBAD CAVERNS N.P.
Largest natural underground chamber in North America
Eunice
TEXAS
Playas Lake
U.S.
MEXICO
Sunland Park
CORONADO NATIONAL FOREST
SONORA
CHIHUAHUA
Economy Symbols
Poultry/eggs
Sheep
Hogs
Dairy cows/products
Beef cattle
Fruits
Vegetables
Peanuts
Nursery stock
Wheat
Corn
Vineyards
Timber/forest products
Mining
Coal
Oil/gas
Hydro-electricity
Computers/electronics
Tourism

THE SOONER STATE:
OKLAHOMA

OKLAHOMA

THE BASICS

STATS

Area
69,898 sq mi (181,036 sq km)

Population
3,751,351

Capital
Oklahoma City
Population 579,999

Largest city
Oklahoma City
Population 579,999

Ethnic/racial groups
72.2% white; 8.6% Native American; 7.4% African American; 1.7% Asian. Hispanic (any race) 8.9%.

Industry
Manufacturing, services, government, finance, insurance, real estate

Agriculture
Cattle, wheat, hogs, poultry, nursery stock

Statehood
November 16, 1907; 46th state

GEO WHIZ

An area of Oklahoma City has earned the nickname Little Saigon. In the 1960s the city opened its doors to tens of thousands of refugees from Vietnam. Today, the area is a thriving business district that includes people of other Asian nationalities.

"Hillbilly Speed Bump" is one of several nicknames for the armadillo. Native to South America, large populations of this armor-plated mammal are found as far north as Oklahoma.

Before it became a state in 1907, Oklahoma was known as Indian Territory. Today 39 tribes, including Cherokees, Osages, Creeks, and Choctaws, have their headquarters in the state.

SCISSOR-TAILED FLYCATCHER
MISTLETOE

OKLAHOMA

The U.S. government declared most of present-day Oklahoma Indian Territory in 1834. To reach this new homeland, southeastern Indians were forced to travel the Trail of Tears, named for its brutal conditions. By 1889 areas were opened for white homesteaders who staked claims in frenzied land runs. White and Indian lands were combined to form the state of Oklahoma in 1907. During the 1930s, many Okies fled drought and dust storms that smothered everything in sight. Some traveled as far as California in search of work. Better farming methods and the return of rain helped agriculture recover, and today cattle and wheat are the chief products. Oil and natural gas wells are found throughout the state. The Red River, colored by the region's iron-rich soils, marks the state's southern boundary. Along the eastern border, the Ozark Plateau and Ouachita Mountains form rugged bluffs and valleys. To the west, rolling plains rise toward the High Plains in the state's panhandle.

⇧ NATURAL LANDSCAPE. A bison herd grazes in the Tallgrass Prairie Preserve, near Pawhuska. In years when rain is abundant, the grasses can grow as tall as 8 feet (2.5 m). Tallgrass prairie once covered 140 million acres (57 million ha), extending from Minnesota to Texas, but today less than 10 percent remains because of urban sprawl and cropland expansion.

WEATHER ALERT

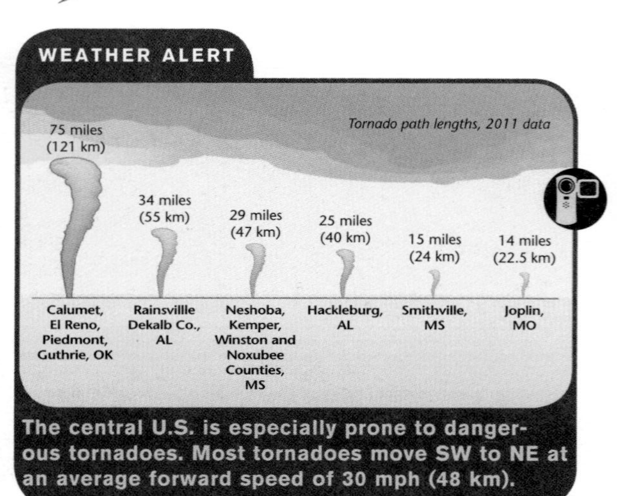

The central U.S. is especially prone to dangerous tornadoes. Most tornadoes move SW to NE at an average forward speed of 30 mph (48 km).

THE SOONER STATE: OKLAHOMA

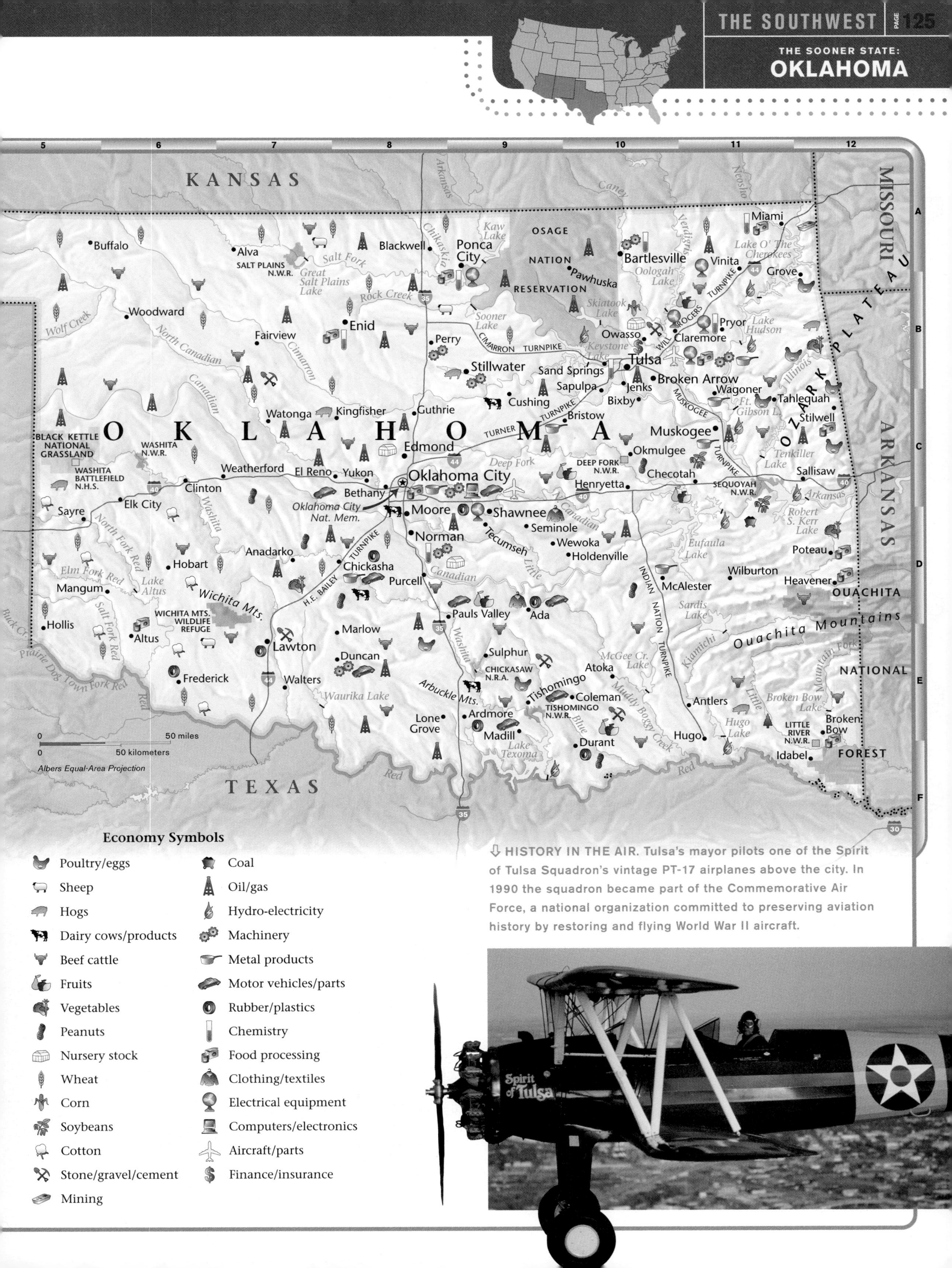

⇩ **HISTORY IN THE AIR.** Tulsa's mayor pilots one of the Spirit of Tulsa Squadron's vintage PT-17 airplanes above the city. In 1990 the squadron became part of the Commemorative Air Force, a national organization committed to preserving aviation history by restoring and flying World War II aircraft.

THE LONE STAR STATE:
TEXAS

TEXAS

Huge size, geographic diversity, and rich natural resources make Texas seem like its own country. In fact, it was an independent republic after throwing off Mexican rule in 1836. A famous battle in the fight for independence produced the Texan battle cry "Remember the Alamo!" In 1845 Texas was annexed by the United States. Texas is the second largest state (behind Alaska) and the second most populous (behind California). It is a top producer of many agricultural products, including cattle, sheep, cotton, citrus fruits, vegetables, rice, and pecans. It also has huge oil and natural gas fields and is a manufacturing powerhouse. Pine forests cover East Texas, the wettest region. The Gulf Coast has swamps and extensive barrier islands. Grassy plains stretch across the northern panhandle, while the rolling Hill Country is famous for beautiful wildflowers. Mountains, valleys, and sandy plains sprawl across dry West Texas. The Rio Grande, sometimes barely a trickle, separates Texas and Mexico.

⇧ BLACK GOLD. Workers plug an oil well. Discovery of oil early in the 20th century transformed life in Texas. Today, the state leads the U.S. in oil and natural gas production.

Chamizal National Memorial
NEW MEXIC
U.S.
MEXICO
El Paso
GUADALUPE MTS. N.P.
Guadalupe Pea
8,749 ft
2,667 m
Highest point in Texas
YSLETA DEL SUR I.R.
Fabens
CHIHUAHUA
Rio Grande
Davis Mts.
FORT D N.H.S.
Alpine
Marfa
Presidio
ROCKY MTS.

THE BASICS

STATS

Area
268,581 sq mi (695,624 sq km)

Population
25,145,561

Capital
Austin
Population 790,390

Largest city
Houston
Population 2,099,451

Ethnic/racial groups
70.4% white; 11.8% African American; 3.8% Asian; .7% Native American. Hispanic (any race) 37.6%.

Industry
Chemicals, machinery, electronics and computers, food products, petroleum and natural gas, transportation equipment

Agriculture
Cattle, sheep, poultry, cotton, sorghum, wheat, rice, hay, peanuts, pecans

Statehood
December 29, 1845; 28th state

GEO WHIZ

The Fossil Rim Wildlife Research Center in the Texas Hill Country is breeding black rhinos and other endangered African animals. The goal is to reintroduce offspring into the wild in their native environment. Meanwhile, visitors get a chance to see a bit of Africa in Texas.

Six national flags have flown over Texas during the course of its history—the Spanish, French, Mexican, Texan, Confederate, and American.

Texas has a long history of Bigfoot sightings. The ape-man creature was part of local Indian lore, and white settlers told stories about a wild woman along the Navidad River. The Texas Bigfoot Research Center has collected hundreds of eyewitness reports, footprint casts, and hair samples of what locals call Wooly Booger.

MOCKINGBIRD
BLUEBONNET

ROUNDUP

2011 data

Texas	Kansas	Nebraska	California	Oklahoma
13.3 million cattle	6.3 million cattle	6.2 million cattle	5.2 million cattle	5.1 million cattle

Texas has more cattle than most states have people. Only California, Texas, New York, and Florida have larger human populations.

⇨ BORDERLAND RELIC. Los Ebanos Ferry, which takes its name from a grove of ebony trees growing nearby, is the last remaining government-licensed, hand-pulled ferry on any U.S. border. The privately owned ferry, near Mission, Texas, can carry three cars at a time across the Rio Grande.

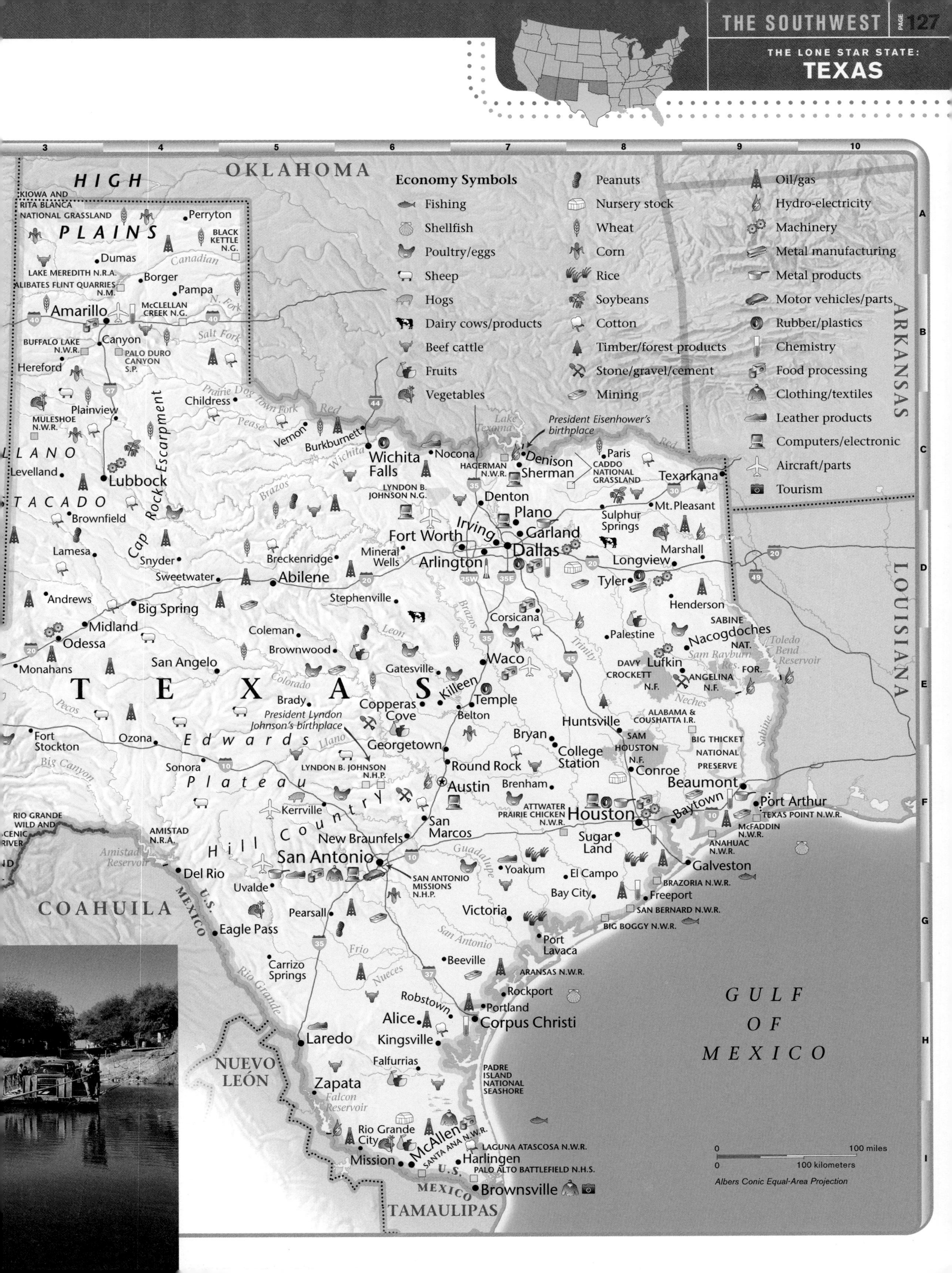
Economy Symbols
Fishing
Shellfish
Poultry/eggs
Sheep
Hogs
Dairy cows/products
Beef cattle
Fruits
Vegetables
Peanuts
Nursery stock
Wheat
Corn
Rice
Soybeans
Cotton
Timber/forest products
Stone/gravel/cement
Mining
Oil/gas
Hydro-electricity
Machinery
Metal manufacturing
Metal products
Motor vehicles/parts
Rubber/plastics
Chemistry
Food processing
Clothing/textiles
Leather products
Computers/electronic
Aircraft/parts
Tourism
OKLAHOMA
ARKANSAS
LOUISIANA
COAHUILA
NUEVO LEÓN
TAMAULIPAS
U.S.
MEXICO
GULF OF MEXICO
TEXAS
HIGH PLAINS
LLANO ESTACADO
Cap Rock Escarpment
Edwards Plateau
Hill Country
KIOWA AND RITA BLANCA NATIONAL GRASSLAND
BLACK KETTLE N.G.
LAKE MEREDITH N.R.A.
ALIBATES FLINT QUARRIES N.M.
McCLELLAN CREEK N.G.
BUFFALO LAKE N.W.R.
PALO DURO CANYON S.P.
MULESHOE N.W.R.
LYNDON B. JOHNSON N.G.
HAGERMAN N.W.R.
CADDO NATIONAL GRASSLAND
President Eisenhower's birthplace
President Lyndon Johnson's birthplace
LYNDON B. JOHNSON N.H.P.
SAN ANTONIO MISSIONS N.H.P.
AMISTAD N.R.A.
RIO GRANDE WILD AND SCENIC RIVER
ATTWATER PRAIRIE CHICKEN N.W.R.
SAM HOUSTON N.F.
DAVY CROCKETT N.F.
ALABAMA & COUSHATTA I.R.
ANGELINA N.F.
SABINE NAT. FOR.
BIG THICKET NATIONAL PRESERVE
TEXAS POINT N.W.R.
McFADDIN N.W.R.
ANAHUAC N.W.R.
BRAZORIA N.W.R.
SAN BERNARD N.W.R.
BIG BOGGY N.W.R.
ARANSAS N.W.R.
PADRE ISLAND NATIONAL SEASHORE
LAGUNA ATASCOSA N.W.R.
SANTA ANA N.W.R.
PALO ALTO BATTLEFIELD N.H.S.
Perryton
Dumas
Borger
Pampa
Amarillo
Canyon
Hereford
Plainview
Childress
Levelland
Lubbock
Brownfield
Lamesa
Snyder
Sweetwater
Abilene
Andrews
Big Spring
Midland
Odessa
Monahans
San Angelo
Fort Stockton
Ozona
Sonora
Vernon
Burkburnett
Wichita Falls
Nocona
Denison
Sherman
Paris
Texarkana
Denton
Plano
Irving
Garland
Fort Worth
Dallas
Arlington
Mineral Wells
Breckenridge
Stephenville
Mt. Pleasant
Sulphur Springs
Marshall
Longview
Tyler
Henderson
Corsicana
Palestine
Nacogdoches
Lufkin
Coleman
Brownwood
Gatesville
Waco
Killeen
Temple
Belton
Brady
Copperas Cove
Georgetown
Round Rock
Austin
Bryan
College Station
Huntsville
Conroe
Beaumont
Port Arthur
Brenham
Houston
Baytown
Sugar Land
Galveston
Kerrville
New Braunfels
San Marcos
San Antonio
Del Rio
Uvalde
Eagle Pass
Pearsall
Yoakum
El Campo
Bay City
Freeport
Victoria
Port Lavaca
Beeville
Carrizo Springs
Rockport
Portland
Robstown
Alice
Corpus Christi
Kingsville
Laredo
Falfurrias
Zapata
Rio Grande City
Mission
McAllen
Harlingen
Brownsville
Canadian
N. Fork
Salt Fork
Prairie Dog Town Fork
Pease
Red
Wichita
Brazos
Lake Texoma
Leon
Colorado
Llano
Pecos
Big Canyon
Trinity
Neches
Sabine
Sam Rayburn Res.
Toledo Bend Reservoir
Guadalupe
San Antonio
Frio
Nueces
Rio Grande
Amistad Reservoir
Falcon Reservoir
0 100 miles
0 100 kilometers
Albers Conic Equal-Area Projection

THE REGION

The West

PHYSICAL

Total area
1,635,555 sq mi (4,236,083 sq km)

Highest point
Mount McKinley (Denali), AK: 20,320 ft (6,194 m)

Lowest point
Death Valley, CA: -282 ft (-86 m)

Longest rivers
Missouri, Yukon, Rio Grande, Colorado

Largest lakes
Great Salt, Iliamna, Becharof

Vegetation
Needleleaf, broadleaf, and mixed forest; grassland; desert; tundra (Alaska); tropical (Hawai'i)

Climate
Mild along the coast, with warm summers and mild winters; semiarid to arid inland; polar in parts of Alaska; tropical in Hawai'i

POLITICAL

Total population
63,494,357

States (11):
Alaska, California, Colorado, Hawai'i, Idaho, Montana, Nevada, Oregon, Utah, Washington, Wyoming

Largest state
Alaska: 663,267 sq mi (1,717,862 sq km)

Smallest state
Hawai'i: 10,931 sq mi (28,311 sq km)

Most populous state
California: 37,253,956

Least populous state
Wyoming: 563,626

Largest city proper
Los Angeles, CA: 3,792,621

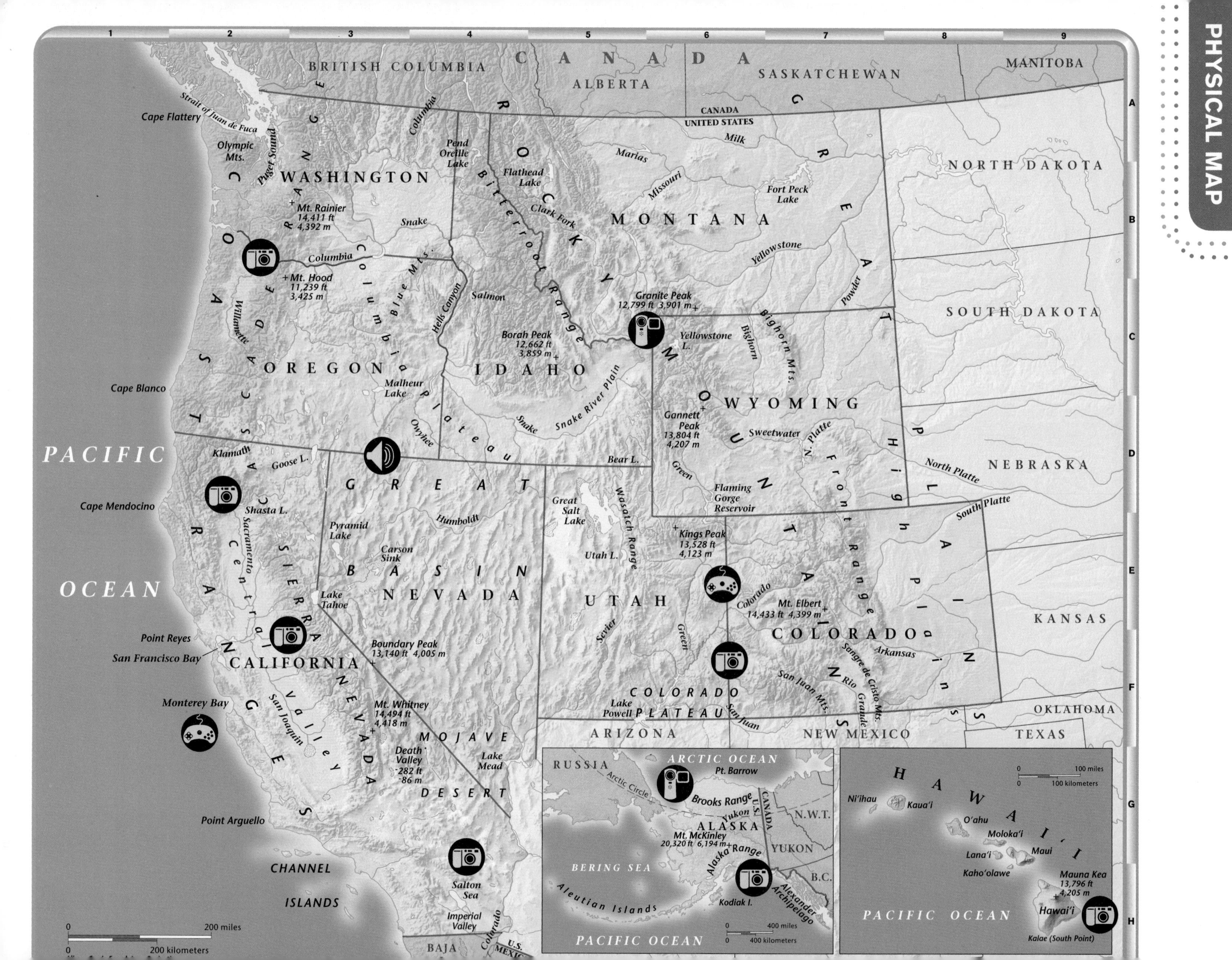
CANADA
BRITISH COLUMBIA
ALBERTA
SASKATCHEWAN
MANITOBA
CANADA
UNITED STATES
WASHINGTON
OREGON
IDAHO
MONTANA
WYOMING
NORTH DAKOTA
SOUTH DAKOTA
NEBRASKA
KANSAS
OKLAHOMA
TEXAS
NEW MEXICO
ARIZONA
UTAH
COLORADO
NEVADA
CALIFORNIA
BAJA
U.S.
MEXICO
PACIFIC OCEAN
CHANNEL ISLANDS
Strait of Juan de Fuca
Cape Flattery
Olympic Mts.
Puget Sound
Mt. Rainier 14,411 ft 4,392 m
Mt. Hood 11,239 ft 3,425 m
Columbia
Snake
Willamette
Blue Mts.
Columbia Plateau
Hells Canyon
Salmon
Pend Oreille Lake
Flathead Lake
Clark Fork
Bitterroot Range
ROCKY MOUNTAINS
CASCADE RANGE
COAST RANGES
GREAT PLAINS
GREAT BASIN
SIERRA NEVADA
Central Valley
MOJAVE DESERT
COLORADO PLATEAU
Marias
Milk
Missouri
Fort Peck Lake
Yellowstone
Powder
Granite Peak 12,799 ft 3,901 m
Yellowstone L.
Bighorn
Bighorn Mts.
Borah Peak 12,662 ft 3,859 m
Snake River Plain
Malheur Lake
Owyhee
Cape Blanco
Klamath
Goose L.
Bear L.
Gannett Peak 13,804 ft 4,207 m
Sweetwater
N. Platte
North Platte
South Platte
High Plains
Front Range
Green
Flaming Gorge Reservoir
Great Salt Lake
Wasatch Range
Utah L.
Kings Peak 13,528 ft 4,123 m
Cape Mendocino
Shasta L.
Sacramento
Pyramid Lake
Humboldt
Carson Sink
Lake Tahoe
Colorado
Mt. Elbert 14,433 ft 4,399 m
Arkansas
Sangre de Cristo Mts.
Rio Grande
San Juan Mts.
San Juan
Sevier
Point Reyes
San Francisco Bay
Boundary Peak 13,140 ft 4,005 m
Monterey Bay
San Joaquin Valley
Mt. Whitney 14,494 ft 4,418 m
Death Valley -282 ft -86 m
Lake Mead
Lake Powell
Point Arguello
Salton Sea
Imperial Valley
0 200 miles
0 200 kilometers
RUSSIA
ARCTIC OCEAN
Pt. Barrow
Arctic Circle
Brooks Range
Yukon
U.S.
CANADA
N.W.T.
ALASKA
Mt. McKinley 20,320 ft 6,194 m
Alaska Range
YUKON
B.C.
BERING SEA
Aleutian Islands
Kodiak I.
Alexander Archipelago
PACIFIC OCEAN
0 400 miles
0 400 kilometers
HAWAI'I
Ni'ihau
Kaua'i
O'ahu
Moloka'i
Lana'i
Maui
Kaho'olawe
Mauna Kea 13,796 ft 4,205 m
Hawai'i
Kalae (South Point)
PACIFIC OCEAN
0 100 miles
0 100 kilometers

BRITISH COLUMBIA
ALBERTA
SASKATCHEWAN
CANADA
UNITED STATES
NORTH DAKOTA
SOUTH DAKOTA
NEBRASKA
KANSAS
OKLAHOMA
TEXAS
NEW MEXICO
ARIZONA
WASHINGTON
OREGON
IDAHO
MONTANA
WYOMING
NEVADA
UTAH
COLORADO
CALIFORNIA
PACIFIC
OCEAN
MEXICO
BAJA CALIF.
SONORA
U.S.
MEXICO
Bellingham
Seattle
Olympia
Tacoma
Spokane
Coeur d'Alene
Yakima
Walla Walla
Lewiston
Vancouver
Portland
Pendleton
Salem
Eugene
Bend
Medford
Klamath Falls
Missoula
Great Falls
Helena
Butte
Bozeman
Billings
Boise
Idaho Falls
Pocatello
Twin Falls
Cody
Gillette
Casper
Rock Springs
Cheyenne
Laramie
Logan
Ogden
Salt Lake City
Provo
St. George
Fort Collins
Boulder
Denver
Grand Junction
Colorado Springs
Pueblo
Eureka
Redding
Elko
Reno
Carson City
Santa Rosa
Sacramento
Stockton
San Francisco
Oakland
San Jose
Salinas
Fresno
Las Vegas
Henderson
Bakersfield
Los Angeles
San Bernardino
Long Beach
Riverside
Oceanside
San Diego
Columbia
Snake
Salmon
Owyhee
Klamath
Marias
Milk
Missouri
Yellowstone
Powder
Bighorn
Sweetwater
Green
North Platte
South Platte
Great Salt Lake
Humboldt
Sacramento
San Joaquin
Sevier
Colorado
Arkansas
Rio Grande
San Juan
0 200 miles
0 200 kilometers
Albers Conic Equal-Area Projection
RUSSIA
ARCTIC OCEAN
Arctic Circle
CANADA
U.S.
N.W.T.
Yukon
Fairbanks
ALASKA
YUKON
Anchorage
BERING SEA
B.C.
Juneau
Aleutian Islands
Kodiak I.
PACIFIC OCEAN
0 400 miles
0 400 kilometers
HAWAI'I
0 100 miles
0 100 kilometers
Ni'ihau
Kaua'i
O'ahu
Honolulu
Moloka'i
Lana'i
Maui
Kaho'olawe
Hilo
Hawai'i
PACIFIC OCEAN
A
B
C
D
E
F
G
H
1
2
3
4
5
6
7
8
9

ABOUT THE **WEST**

⇨ OLD AND NEW. A cable car carries passengers on a steep hill in San Francisco. In the background modern buildings, including the Transamerica Pyramid, rise above older neighborhoods in this earthquake-prone city.

The West

THE HIGH FRONTIER

The western states, which make up almost half of the country's land area, have diverse landscapes and climates, ranging from the frozen heights of Denali, in Alaska, to the desolation of Death Valley, in California, and the lush, tropical islands of Hawai'i. More than half the region's population lives in California, and the Los Angeles metropolitan area is second only to New York City. Yet many parts of the region are sparsely populated, and much of the land is set aside as parkland and military bases. The region also faces many natural hazards—earthquakes, landslides, wildfires, and even volcanic eruptions.

⇨ NORTHERN GIANT. Mount McKinley, called Denali—the "High One"—by native Athabascans, is North America's highest peak, rising more than 20,000 feet (6,100 m) in the Alaska Range. The same tectonic forces that trigger earthquakes in Alaska are slowly pushing this huge block of granite ever higher.

ABOUT THE
WEST

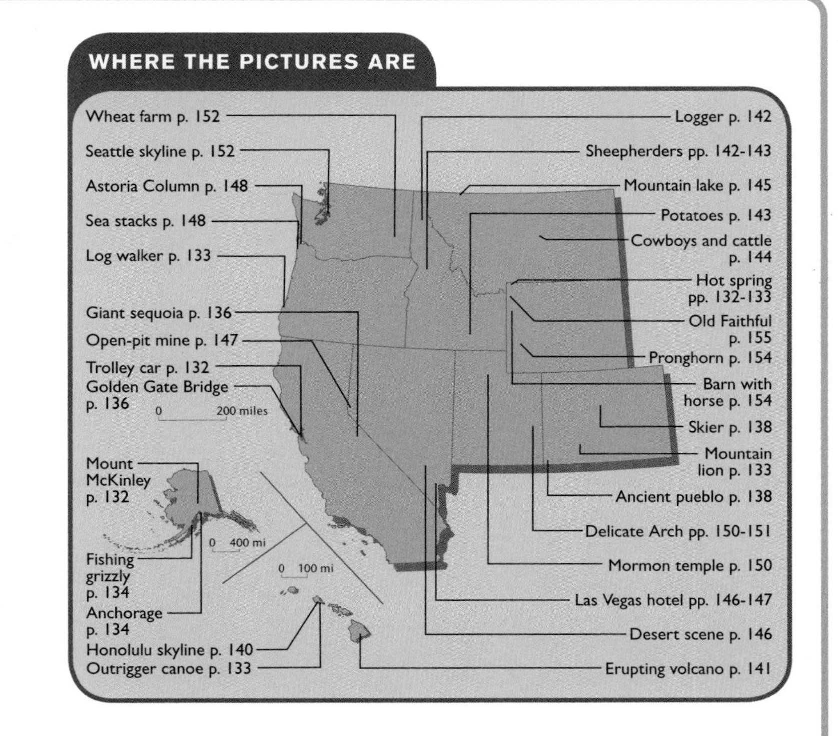

⇧ ELUSIVE PREDATOR. Known by many names, including cougar and mountain lion, these big cats are found mainly in remote mountainous areas of the West, where they hunt deer and smaller animals.

⇦ STEAMY BATH. Colorful, mineral-rich hot springs are just one geothermal feature of Yellowstone National Park. Runoff from rain and snowmelt seeps into cracks in the ground, sinking to a depth of 10,000 feet (3,050 m), where it is heated by molten rock before rising back to the surface.

⇩ BALANCING ACT. For many years, rivers have been used to move logs from forest to market, taking advantage of the buoyancy of logs and the power of moving water. A logger stands on a floating log raft in Coos Bay, Oregon.

⇧ TRADITIONAL SAILING CRAFT. A Hawaiian outrigger canoe on Waikiki Beach promises fun in the surf for visitors to the 50th state. An important part of Polynesian culture, the canoes were once used to travel from island to island.

THE LAST FRONTIER STATE:
ALASKA

ALASKA

THE BASICS

STATS

Area
663,267 sq mi (1,717,862 sq km)

Population
710,231

Capital
Juneau
Population 31,275

Largest city
Anchorage
Population 291,826

Ethnic/racial groups
66.7% white; 14.8% Native American; 5.4% Asian; 3.3% African American. Hispanic (any race) 5.5%.

Industry
Petroleum products, government, services, trade

Agriculture
Shellfish, seafood, nursery stock, vegetables, dairy products, feed crops

Statehood
January 3, 1959; 49th state

GEO WHIZ

During the summer humpback whales migrate to Alaskan waters, where they work together to catch fish. While swimming in circles, the whales blow bubbles that form a net around schools of herring. Each whale can eat hundreds of fish in one gulp.

Global warming and population growth are changing the route of the Iditarod, the world's most famous sled-dog race. Since 2002 lack of snow in Wasilla has forced the starting point for the competition to move 30 miles (48 km) farther north to Willow.

The Tongass National Forest, where conservationists are battling to stop the harvesting of 1,000-year-old trees, is the largest national forest in the United States.

WILLOW PTARMIGAN
FORGET-ME-NOT

Alaska—from *Alyeska*, an Aleut word meaning "great land"—was purchased by the U.S. from Russia in 1867 for just two cents an acre. Many people thought it was a bad investment, but it soon paid off when gold was discovered, and again when major petroleum deposits were discovered in 1968. Today, an 800-mile-long pipeline (1,287 km) links North Slope oil fields to the ice-free port at Valdez, but opponents worry about long-term environmental impact. Everything is big in Alaska. It is the largest state, with one-sixth of the country's land area; it has the highest peak in the U.S., Mt. McKinley (Denali); and the largest earthquake ever recorded in the U.S.—a 9.2 magnitude—occurred there in 1964. It is first in forestland, a leading source of seafood, and a major oil producer. Alaska's population includes a higher percentage of native people than that of any other state.

⇧ TIME FOR LUNCH. A grizzly bear wades into the rushing waters of Brooks Falls, in Katmai National Park, to catch a leaping salmon.

⇦ NORTHERN METROPOLIS. Anchorage, established in 1915 as a construction port for the Alaska Railroad, sits in the shadow of the snow-covered Chugach Mountains.

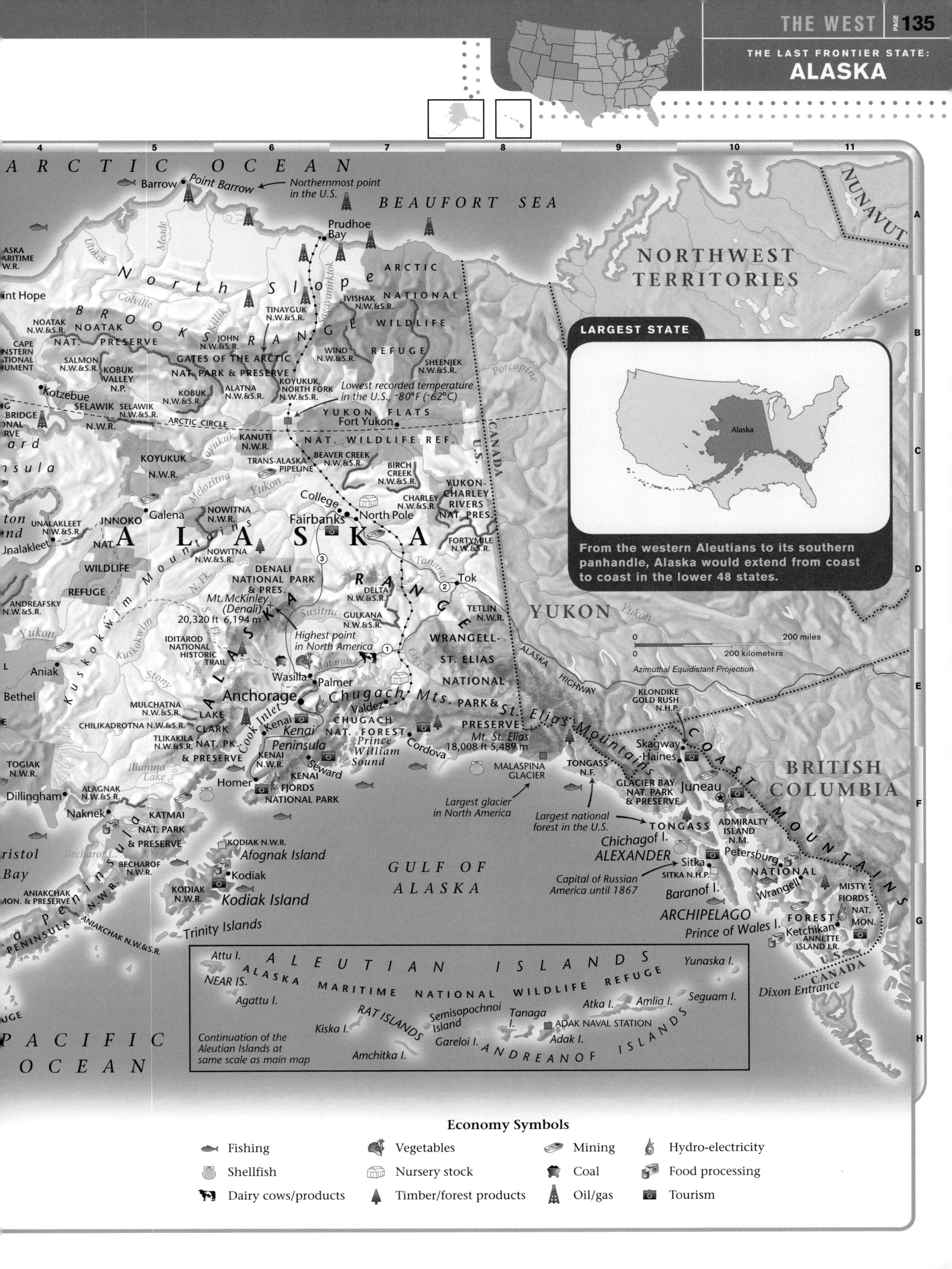
ARCTIC OCEAN
BEAUFORT SEA
Barrow
Point Barrow
Northernmost point in the U.S.
Prudhoe Bay
North Slope
BROOKS RANGE
ARCTIC NATIONAL WILDLIFE REFUGE
NORTHWEST TERRITORIES
NUNAVUT
NOATAK N.W.&S.R.
NOATAK NAT. PRESERVE
SALMON N.W.&S.R.
KOBUK VALLEY N.P.
GATES OF THE ARCTIC NAT. PARK & PRESERVE
JOHN N.W.&S.R.
TINAYGUK N.W.&S.R.
IVISHAK N.W.&S.R.
WIND N.W.&S.R.
SHEENJEK N.W.&S.R.
KOBUK N.W.&S.R.
ALATNA N.W.&S.R.
KOYUKUK, NORTH FORK N.W.&S.R.
Lowest recorded temperature in the U.S., -80°F (-62°C)
Kotzebue
SELAWIK N.W.R.
SELAWIK N.W.&S.R.
ARCTIC CIRCLE
YUKON FLATS NAT. WILDLIFE REF.
Fort Yukon
KANUTI N.W.R.
KOYUKUK N.W.R.
TRANS-ALASKA PIPELINE
BEAVER CREEK N.W.&S.R.
BIRCH CREEK N.W.&S.R.
YUKON-CHARLEY RIVERS NAT. PRES.
CHARLEY N.W.&S.R.
FORTYMILE N.W.&S.R.
U.S.
CANADA
LARGEST STATE
Alaska
From the western Aleutians to its southern panhandle, Alaska would extend from coast to coast in the lower 48 states.
College
Fairbanks
North Pole
Galena
NOWITNA N.W.R.
NOWITNA N.W.&S.R.
INNOKO NAT. WILDLIFE REFUGE
UNALAKLEET N.W.&S.R.
Unalakleet
ALASKA
Kuskokwim Mountains
DENALI NATIONAL PARK & PRES.
Mt. McKinley (Denali) 20,320 ft 6,194 m
Highest point in North America
ALASKA RANGE
DELTA N.W.&S.R.
GULKANA N.W.&S.R.
Tok
TETLIN N.W.R.
YUKON
0 200 miles
0 200 kilometers
Azimuthal Equidistant Projection
ANDREAFSKY N.W.&S.R.
IDITAROD NATIONAL HISTORIC TRAIL
WRANGELL-ST. ELIAS NATIONAL PARK & PRESERVE
ALASKA HIGHWAY
KLONDIKE GOLD RUSH N.H.P.
Aniak
Bethel
Wasilla
Palmer
Anchorage
Chugach Mts.
Valdez
MULCHATNA N.W.&S.R.
LAKE CLARK NAT. PK. & PRESERVE
CHILIKADROTNA N.W.&S.R.
TLIKAKILA N.W.&S.R.
Cook Inlet
Kenai
Kenai Peninsula
KENAI N.W.R.
KENAI FJORDS NATIONAL PARK
Seward
CHUGACH NAT. FOREST
Prince William Sound
Cordova
Mt. St. Elias 18,008 ft 5,489 m
St. Elias Mountains
MALASPINA GLACIER
Largest glacier in North America
TONGASS N.F.
Largest national forest in the U.S.
Skagway
Haines
GLACIER BAY NAT. PARK & PRESERVE
Juneau
COAST MOUNTAINS
BRITISH COLUMBIA
TOGIAK N.W.R.
Iliamna Lake
Homer
Dillingham
ALAGNAK N.W.&S.R.
Naknek
KATMAI NAT. PARK & PRESERVE
Bristol Bay
Becharof L.
BECHAROF N.W.R.
KODIAK N.W.R.
Afognak Island
Kodiak
KODIAK N.W.R.
Kodiak Island
Alaska Peninsula N.W.R.
ANIAKCHAK NAT. MON. & PRESERVE
ANIAKCHAK N.W.&S.R.
Trinity Islands
GULF OF ALASKA
TONGASS
ADMIRALTY ISLAND N.M.
Chichagof I.
ALEXANDER ARCHIPELAGO
Sitka
SITKA N.H.P.
Capital of Russian America until 1867
Petersburg
NATIONAL FOREST
Baranof I.
Wrangell
MISTY FIORDS NAT. MON.
Prince of Wales I.
Ketchikan
ANNETTE ISLAND I.R.
Dixon Entrance
PACIFIC OCEAN
Attu I.
NEAR IS.
Agattu I.
ALEUTIAN ISLANDS
ALASKA MARITIME NATIONAL WILDLIFE REFUGE
Yunaska I.
Seguam I.
Amlia I.
Atka I.
Kiska I.
RAT ISLANDS
Semisopochnoi Island
Tanaga I.
ADAK NAVAL STATION
Adak I.
Gareloi I.
Amchitka I.
ANDREANOF ISLANDS
Continuation of the Aleutian Islands at same scale as main map
Economy Symbols
Fishing
Shellfish
Dairy cows/products
Vegetables
Nursery stock
Timber/forest products
Mining
Coal
Oil/gas
Hydro-electricity
Food processing
Tourism

THE GOLDEN STATE:
CALIFORNIA

THE BASICS

STATS

Area
163,696 sq mi (423,972 sq km)

Population
37,253,956

Capital
Sacramento
Population 466,488

Largest city
Los Angeles
Population 3,792,621

Ethnic/racial groups
57.6% white; 13.0% Asian; 6.2% African American; 1.0% Native American. Hispanic (any race) 37.6%.

Industry
Electronic components and equipment, computers and computer software, tourism, food processing, entertainment, clothing

Agriculture
Fruits and vegetables, dairy products, cattle, forest products, commercial fishing

Statehood
September 9, 1850; 31st state

GEO WHIZ

Every December one of the largest gatherings of northern elephant seals in the world converges on the beaches of Año Nuevo State Reserve, south of San Francisco, to rest, mate, and give birth.

The Monterey Bay Aquarium has been working to save endangered sea otters for 20 years. Rescued animals that cannot be rehabilitated for re-release into the wild find a permanent home at the aquarium.

Castroville, known as the Artichoke Capital of the World, crowned future movie legend Marilyn Monroe its first-ever artichoke queen in 1947.

CALIFORNIA QUAIL
GOLDEN POPPY

CALIFORNIA

The coast of what is now California was visited by Spanish and English explorers in the mid-1500s, but colonization did not begin until 1769 when the first of 21 Spanish missions was established at San Diego. The missions, built to bring Christianity to the many native people living in the area, eventually extended up the coast as far as Sonoma along a road known as El Camino Real. The U.S. gained control of California in 1847, following a war with Mexico. The next year gold was discovered near Sutter's Mill, triggering a gold rush and migration from the eastern U.S. and around the world. Today, California is the most populous state, and its economy ranks above that of most of the world's countries. It is a major source of fruits, nuts, and vegetables, accounting for more than half of the U.S. output. The state is an industrial leader, producing jet aircraft, ships, and high-tech equipment. It is also a center for the entertainment industry.

⇧ ENGINEERING WONDER. Stretching more than a mile (1.6 km) across the entrance to San Francisco Bay, the Golden Gate Bridge opened to traffic in 1937. The bridge is painted vermilion orange, a color chosen in part because it is visible in fog.

BOUNTIFUL HARVEST

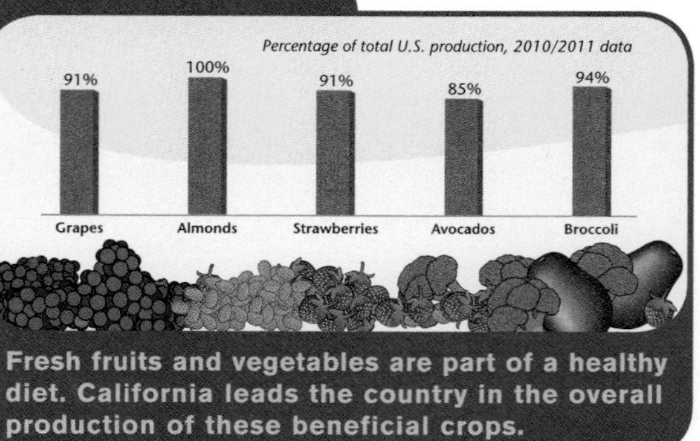

Fresh fruits and vegetables are part of a healthy diet. California leads the country in the overall production of these beneficial crops.

⇦ FOREST GIANT. Sequoias in Yosemite National Park's Mariposa Grove exceed 200 feet (61 m), making them the world's tallest trees. The trees, some of which are 3,000 years old, grow in isolated groves on the western slopes of the Sierra Nevada.

THE GOLDEN STATE: CALIFORNIA

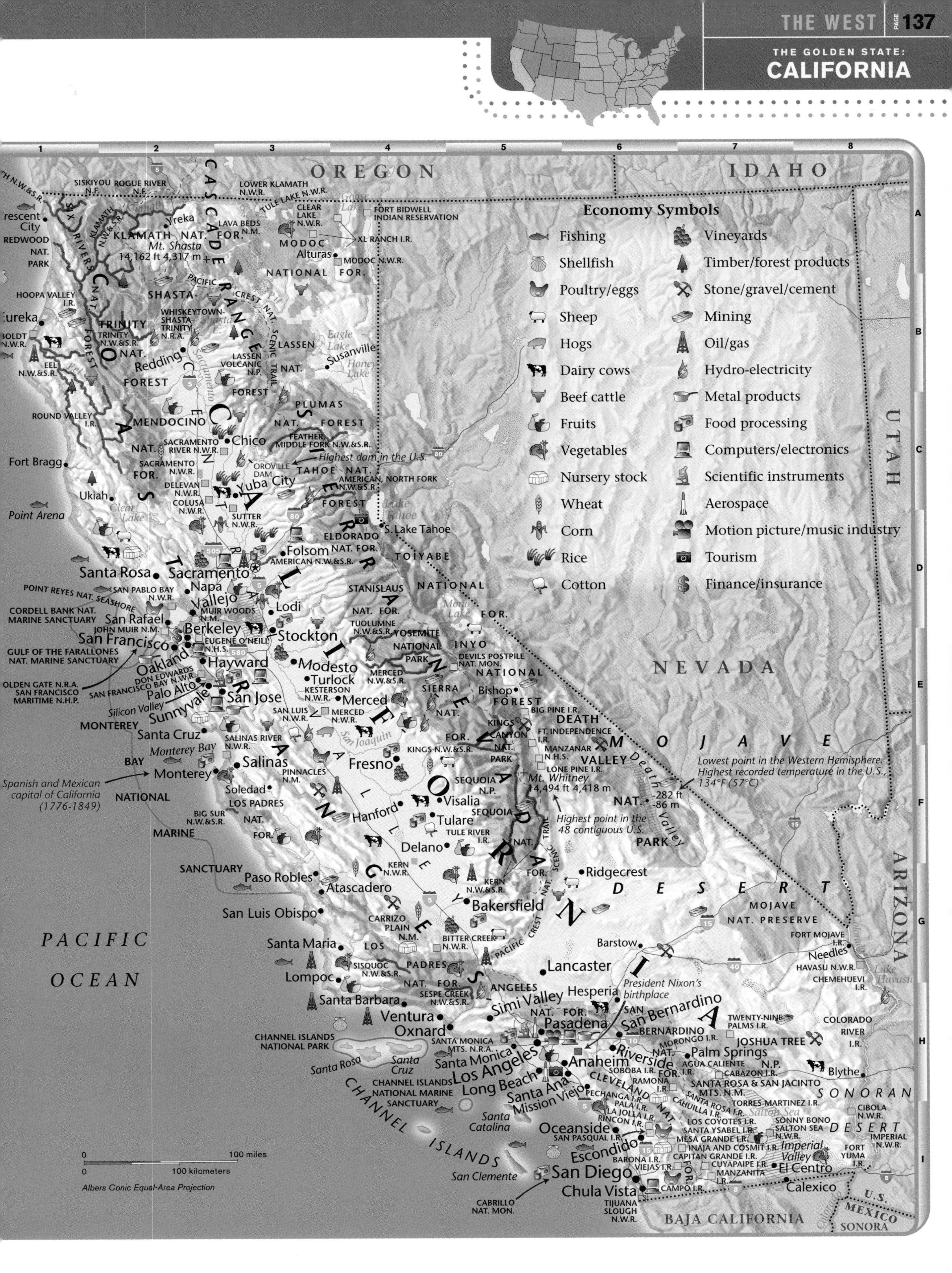

THE CENTENNIAL STATE:
COLORADO

THE BASICS

STATS

Area
104,094 sq mi (269,602 sq km)

Population
5,029,196

Capital
Denver
Population 600,158

Largest city
Denver
Population 600,158

Ethnic/racial groups
81.3% white; 4.0% African American; 2.8% Asian; 1.1% Native American. Hispanic (any race) 20.7%.

Industry
Real estate, government, durable goods, communications, health and other services, nondurable goods, transportation

Agriculture
Cattle, corn, wheat, dairy products, hay

Statehood
August 1, 1876; 38th state

GEO WHIZ

The Black Canyon of the Gunnison is one of the newest national parks in the Rockies. As it flows through the canyon, the Gunnison River drops an average of 95 feet (29 m) per mile—one of the steepest descents in North America. The craggy rock walls are a mecca for rock climbers.

Colorado's lynx population is making a comeback, thanks to a program that releases wild cats captured in Canada into Colorado's southern Rockies. Since the program began in 1999, more than 200 cats have been released and at least 141 lynx kittens have been born.

LARK BUNTING
COLUMBINE

COLORADO

Indians were the earliest inhabitants of present-day Colorado. Some were cliff dwellers; others were plains dwellers. Spanish explorers arrived in Colorado in 1541. In 1803 eastern Colorado became U.S. territory as part of the Louisiana Purchase. Gold was discovered in 1858, and thousands were attracted by the prospect of quick wealth. The sudden jump in population led to conflict with native Cheyennes and Arapahos over control of the land, but the settlers prevailed. Completion of the transcontinental railroad in 1869 helped link Colorado to the eastern states and opened its doors for growth. Cattle ranching and farming developed on the High Plains of eastern Colorado, while the mountainous western part of the state focused on mining. Today, mining is still important in Colorado, but the focus has shifted to energy resources—oil, natural gas, and coal. Agriculture is also an important source of income, with cattle accounting for almost half of farm income. And Colorado's majestic mountains attract thousands of tourists each year.

⇧ THRILLING SPORT. Colorado's snow-covered mountains attract winter sports enthusiasts from near and far. In the past skis were used by gold prospectors. Today, skiing and snowboarding are big moneymakers in the state's recreation and tourism industry.

⇦ ANCIENT CULTURE. Ancestral Puebloans lived from about A.D. 600 to A.D. 1300 in the canyons that today are a part of Mesa Verde National Park. More than 600 stone structures were built on protected cliffs of the canyon walls; others were located on mesas. These dwellings hold many clues to a past way of life.

THE CENTENNIAL STATE: COLORADO

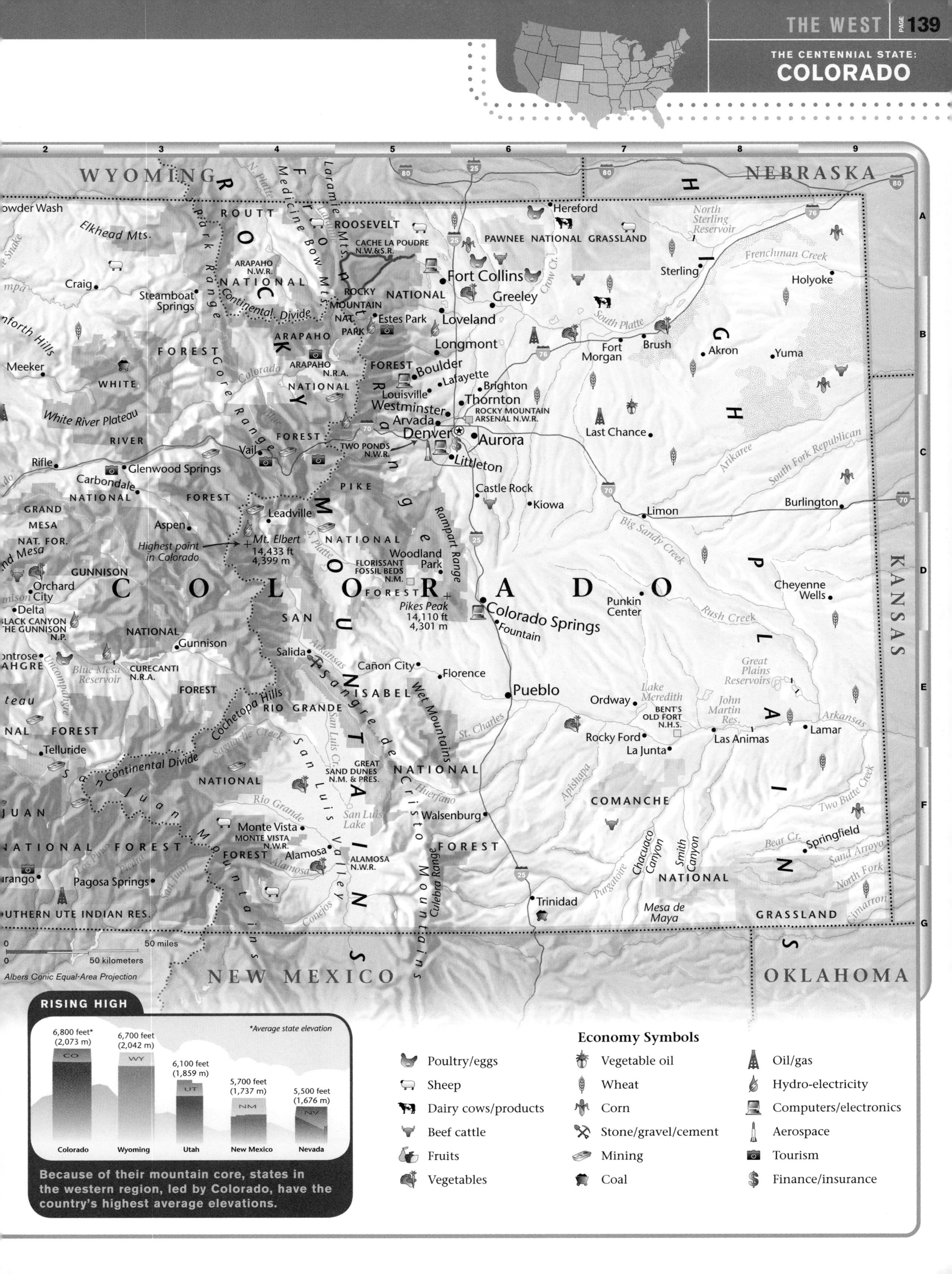

THE ALOHA STATE:
HAWAI'I

HAWAI'I

THE BASICS

STATS

Area
10,931 sq mi (28,311 sq km)

Population
1,360,301

Capital
Honolulu
Population 337,256

Largest city
Honolulu
Population 337,256

Ethnic/racial groups
38.6% Asian; 24.7% white; 10.0% Hawaiian/Pacific Islander; 1.6% African American. Hispanic (any race) 10.5%.

Industry
Tourism, trade, finance, food processing, petroleum refining, stone, clay, glass products

Agriculture
Sugarcane, pineapples, nursery stock, tropical fruit, livestock, macadamia nuts

Statehood
August 21, 1959; 50th state

GEO WHIZ

The shallow waters off the coast of Hawai'i are home to some of the world's most interesting sea creatures: marine worms. They were among the first sea animals more than 500 million years ago.

Hawai'i is the most isolated population center on Earth. It is more than 2,300 miles (3,700 km) from California, 3,850 miles (6,196 km) from Japan, and 4,900 miles (7,886 km) from China.

Everywhere else in the world caterpillars feed on plants. In Hawai'i there are 20 species that eat meat. Scientists have recorded the world's only known carnivorous caterpillars munching on ants.

You can ski two different ways on the same day in Hawai'i: on water at the beach and on snow on the slopes of Mauna Kea, a 13,796-foot-high volcano (4,205 m) on the Big Island.

HAWAIIAN GOOSE (NENE)
HIBISCUS

Some 1,500 years ago, Polynesians traveling in large canoes arrived from the south to settle the volcanic islands that make up Hawai'i. In 1778 Captain James Cook claimed the islands for Britain, and soon Hawai'i became a center of the whaling industry and a major producer of sugarcane. The spread of sugarcane plantations led to the importation of workers from Asia. Hawai'i became a U.S. territory in 1900. Naval installations, established as fueling depots and to protect U.S. interests in the Pacific, were attacked by the Japanese in 1941, an act that officially brought the U.S. into World War II. In 1959 Hawai'i became the 50th state. Tourism, agriculture, and the military, with bases centered on O'ahu's Pearl Harbor, are the cornerstone of Hawai'i's economy today. Jet airline service makes the distant islands accessible to tourists from both the mainland U.S. and Asia as well as from Australia and New Zealand. Hawai'i is still a major producer of sugarcane, along with nursery products and pineapples.

⇧ ISLAND PARADISE. High-rise hotels light up Waikiki, the center of Honolulu's tourist industry. Thousands of visitors flock to the islands each year to enjoy the warm climate, sandy beaches, and rich, multicultural heritage of Hawai'i.

DANGER FROM BELOW

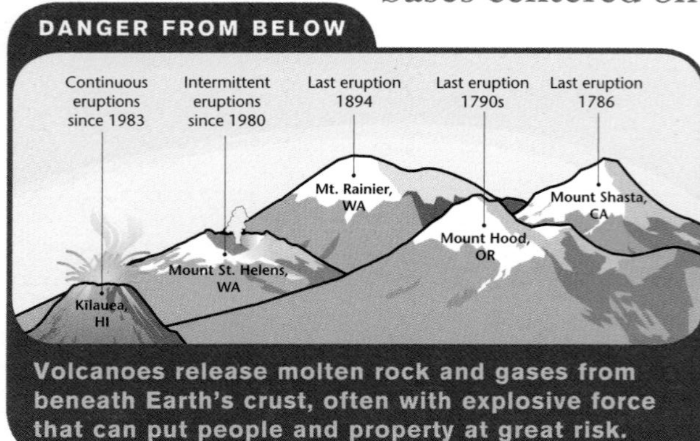

Volcanoes release molten rock and gases from beneath Earth's crust, often with explosive force that can put people and property at great risk.

THE ALOHA STATE:
HAWAI'I

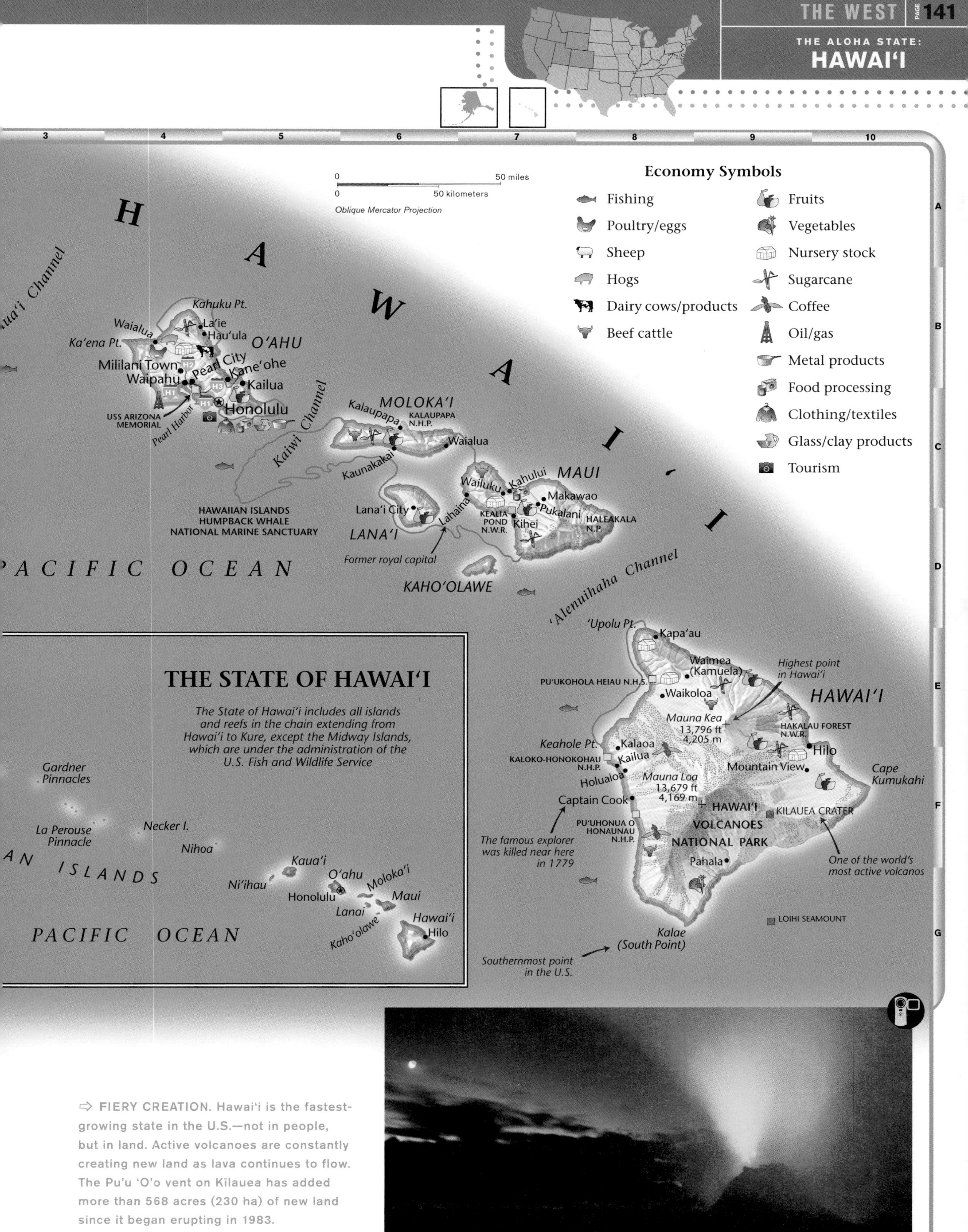

⇨ FIERY CREATION. Hawai'i is the fastest-growing state in the U.S.—not in people, but in land. Active volcanoes are constantly creating new land as lava continues to flow. The Pu'u 'O'o vent on Kīlauea has added more than 568 acres (230 ha) of new land since it began erupting in 1983.

THE GEM STATE:
IDAHO

IDAHO

THE BASICS

STATS

Area
83,570 sq mi (216,447 sq km)

Population
1,567,582

Capital
Boise
Population 205,671

Largest city
Boise
Population 205,671

Ethnic/racial groups
89.1% white; 1.4% Native American; 1.2% Asian; .6% African American. Hispanic (any race) 11.2%.

Industry
Electronics and computer equipment, tourism, food processing, forest products, mining, chemicals

Agriculture
Potatoes, dairy products, cattle, wheat, alfalfa hay, sugar beets, barley, trout

Statehood
July 3, 1890; 43rd state

GEO WHIZ

Before the last ice age, mammoths, woolly rhinos, giant ground sloths, and other huge mammal species roamed what is now Idaho. Fossils of these prehistoric creatures are on display at the Museum of Idaho, in Idaho Falls.

Wood duck chicks born in Idaho and other Rocky Mountain states undergo an amazing rite of passage the day after they are born. If they want to eat, they have to jump as much as 60 feet (18 m) from their tree-hole nest to the water below, where their mother waits for them.

In preparation for their mission to the Moon, Apollo astronauts visited Craters of the Moon National Monument to study its volcanic geology and experience firsthand its harsh environment.

MOUNTAIN BLUEBIRD
SYRINGA (MOCK ORANGE)

Some of the earliest Native American sites in what is now Idaho date back 10,000 to 12,000 years. In the 18th and early 19th centuries, contact between native people and Europeans brought not only trade and cultural change but also diseases that wiped out many native groups. Present-day Idaho was part of the 1803 Louisiana Purchase, and in 1805 it was explored during the famous Lewis and Clark expedition. In 1843 wagons crossed into Idaho on the Oregon Trail. The arrival of white settlers brought conflict with the Indians, which continued until 1890 when Idaho became a state. Today, farming plays an important role in Idaho's economy. More than one-fifth of the land is planted with crops, especially wheat, sugar beets, barley, and potatoes. The state supports the use of alternative sources of energy, including geothermal, ethanol, wind, and biomass. The economy has diversified to include manufacturing and high-tech industries. The state's rugged natural beauty also attracts tourists year-round.

⇧ WOOLLY RUSH HOUR. Sheep fill a roadway in Idaho's Salmon River Valley. The herds move twice a year. In the spring they migrate north to mountain pastures. In the fall they return to the Snake River plains in the south.

ANCIENT STAPLE FOOD

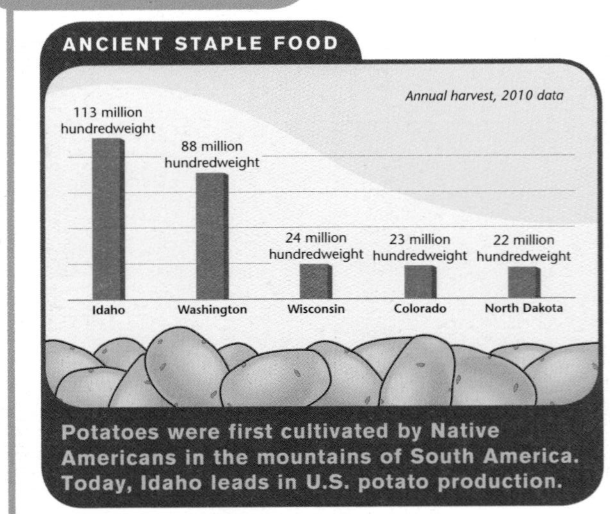

Potatoes were first cultivated by Native Americans in the mountains of South America. Today, Idaho leads in U.S. potato production.

⇧ TIMBER! More than 40 percent of Idaho's land area is tree-covered, much of it in national forests. Lumber and paper products, most of which are sold to other states, are important to the state economy.

THE GEM STATE: IDAHO

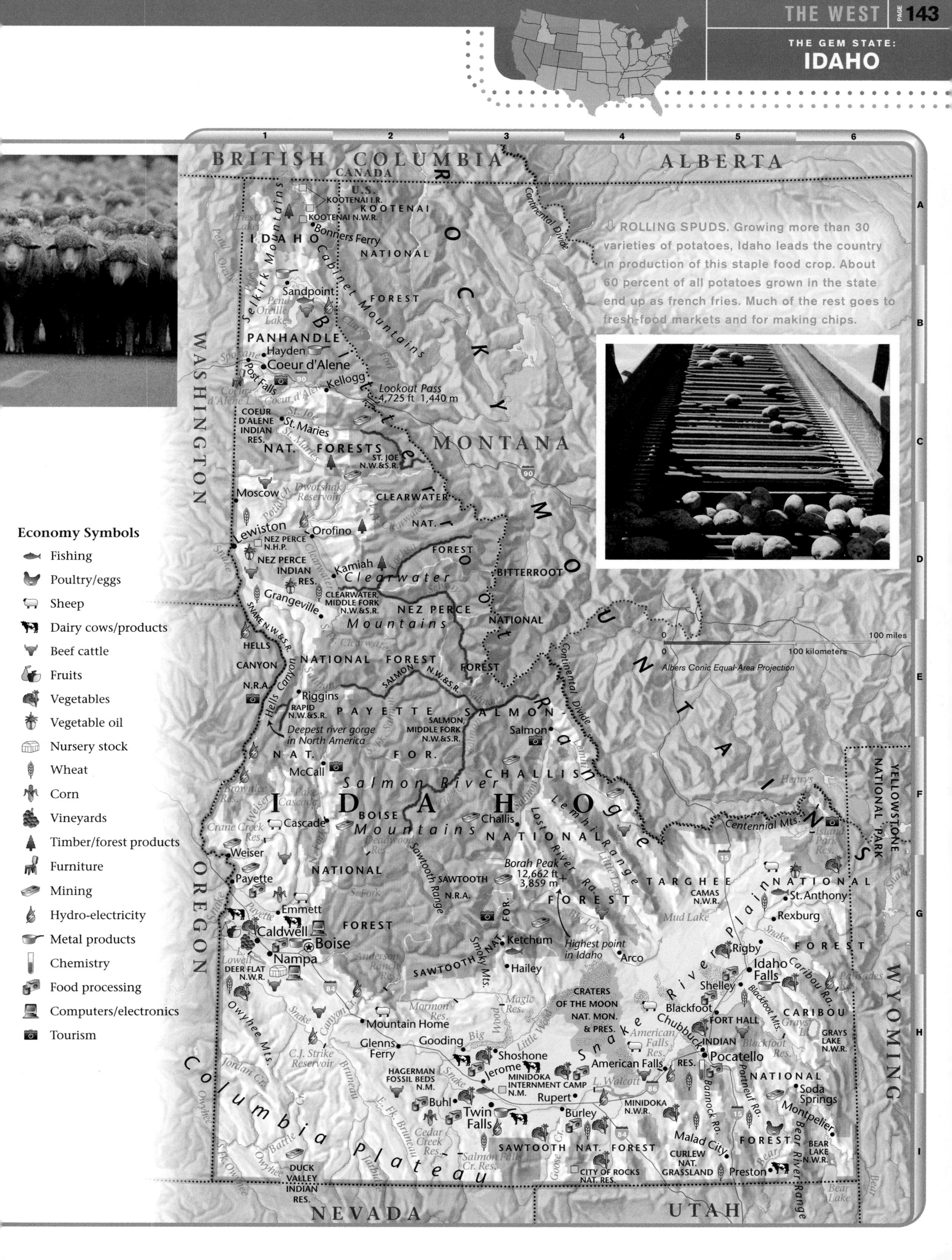

⇩ ROLLING SPUDS. Growing more than 30 varieties of potatoes, Idaho leads the country in production of this staple food crop. About 60 percent of all potatoes grown in the state end up as french fries. Much of the rest goes to fresh-food markets and for making chips.

Economy Symbols

- Fishing
- Poultry/eggs
- Sheep
- Dairy cows/products
- Beef cattle
- Fruits
- Vegetables
- Vegetable oil
- Nursery stock
- Wheat
- Corn
- Vineyards
- Timber/forest products
- Furniture
- Mining
- Hydro-electricity
- Metal products
- Chemistry
- Food processing
- Computers/electronics
- Tourism

THE TREASURE STATE:
MONTANA

MONTANA

Long before the arrival of Europeans, numerous native groups lived and hunted in the plains and mountains of present-day Montana. While contact between European explorers and Native Americans was often peaceful, Montana was the site of the historic 1876 Battle of the Little Bighorn, in which Lakota (Sioux) and Cheyenne warriors defeated George Armstrong Custer's troops. In the mid-19th century the discovery of gold and silver attracted many prospectors, and later cattle ranching became big business, adding to tensions with the Indians. Montana became the 41st state in 1889. Today, Indians still make up more than 6 percent of the state's population—only four other states have a larger percent. Agriculture is an important part of the economy, producing wheat, hay, and barley as well as beef cattle. Mining and timber industries have seen a decline, but service industries and tourism are growing. Montana's natural environment, including Glacier and Yellowstone National Parks, remains one of its greatest resources.

MONTANA

THE BASICS

STATS

Area
147,042 sq mi (380,840 sq km)

Population
989,415

Capital
Helena
Population 28,190

Largest city
Billings
Population 104,170

Ethnic/racial groups
89.4% white; 6.3% Native American .6% Asian; .4% African American. Hispanic (any race) 2.9%.

Industry
Forest products, food processing, mining, construction, tourism

Agriculture
Wheat, cattle, barley, hay, sugar beets, dairy products

Statehood
November 8, 1889; 41st state

GEO WHIZ

The fossil of a dinosaur about the size of a large turkey is being called the missing link between Asian and North American horned dinosaurs. Paleontologist Jack Horner, who served as the model for the character of Alan Grant in the *Jurassic Park* movies, discovered the fossil while sitting on it during a lunch break at a dig near Choteau.

Montana is the only state with river systems that empty into the Gulf of Mexico, Hudson Bay, and the Pacific Ocean.

Grasshopper Glacier is littered with the bodies of thousands of grasshoppers that became trapped in the ice sometime before the species became extinct 200 years ago.

WESTERN MEADOWLARK
BITTERROOT

⇧ STEP BACK IN TIME. Just like in the past, Montana ranchers move their cattle herds from low winter pastures to higher elevations for summer grazing. Some ranches allow adventurous tourists to participate in the drives.

ECONOMIC CORNERSTONE

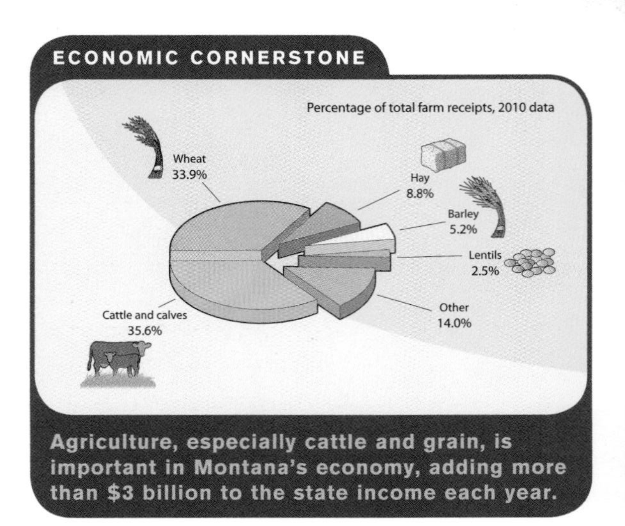

Agriculture, especially cattle and grain, is important in Montana's economy, adding more than $3 billion to the state income each year.

THE TREASURE STATE: MONTANA

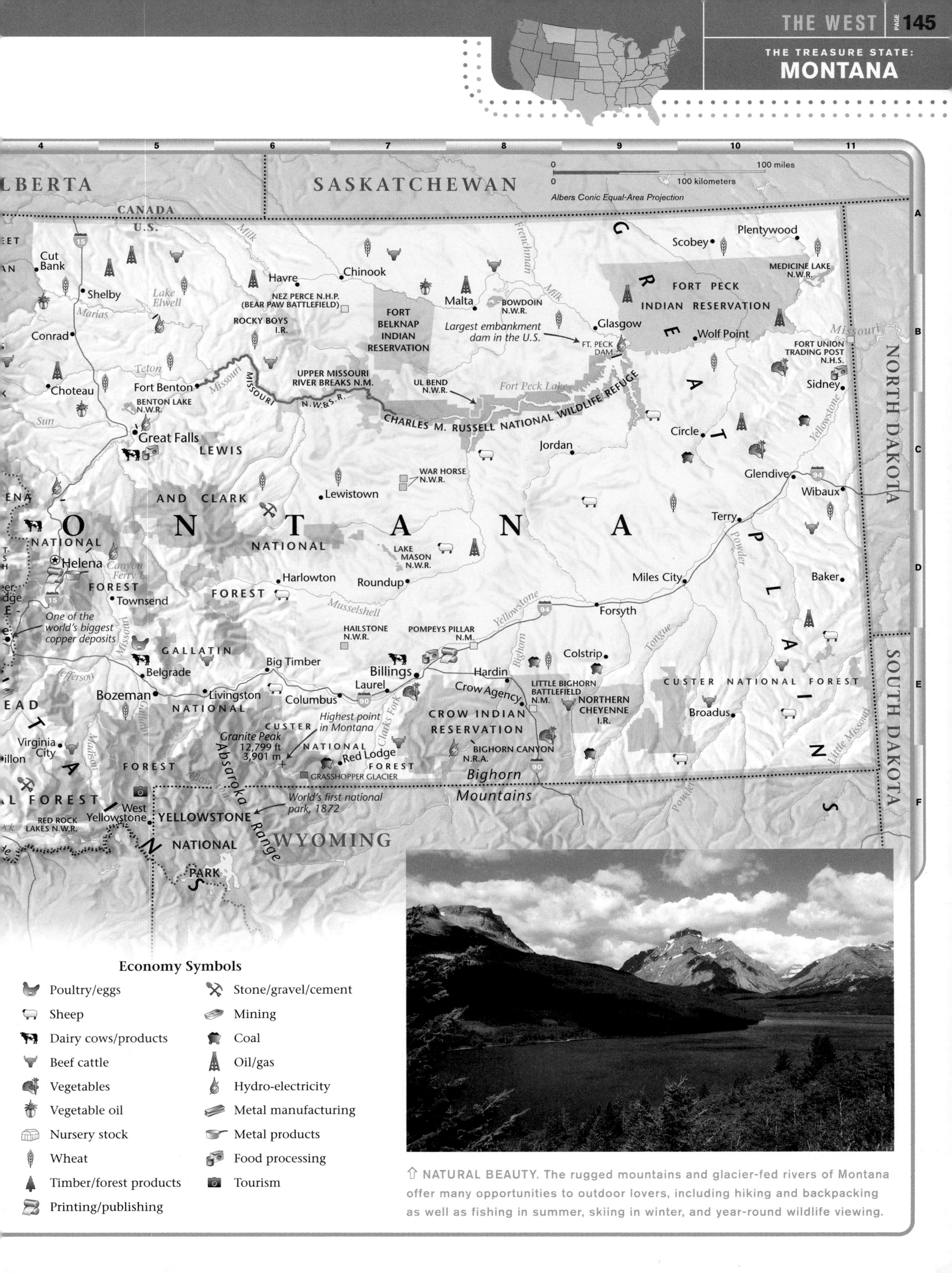

⇧ NATURAL BEAUTY. The rugged mountains and glacier-fed rivers of Montana offer many opportunities to outdoor lovers, including hiking and backpacking as well as fishing in summer, skiing in winter, and year-round wildlife viewing.

THE SILVER STATE:
NEVADA

NEVADA

Nevada's earliest settlers were native people about whom little is known. Around two thousand years ago, they began establishing permanent dwellings of clay and stone perched atop rocky ledges in what is today the state of Nevada. This was what Spanish explorers saw when they arrived in 1776. In years following, many expeditions passing through the area faced challenges of a difficult environment and native groups protecting their land. In the mid-1800s, gold and silver were discovered. In 1861, the Nevada Territory was created, and three years later statehood was granted. Today, the Nevada landscape is dotted with ghost towns—places once prosperous, but now abandoned except for curious tourists. Mining is now overshadowed by other economic activities. Casinos, modern hotels, and lavish entertainment attract thousands of visitors each year. Hoover Dam, on the Colorado River, supplies water and power to much of Nevada as well as two adjoining states. But water promises to be a challenge to Nevada's future growth.

⇧ TURNING BACK TIME. The Luxor, recreating a scene from ancient Egypt, is one of the many hotel-casinos that attract thousands of tourists to the four-mile (7-km) section of Las Vegas known as the Strip.

THE BASICS

STATS

Area
110,561 sq mi (286,352 sq km)

Population
2,700,551

Capital
Carson City
Population 55,274

Largest city
Las Vegas
Population 583,756

Ethnic/racial groups
66.2% white; 8.1% African American; 7.2% Asian; 1.2% Native American. Hispanic (any race) 26.5%.

Industry
Tourism and gaming, mining, printing and publishing, food processing, electrical equipment

Agriculture
Cattle, hay, dairy products

Statehood
October 31, 1864; 36th state

GEO WHIZ

Lehman Caves, in Great Basin National Park, contains the best collection of shield, or angel wing, formations in the country.

The Applegate Trail, named for two brothers who first traveled it in 1846, offered a shorter alternative to the Oregon Trail. The trail headed south from Idaho, across Nevada's Black Rock Desert into northern California and then north into Oregon.

So many people claim to have seen extraterrestrials along a 98-mile (158-km) stretch of Nevada Highway 375 that the state transportation board named it Extraterrestrial Highway in 1996.

MOUNTAIN BLUEBIRD
SAGEBRUSH

THIRSTY LAND

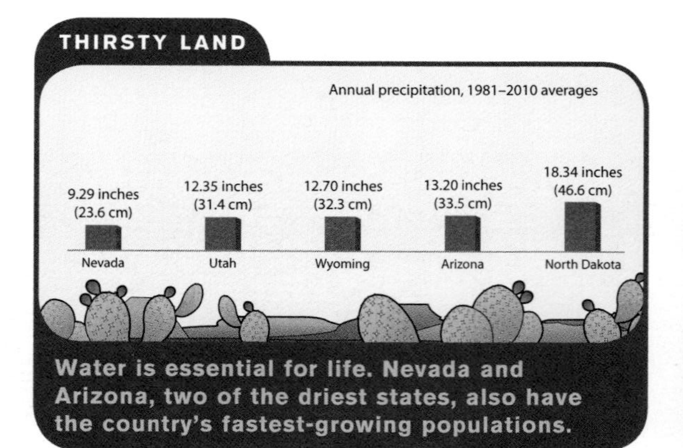

Water is essential for life. Nevada and Arizona, two of the driest states, also have the country's fastest-growing populations.

⇦ PRICKLY GARDEN. Nevada's desert environment includes many varieties of cactuses. Saguaro and aloe plants as well as other xerophytes—plants that tolerate very dry conditions—thrive in this rocky garden.

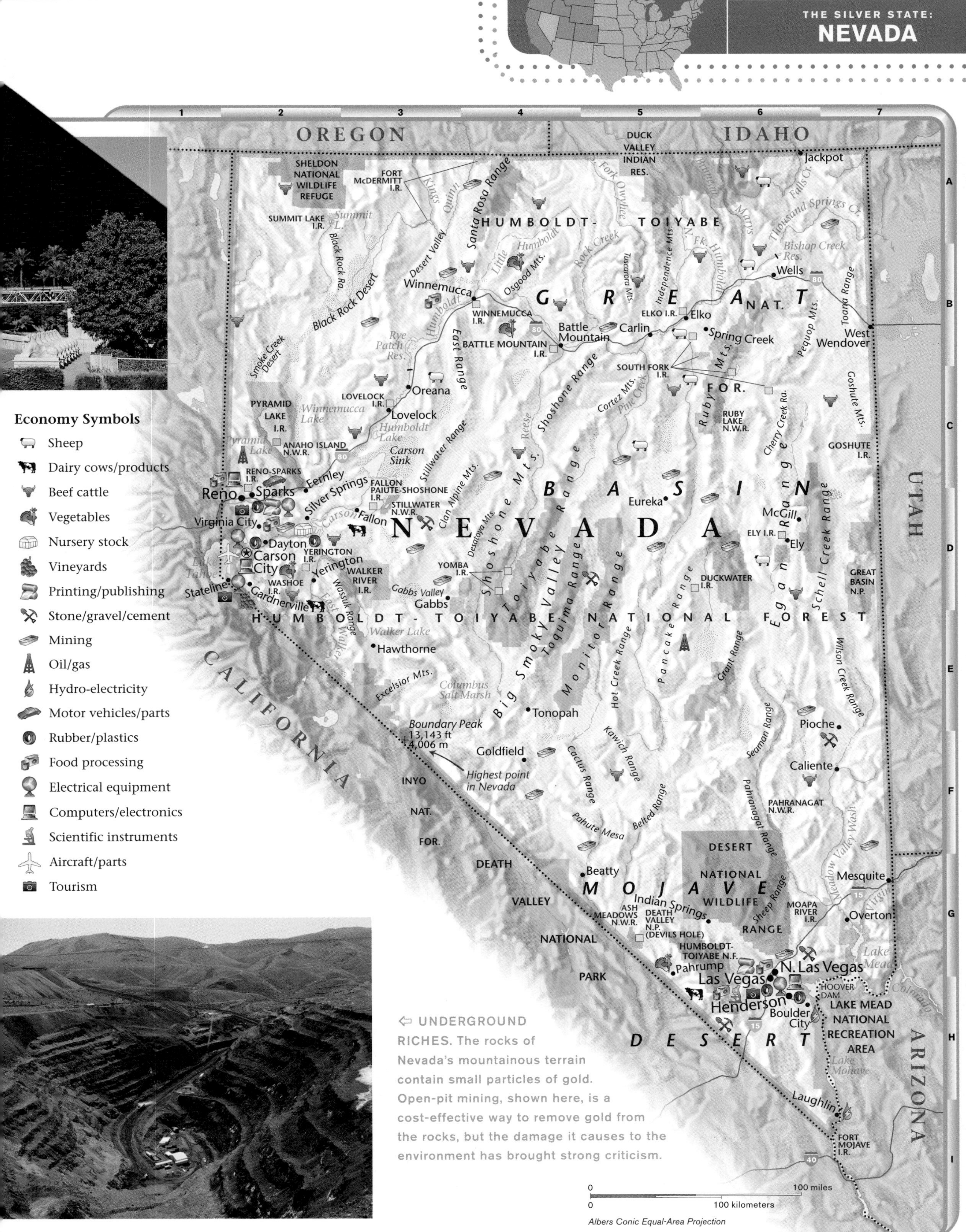

⇦ UNDERGROUND RICHES. The rocks of Nevada's mountainous terrain contain small particles of gold. Open-pit mining, shown here, is a cost-effective way to remove gold from the rocks, but the damage it causes to the environment has brought strong criticism.

THE BEAVER STATE:
OREGON

STATE OF OREGON
1859

OREGON

Long before the Oregon Trail brought settlers from the eastern U.S., Indians fished and hunted in Oregon's coastal waters and forested valleys. Spanish explorers sailed along Oregon's coast in 1543, and in the 18th century fur traders from Europe set up forts in the region. In the mid-1800s settlers began farming the rich soil of the Willamette Valley. Oregon achieved statehood in 1859, and by 1883 Oregon was linked to the East by railroad, and Portland had become an important shipping center. Today, forestry, fishing, and agriculture make up an important part of the state's economy, but Oregon is making an effort to diversify into manufacturing and high-tech industries, as well. Dams on the Columbia River generate inexpensive electricity to support energy-hungry industries, such as aluminum production. Computers, electronics, and research-based industries are expanding. The state's natural beauty—snow-capped volcanoes, old-growth forests, and rocky coastline—makes tourism an important growth industry.

⇧ TOWER OF HISTORY. The 125-foot (38-m) Astoria Column, built in 1926 near the mouth of the Columbia River, is decorated with historic scenes of exploration and settlement along the Pacific Northwest coast.

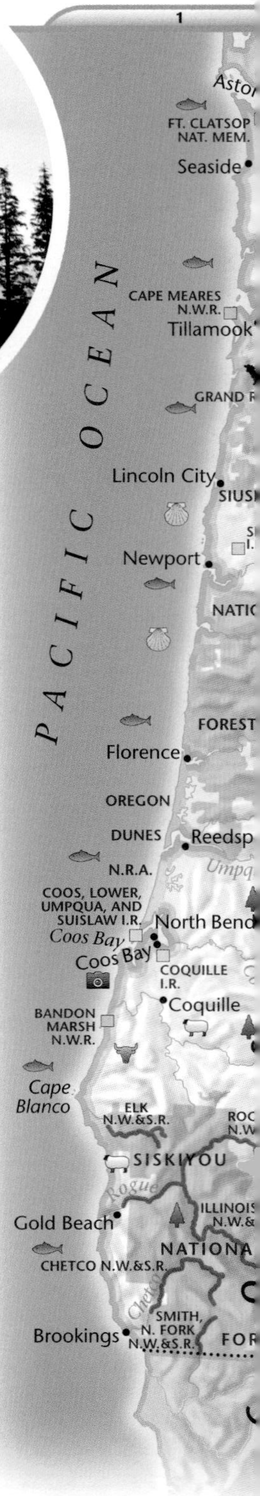

THE BASICS

STATS

Area
98,381 sq mi (254,806 sq km)

Population
3,831,074

Capital
Salem
Population 154,637

Largest city
Portland
Population 583,776

Ethnic/racial groups
83.6% white; 3.7% Asian; 1.8% African American; 1.4% Native American. Hispanic (any race) 11.7%.

Industry
Real estate, retail and wholesale trade, electronic equipment, health services, construction, forest products, business services

Agriculture
Nursery stock, hay, cattle, grass seed, wheat, dairy products, potatoes

Statehood
February 14, 1859; 33rd state

GEO WHIZ

To recover wetlands and save two endangered fish species, 100 tons of explosives were used to blast through levees so that water from the Williamson River could again flow into Upper Klamath Lake.

Crater Lake, at 1,943 feet (592 m), is the deepest in the United States. It fills a depression created when an eruption caused the top of a mountain to collapse. Wizard Island, at the center of the 6-mile-wide lake (10 km), is the top of a volcano.

Snow-covered Mount Hood dominates the Portland skyline. The peak is one of the most active volcanoes in the Cascade Range. Its last eruption occurred just a few years before Lewis and Clark reached the region.

WESTERN MEADOWLARK
OREGON GRAPE

⇦ CHANGING LANDSCAPE. Oregon's Pacific coast is a lesson on erosion and deposition. Rocky outcrops called sea stacks are leftovers of a former coastline that has been eroded by waves. The sandy beach is a result of eroded material being deposited along the shore.

THE BEAVER STATE:
OREGON

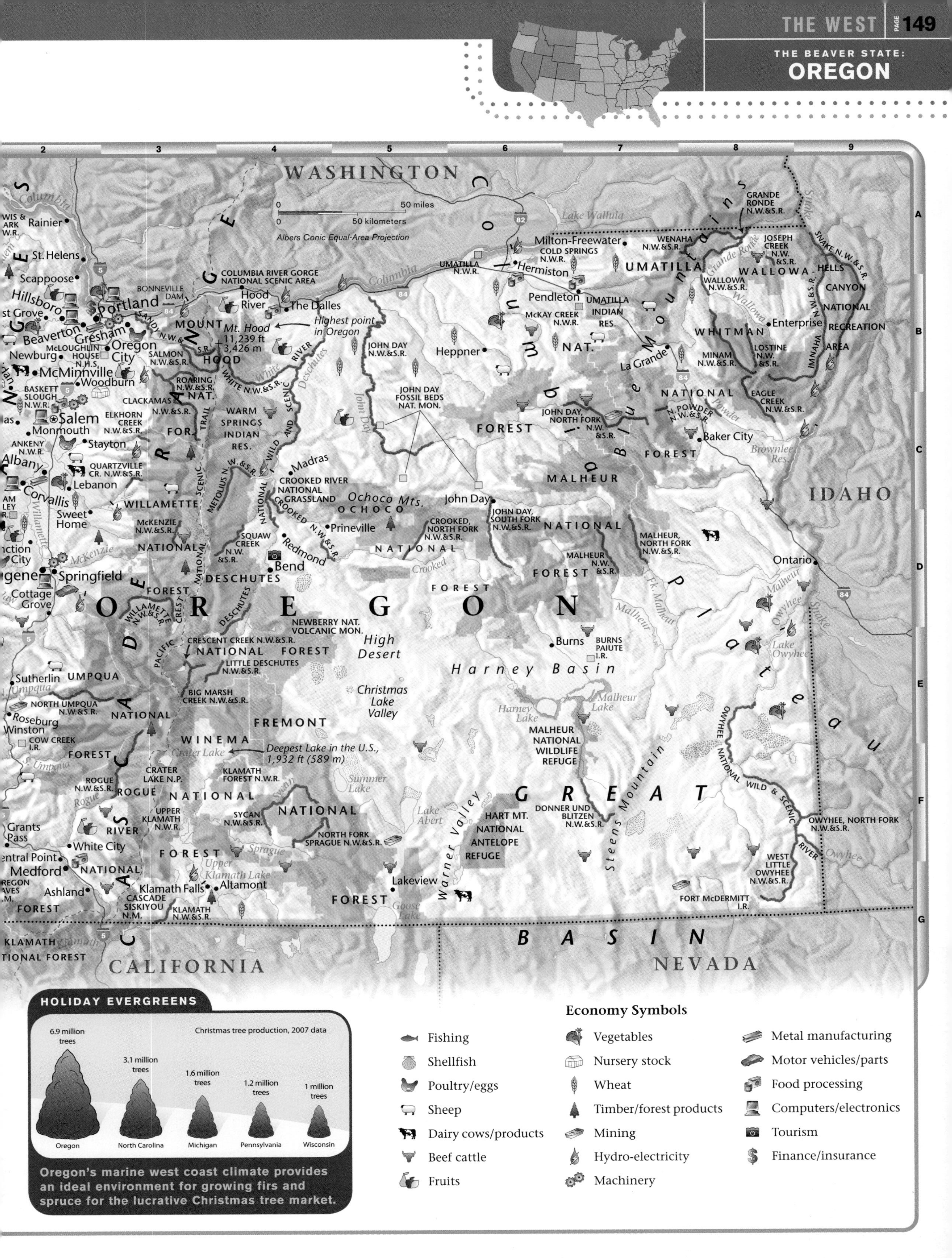

THE BEEHIVE STATE:
UTAH

UTAH

For thousands of years, present-day Utah was populated by Native Americans living in small hunter-gatherer groups, including the Utes for whom the state is named. Spanish explorers passed through Utah in 1776, and in the early 19th century trappers came from the East searching for beavers. In 1847, the arrival of Mormons seeking freedom to practice their religion marked the beginning of widespread settlement of the territory. They established farms and introduced irrigation. Discovery of precious metals in the 1860s brought miners to the territory. Today, almost 70 percent of Utah's land is set aside by the federal government for use by the military and defense industries and as national parks, which attract large numbers of tourists annually. As a result, government is a leading employer in the state. Another important force in Utah is the Church of Latter-day Saints (Mormons), which has influenced culture and politics in the state for more than a century. More than half the state's population is Mormon.

⇧ NATURE'S HANDIWORK. Arches National Park includes more than 2,000 arches carved by forces of water and ice, extreme temperatures, and the shifting of underground salt beds over a period of 100 million years. Delicate Arch stands on the edge of a canyon, with the La Sal Mountains in the distance.

THE BASICS

STATS

Area
84,899 sq mi (219,888 sq km)

Population
2,763,885

Capital
Salt Lake City
Population 186,440

Largest city
Salt Lake City
Population 186,440

Ethnic/racial groups
86.1% white; 2.0% Asian; 1.2% Native American; 1.1% African American. Hispanic (any race) 13.0%.

Industry
Government, manufacturing, real estate, construction, health services, business services, banking

Agriculture
Cattle, dairy products, hay, poultry and eggs, wheat

Statehood
January 4, 1896; 45th state

GEO WHIZ

A giant, duck-billed dinosaur is among the many kinds of dinosaur fossils that have been found in the Grand Staircase–Escalante National Monument. Scientists think the plant eater was at least 30 feet (9 m) long and had a mouthful of 300 teeth.

Drought has caused the level of Lake Powell to drop by more than 100 feet (30 meters), revealing much of the spectacular scenery of Glen Canyon that was drowned in 1963 when a dam created the lake.

Great Salt Lake is the largest natural lake west of the Mississippi River. The lake, which has a high level of evaporation, is about eight times saltier than the ocean.

CALIFORNIA GULL
SEGO LILY

SPREADING THE FAITH

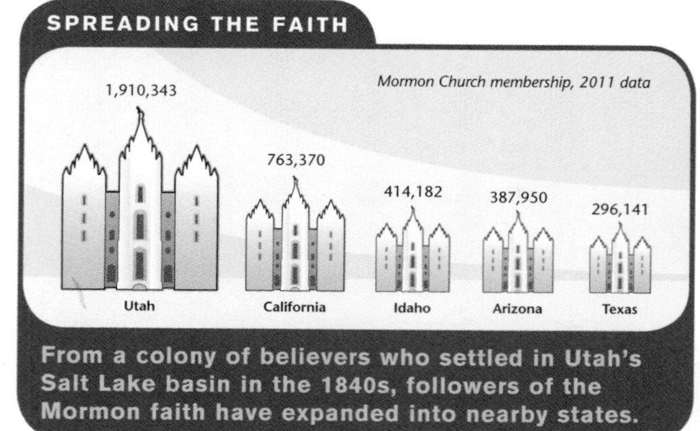

From a colony of believers who settled in Utah's Salt Lake basin in the 1840s, followers of the Mormon faith have expanded into nearby states.

⇦ MONUMENT TO FAITH. Completed in 1893, the Salt Lake Temple is where Mormons gather to worship and participate in religious ceremonies. Church members regard temples as the most sacred places on Earth.

THE BEEHIVE STATE:
UTAH

THE EVERGREEN STATE:
WASHINGTON

WASHINGTON

THE BASICS

STATS

Area
71,300 sq mi (184,666 sq km)

Population
6,724,540

Capital
Olympia
Population 46,478

Largest city
Seattle
Population 608,660

Ethnic/racial groups
77.3% white; 7.2% Asian; 3.6% African American; 1.5% Native American. Hispanic (any race) 11.2%.

Industry
Aerospace, tourism, food processing, forest products, paper products, industrial machinery, printing and publishing, metals, computer software

Agriculture
Seafood, apples, dairy products, wheat, cattle, potatoes, hay

Statehood
November 11, 1889; 42nd state

GEO WHIZ

The forests of the Olympic Peninsula are among the world's rainiest places. The Hoh Rain Forest is one of the planet's few temperate rain forests.

Mount St. Helens, the most active volcano in the lower 48 states, is close to both Seattle and Portland, Oregon. The eruption in May 1980 reduced its elevation by 1,314 feet (401 m), triggering the largest landslide in recorded history.

Orcas, also known as killer whales, are the world's largest dolphins. The 90 or so that call the waters of Puget Sound home have been placed on the government's Endangered Species List.

AMERICAN GOLDFINCH
COAST RHODODENDRON

Long before Europeans explored the coast of the Pacific Northwest, Native Americans inhabited the area, living mainly off abundant seafood found in coastal waters and rivers. In the late 18th century, first Spanish sailors and then British explorers, including Captain James Cook, visited the region. Under treaties with Spain (1819) and Britain (1846), the U.S. gained control of the land, and in 1853 the Washington Territory was formally separated from the Oregon Territory. Settlers soon based their livelihood on fishing, farming, and lumbering. Washington became the 42nd state in 1889. The 20th century was a time of growth and development in Washington. Seattle became a major Pacific seaport. The Grand Coulee Dam, completed in 1941, provided the region with inexpensive electricity. Today, manufacturing, led by Boeing and Microsoft, is a mainstay of the economy. Washington leads the country in production of apples and sweet cherries, and the state is home to the headquarters of the popular Starbucks chain of coffee shops.

⇩ HARVEST TIME. Once a semiarid grassland, the Palouse region north of the Snake River in eastern Washington is now a major wheat-producing area.

⇧ PACIFIC GATEWAY. The city of Seattle, easily recognizable by its distinctive Space Needle tower, is a major West Coast port and home to the North Pacific fishing fleet.

THE EVERGREEN STATE: WASHINGTON

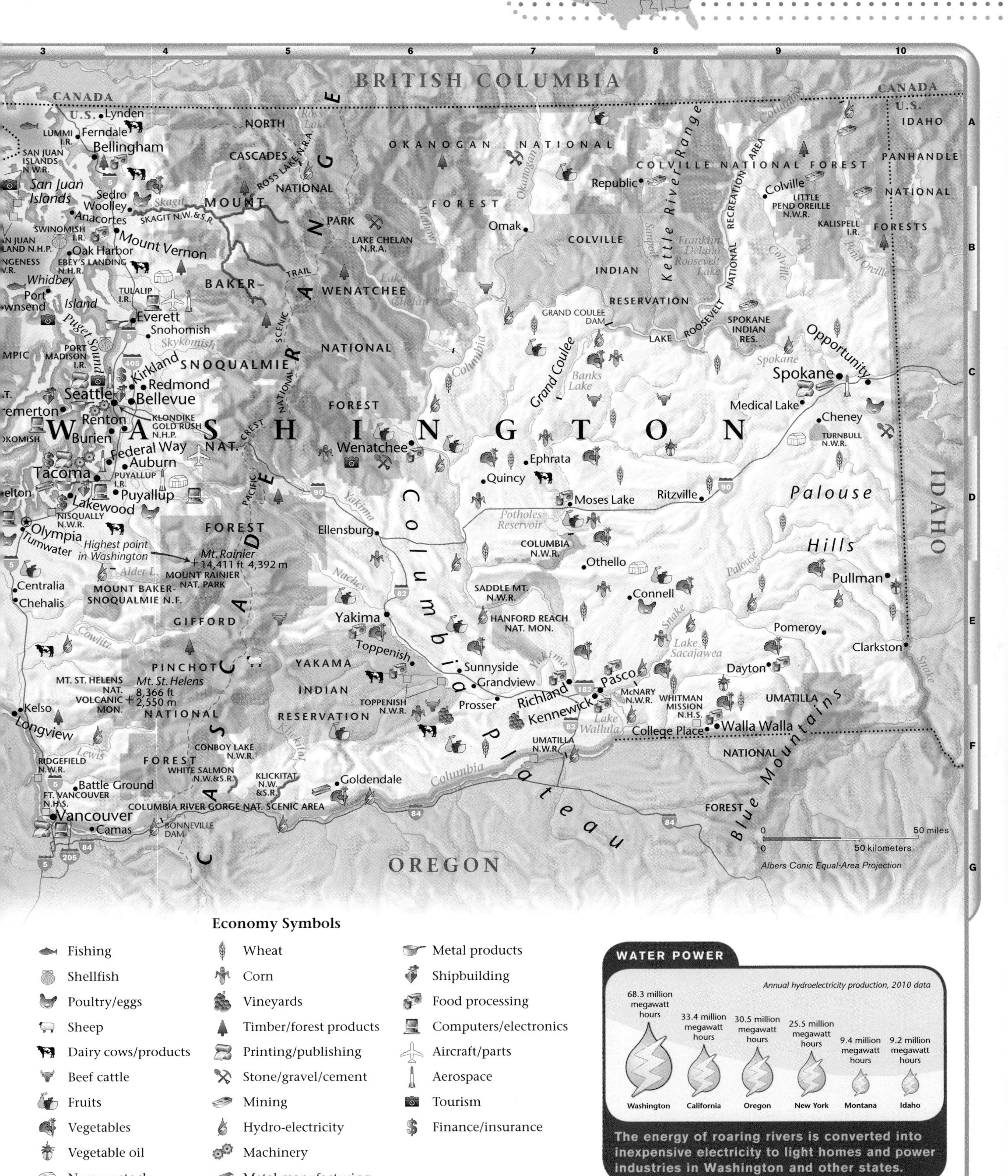

THE EQUALITY STATE:
WYOMING

WYOMING

THE BASICS

STATS

Area
97,814 sq mi (253,337 sq km)

Population
563,626

Capital
Cheyenne
Population 59,466

Largest city
Cheyenne
Population 59,466

Ethnic/racial groups
90.7% white; 2.4% Native American; .8% African American; .8% Asian. Hispanic (any race) 8.9%.

Industry
Oil and natural gas, mining, generation of electricity, chemicals, tourism

Agriculture
Cattle, sugar beets, sheep, hay, wheat

Statehood
July 10, 1890; 44th state

GEO WHIZ

The successful reintroduction of wolves into Yellowstone National Park, a program that began in the mid-1990s, has become a model for saving endangered carnivores around the world. In 2010 there were almost 350 wolves in 45 packs living in the Northern Rockies of Wyoming.

The National Elk Refuge, in Jackson Hole, provides a winter home for some 5,000 elk. The herd's migration from the refuge to their summer home in Yellowstone National Park is the longest elk herd migration in the lower 48 states.

Devils Tower, a huge formation of igneous rock near Sundance, was the country's first national monument. It was featured in the science-fiction classic *Close Encounters of the Third Kind.*

WESTERN MEADOWLARK
INDIAN PAINTBRUSH

When Europeans arrived in the 18th century in what would become Wyoming, various native groups were already there, living as nomads following herds of deer and bison across the plains. In the early 19th century fur traders moved into Wyoming, and settlers followed later along the Oregon Trail. Laramie and many of the state's other towns developed around old army forts built to protect wagon trains traveling through Wyoming. Today, fewer than 600,000 people live in all of Wyoming. The state's economy is based on agriculture—mainly grain and livestock production—and mining, especially energy resources. The state has some of the world's largest surface coal mines. In addition, it produces petroleum, natural gas, industrial metals, and precious gems. The natural environment is also a major resource. People come to Wyoming for fishing and hunting, for rodeos, and for the state's majestic mountains and parks. Yellowstone, established in 1872, was the world's first national park.

⇧ WANT TO RACE? Unique to the High Plains of the West, the pronghorn can sprint up to 60 miles per hour (97 kmph).

⇩ DRAMATIC LANDSCAPE. Rising more than 13,000 feet (3,900 m), the jagged peaks of the Tetons, one of the youngest mountain ranges of the West, tower over a barn on the valley floor.

HOME ON THE RANGE

More than half of Wyoming's land is in agriculture, mainly pasture. Cattle account for more than 60 percent of the state's agriculture income.

THE EQUALITY STATE: WYOMING

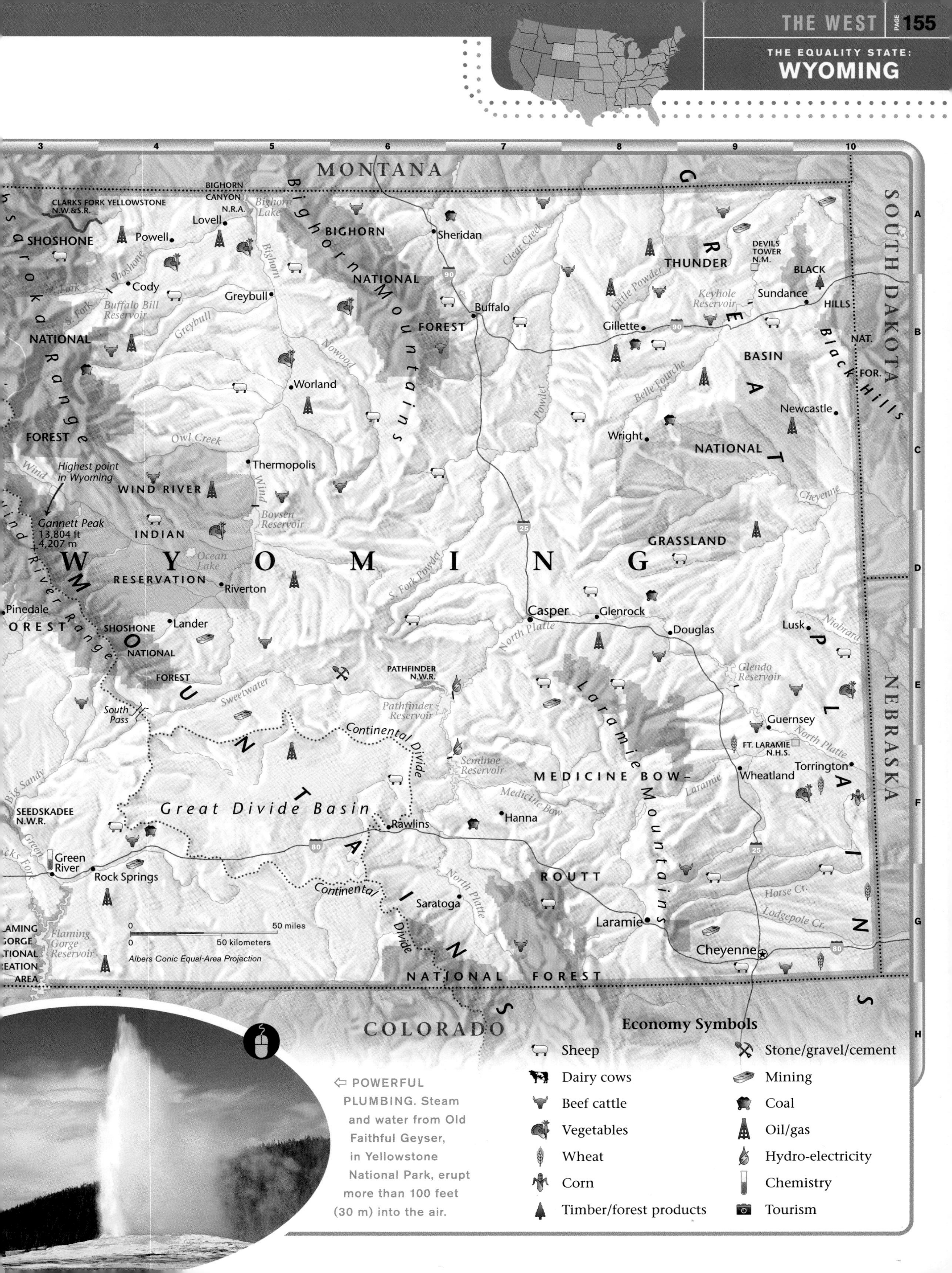

⇦ POWERFUL PLUMBING. Steam and water from Old Faithful Geyser, in Yellowstone National Park, erupt more than 100 feet (30 m) into the air.

The Territories

ACROSS TWO SEAS

Listed below are the 5 largest of the 14 U.S. territories, along with their flags and key information. Two of these are in the Caribbean Sea, and the other three are in the Pacific Ocean. Can you find the other 9 U.S. territories on the map?

U.S. CARIBBEAN TERRITORIES

PUERTO RICO

Area: 3,508 sq mi (9,086 sq km)
Population: 3,989,133
Capital: San Juan
Population 2,730,000
Languages: Spanish, English

U.S. VIRGIN ISLANDS

Area: 149 sq mi (386 sq km)
Population: 109,666
Capital: Charlotte Amalie
Population 54,000
Languages: English, Spanish or Spanish Creole, French or French Creole

U.S. PACIFIC TERRITORIES

AMERICAN SAMOA

Area: 77 sq mi (199 sq km)
Population: 67,242
Capital: Pago Pago
Population 60,000
Language: Samoan

GUAM

Area: 217 sq mi (561 sq km)
Population: 183,286
Capital: Hagåtña (Agana)
Population 153,000
Languages: English, Chamorro, Philippine languages

NORTHERN MARIANA ISLANDS

Area: 184 sq mi (477 sq km)
Population: 46,050
Capital: Saipan (Capitol Hill)
Population 1,500
Languages: Philippine languages, Chinese, Chamorro, English

OTHER U.S. TERRITORIES

Baker Island, Howland Island, Jarvis Island, Johnston Atoll, Kingman Reef, Midway Islands, Navassa Island, Palmyra Atoll, Wake Island

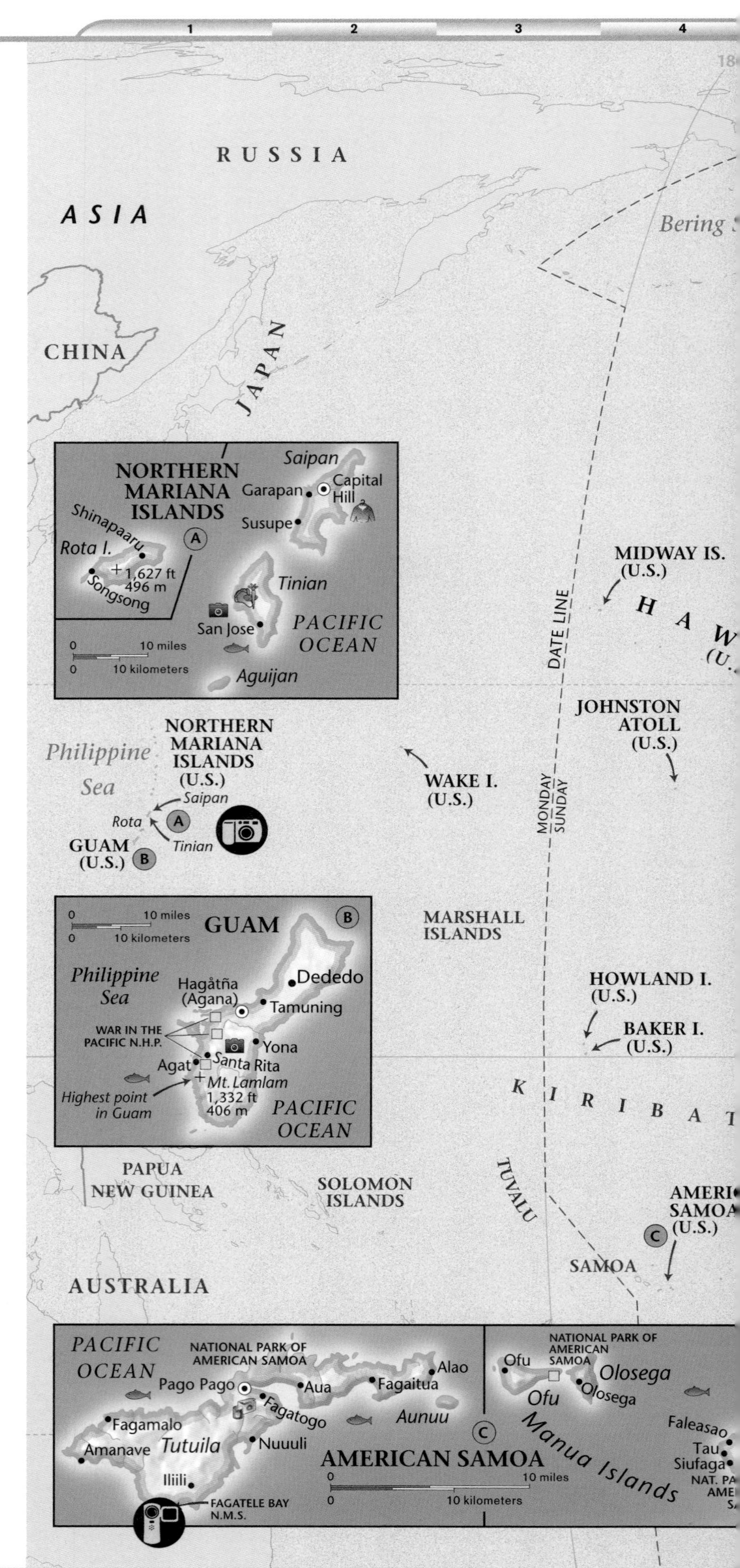

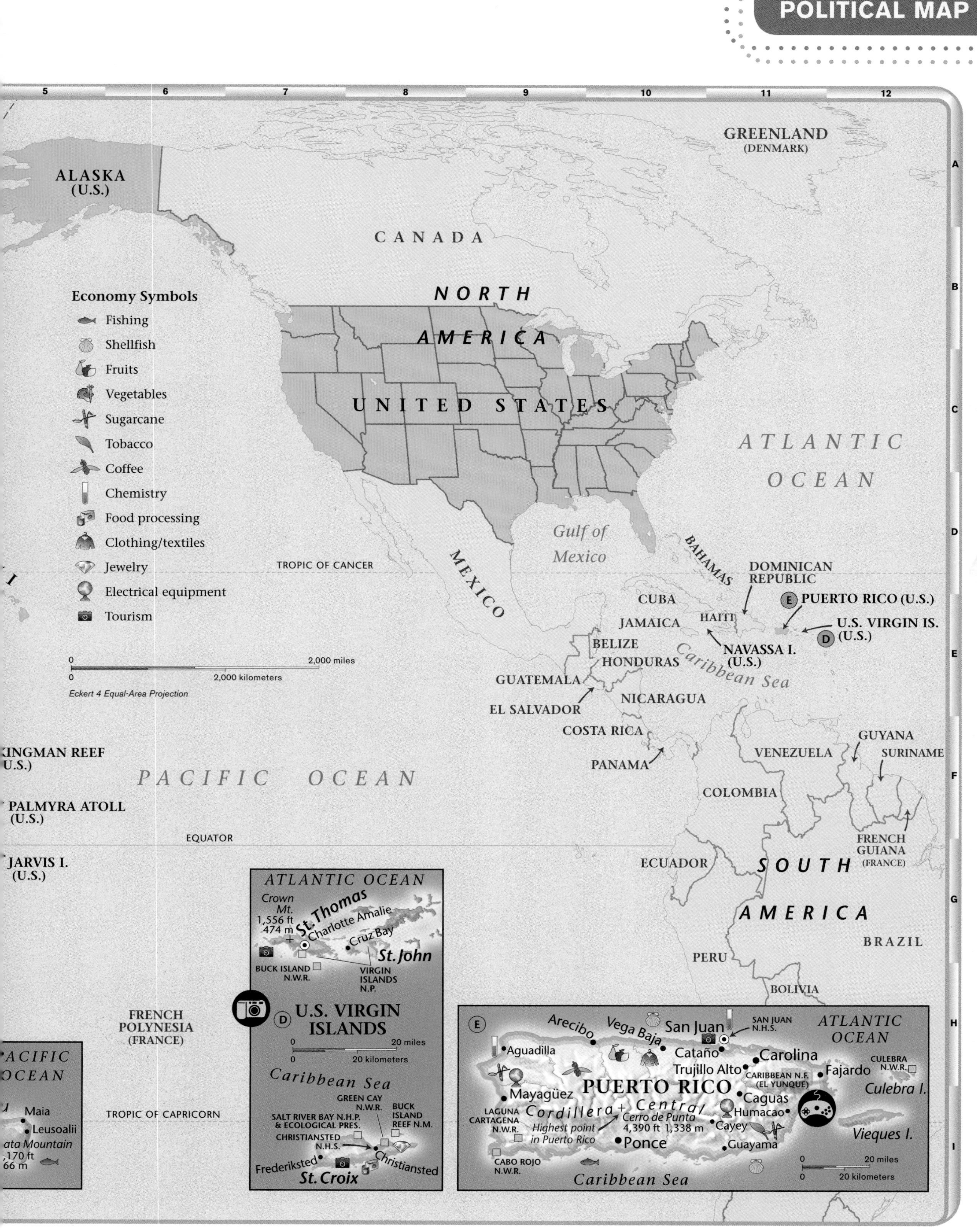

5
6
7
8
9
10
11
12
A
B
C
D
E
F
G
H
I
GREENLAND
(DENMARK)
ALASKA
(U.S.)
CANADA
NORTH
AMERICA
UNITED STATES
ATLANTIC
OCEAN
Economy Symbols
Fishing
Shellfish
Fruits
Vegetables
Sugarcane
Tobacco
Coffee
Chemistry
Food processing
Clothing/textiles
Jewelry
Electrical equipment
Tourism
TROPIC OF CANCER
Gulf of
Mexico
MEXICO
BAHAMAS
DOMINICAN
REPUBLIC
PUERTO RICO (U.S.)
U.S. VIRGIN IS.
(U.S.)
CUBA
JAMAICA
HAITI
NAVASSA I.
(U.S.)
BELIZE
HONDURAS
Caribbean Sea
GUATEMALA
EL SALVADOR
NICARAGUA
COSTA RICA
PANAMA
0
2,000 miles
0
2,000 kilometers
Eckert 4 Equal-Area Projection
KINGMAN REEF
(U.S.)
PACIFIC OCEAN
PALMYRA ATOLL
(U.S.)
EQUATOR
JARVIS I.
(U.S.)
GUYANA
VENEZUELA
SURINAME
COLOMBIA
FRENCH
GUIANA
(FRANCE)
ECUADOR
SOUTH
AMERICA
BRAZIL
PERU
BOLIVIA
FRENCH
POLYNESIA
(FRANCE)
TROPIC OF CAPRICORN
PACIFIC
OCEAN
Maia
Leusoalii
Mountain
170 ft
66 m
ATLANTIC OCEAN
Crown
Mt.
1,556 ft
474 m
St. Thomas
Charlotte Amalie
Cruz Bay
St. John
BUCK ISLAND
N.W.R.
VIRGIN
ISLANDS
N.P.
U.S. VIRGIN
ISLANDS
0
20 miles
0
20 kilometers
Caribbean Sea
GREEN CAY
N.W.R.
BUCK
ISLAND
REEF N.M.
SALT RIVER BAY N.H.P.
& ECOLOGICAL PRES.
CHRISTIANSTED
N.H.S.
Frederiksted
Christiansted
St. Croix
Arecibo
Vega Baja
San Juan
SAN JUAN
N.H.S.
ATLANTIC
OCEAN
Aguadilla
Cataño
Carolina
CULEBRA
N.W.R.
Trujillo Alto
CARIBBEAN N.F.
(EL YUNQUE)
Fajardo
Culebra I.
Mayagüez
PUERTO RICO
Caguas
LAGUNA
CARTAGENA
N.W.R.
Cordillera Central
Cerro de Punta
4,390 ft 1,338 m
Highest point
in Puerto Rico
Humacao
Cayey
Vieques I.
Ponce
Guayama
CABO ROJO
N.W.R.
Caribbean Sea
0
20 miles
0
20 kilometers

⇨ PRESERVING TRADITION. Young dancers from American Samoa, dressed in costumes of feathers and pandanus leaves, prepare to perform in the Pacific Arts Festival, which is held once every four years to promote Pacific cultures.

The Territories

ISLANDS IN THE FAMILY

Fourteen territories and commonwealths scattered across the Pacific and Caribbean came under U.S. influence after wars or various international agreements. Because they are neither states nor independent countries, the U.S. government provides economic and military aid. Puerto Rico's nearly four million residents give it a population greater than that of 24 U.S. states. Many tourists seeking sunny beaches visit the Virgin Islands, purchased from Denmark for $25 million in 1917. American Samoa, Guam, and the Northern Mariana Islands in the Pacific have sizable populations, but several tiny atolls have no civilian residents and are administered by the U.S. military or government departments. In most cases, citizens of these territories are also eligible for American citizenship.

⇧ RELIC OF THE PAST. Sugar mill ruins on St. John, in the U.S. Virgin Islands, recall a way of life that dominated the Caribbean in the 18th and 19th centuries. Plantations used slave labor to grow cane and make it into sugar and molasses.

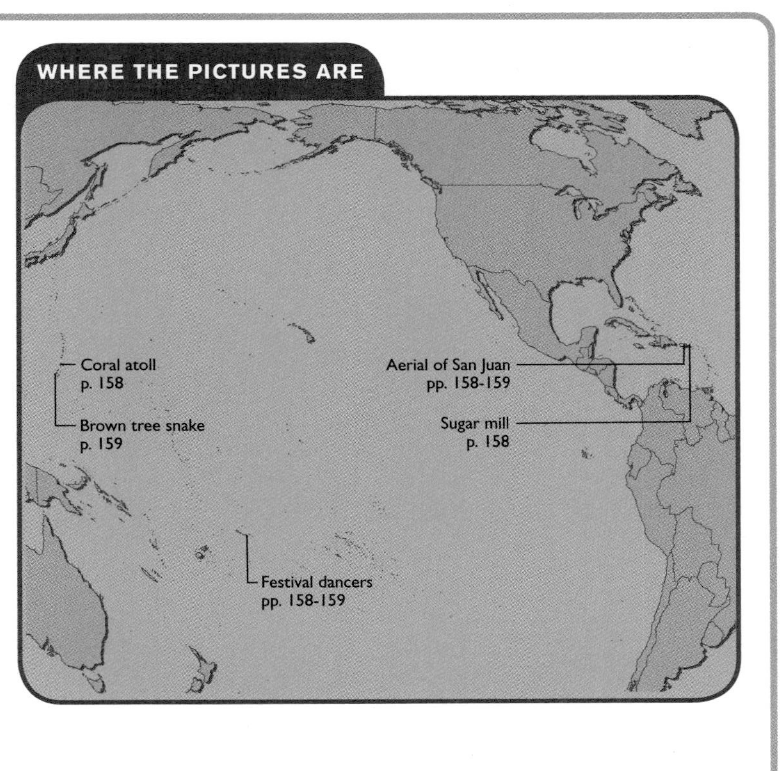

⇦ PACIFIC JEWEL. Managaha Island sits in the blue-green waters of a lagoon formed by a long reef along Saipan's western coast. Marine biologists fear that portions of the reef are dying due to pollution. The lagoon holds wrecks from battles fought in Northern Mariana waters during World War II.

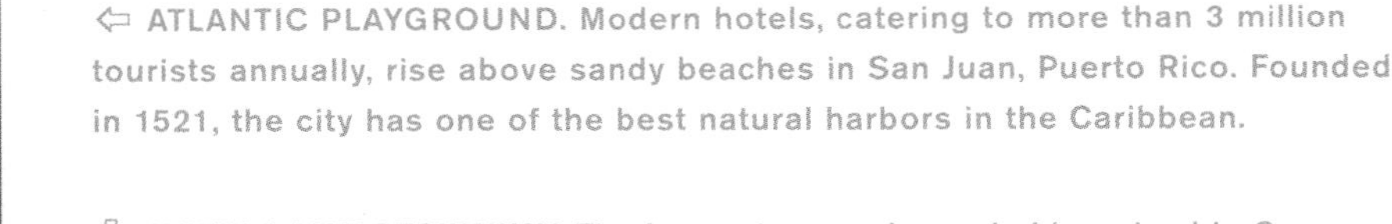

⇦ ATLANTIC PLAYGROUND. Modern hotels, catering to more than 3 million tourists annually, rise above sandy beaches in San Juan, Puerto Rico. Founded in 1521, the city has one of the best natural harbors in the Caribbean.

⇩ UNWELCOME STOWAWAY. The brown tree snake probably arrived in Guam on cargo ships in the 1950s. The snake has greatly reduced the island's bird and small mammal populations and causes power outages when it climbs electric poles.

U.S. FACTS & FIGURES

THE COUNTRY

STATS

Founding
1776

Area
3,794,083 sq mi (9,826,675 sq km)

Population (December 2011)
312,782,167

Capital
Washington, D.C.

Population
601,723

Largest city
New York

Population
8,782,166

Ethnic/racial groups
72.4% white; 12.6% African American; 4.8% Asian; .9% Native American. Hispanic (any race) 16.3%.

Languages (most widely spoken)
English, Spanish

Economy
Services: 76.7% of GDP
Industry: 22.2% of GDP
Agriculture: 1.2% of GDP

BALD EAGLE, NATIONAL SYMBOL

Top States

Listed below are major farm products, fish, and minerals and the states that currently lead in their production. Following each list is a ranking of the top states in each category.

Farm Products

Cattle and calves: Texas, Kansas, Nebraska, Iowa
Dairy products: California, Wisconsin, New York, Pennsylvania
Soybeans: Iowa, Illinois, Minnesota, Nebraska
Corn for grain: Iowa, Illinois, Nebraska, Minnesota
Hogs and pigs: Iowa, North Carolina, Minnesota, Illinois
Broiler chickens: Georgia, Arkansas, Alabama, North Carolina
Wheat: North Dakota, Kansas, Montana, Washington
Cotton: Texas, Georgia, North Carolina, Arkansas
Eggs: Iowa, Ohio, Pennsylvania, Indiana
Hay: Texas, California, Missouri, South Dakota
Tobacco: North Carolina, Kentucky, Tennessee, Virginia
Turkeys: Minnesota, North Carolina, Missouri, Indiana
Oranges: Florida, California, Texas, Arizona
Potatoes: Idaho, Washington, Wisconsin, Colorado
Grapes: California, Washington, New York
Tomatoes (processed): Florida, Georgia, California
Rice: Arkansas, California, Louisiana, Mississippi

Top Ten in Farm Products (by net farm income)

1. California
2. Iowa
3. Illinois
4. Nebraska
5. Minnesota
6. North Carolina
7. Indiana
8. South Dakota
9. Kansas
10. Georgia

Fish

Shrimp: Louisiana, Texas, Florida, Alabama
Crabs: Alaska, Louisiana, Oregon, Maryland, California
Lobsters: Maine, Massachusetts, Florida, Rhode Island
Salmon: Alaska, Washington, Oregon, California
Pollock: Alaska, Massachusetts, Maine, New Hampshire

Top Five in Fisheries (by value of catch)

1. Alaska
2. Massachusetts
3. Maine
4. Louisiana
5. Washington

Minerals

Crude oil: Texas, Alaska, California, North Dakota, New Mexico
Natural gas: Texas, Wyoming, Oklahoma, Louisiana, Colorado
Coal: Wyoming, West Virginia, Kentucky, Pennsylvania, Montana
Crushed stone: Texas, Pennsylvania, Missouri, Illinois, Florida
Copper: Arizona, Utah, Nevada, New Mexico, Montana
Cement: Texas, California, Missouri, Pennsylvania, Alabama
Construction sand and gravel: Texas, California, Arizona, Colorado, Wisconsin
Gold: Nevada, Alaska, Utah, Colorado, California
Iron ore: Michigan, Minnesota
Clay: Georgia, Wyoming, Alabama, Texas, North Carolina
Phosphate rock: Florida, North Carolina, Idaho, Utah
Lime: Alabama, Kentucky, Missouri, Nevada, Ohio
Salt: Louisiana, Texas, New York, Kansas, Utah
Sulfur: Louisiana, Texas

Top Ten in Minerals

1. Nevada
2. Arizona
3. Florida
4. Utah
5. California
6. Texas
7. Alaska
8. Minnesota
9. Missouri
10. Wyoming

Extremes

World's Strongest Surface Wind
231 mph (372 kmph), Mount Washington, New Hampshire, April 12, 1934

World's Tallest Living Tree
"Hyperion," a coast redwood in Redwood National Park, California, 379.1 ft (115.55 m) high

World's Oldest Living Tree
Methuselah bristlecone pine, California; 4,789 years old

World's Largest Gorge
Grand Canyon, Arizona; 290 mi (466 km) long, 600 ft to 18 mi (183 m to 29 km) wide, 1 mile (1.6 km) deep

Highest Temperature in U.S.
134°F (56.6°C), Death Valley, California, July 10, 1913

Lowest Temperature in U.S.
Minus 80°F (-62.2°C) at Prospect Creek, Alaska, January 23, 1971

Highest Point in U.S.
Mount McKinley (Denali), Alaska; 20,320 ft (6,194 m)

Lowest Point in U.S.
Death Valley, California; 282 feet (86 m) below sea level

Longest River System in U.S.
Mississippi-Missouri; 3,710 mi (5,971 km) long

Rainiest Spot in U.S.
Wai'ale'ale (mountain), Hawai'i: average annual rainfall 460 in (1,168 cm)

Metropolitan Areas With More Than Five Million People
A metropolitan area is a city and its surrounding suburban areas. (2010 data)

1. New York, pop. 18,897,109
2. Los Angeles, pop. 12,828,837
3. Chicago, pop. 9,461,105
4. Dallas–Fort Worth, pop. 6,371,773
5. Philadelphia, pop. 5,965,343
6. Houston, pop. 5,946,800
7. Washington, D.C., pop. 5,582,170
8. Miami, pop. 5,564,635
9. Atlanta, pop. 5,268,860

GLOSSARY

aquaculture raising fish or shellfish in controlled ponds or waterways for commercial use
atoll a circular coral reef enclosing a tropical lagoon
arid climate type of dry climate in which annual precipitation is often less than 10 inches (25 cm)
biomass total weight of all organisms found in a given area
bituminous coal a soft form of coal used in industries and power plants
bog a poorly drained area with wet, spongy ground
broadleaf forest trees with wide leaves that are shed during the winter season
butte a high, steep-sided rock formation created by the erosion of a mesa
canal an artificial waterway that is used by ships or to carry water for irrigation
center-pivot irrigation an irrigation system that rotates around a piped water source at its middle, often resulting in circular field patterns
continental climate temperature extremes with long cold winters and heavy snowfall
continental divide an elevated area that separates rivers flowing toward opposite sides of a continent; in the U.S. this divide follows the crest of the Rocky Mountains
copra dried coconut meat from which oil is extracted to make a variety of products, including soap, candles, and cosmetics
Creole a simplified or modified form of a language, such as French or Spanish, used for communication between two groups; spoken in some Caribbean islands
delta lowland formed by silt, sand, and gravel deposited by a river at its mouth
desert vegetation plants such as cactus and dry shrubs that have adapted to conditions of low, often irregular precipitation
fork in a river, the place where two streams join
Fortune 500 company ranking of the top 500 U.S. companies based on total revenue
fossil remains of or an impression left by the remains of plants or animals preserved in rock
geothermal energy a clean, renewable form of energy derived from heat that flows continuously from Earth's interior
grassland areas with medium to short grasses; found where precipitation is not sufficient to support tree growth
gross domestic product (GDP) the total value of goods and services produced in a country in a year
highland climate found in association with high mountains where elevation affects temperature and precipitation
hundredweight in the U.S., a commercial unit of measure equal to 100 pounds
ice age a very long period of cold climate when glaciers often cover large areas of land
intermittent river/lake a stream or lake that contains water only part of the time, usually after heavy rain or snowmelt
lava molten rock from Earth's interior that flows out on the surface during volcanic activity
levee an embankment, usually earth or concrete, built to prevent a river from overflowing
lignite low-grade coal used mainly to produce heat in thermal-electric generators
marine west coast climate type of mild climate found on the mid-latitude West Coast of the U.S.
Mediterranean climate type of mild climate found on the West Coast of the U.S., south of the marine west coast climate
mesa an eroded plateau, broader than it is high, that is found in arid or semiarid regions
metropolitan area a city and its surrounding suburbs or communities
mild climate moderate temperatures with distinct seasons and ample precipitation
nursery stock young plants, including fruits, vegetables, shrubs, and trees, raised in a greenhouse or nursery
pinnacle a tall pillar of rock standing alone or on a summit
plain a large area of relatively flat land that is often covered with grasses
plateau a relatively flat area, larger than a mesa, that rises above the surrounding landscape
population density the average number of people living on each square mile or square kilometer of a specific land area
precipitate process of depositing dissolved minerals as water evaporates, as in limestone caves
rangeland areas of grass prairie that are used for grazing livestock
reactor a device that uses controlled nuclear fission to divide an atomic nucleus to generate power
Richter scale ranking of the power of an earthquake; the higher the number, the stronger the quake
Rust Belt a region made up of northeastern and midwestern states that have experienced a decline in heavy industry and an out-migration of population
scale on a map, a means of explaining the relationship between distances on the map and actual distances on Earth's surface
stalactite column of limestone hanging from the ceiling of a cave that forms as underground water drips down and evaporates, leaving dissolved minerals behind
stalagmite column of limestone that forms on the floor of a cave when underground water drips down and evaporates, leaving dissolved minerals behind
staple main item in an economy; also, main food for domestic consumption
Sunbelt a region made up of southern and western states that are experiencing major in-migration of population and rapid economic growth
territory land that is under the jurisdiction of a country but that is not a state or a province
tropical zone the area bounded by the Tropic of Cancer and the Tropic of Capricorn, where it is usually warm year-round
tundra vegetation plants, often stunted in size, that have adapted to periods of extreme cold and a short growing season; found in polar regions and high elevations
urban areas in which natural vegetation has been replaced by towns or cities, where the main economic activity is nonagricultural
volcanic pipe a vertical opening beneath a volcano through which molten rock has passed
wetland land that is either covered with or saturated by water; includes swamps, marshes, and bogs

OUTSIDE WEB SITES

The following Web sites will provide you with additional valuable information about various topics discussed in this atlas. You can find direct links to each by going to the atlas URL (www.nationalgeographic.com/kids-usa-atlas) and clicking on "Resources."

General information:
States: www.state.al.us (This is for Alabama; for each state insert the two-letter state abbreviation where "al" is now.)

D.C. and the Territories:
Washington, D.C.: kids.dc.gov/kids_main_content.html
American Samoa: www.samoanet.com
Guam: ns.gov.gu
Northern Marianas: www.saipan.com/gov
Puerto Rico: www.prstar.net
U.S. Virgin Islands: www.gov.vi

Natural Environment:
Biomes: www.blueplanetbiomes.org
Climate: www.eoearth.org
Global Warming: www.nrdc.org/globalWarming

Climate:
www.noaa.gov/climate.html
www.worldclimate.com (for cities)
www.cpc.noaa.gov

Natural Hazards:
General: www.usgs.gov/hazards
Droughts: www.drought.unl.edu/DM/monitor.html
Earthquakes: earthquake.usgs.gov
Hurricanes: hurricanes.noaa.gov
Tornadoes: www.tornadoproject.com
Tsunamis: www.noaa.gov/tsunamis.html
Volcanoes: www.geo.mtu.edu/volcanoes
Wildfires: www.nifc.gov/ and www.fs.fed.us/fire

Population:
States: quickfacts.census.gov/qfd
Cities: www.city-data.com
Population migration: www.census.gov/prod/2001pubs/p23-204.pdf
Hispanic population: www.census.gov/prod/2003pubs/p20-545.pdf

Getting Green:
www.epa.gov/
www.earthday.org
www.footprintnetwork.org/index.php

Bird sounds:
www.animalbehaviorarchive.org/loginPublic.do

Mapping site:
earth.google.com

PLACE-NAME INDEX

Map references are in boldface (**50**) type. Letters and numbers following in lightface (D12) locate the place-names using the map grid. (Refer to page 7 for more details.)

A
Abbeville, AL **61** G6
Abbeville, LA **71** G4
Abbeville, SC **76** C2
Aberdeen, MD **39** A8
Aberdeen, MS **73** C5
Aberdeen, SD **111** B8
Aberdeen, WA **152** D2
Abert, Lake, OR **149** F5
Abilene, KS **97** C7
Abilene, TX **127** D5
Abingdon, VA **80** E3
Abraham Lincoln Birthplace National Historic Site, KY **69** D6
Absaroka Range, MT, WY **155** A3
Absecon, NJ **45** H3
Acadia N.P., ME **37** G6
Ada, OK **125** D9
Adak Island, AK **135** H8
Adams, MA **40** A1
Adamsville, RI **51** E7
Adel, GA **67** H4
Adirondack Mountains, NY **47** B7
Adirondack Park, NY **47** C7
Admiralty Island Nat. Mon., AK **135** F10
Adrian, MI **99** I7
Afognak Island, AK **135** F6
Afton, WY **154** E1
Agana *see* Hagåtña, GU **156** F1
Agat, GU **156** G1
Agate Fossil Beds Nat. Mon., NE **104** B1
Agattu Island, AK **135** H6
Agawam, MA **41** D3
Agua Fria (river), AZ **121** E4
Agua Fria Nat. Mon., AZ **121** E4
Aguadilla, PR **157** H9
Aguijan (island), MP **156** D1
Ahoskie, NC **75** B9
Aiken, SC **77** E4
Ainsworth, NE **105** B5
Aitkin, MN **101** D4
Ajo, AZ **121** G3
Akron, CO **139** B8
Akron, OH **109** B6
Alabama (river), AL **61** F3
Alabaster, AL **61** D3
Alagnak N.W.&S.R., AK **135** F5
Alamogordo, NM **123** G5
Alamosa, CO **139** F4
Alamosa (river), CO **139** F4
Alao, AS **156** H2
Alapaha (river), GA **67** H4
Alaska Highway, AK **135** E8
Alaska Peninsula, AK **134** G3
Alaska Range, AK **135** E6
Alaska, Gulf of, AK **135** G7
Alatna N.W.&S.R., AK **135** B6
Albany, GA **67** G3
Albany, KY **69** E7
Albany, NY **47** E8
Albany, OR **149** C2
Albemarle, NC **75** C5
Albemarle Sound, NC **75** B10
Albert Lea, MN **101** H4
Albertville, AL **61** B4
Albion, MI **99** H6
Albion, NE **105** C7
Albuquerque, NM **123** D4
Alburg, VT **53** A1
Alcoa, TN **79** C8
Alder Lake, WA **153** E4
'Alenuihaha Channel, HI **141** D7
Aleutian Islands, AK **135** G6
Aleutian World War II National Historic Area, AK **134** H2
Alexander Archipelago, AK **135** F9
Alexander City, AL **61** D5
Alexandria, IN **93** D4
Alexandria, LA **71** D4
Alexandria, MN **101** E2
Alexandria, SD **111** E9
Alexandria, VA **81** B10
Algoma, WI **113** E7
Algona, IA **95** B4
Alibates Flint Quarries Nat. Mon., TX **127** B4
Alice, TX **127** H6
Aliceville, AL **61** D1
Aliquippa, PA **48** D1
Allagash (river), ME **37** B4
Allagash, ME **37** A4
Allagash Lake, ME **37** C4
Allagash Wilderness Waterway, ME **37** C4
Allatoona Lake, GA **67** C2
Allegheny (river), PA **48** D2
Allegheny Mountains, **28** G2
Allegheny N.W.&S.R., PA **49** B3
Allegheny Portage Railroad National Historic Site, PA **49** D4
Allegheny Reservoir, PA **49** A3
Allendale, SC **77** F4
Allenton, RI **51** E4
Allentown, PA **49** D9
Alliance, NE **104** B2
Alliance, OH **109** C7
Alligator (river), NC **75** B10
Alma, MI **99** G6
Alma, NE **105** E6
Alpena, MI **99** E7
Alpine, TX **126** F2
Altamaha (river), GA **67** G6
Altamont, OR **149** G3
Altavista, VA **81** E7
Alton, IL **91** F3
Alton Bay, NH **43** G4
Altoona, PA **49** D4
Altoona, WI **113** D3
Alturas, CA **137** A4
Altus, OK **125** E6
Altus, Lake, OK **125** D6
Alva, OK **125** A7
Amana Colonies (site), IA **95** D8
Amanave, AS **156** I1
Amarillo, TX **127** B3
Amchitka Island, AK **135** H7
American Falls, ID **143** H4
American Falls Reservoir, ID **143** H4
American N.W.&S.R., CA **137** D3
American Samoa (territory), US **156** G4
American, North Fork N.W.&S.R., CA **137** C4
Americus, GA **67** F3
Ames, IA **95** D5
Amesbury, MA **41** A7
Amherst, MA **41** C3
Amherst, NY **46** D2
Amistad N.R.A., TX **127** F4
Amistad Reservoir, TX **127** F4
Amite, LA **71** F7
Amlia Island, AK **135** H9
Ammonoosuc (river), NH **43** D3
Amory, MS **73** C5
Amsterdam, NY **47** D8
Anaconda, MT **144** D3
Anacortes, WA **153** B3
Anadarko, OK **125** D7
Anamosa, IA **95** C9
Anchorage, AK **135** E6
Andalusia, AL **61** G4
Anderson, IN **93** D4
Anderson, SC **76** C2
Anderson Ranch Reservoir, ID **143** G2
Andersonville National Historic Site, GA **67** F3
Andreafsky N.W.&S.R., AK **135** D4
Andreanof Islands, AK **135** H8
Andrew Johnson National Historic Site, TN **79** B10
Andrews, TX **127** D3
Androscoggin (river), ME, NH **43** C4
Angola, IN **93** A5
Aniak, AK **135** E4
Aniakchak N.W.&S.R., AK **135** G4
Aniakchak Nat. Mon. and Preserve, AK **135** G4
Ankeny, IA **95** D5
Ann Arbor, MI **99** H7
Ann, Cape, MA **41** A8
Anna, IL **91** I4
Anna, Lake, VA **81** C9
Annapolis, MD **39** C8
Anniston, AL **61** C5
Ansonia, CT **33** D3
Anthony, KS **97** E6
Anthony, NM **123** H4
Anthony, RI **51** D4
Antietam N.B., MD **39** B5
Antigo, WI **113** D5
Antlers, OK **125** E11
Antrim, NH **43** H2
Apache-Sitgreaves National Forests, AZ, NM **121** E7
Apalachicola (river), FL **65** B3
Apishapa (river), CO **139** F7
Apostle Islands, WI **113** A4
Apostle Islands National Lakeshore, WI **113** A3
Appalachian Mountains, **56** C5
Appalachian National Scenic Trail, **47** G7
Appalachian Plateau, **28** F2
Apple (river), WI **113** D2
Appleton, WI **113** E6
Appomattox, VA **81** D7
Appomattox (river), VA **81** D8
Appomattox Court House N.H.P., VA **81** D7
Arapaho N.R.A., CO **139** B5
Arbuckle Mountains, OK **125** E8
Arcadia, FL **65** F7
Archbald, PA **49** B9
Arches N.P., UT **151** E6
Arco, ID **143** G4
Ardmore, OK **125** E9
Arecibo, PR **157** H10
Arena, Point, CA **137** D1
Arikaree (river), CO **139** C8
Arkabutla Lake, MS **73** A3
Arkadelphia, AR **63** E3
Arkansas (river), **56** C1
Arkansas City, KS **97** F7
Arkansas Post National Memorial, AR **63** E6
Arlington, TX **127** D7
Arlington, VA **81** B10
Arlington, VT **53** H2
Arlington Heights, IL **91** B5
Armour, SD **111** E8
Aroostook (river), ME **37** C5
Arroyo del Macho (river), NM **123** F5
Artesia, NM **123** G6
Arvada, CO **139** C5
Arvon, Mount, MI **99** C3
Asbury Park, NJ **45** E5
Ash Lawn-Highland (site), VA **81** C8
Ashaway, RI **51** F2
Ashdown, AR **63** F1
Asheboro, NC **75** B6
Asheville, NC **74** C2
Ashland, KY **69** B10
Ashland, ME **37** B5
Ashland, NE **105** D9
Ashland, NH **43** F3
Ashland, OH **109** C5
Ashland, OR **149** G2
Ashland, VA **81** D9
Ashland, WI **113** A3
Ashley, ND **107** F7
Ashtabula, OH **109** A7
Ashtabula, Lake, ND **107** D9
Ashton, RI **51** A4
Ashuelot (river), NH **43** I1
Ashwaubenon, WI **113** E7
Aspen, CO **139** D3
Assateague Island, MD **39** F11
Assateague Island National Seashore, MD, VA **39** F11
Assawoman Canal, DE **35** I7
Assawompset Pond, MA **41** D8
Astoria, OR **148** A1
Atascadero, CA **137** G3
Atchafalaya (river), LA **71** F5
Atchafalaya Bay, LA **71** H5
Atchison, KS **97** B9
Athens, AL **61** A3
Athens, GA **67** C4
Athens, OH **109** F5
Athens, TN **79** C8
Athol, MA **41** B4
Atka Island, AK **135** H9
Atkinson, NE **105** B6
Atkinson, NH **43** I4
Atlanta, GA **67** C2
Atlantic, IA **95** E3
Atlantic City, NJ **45** H4
Atlantic City Expressway, NJ **45** G2
Atmore, AL **61** H2
Atoka, OK **125** E10
Attleboro, MA **41** D6
Attu Island, AK **135** G6
Atwood Lake, OH **109** C7
Au Sable (river), MI **99** E6
Au Sable N.W.&S.R., MI **99** E7
Aua, AS **156** I2
Aubrey Cliffs, AZ **121** B3
Auburn, AL **61** E5
Auburn, IN **93** B5
Auburn, MA **41** C5
Auburn, ME **37** G3
Auburn, NE **105** D9
Auburn, NY **47** D5
Auburn, WA **153** D4
Audubon Lake, ND **107** C5
Auglaize (river), OH **109** B2
Augusta, GA **67** D6
Augusta, KS **97** E7
Augusta, ME **37** G3
Aunuu (island), AS **156** I2
Aurora, CO **139** C6
Aurora, IL **91** B5
Aurora, MO **103** F3
Aurora, NE **105** D7
Austin, MN **101** H5
Austin, RI **51** E3
Austin, TX **127** F6
Austintown, OH **109** B8
Ava, MO **103** F4
Avery Island, LA **71** G4
Aziscohos Lake, ME **37** E2
Aztec, NM **123** A2
Aztec Ruins Nat. Mon., NM **123** A2
B
B. Everett Jordan Lake, NC **75** B6
Backbone Mountain, MD **38** B1
Bad (river), SD **111** D4
Bad Axe, MI **99** F8
Badlands (region), ND **106** E2
Badlands N.P., SD **110** E2
Bainbridge, GA **67** H2
Baker, MT **145** D11
Baker (river), NH **43** F2
Baker City, OR **149** C8
Baker Island (territory), US **156** F4
Bakersfield, CA **137** G5
Bald Knob, AR **63** C5
Baldwyn, MS **73** B5
Baltic, CT **33** C7
Baltimore, MD **39** B7
Bamberg, SC **77** E5
Bandelier Nat. Mon., NM **123** C4
Bangor, ME **37** F5
Bangor, PA **49** E9
Banks Lake, WA **153** C7
Bannock Range, ID **143** H5
Bantam Lake, CT **33** B3
Bar Harbor, ME **37** G6
Baraboo, WI **113** F5
Baranof Island, AK **135** G10
Barataria Bay, LA **71** H8
Barberton, OH **109** C6
Bardstown, KY **69** C6
Barkhamsted Reservoir, CT **33** A4
Barkley, Lake, KY, TN **68** E3
Barnegat Bay, NJ **45** F5
Barnstable, MA **41** E9
Barnwell, SC **77** E4
Barre, VT **53** D3
Barren (river), KY **69** D5
Barren River Lake, KY **69** E5
Barrington, RI **51** C5
Barrow, AK **135** A5
Barrow, Point, AK **135** A5
Barstow, CA **137** G6
Bartholomew, Bayou (river), LA **71** B4
Bartlesville, OK **125** A10
Bartlett, TN **78** C1
Barton, VT **53** B4
Bastrop, LA **71** A5
Batavia, NY **46** D3
Batesburg-Leesville, SC **77** D4
Batesville, AR **63** B5
Batesville, MS **73** B3
Bath, ME **37** H3
Bath, NY **47** E4
Baton Rouge, LA **71** F6
Batten Kill (river), VT **53** H1
Battle Creek, ID **143** I1
Battle Creek, MI **99** H5
Battle Ground, WA **153** F3
Battle Mountain, NV **147** B4
Baudette, MN **101** A3
Baxter Springs, KS **97** E10
Bay City, MI **99** G7
Bay City, TX **127** G8
Bay Minette, AL **61** H2
Bay St. Louis, MS **73** I4
Bayard, NM **123** G2
Bayonet Point, FL **65** D6
Bayonne, NJ **45** C5
Bayou Bartholomew (river), AR **63** E5
Bayou La Batre, AL **61** I1
Baytown, TX **127** F8
Beach, ND **106** D1
Beach Haven, NJ **45** G4
Beacon, NY **47** G8
Bear, DE **35** B4
Bear (river), ID, WY **143** I5
Bear Creek, AL **61** B2
Bear Creek, CO, KS **139** F8
Bear Creek N.W.&S.R., MI **99** F5
Bear Lake, ID, UT **151** A5
Bear River Migratory Bird Refuge, UT **151** B3
Bear River Range, ID **143** I6
Bearcamp (river), NH **43** F4
Beardstown, IL **91** E2
Beatrice, NE **105** E9
Beatty, NV **147** G5
Beaufort, SC **77** G6
Beaufort Sea, AK **135** A7
Beaumont, TX **127** F9
Beaver, OK **124** A4
Beaver, UT **151** F3
Beaver (river), OK **124** A4
Beaver (river), PA **48** C1
Beaver Creek, KS **96** B1
Beaver Creek, ND **107** F6
Beaver Creek N.W.&S.R., AK **135** C7
Beaver Dam, WI **113** G6
Beaver Falls, PA **48** D1
Beaver Island, MI **99** D5
Beaver Lake (lake), AR **63** A2
Beaverton, OR **149** B2
Becharof Lake, AK **135** F5
Beckley, WV **83** G4
Bedford, IA **95** F4
Bedford, IN **93** G3
Bedford, PA **49** E4
Bedford, VA **81** D6
Beebe, AR **63** C5
Beech Grove, IN **93** E4
Beeville, TX **127** G6
Bel Air, MD **39** A8
Belcourt, ND **107** A6
Belding, MI **99** G5
Belen, NM **123** D4
Belfast, ME **37** G4
Belgrade, MT **145** E5
Bella Vista, AR **63** A1
Bellaire, OH **109** E8
Belle Fourche, SD **110** C1
Belle Fourche (river), SD, WY **110** C2
Belle Glade, FL **65** F9
Bellefontaine, OH **109** D3
Bellefonte, DE **35** A5
Belleville, IL **91** G3
Belleville, KS **97** A6
Bellevue, NE **105** C9
Bellevue, OH **109** B4
Bellevue, WA **153** C4
Bellingham, MA **41** D6
Bellingham, WA **153** A3
Bellows Falls, VT **53** H4
Belmar, NJ **45** E5
Beloit, KS **97** B6
Beloit, WI **113** H6
Belpre, OH **109** F6
Belted Range, NV **147** F5
Belton, MO **103** C2
Belton, SC **76** C2
Belton, TX **127** E7
Belvidere, IL **91** A4
Bemidji, MN **101** C3
Bend, OR **149** D4
Bennettsville, SC **77** B8
Bennington, VT **53** I1
Benson, AZ **121** H6
Benson, MN **101** F2
Benton, AR **63** D4
Benton, IL **91** H4
Benton Harbor, MI **99** H4
Bentonville, AR **63** A1
Bent's Old Fort National Historic Site, CO **139** E7
Berea, KY **69** D8
Beresford, SD **111** F10
Bering Sea, AK **134** F2
Bering Strait, AK **134** C2
Berkeley, CA **137** E2
Berkeley (site), VA **81** D10
Berkeley Heights, NJ **45** C4
Berlin, MD **39** E11
Berlin, NH **43** C4
Berlin Lake, OH **109** C7
Bernalillo, NM **123** C4
Bernardsville, NJ **45** C3
Berryville, AR **63** A2
Bessemer, AL **61** D3
Bethany, MO **103** A3
Bethany, OK **125** C8
Bethany Beach, DE **35** I7
Bethel, AK **135** E4
Bethel, CT **33** D2
Bethel, ME **37** G2
Bethesda, MD **39** C6
Bethlehem, CT **33** C3
Bethlehem, PA **49** D9
Bettendorf, IA **95** D10

Beulah — Cascade

Beulah, ND **107** D4
Beverly, MA **41** B8
Biddeford, ME **37** H2
Big Bend N.P., TX **127** F3
Big Black (river), MS **73** E2
Big Blue (river), KS, NE **97** A7
Big Blue (river), IN **93** E4
Big Canyon (river), TX **127** F3
Big Coal (river), WV **83** G3
Big Cypress National Preserve, FL **65** G8
Big Cypress Swamp, FL **65** G8
Big Darby Creek, OH **109** D3
Big Darby Creek National Scenic River, OH **109** E4
Big Eau Pleine Reservoir, WI **113** D4
Big Fork (river), MN **101** B4
Big Hole N.B., MT **144** E3
Big Lake, ME **37** E6
Big Lost (river), ID **143** G4
Big Marsh Creek N.W.&S.R., OR **149** E3
Big Muddy (river), IL **91** H4
Big Nemaha (river), NE **105** E9
Big Piney (river), MO **103** F5
Big Piney Creek, AR **63** C3
Big Piney Creek N.W.&S.R., AR **63** B3
Big Raccoon Creek, IN **93** E2
Big Rapids, MI **99** G5
Big Sandy (river), AZ **121** D3
Big Sandy (river), KY, WV **82** F1
Big Sandy (river), WY **155** F3
Big Sandy Creek, CO **139** D7
Big Sioux (river), IA, SD **94** B1
Big Smoky Valley, NV **147** E4
Big South Fork National River and Recreation Area, KY, TN **79** A7
Big Spring, TX **127** D4
Big Stone Gap, VA **80** E2
Big Stone Lake, MN, SD **101** F1
Big Sunflower (river), MS **73** C2
Big Sur N.W.&S.R., CA **137** F3
Big Thicket National Preserve, TX **127** E9
Big Timber, MT **145** E6
Big Wood (river), ID **143** H3
Bighorn (river), MT, WY **130** C6
Bighorn Canyon N.R.A., MT, WY **145** F8
Bighorn Lake, WY **155** A5
Bighorn Mountains, MT, WY **155** A5
Bill Williams (river), AZ **121** E2
Billings, MT **145** E7
Biloxi, MS **73** I5
Biltmore House (site), NC **74** C2
Bingham, ME **37** E3
Binghamton, NY **47** F6
Birch Creek N.W.&S.R., AK **135** C7
Birmingham, AL **61** C3
Bisbee, AZ **121** H7
Biscayne Bay, FL **65** H9
Biscayne N.P., FL **65** H9
Bishop, CA **137** E5
Bishop Creek Reservoir, NV **147** B6
Bismarck, ND **107** E5
Bison, SD **111** B3
Bistineau, Lake, LA **70** B2
Bitter Creek, UT **151** D7
Bitterroot Range, ID, MT **143** B1
Bixby, OK **125** C10
Black (river), VT **53** G3
Black (river), AR, MO **63** B6
Black (river), AZ **121** F7
Black (river), MI **99** G8
Black (river), NY **47** C6
Black (river), SC **77** E8
Black (river), WI **113** E3
Black Belt (region), AL **61** E2
Black Canyon of the Gunnison N.P., CO **139** D2
Black Creek, MS **73** H5
Black Creek N.W.&S.R., MS **73** H4
Black Hawk, SD **110** D2
Black Hills, SD **110** D1
Black Hills, WY **155** B10
Black Mesa (peak), OK **124** A1
Black Mesa, AZ **121** B6
Black Mountain, KY **69** E10
Black Mountain, NC **74** C3
Black Mountains, AZ **121** C2
Black N.W.&S.R., MI **99** C1
Black Range, NM **123** G2
Black River Falls, WI **113** E3
Black Rock Desert, NV **147** B2
Black Rock Range, NV **147** A2
Black Warrior (river), AL **61** E2
Blackfoot, ID **143** H5
Blackfoot Mountains, ID **143** H5
Blackfoot Reservoir, ID **143** H5
Blacks Fork (river), WY **154** G2
Blacksburg, VA **81** E5
Blackstone, VA **81** E9
Blackstone (river), MA, RI **51** A4
Blackwater (river), MO **103** C3
Blackwell, OK **125** A8
Blades, DE **35** H5
Blair, NE **105** C9
Blakely, GA **67** G1
Blanchard, IA **95** F3
Blanchard (river), OH **109** C2
Blanco, Cape, OR **148** F1
Blanding, UT **151** G6
Block Island, RI **51** I3
Block Island, RI **51** H3
Block Island Sound, NY **47** G11
Bloodsworth Island, MD **39** F9
Bloomfield, CT **33** B5
Bloomfield, IA **95** F7
Bloomfield, NM **123** A2
Blooming Grove, OH **109** C4
Bloomington, IL **91** D4
Bloomington, IN **93** F3
Bloomington, MN **101** F4
Bloomsburg, PA **49** C7
Blue (river), CO **139** C4
Blue (river), IN **93** H3
Blue (river), OK **125** E10
Blue Earth (river), MN **101** H4
Blue Grass Parkway, KY **69** C6
Blue Hill Bay, ME **37** G5
Blue Mesa Reservoir, CO **139** E3
Blue Mountain, NH **43** B3
Blue Mountain, PA **49** D7
Blue Mountains, OR **149** C7
Blue Ridge, GA, NC, VA **56** C5
Blue Ridge Parkway, VA **81** F5
Blue Springs, MO **103** C2
Bluefield, VA **80** E4
Bluefield, WV **83** H3
Bluegrass Region, KY **69** B7
Bluestone (river), WV **83** H3
Bluestone Lake, WV **83** H4
Bluestone National Scenic River, WV **83** H4
Blythe, CA **137** H8
Blytheville, AR **63** B8
Boaz, AL **61** B4
Boca Raton, FL **65** G9
Bogalusa, LA **71** E8
Bogue Chitto (river), LA, MS **71** E8
Bois Blanc Island, MI **99** D6
Bois Brule (river), WI **113** B3
Bois de Sioux (river), MN **101** E1
Boise, ID **143** G1
Boise City, OK **124** A2
Bolivar, MO **103** E3
Bolivar, TN **78** C2
Bombay Hook Island, DE **35** D5
Bomoseen, Lake, VT **53** F1
Bonne Springs, KS **97** B10
Bonners Ferry, ID **143** A1
Bonneville Dam, OR, WA **149** B3
Booker T. Washington Nat. Mon., VA **81** E6
Boone, IA **95** C5
Boone, NC **74** B3
Boone (river), IA **95** B5
Booneville, AR **63** C2
Booneville, MS **73** A5
Boonsboro, MD **39** A5
Boonville, IN **93** I2
Boonville, MO **103** C4
Boothbay Harbor, ME **37** H4
Borah Peak, ID **143** G3
Borger, TX **127** B4
Borgne, Lake, LA **71** G8
Bossier City, LA **70** B1
Boston, MA **41** C7
Boston Harbor Islands N.R.A., MA **41** C7
Boston Mountains, AR **63** B2
Boston N.H.P., MA **41** B7
Bottineau, ND **107** A5
Boulder, CO **139** B5
Boulder City, NV **147** H6
Boundary Peak, NV **147** E3
Boundary Waters Canoe Area Wilderness, MN **101** B5
Bountiful, UT **151** B4
Bow Lake (lake), NH **43** H4
Bowers Beach, DE **35** F6
Bowie, MD **39** C7
Bowling Green, KY **69** E5
Bowling Green, OH **109** B3
Bowman, ND **106** F2
Boyer (river), IA **95** D3
Boyne City, MI **99** E6
Boysen Reservoir, WY **155** D5
Bozeman, MT **145** E5
Bradenton, FL **65** E6
Bradford, PA **49** A4
Bradford, RI **51** F2
Bradford, VT **53** E4
Brady, TX **127** E5
Brainerd, MN **101** D4
Brandenburg, KY **69** C5
Brandon, MS **73** F3
Brandon, VT **53** E2
Brandywine, DE **35** A5
Brandywine Creek, DE **35** A5
Branford, CT **33** E4
Branson, MO **103** F3
Brantley Lake, NM **123** G7
Brasstown Bald (peak), GA **67** A3
Brattleboro, VT **53** I3
Brazil, IN **93** F2
Brazos (river), TX **127** C5
Breaks Interstate Park, KY **69** D11
Breaux Bridge, LA **71** F4
Breckenridge, TX **127** D5
Bremerton, WA **153** C3
Brenham, TX **127** F7
Brentwood, NY **47** H9
Brentwood, TN **79** B5
Breton Islands, LA **71** H10
Breton Sound, LA **71** H9
Brevard, NC **74** C2
Brewer, ME **37** F5
Brewton, AL **61** H3
Brices Cross Roads National Battlefield Site, MS **73** B5
Bridgeport, CT **33** E3
Bridgeport, NE **104** C2
Bridgeport, WV **83** D5
Bridgeton, NJ **45** H1
Bridgeville, DE **35** H5
Bridgewater, MA **41** D7
Bridgewater, VA **81** C7
Bridgton, ME **37** G2
Brigantine, NJ **45** H4
Brigham City, UT **151** A4
Brighton, CO **139** B6
Brinkley, AR **63** D6
Bristol, NH **43** F3
Bristol, RI **51** D6
Bristol, TN **79** A11
Bristol, VA **80** F3
Bristol, VT **53** D2
Bristol Bay, AK **135** F4
Bristow, OK **125** C10
Britton, SD **111** A8
Britton Hill (peak), FL **64** A2
Broad (river), GA **67** C5
Broad (river), NC, SC **77** A4
Broad Brook, CT **33** A5
Broadkill Beach, DE **35** G7
Broadus, MT **145** E10
Brockton, MA **41** D7
Broken Arrow, OK **125** B10
Broken Bow, NE **105** C5
Broken Bow, OK **125** E12
Broken Bow Lake, OK **125** E12
Bromley Mountain, VT **53** G2
Brookfield, MO **103** B4
Brookfield, WI **113** G7
Brookhaven, MS **73** G2
Brookings, OR **148** G1
Brookings, SD **111** D10
Brookline, MA **41** C7
Brooklyn, CT **33** B8
Brooklyn Park, MN **101** F4
Brooks Range, AK **135** B4
Brookside, DE **35** B4
Brookville Lake, IN **93** F5
Brown v. Board of Education N.H.S., KS **97** C8
Brownfield, TX **127** D3
Browning, MT **144** B3
Brownlee Reservoir, ID, OR **143** F1
Browns Mills, NJ **45** F3
Brownsville, TN **78** C2
Brownsville, TX **127** I7
Brownville Junction, ME **37** E4
Brownwood, TX **127** E5
Brule (river), MI, WI **113** B6
Bruneau (river), ID, NV **143** H2
Bruneau, East Fork (river), ID **143** I2
Brunswick, GA **67** H7
Brunswick, MD **39** B5
Brunswick, ME **37** H3
Brunswick, OH **109** B6
Brush, CO **139** B7
Bryan, OH **109** B2
Bryan, TX **127** E7
Bryant, AR **63** D4
Bryant Creek, MO **103** F4
Bryce Canyon N.P., UT **151** G3
Buck Creek, OK **125** D5
Buck Island Reef Nat. Mon., VI **157** I8
Buckeye Lake, OH **109** E5
Buckhannon, WV **83** D5
Buckner Creek, KS **97** D3
Bucksport, ME **37** F5
Bucktown, MD **39** E9
Bucyrus, OH **109** C4
Budd Lake, NJ **45** B3
Buena Vista, VA **81** D7
Buffalo, NY **46** D2
Buffalo, OK **125** A5
Buffalo, SD **110** A2
Buffalo (river), TN **79** C4
Buffalo, WY **155** B7
Buffalo (river), AR **63** B2
Buffalo Bill Reservoir, WY **155** B4
Buffalo N.W.&S.R., AR **63** B2
Buffalo National River, AR **63** B3
Buhl, ID **143** I3
Bull Shoals Lake, AR, MO **63** A3
Bullfrog Creek, UT **151** G5
Bullhead City, AZ **121** D2
Bunkie, LA **71** E4
Burien, WA **153** C4
Burkburnett, TX **127** C6
Burke, SD **111** F7
Burley, ID **143** I5
Burlington, CO **139** C9
Burlington, IA **95** F9
Burlington, KS **97** D9
Burlington, NC **75** B6
Burlington, NJ **45** E2
Burlington, VT **53** C1
Burlington, WI **113** H6
Burns, OR **149** E6
Burt Lake, MI **99** D6
Burton, MI **99** G7
Burton, SC **77** G6
Burwell, NE **105** C6
Butler, MO **103** D2
Butler, PA **48** C2
Butte, MT **145** E4
Buzzards Bay, MA **41** E8

C

C.J. Strike Reservoir, ID **143** H1
C.W. McConaughy, Lake, NE **105** C3
Caballo Reservoir, NM **123** G3
Cabinet Mountains, ID, MT **144** A1
Cabot, AR **63** D5
Cabot, Mount, NH **43** C4
Cabrillo Nat. Mon., CA **137** I5
Cacapon (river), WV **83** D8
Cache (river), AR **63** C6
Cache La Poudre N.W.&S.R., CO **139** A5
Cactus Range, NV **147** F4
Caddo Lake, LA **70** A1
Cadillac, MI **99** F5
Cadillac Mountain, ME **37** G6
Caesar Creek Lake, OH **109** F2
Cagles Mill Lake, IN **93** F2
Caguas, PR **157** I11
Cahaba (river), AL **61** E3
Cairo, GA **67** H3
Cairo, IL **91** I4
Calais, ME **37** E7
Calamus (river), NE **105** B5
Calamus Reservoir, NE **105** B6
Calcasieu (river), LA **71** F3
Calcasieu Lake, LA **70** G2
Caldwell, ID **143** G1
Caldwell, NJ **45** C4
Caledonia, MN **101** H6
Calexico, CA **137** I7
Calhoun, GA **67** B2
Caliente, NV **147** F7
California, MO **103** D4
California, Gulf of, **116** F1
Caloosahatchee (river), FL **65** F8
Calvert City, KY **68** E2
Camas, WA **153** G3
Cambridge, MA **41** B7
Cambridge, MD **39** D9
Cambridge, NE **105** E5
Cambridge, OH **109** E6
Camden, AR **63** F3
Camden, DE **35** E5
Camden, ME **37** G4
Camden, NJ **45** F2
Camden, SC **77** C6
Camels Hump (peak), VT **53** C2
Cameron, MO **103** B2
Camilla, GA **67** H3
Campbell Hill (peak), OH **109** D3
Campbellsville, KY **69** D6
Campe Verde, AZ **121** D5
Canaan, CT **33** A2
Canaan, NH **43** F2
Canaan, VT **53** A6
Canadian (river), NM, OK, TX **116** C6
Canadian, North (river), OK **125** B6
Canandaigua, NY **47** D4
Canaveral National Seashore, FL **65** C8
Canaveral, Cape, FL **65** D9
Candlewood, Lake, CT **33** D2
Cando, ND **107** B7
Cane River Creole N.H.P. and Heritage Area, LA **70** D2
Caney (river), KS, OK **125** A10
Caney Fork (river), TN **79** C6
Cannonball (river), ND **107** E3
Cañon City, CO **139** E5
Cañon Largo (river), NM **123** B3
Canoochee (river), GA **67** F6
Canterbury, NH **43** G3
Canton, IL **91** D3
Canton, MO **103** A5
Canton, MS **73** E3
Canton, OH **109** C7
Canton, SD **111** E10
Canyon, TX **127** B3
Canyon Creek, ID **143** H1
Canyon de Chelly Nat. Mon., AZ **121** B7
Canyon Ferry Lake, MT **145** D5
Canyonlands N.P., UT **151** F6
Canyons of the Ancients Nat. Mon., CO **138** F1
Cap Rock Escarpment, TX **127** D4
Cape Charles, VA **81** D11
Cape Cod Bay, MA **41** D9
Cape Cod Canal, MA **41** D8
Cape Cod National Seashore, MA **41** D10
Cape Coral, FL **65** G7
Cape Elizabeth, ME **37** H3
Cape Fear (river), NC **75** D7
Cape Girardeau, MO **103** E8
Cape Hatteras National Seashore, NC **75** C11
Cape Island, SC **77** F8
Cape Krusenstern Nat. Mon., AK **135** B4
Cape Lookout National Seashore, NC **75** D10
Cape May, NJ **45** I2
Cape May Canal, NJ **45** I2
Cape May Court House, NJ **45** I3
Capitol Hill, MP **156** C2
Capitol Reef N.P., UT **151** F5
Captain Cook, HI **141** F8
Capulin Volcano Nat. Mon., NM **123** A7
Carbondale, CO **139** C3
Carbondale, IL **91** H4
Carbondale, PA **49** B9
Caribou, ME **37** B6
Caribou Range, ID **143** G6
Carl Sandburg Home National Historic Site, NC **74** C3
Carlin, NV **147** B5
Carlinville, IL **91** F3
Carlisle, PA **49** E6
Carlsbad, NM **123** G7
Carlsbad Caverns N.P., NM **123** H6
Carlyle Lake, IL **91** G4
Carmel, IN **93** E4
Carmi, IL **91** H5
Caro, MI **99** G7
Carolina, PR **157** H11
Carolina, RI **51** F3
Carp N.W.&S.R., MI **99** D5
Carrington, ND **107** D7
Carrizo Creek, NM **123** B7
Carrizo Plain Nat. Mon., CA **137** G4
Carrizo Springs, TX **127** G5
Carrizozo, NM **123** F5
Carroll, IA **95** C3
Carrollton, GA **67** D1
Carson (river), NV **147** D2
Carson City, NV **147** D2
Carson Sink (river), NV **147** C3
Carthage, IL **91** D2
Carthage, MO **103** F2
Carthage, MS **73** E4
Caruthersville, MO **103** G8
Cary, NC **75** B7
Casa Grande, AZ **121** F5
Casa Grande Ruins Nat. Mon., AZ **121** F5
Cascade, ID **143** F1

Cascade Range — Crossville

Cascade Range, **130** C2
Cascade Siskiyou Nat. Mon., OR **149** G3
Cascade, Lake, ID **143** F1
Casco Bay, ME **37** H3
Casper, WY **155** D7
Cass (river), MI **99** G7
Casselman (river), PA **49** F3
Casselton, ND **107** D9
Castillo de San Marcos Nat. Mon., FL **65** B8
Castine, ME **37** G5
Castle Dale, UT **151** E5
Castle Rock, CO **139** C6
Castle Rock Lake, WI **113** F5
Castleton, VT **53** F2
Catahoula Lake, LA **71** D4
Catalina, AZ **121** G6
Cataño, PR **157** H11
Catawba (river), NC, SC **77** B5
Cathedral Bluffs, CO **138** B1
Catoctin Mountain Park, MD **39** A5
Catonsville, MD **39** B7
Catskill, NY **47** E8
Catskill Mountains, NY **47** F8
Catskill Park, NY **47** F7
Cattaraugus Creek, NY **46** E2
Cavalier, ND **107** A9
Cave City, KY **69** D6
Cave Run Lake, KY **69** C9
Cayce, SC **77** D5
Cayey, PR **157** I11
Cayuga Lake, NY **47** E5
Cecil M. Harden Lake, IN **93** E2
Cedar (river), NE **105** C6
Cedar (river), IA **95** A6
Cedar (river), MI **99** D3
Cedar Bluff Reservoir, KS **97** C3
Cedar Breaks Nat. Mon., UT **151** G2
Cedar City, UT **151** G2
Cedar Creek, ND **106** E2
Cedar Creek, IN **93** B5
Cedar Creek Reservoir, ID **143** I2
Cedar Falls, IA **95** C7
Cedar Rapids, IA **95** D8
Celina, OH **109** D2
Centennial Mountains, ID **143** F5
Center, ND **107** D4
Center Hill Lake, TN **79** B6
Center Ossipee, NH **43** F4
Center Point, AL **61** C3
Center Sandwich, NH **43** F4
Centereach, NY **47** H9
Centerville, IA **95** F6
Centerville, OH **109** E2
Centerville, UT **151** B4
Central City, IA **95** C8
Central City, NE **105** C7
Central Falls, RI **51** B5
Central Lowland (plain), **86** E5
Central Point, OR **149** F2
Central Valley, CA **137** B2
Centralia, IL **91** G4
Centralia, MO **103** C5
Centralia, WA **153** E3
Centreville, MS **73** H1
Cerro de Punta (mountains), PR **157** I10
Chaco Culture N.H.P., NM **123** B2
Chacuaco Canyon, CO **139** F7
Chadron, NE **104** A2
Challis, ID **143** F3
Chalmette, LA **71** G8
Chama, NM **123** A4
Chamberlain, SD **111** D7
Chamberlain Lake, ME **37** C4
Chambersburg, PA **49** E5
Champaign, IL **91** E5
Champlain, Lake, NY, VT **47** B9
Chandeleur Islands, LA **71** G10
Chandeleur Sound, LA **71** G10
Chandler, AZ **121** F5
Channel Islands, CA **137** H3
Channel Islands N.P., CA **137** H3
Channel Islands National Marine Sanctuary, CA **137** H4
Chanute, KS **97** E9
Chaparral, NM **123** H4
Chapel Hill, NC **75** B6
Chappaquiddick Island, MA **41** F9
Chariton, IA **95** E6
Chariton (river), IA, MO **103** B4
Charles (river), MA **41** C6
Charles City, IA **95** B7
Charles Mound, IL **91** A3
Charles Pinckney National Historic Site, SC **77** F8
Charles Town, WV **83** D10
Charleston, IL **91** F5
Charleston, MO **103** F8
Charleston, SC **77** G7
Charleston, WV **83** F3
Charlestown, IN **93** H4
Charlestown, NH **43** G1
Charlestown, RI **51** G3
Charley N.W.&S.R., AK **135** C7
Charlotte, MI **99** H6
Charlotte, NC **75** C4
Charlotte Amalie, VI **157** G7
Charlotte Harbor, FL **65** F7
Charlottesville, VA **81** C8
Chatham, MA **41** E10
Chattahoochee (river), AL, GA **56** D5
Chattahoochee River N.R.A., GA **67** C2
Chattanooga, TN **79** D6
Chattooga (river), SC **76** B1
Chattooga N.W.&S.R., GA, NC, SC **67** A4
Chautauqua Lake, NY **46** E1
Cheaha Mountain, AL **61** C5
Cheat (river), WV **83** C6
Cheat Mountain, WV **83** F6
Cheboygan, MI **99** D6
Checotah, OK **125** C11
Cheektowaga, NY **46** D2
Cheesequake, NJ **45** D4
Chehalis, WA **153** E3
Chehalis (river), WA **152** D2
Chelan, Lake, WA **153** B6
Chelmsford, MA **41** B6
Chemung (river), NY **47** E4
Cheney, WA **153** C9
Cheney Reservoir, KS **97** D6
Chepachet, RI **51** B3
Cheraw, SC **77** B7
Cherokee, IA **94** B2
Cherokee Lake, TN **79** A9
Cherokee Village, AR **63** A5
Cherokees, Lake O' The, OK **125** A11
Cherry Creek, SD **111** C3
Cherry Creek Range, NV **147** C6
Cherry Hill, NJ **45** F2
Chesapeake, VA **81** E11
Chesapeake and Delaware Canal, DE, MD **35** C4
Chesapeake and Ohio Canal, MD **38** A2
Chesapeake and Ohio Canal N.H.P., MD **39** B5
Chesapeake Bay, MD, VA **28** H4
Chesapeake Bay Bridge *see* William Preston Lane Jr. Memorial Bridge, MD **39** C8
Chesapeake Bay Bridge-Tunnel, VA **81** E11
Chesapeake Beach, MD **39** D8
Cheshire, CT **33** D4
Cheshire Reservoir, MA **40** B1
Chester, IL **91** H3
Chester, PA **49** F9
Chester, SC **77** B5
Chester, VA **81** D9
Chester, VT **53** G3
Chester, WV **83** A5
Chester (bay), MD **39** C8
Chesterfield, CT **33** D7
Chestertown, MD **39** B9
Chesuncook Lake, ME **37** D4
Cheswold, DE **35** E5
Chetco (river), OR **148** G1
Chetco N.W.&S.R., OR **148** G1
Chevelon Creek, AZ **121** D6
Cheyenne, WY **155** G9
Cheyenne (river), SD, WY **111** C3
Cheyenne Bottoms (lake), KS **97** C5
Cheyenne Wells, CO **139** D9
Chicago, IL **91** B6
Chichagof Island, AK **135** F9
Chickamauga and Chattanooga N.M.P., GA, TN **67** A1
Chickamauga Lake, TN **79** C7
Chickasaw N.R.A., OK **125** E9
Chickasawhay (river), MS **73** G5
Chickasha, OK **125** D8
Chico, CA **137** C3
Chicopee (river), MA **41** C3
Chicopee, MA **41** C3
Chikaskia (river), OK **125** A8
Childress, TX **127** C5
Chilikadrotna N.W.&S.R., AK **135** E5
Chillicothe, IL **91** C3
Chillicothe, MO **103** B3
Chillicothe, OH **109** F4
Chimayo, NM **123** B5
Chimney Rock National Historic Site, NE **104** C1
Chincoteague, VA **81** C12
Chincoteague Bay, MD **39** F11
Chinle, AZ **121** B7
Chinle Wash (river), AZ **121** A7
Chino Valley, AZ **121** D4
Chinook, MT **145** B7
Chippewa (river), MN **101** E2
Chippewa (river), WI **113** C3
Chippewa Falls, WI **113** D3
Chippewa, Lake, WI **113** B3
Chiputneticook Lakes, ME **37** D6
Chiricahua Nat. Mon., AZ **121** H7
Chisholm, MN **101** C5
Chittenden Reservoir, VT **53** E2
Choctawhatchee (river), AL, FL **64** B2
Choptank (bay), MD **39** D8
Choptank (river), MD **39** D9
Choteau, MT **145** B4
Chowan (river), NC **75** A9
Christiansburg, VA **81** E5
Christiansted, VI **157** I8
Christiansted National Historic Site, VI **157** I7
Christina (river), DE **35** B4
Christmas Lake Valley, OR **149** E5
Chubbuck, ID **143** H5
Chugach Mountains, AK **135** E7
Chukchi Sea, AK **134** A3
Chula Vista, CA **137** I6
Church Hill, TN **79** A10
Churchill Lake, ME **37** C4
Cicero, IL **91** B5
Cimarron (river), CO, KS, OK **125** B7
Cimarron Turnpike, OK **125** B9
Cimarron, North Fork (river), CO, KS **96** E1
Cincinnati, OH **109** G1
Cinnaminson, NJ **45** F2
Circle, MT **145** C10
Circleville, OH **109** F4
Citronelle, AL **61** H1
City of Rocks National Reserve, ID **143** I4
Clackamas N.W.&S.R., OR **149** C3
Clan Alpine Mountains, NV **147** D3
Clanton, AL **61** E3
Clara Barton National Historic Site, MD **39** C6
Claremont, NH **43** G1
Claremore, OK **125** B10
Clarinda, IA **95** F3
Clarion, PA **49** C3
Clarion (river), PA **49** C3
Clarion N.W.&S.R., PA **49** C3
Clark, SD **111** C9
Clark Fork (river), MT **144** B1
Clarks Fork (river), MT **145** E7
Clarks Fork Yellowstone N.W.&S.R., WY **155** A3
Clarksburg, WV **83** D5
Clarksdale, MS **73** B2
Clarkston, WA **153** E10
Clarksville, AR **63** C2
Clarksville, TN **79** A4
Clay Center, KS **97** B7
Claymont, DE **35** A6
Clayton, DE **35** D4
Clayton, NM **123** B8
Clear Creek, AZ **121** D5
Clear Creek, WY **155** A7
Clear Lake, CA **137** C2
Clear Lake, IA **95** A5
Clear Lake, SD **111** C10
Clearfield, PA **49** C4
Clearfield, UT **151** B3
Clearwater, FL **65** E6
Clearwater, SC **77** E3
Clearwater (river), ID **143** D1
Clearwater Mountains, ID **143** D2
Clearwater, Middle Fork N.W.&S.R., ID **143** D2
Clearwater, North Fork (river), ID **143** D2
Clearwater, South Fork (river), ID **143** E2
Clemson, SC **76** B2
Cleveland, MS **73** C2
Cleveland, OH **109** B6
Cleveland, TN **79** D7
Clifton, AZ **121** F7
Clifton, NJ **45** B4
Clifton Forge, VA **81** D6
Clinch (river), TN, VA **79** A9
Clinch Mountain, VA **80** E3
Clingmans Dome (peak), TN **79** C9
Clinton, AR **63** B4
Clinton, CT **33** E5
Clinton, IA **95** D10
Clinton, IL **91** E4
Clinton, IN **93** E2
Clinton, MO **103** D3
Clinton, MS **73** E2
Clinton, NC **75** C7
Clinton, OK **125** C6
Clinton, SC **77** C3
Clinton, TN **79** B8
Cloquet, MN **101** D5
Clovis, NM **123** E8
Clyde (river), VT **53** A5
Coast Mountains, AK **135** E10
Coast Ranges, CA **137** B2
Coast Ranges, **130** B2
Coastal Plain, **56** E2
Coatesville, PA **49** E8
Cobble Mountain Reservoir, MA **40** C2
Cobleskill, NY **47** E7
Cocheco (river), NH **43** G5
Cochetopa Hills, CO **139** E4
Cockeysville, MD **39** A7
Coconino Plateau, AZ **121** C4
Cod, Cape, MA **41** E9
Cody, WY **155** B4
Coeur d'Alene, ID **143** B1
Coeur d'Alene (river), ID **143** C1
Coeur d'Alene Lake, ID **143** C1
Coffeyville, KS **97** F9
Cohansey (river), NJ **45** H1
Colby, KS **96** B2
Colchester, CT **33** C6
Cold Spring, MN **101** F3
Coldwater, MI **99** I6
Coldwater (river), MS **73** B2
Colebrook, NH **43** B3
Coleman, OK **125** E10
Coleman, TX **127** E5
College, AK **135** C7
College Place, WA **153** F8
College Station, TX **127** E7
Collierville, TN **78** D1
Collins, MS **73** G4
Collinsville, CT **33** B4
Collinsville, VA **81** E6
Colonial Beach, VA **81** C10
Colonial N.H.P., VA **81** D10
Colorado (river), **130** H4
Colorado City, AZ **121** A3
Colorado Nat. Mon., CO **138** D1
Colorado Plateau, AZ **116** B2
Colorado Springs, CO **139** D6
Colstrip, MT **145** E9
Columbia, MD **39** B7
Columbia, MO **103** C4
Columbia, MS **73** G3
Columbia, PA **49** E7
Columbia, SC **77** D5
Columbia, TN **79** C4
Columbia (river), OR, WA **149** A2
Columbia City, IN **93** B5
Columbia Falls, MT **144** B2
Columbia Plateau, OR **130** B3
Columbia River Gorge National Scenic Area, OR, WA **153** F4
Columbus, GA **67** F1
Columbus, IN **93** F4
Columbus, KS **97** E10
Columbus, MS **73** C5
Columbus, MT **145** E7
Columbus, NE **105** C8
Columbus, OH **109** E4
Columbus Salt Marsh (river), NV **147** E3
Colville, WA **153** B9
Colville (river), AK **135** B5
Colville (river), WA **153** B9
Combahee (river), SC **77** G6
Combs Mountain Parkway, KY **69** C9
Compensating Reservoir, CT **33** B4
Conanicut Island, RI **51** E5
Conchas (river), NM **123** C6
Conchas Lake, NM **123** C7
Concord, MA **41** B6
Concord, NC **75** C5
Concord, NH **43** H3
Concord (river), MA **41** B6
Concordia, KS **97** B6
Conecuh (river), AL **61** G4
Conejos (river), CO **139** G4
Conemaugh (river), PA **49** D3
Confusion Range, UT **151** D1
Congamond Lakes, CT **33** A4
Congaree (river), SC **77** D5
Congaree N.P., SC **77** D5
Conneaut, OH **109** A8
Connecticut (river), CT, MA, NH, VT **28** D6
Connell, WA **153** E8
Connellsville, PA **48** E2
Connersville, IN **93** E5
Conrad, MT **145** B4
Conroe, TX **127** F8
Continental Divide, CO, ID, MT, NM, WY **143** E4
Contoocook, NH **43** H3
Contoocook (river), NH **43** H3
Conway, AR **63** C4
Conway, NH **43** E4
Conway, SC **77** D9
Conway Lake, NH **43** E4
Cook Inlet, AK **135** E6
Cookeville, TN **79** B6
Coolidge, AZ **121** F5
Coon Rapids, MN **101** F4
Cooper (river), SC **77** F7
Cooperstown, ND **107** D8
Cooperstown, NY **47** E7
Coos (river), OR **148** E1
Coos Bay, OR **148** E1
Coosa (river), AL, GA **61** D4
Coosawattee (river), GA **67** B2
Coosawhatchie (river), SC **77** F5
Copper (river), AK **135** E7
Copperas Cove, TX **127** E6
Coquille, OR **148** E1
Coral Springs, FL **65** G9
Coralville, IA **95** D8
Coram, NY **47** H9
Corbin, KY **69** E8
Cordele, GA **67** F3
Cordell Bank National Marine Sanctuary, CA **137** D1
Cordillera Central (mountains), PR **157** I9
Cordova, AK **135** E7
Core Sound, NC **75** D10
Corinth, MS **73** A5
Corning, AR **63** A7
Corning, NY **47** F4
Coronado Nat. Mon., AZ **121** H6
Corpus Christi, TX **127** H7
Corpus Christi Bay, TX **116** G8
Corrumpa Creek, NM **123** A7
Corry, PA **48** A2
Corsicana, TX **127** D7
Cortez, CO **138** F1
Cortez Mountains, NV **147** C5
Cortland, NY **47** E5
Corvallis, OR **149** C2
Corydon, IN **93** H4
Coshocton, OH **109** D6
Cossatot (river), AR **63** E1
Cossatot N.W.&S.R., AR **63** E1
Coteau des Prairies, SD **111** A9
Cottage Grove, OR **149** D2
Cottonwood, AZ **121** D4
Coudersport, PA **49** B5
Council Bluffs, IA **94** E2
Council Grove, KS **97** C8
Coventry, CT **33** B6
Coventry Center, RI **51** D3
Covington, GA **67** D3
Covington, KY **69** A8
Covington, LA **71** F8
Covington, VA **81** D6
Cowlitz (river), WA **153** E3
Cowpasture (river), VA **81** C6
Cowpens N.B., SC **77** A4
Cozad, NE **105** D5
Craig, CO **139** B2
Crane Creek Reservoir, ID **143** F1
Cranston, RI **51** C4
Crater Lake, OR **149** F3
Crater Lake N.P., OR **149** F3
Craters of the Moon Nat. Mon. and Preserve, ID **143** H4
Crawford, NE **104** A1
Crawfordsville, IN **93** D2
Crazy Horse Memorial, SD **110** D1
Crescent City, CA **137** A1
Crescent Creek N.W.&S.R., OR **149** E3
Cresco, IA **95** A7
Creston, IA **95** E4
Crestview, FL **64** A2
Crestwood Village, NJ **45** F4
Crete, NE **105** D8
Crisfield, MD **39** F9
Crooked (river), OR **149** D5
Crooked N.W.&S.R., OR **149** C4
Crooked, North Fork N.W.&S.R., OR **149** D5
Crookston, MN **101** C1
Crosby, ND **106** A2
Crossett, AR **63** G5
Crossville, TN **79** B7

Crow Agency — Fall

Crow Agency, MT **145** E8
Crow Creek, CO **139** B6
Crow Creek, SD **111** D7
Crow Wing (river), MN **101** D3
Crow, North Fork (river), MN **101** E3
Crow, South Fork (river), MN **101** F3
Crowley, LA **71** G4
Crowleys Ridge, AR **63** C7
Crown Mountain, VI **157** G7
Crown Point, IN **93** B2
Crownpoint, NM **123** C2
Cruz Bay, VI **157** G8
Crystal Lake, NH **43** G4
Crystal Springs, MS **73** F2
Cuivre (river), MO **103** C6
Culebra Island, PR **157** I12
Culebra Range, CO **139** G5
Cullman, AL **61** B3
Culpeper, VA **81** B8
Cumberland, KY **69** E10
Cumberland, MD **38** A2
Cumberland (river), KY, TN **56** C4
Cumberland Gap, KY, VA **69** E9
Cumberland Gap N.H.P., KY, TN, VA **69** E9
Cumberland Hill, RI **51** A4
Cumberland Island, GA **67** H7
Cumberland Island National Seashore, GA **67** H7
Cumberland Mountains, KY **69** E9
Cumberland Plateau, **56** C5
Cumberland, Lake, KY **69** E7
Curecanti N.R.A., CO **139** E3
Current (river), MO **103** E5
Currituck Sound, NC **75** A10
Cushing, OK **125** C9
Custer, SD **110** D1
Cut Bank, MT **145** A4
Cuyahoga (river), OH **109** B7
Cuyahoga Falls, OH **109** B6
Cuyahoga Valley N.P., OH **109** B6
Cynthiana, KY **69** B8
Cypress Swamp, DE **35** I6

D

Dagsboro, DE **35** I6
Dahlonega, GA **67** B3
Dale City, VA **81** B9
Dale Hollow Lake, KY,TN **79** A7
Daleville, AL **61** G5
Dallas, OR **149** C2
Dallas, TX **127** D7
Dalton, GA **67** B2
Dalton, MA **40** B1
Dan (river), NC, VA **75** A6
Danbury, CT **33** D2
Danforth, ME **37** D6
Danielson, CT **33** B8
Dannemora, NY **47** A8
Dansville, NY **46** E3
Danvers, MA **41** B7
Danville, IL **91** E6
Danville, KY **69** D7
Danville, VA **81** F7
Daphne, AL **61** I1
D'Arbonne, Bayou (river), LA **71** B3
Dardanelle, AR **63** C3
Dardanelle, Lake, AR **63** C2
Darien, CT **33** F2
Darling, Lake, ND **107** B4
Darlington, SC **77** C7
Daufuskie Island, SC **77** H5
Dauphin Island, AL **61** I1
Davenport, IA **95** D9
David Berger National Memorial, OH **109** B6
David City, NE **105** C8
Davis Mountains, TX **126** F2
Davis, Mount, PA **49** F3
Dawson, GA **67** G2
Dayton, NV **147** D2
Dayton, OH **109** E2
Dayton, TN **79** C7
Dayton, WA **153** E9
Dayton Aviation Heritage N.H.P., OH **109** E2
Daytona Beach, FL **65** C8
Dayville, CT **33** B8
De Gray Lake, AR **63** E3
De Land, FL **65** C8
De Pere, WI **113** E7
De Queen, AR **63** E1
De Quincy, LA **70** F2
De Ridder, LA **70** E2
De Smet, SD **111** C9
De Soto, MO **103** D6
De Soto National Memorial, FL **65** E6
De Witt, AR **63** E6
De Witt, IA **95** D9
Dead (river), ME **37** E3
Deadwood, SD **110** C1
Deadwood Reservoir, ID **143** F2
Deale, MD **39** D8
Dearborn, MI **99** H7
Death Valley, CA **137** F6
Death Valley N.P., CA, NV **137** E6
Decatur, AL **61** B3
Decatur, IL **91** E4
Decatur, IN **93** C6
Decorah, IA **95** A8
Dededo, GU **156** F2
Deep (river), NC **75** C6
Deep Creek Lake, MD **38** A1
Deep Fork (river), OK **125** C9
Deep River, CT **33** D6
Deepwater Point, DE **35** E6
Deer Creek, OH **109** F4
Deer Creek, MS **73** E2
Deer Creek Lake, OH **109** F4
Deer Isle, ME **37** G5
Deer Lodge, MT **145** D4
Deerfield, MA **41** B3
Deerfield (river), MA **40** B2
Defiance, OH **109** B2
DeKalb, IL **91** B4
Del Rio, TX **127** G4
Delano, CA **137** F4
Delaware, OH **109** D4
Delaware (river), DE, NJ, PA **28** F4
Delaware and Raritan Canal, NJ **45** E3
Delaware Bay, DE, NJ **28** G4
Delaware City, DE **35** B5
Delaware Lake, OH **109** D4
Delaware Memorial Bridge, DE **35** B5
Delaware Water Gap N.R.A., NJ, PA **45** B2
Delaware, East Branch (river), NY **47** F7
Delaware, West Branch (river), NY **47** F7
Delmar, DE **35** I5
Delmarva Peninsula, DE, MD, VA **28** H4
Delphos, OH **109** C2
Delray Beach, FL **65** G9
Delta, CO **139** D2
Delta, UT **151** E3
Delta N.W.&S.R., AK **135** D7
Deltona, FL **65** D8
Deming, NM **123** H2
Demopolis, AL **61** E2
Denali (peak) *see* McKinley, Mount, AK **135** D6
Denali N.P. and Preserve, AK **135** D6
Denham Springs, LA **71** F6
Denison, IA **95** C3
Denison, TX **127** C7
Dennis, MA **41** E10
Denton, MD **39** C9
Denton, TX **127** C7
Denver, CO **139** C6
Derby, KS **97** E7
Derby Center, VT **53** A4
Derby Line, VT **53** A4
Dermott, AR **63** F6
Derry, NH **43** I4
Des Lacs (river), ND **107** B4
Des Moines, IA **95** D5
Des Moines (river), IA, MN **95** B4
Des Plaines (river), IL **91** B5
Desatoya Mountains, NV **147** D4
Deschutes (river), OR **149** B4
Deschutes N.W.&S.R., OR **149** D4
Desert National Wildlife Range, NV **147** F6
Desert Valley, NV **147** B3
Desolation Canyon, UT **151** D6
Detroit, MI **99** H8
Detroit (river), MI **99** H8
Detroit Lakes, MN **101** D2
Devils Lake (lake), ND **107** B7
Devils Lake, ND **107** B7
Devils Postpile Nat. Mon., CA **137** E5
Devils Tower Nat. Mon., WY **155** A9
Dewey Beach, DE **35** H7
Dexter, ME **37** E4
Dexter, MO **103** F7
Dickinson, ND **106** D2
Dickson, TN **79** B4
Dillingham, AK **135** F4
Dillon, MT **145** F4
Dillon, SC **77** C8
Dinosaur Nat. Mon., CO, UT **138** A1
Dirty Devil (river), UT **151** F5
Disappointment, Cape, WA **152** E1
Dismal (river), NE **105** C4
Dixon, IL **91** B3
Dixon Entrance (strait), AK **135** H10
Dodge City, KS **97** D3
Dodgeville, WI **113** G4
Dolan Springs, AZ **121** C2
Dolores, CO **138** E1
Donaldsonville, LA **71** G6
Donner Und Blitzen N.W.&S.R., OR **149** F7
Door Peninsula, WI **113** E7
Dothan, AL **61** G5
Double Trouble, NJ **45** F4
Douglas, AZ **121** H7
Douglas, GA **67** G5
Douglas, WY **155** E8
Douglas Lake, TN **79** B9
Dover, DE **35** E5
Dover, NH **43** H5
Dover, NJ **45** B3
Dover, OH **109** D6
Dover-Foxcroft, ME **37** E4
Dowagiac, MI **99** I5
Doylestown, PA **49** E10
Dracut, MA **41** A6
Drayton, ND **107** A9
Drift Prairie, ND **107** B7
Driskill Mountain, LA **71** B3
Drummond Island, MI **99** D7
Dry Cimarron (river), NM **123** A7
Dry Lake, ND **107** B7
Dry Tortugas N.P., FL **65** I6
Du Bay, Lake, WI **113** D5
Du Bois, PA **49** C4
Du Quoin, IL **91** H4
Dublin, GA **67** E5
Dublin, OH **109** E4
Dubuque, IA **95** C9
Duck (river), TN **79** C4
Dulce, NM **123** A3
Duluth, MN **101** D5
Dumas, AR **63** F6
Dumas, TX **127** A3
Dunbar, WV **83** F3
Duncan, OK **125** E8
Dundalk, MD **39** B8
Dunkirk, NY **46** E1
Dunmore, PA **49** B9
Dunmore, Lake, VT **53** E2
Dunn, NC **75** C7
Dupree, SD **111** B4
Durango, CO **139** G2
Durant, OK **125** F10
Durham, CT **33** D5
Durham, NC **75** B7
Durham, NH **43** H5
Dutch Harbor, AK **134** H2
Dworshak Reservoir, ID **143** C2
Dyersburg, TN **78** B1
Dyersville, IA **95** C9

E

Eagan, MN **101** F5
Eagar, AZ **121** E7
Eagle Creek, KY **69** B7
Eagle Creek N.W.&S.R., OR **149** C8
Eagle Lake, CA **137** B4
Eagle Lake, ME **37** B5
Eagle Lake, ME **37** C4
Eagle Lake, ME **37** A5
Eagle Mountain, MN **101** B7
Eagle Pass, TX **127** G4
Eagle River, WI **113** C5
Earle, AR **63** C7
Easley, SC **76** B2
East Brunswick, NJ **45** D4
East Chicago, IN **93** A2
East Derry, NH **43** I4
East Falmouth, MA **41** E9
East Fork Lake, OH **109** G2
East Grand Forks, MN **101** B1
East Greenwich, RI **51** D4
East Hampton, CT **33** C6
East Hartford, CT **33** B5
East Hartland, CT **33** A4
East Haven, CT **33** E4
East Lansing, MI **99** H6
East Liverpool, OH **109** C8
East Millinocket, ME **37** D5
East Mountain, VT **53** B5
East Okoboji Lake, IA **95** A3
East Point, GA **67** C2
East Providence, RI **51** B5
East Range, NV **147** B3
East Ridge, TN **79** D7
East River, CT **33** E5
East St. Louis, IL **91** G3
East Tavaputs Plateau, UT **151** D6
Eastern Bay, MD **39** C8
Easthampton, MA **40** C2
Eastman, GA **67** F4
Easton, MD **39** D9
Easton, PA **49** D9
Eastport, ME **37** F7
Eatonton, GA **67** D4
Eatontown, NJ **45** D5
Eau Claire, WI **113** D3
Ebey's Landing National Historical Reserve, WA **153** B3
Eden, NC **75** A6
Edenton, NC **75** B9
Edgartown, MA **41** F9
Edgefield, SC **77** D3
Edgemont, SD **110** E1
Edgewood, MD **39** B8
Edison, NJ **45** D4
Edison National Historic Site, NJ **45** C4
Edisto (river), SC **77** F6
Edisto Island, SC **77** G6
Edisto, North Fork (river), SC **77** E5
Edisto, South Fork (river), SC **77** E4
Edmond, OK **125** C8
Edward T. Breathitt Parkway, KY **68** D3
Edwards Plateau, TX **127** E5
Edwardsville, IL **91** G3
Eel (river), CA **137** B1
Eel (river), IN **93** B4
Eel (river), IN **93** F2
Eel N.W.&S.R., CA **137** B1
Effigy Mounds Nat. Mon., IA **95** A8
Effingham, IL **91** F5
Egan Range, NV **147** E6
Egg Harbor City, NJ **45** G3
Eisenhower National Historic Site, PA **49** F6
El Campo, TX **127** G7
El Centro, CA **137** I7
El Dorado, AR **63** G4
El Dorado, KS **97** D7
El Dorado Lake, KS **97** D7
El Malpais Nat. Mon., NM **123** D2
El Morro Nat. Mon., NM **123** D2
El Paso, TX **126** D1
El Reno, OK **125** C7
Elbert, Mount, CO **139** D4
Elberton, GA **67** C5
Eldon, MO **103** D4
Eldora, IA **95** C6
Eleanor Roosevelt National Historic Site, NY **47** F8
Elephant Butte Reservoir, NM **123** F3
Eleven Point (river), MO **103** F5
Eleven Point N.W.&S.R., MO **103** F6
Elgin, IL **91** B5
Elizabeth, NJ **45** C4
Elizabeth City, NC **75** A10
Elizabeth Islands, MA **41** F7
Elizabethton, TN **79** B11
Elizabethtown, KY **69** C6
Elizabethtown, PA **49** E7
Elk (river), KS **97** E8
Elk (river), WV **83** F5
Elk City, OK **125** C6
Elk City Lake, KS **97** E9
Elk N.W.&S.R., OR **148** F1
Elk Point, SD **111** F10
Elkhart, IN **93** A4
Elkhart, KS **96** F1
Elkhead Mountains, CO **139** A2
Elkhorn (river), NE **105** B7
Elkhorn Creek N.W.&S.R., OR **149** C3
Elkins, WV **83** E6
Elko, NV **147** B5
Elkton, MD **39** A9
Ellendale, DE **35** G6
Ellendale, ND **107** F8
Ellensburg, WA **153** D6
Ellicott City, MD **39** B7
Ellington, CT **33** A6
Ellis (river), NH **43** D4
Ellis Island, NY, NJ **47** H8
Ellisville, MS **73** G4
Ellsworth, KS **97** C5
Ellsworth, ME **37** F5
Elmira, NY **47** F4
Eloy, AZ **121** G5
Elsmere, DE **35** A5
Elwell, Lake, MT **145** B5
Elwood, IN **93** D4
Ely, MN **101** C6
Ely, NV **147** D6
Elyria, OH **109** B5
Embarras (river), IL **91** F5
Emmetsburg, IA **95** A4
Emmett, ID **143** G1
Emmonak, AK **134** D3
Emporia, KS **97** C8
Emporia, VA **81** E9
Emporium, PA **49** B5
Endicott, NY **47** F5
Endwell, NY **47** F6
Enfield, CT **33** A5
Enfield, NH **43** F2
England, AR **63** D5
Englewood, OH **109** E2
Enid, OK **125** B8
Enid Lake, MS **73** B3
Enosburg Falls, VT **53** A3
Enterprise, AL **61** G5
Enterprise, OR **149** B8
Ephraim, UT **151** E4
Ephrata, PA **49** E8
Ephrata, WA **153** D7
Equinox, Mount, VT **53** H2
Erie, PA **48** A2
Erie Canal, NY **46** D2
Erie, Lake, **86** E9
Erling, Lake, AR **63** G2
Erwin, TN **79** B10
Escalante (river), UT **151** G4
Escanaba, MI **99** D4
Escondido, CA **137** I6
Esmond, RI **51** B4
Espanola, NM **123** B4
Essex, CT **33** D6
Essex, MD **39** B8
Essex Junction, VT **53** C2
Estancia, NM **123** D4
Estes Park, CO **139** B5
Estherville, IA **95** A3
Etowah (river), GA **67** B1
Euclid, OH **109** A6
Eudora, AR **63** G6
Eufaula, AL **61** F6
Eufaula Lake, OK **125** D11
Eugene, OR **149** D2
Eugene O'Neill National Historic Site, CA **137** E2
Eunice, LA **71** F4
Eunice, NM **123** G8
Eureka, CA **137** B1
Eureka, KS **97** D8
Eureka, MT **144** A2
Eureka, NV **147** D5
Eureka, SD **111** A6
Eureka Springs, AR **63** A2
Evangeline, LA **71** F3
Evans, GA **67** D6
Evanston, IL **91** B6
Evanston, WY **154** G1
Evansville, IN **93** I1
Everett, WA **153** C4
Everglades N.P., FL **65** H9
Evergreen, AL **61** G3
Ewing, NJ **45** E3
Excelsior Mountains, NV **147** E3
Exeter, NH **43** H5
Exeter, RI **51** E4

F

Fabens, TX **126** E1
Fabius, Middle (river), MO **103** A4
Fabius, South (river), MO **103** B5
Fagaitua, AS **156** H2
Fagamalo, AS **156** I1
Fagatele Bay National Marine Sanctuary, AS **156** I1
Fagatogo, AS **156** I1
Fair Haven, VT **53** F1
Fairbanks, AK **135** D7
Fairborn, OH **109** E2
Fairbury, NE **105** E8
Fairfield, CT **33** E2
Fairfield, IA **95** E8
Fairfield, IL **91** G5
Fairfield, OH **109** F1
Fairfield, VT **53** B3
Fairfield Bay, AR **63** B4
Fairhaven, MA **41** E8
Fairhope, AL **61** I1
Fairmont, MN **101** H3
Fairmont, WV **83** C5
Fairmount, NY **47** D5
Fairview, KY **69** E4
Fairview, OK **125** B7
Fajardo, PR **157** H12
Falcon Reservoir, TX **127** H5
Faleasao, AS **156** I4
Falfurrias, TX **127** H6
Fall (river), KS **97** D8

Fall Line — Green River

Fall Line (escarpment), NJ, PA **28** G4
Fall River, MA **41** E7
Fallon, NV **147** D3
Falls City, NE **105** E10
Falls Creek, NV **147** A6
Falls Lake, NC **75** B7
Falmouth, MA **41** F8
Falmouth, ME **37** H3
Fargo, ND **107** D10
Faribault, MN **101** G4
Farmington, ME **37** F3
Farmington, MO **103** E7
Farmington, NH **43** G5
Farmington, NM **123** A2
Farmington, UT **151** B4
Farmington (river), CT **33** B4
Farmington N.W.&S.R., CT **33** A3
Farmington, East Branch (river), CT **33** A4
Farmington, West Branch (river), CT, MA **33** A3
Farmville, VA **81** D8
Farragut, TN **79** B8
Father Marquette National Memorial, MI **99** D6
Faulkton, SD **111** B7
Fayette, AL **61** C2
Fayetteville, AR **63** B1
Fayetteville, NC **75** C7
Fayetteville, TN **79** D5
Fayetteville, WV **83** G4
Fear, Cape, NC **75** E8
Feather, Middle Fork N.W.&S.R., CA **137** C3
Federal Way, WA **153** D4
Federalsburg, MD **39** D9
Felton, DE **35** F5
Fenwick Island, DE **35** I7
Fergus Falls, MN **101** D2
Ferguson, MO **103** C7
Fernandina Beach, FL **65** A8
Ferndale, WA **153** A3
Fernley, NV **147** C2
Ferriday, LA **71** D5
Festus, MO **103** D7
Fillmore, UT **151** E3
Findlay, OH **109** C3
Finger Lakes, NY **47** E4
Fire Island National Seashore, NY **47** H9
First Connecticut Lake, NH **43** A4
First Ladies National Historic Site, OH **109** C7
Fish (river), ME **37** B5
Fish Creek, WV **83** C4
Fishing Bay, MD **39** E9
Fitchburg, MA **41** B5
Fitzgerald, GA **67** G4
Flagstaff, AZ **121** C5
Flagstaff Lake, ME **37** E2
Flambeau (river), WI **113** C3
Flaming Gorge N.R.A., WY **155** G3
Flaming Gorge Reservoir, UT, WY **155** G3
Flandreau, SD **111** D10
Flat N.W.&S.R., MI **99** G5
Flat River Reservoir, RI **51** D3
Flathead (river), MT **144** C2
Flathead Lake, MT **144** B3
Flathead N.W.&S.R., MT **144** B3
Flathead, South Fork (river), MT **144** B3
Flatrock (river), IN **93** F4
Flattery, Cape, WA **152** B1
Flatwoods, KY **69** B10
Flemington, NJ **45** D2
Flint, MI **99** G7
Flint (river), GA **67** E2
Flint (river), MI **99** G7
Flint Hills, KS **97** E7
Flora, IL **91** G5
Florence, AL **61** A2
Florence, AZ **121** F5
Florence, CO **139** E5
Florence, KY **69** A7
Florence, OR **148** D1
Florence, SC **77** C8
Florida Bay, FL **65** H9
Florida Keys (islands), FL **65** I8
Florida Keys National Marine Sanctuary, FL **65** I7
Florida, Straits of, FL **65** I9
Florida's Turnpike, FL **65** E8
Florissant, MO **103** C7
Florissant Fossil Beds Nat. Mon., CO **139** D5
Floyd (river), IA **94** B2
Foley, AL **61** I2
Follansbee, WV **83** A5
Folsom, CA **137** D3
Fond du Lac, WI **113** F6
Fontana Lake, NC **74** C1
Fontenelle Reservoir, WY **154** F2
Ford (river), MI **99** C3
Fordyce, AR **63** F4
Forest, MS **73** E4
Forest Acres, SC **77** D5
Forest City, IA **95** A5
Forest City, NC **74** C3
Forest Grove, OR **149** B2
Forrest City, AR **63** D7
Forsyth, MT **145** D9
Fort Atkinson, WI **113** G6
Fort Benton, MT **145** B5
Fort Bowie National Historic Site, AZ **121** G7
Fort Bragg, CA **137** C1
Fort Caroline National Memorial, FL **65** B8
Fort Clatsop National Memorial, OR **148** A1
Fort Collins, CO **139** B5
Fort Davis National Historic Site, TX **126** E2
Fort Defiance, AZ **121** C7
Fort Dodge, IA **95** C4
Fort Donelson N.B., TN **78** A3
Fort Fairfield, ME **37** B6
Fort Foote Park, MD **39** D6
Fort Frederica Nat. Mon., GA **67** H7
Fort Gibson Lake, OK **125** C11
Fort Kent, ME **37** A5
Fort Knox (site), KY **69** C6
Fort Laramie National Historic Site, WY **155** F9
Fort Larned National Historic Site, KS **97** D4
Fort Lauderdale, FL **65** G9
Fort Lee, NJ **45** C5
Fort Loudoun Lake, TN **79** B8
Fort Madison, IA **95** F8
Fort Matanzas Nat. Mon., FL **65** B8
Fort McHenry Nat. Mon. and Historic Shrine, MD **39** B8
Fort Mill, SC **77** A5
Fort Morgan, CO **139** B7
Fort Myers, FL **65** F7
Fort Necessity N.B., PA **48** F2
Fort Payne, AL **61** B5
Fort Peck Dam, MT **145** B9
Fort Peck Lake, MT **145** B8
Fort Pickens, FL **64** B1
Fort Pierce, FL **65** E9
Fort Pierre, SD **111** D5
Fort Pulaski Nat. Mon., GA **67** F8
Fort Raleigh National Historic Site, NC **75** B10
Fort Scott, KS **97** D10
Fort Scott National Historic Site, KS **97** D10
Fort Smith, AR **63** C1
Fort Smith National Historic Site, AR **63** B1
Fort Stanwix Nat. Mon., NY **47** C6
Fort Stockton, TX **127** E3
Fort Sumner, NM **123** D7
Fort Sumter Nat. Mon., SC **77** G7
Fort Thompson, SD **111** D6
Fort Ticonderoga, NY **47** C9
Fort Union Nat. Mon., NM **123** B6
Fort Union Trading Post National Historic Site, MT, ND **145** B11
Fort Vancouver National Historic Site, WA **153** F3
Fort Walton Beach, FL **64** B2
Fort Washington Park, MD **39** D6
Fort Wayne, IN **93** B5
Fort Worth, TX **127** D7
Fort Yates, ND **107** F5
Fort Yukon, AK **135** C7
Fortymile N.W.&S.R., AK **135** D8
Fossil Butte Nat. Mon., WY **154** F2
Foster Center, RI **51** C2
Foster Creek, SD **111** C8
Fostoria, OH **109** B3
Fountain, CO **139** D6
Four Corners (site), AZ, CO, NM, UT **121** A7
Four Mountains, Islands of, AK **134** H1
Fox, IL, WI **91** B5
Framingham, MA **41** C6
Francis Case, Lake, SD **111** E7
Francis, Lake, NH **43** B4
Franconia, NH **43** D3
Frankford, DE **35** I7
Frankfort, IN **93** D3
Frankfort, KY **69** B7
Franklin, IN **93** F4
Franklin, KY **69** E5
Franklin, LA **71** G5
Franklin, MA **41** D6
Franklin, NC **74** C1
Franklin, NH **43** G3
Franklin, NJ **45** B3
Franklin, TN **79** B5
Franklin, VA **81** E10
Franklin Delano Roosevelt Lake, WA **153** B9
Frederica, DE **35** F5
Frederick, MD **39** B5
Frederick, OK **125** E6
Fredericksburg, VA **81** C9
Fredericksburg and Spotsylvania County Battlefields Memorial N.M.P., VA **81** C9
Fredericktown, MO **103** E7
Frederiksted, VI **157** I7
Fredonia, KS **97** E8
Fredonia, NY **46** E1
Freehold, NJ **45** E4
Freeman, SD **111** E9
Freeman, Lake, IN **93** C3
Freeport, IL **91** A3
Freeport, TX **127** G8
Freeport, NY **47** H9
Fremont, MI **99** G5
Fremont, NE **105** C9
Fremont, OH **109** B4
Fremont (river), UT **151** F5
French Broad (river), TN **79** B10
Frenchman (river), MT **145** A8
Frenchman Creek, CO, NE **105** E4
Frenchville, ME **37** A5
Fresno, CA **137** F4
Friendship Hill National Historic Site, PA **48** F2
Frio (river), TX **127** G6
Frissell, Mount, CT **33** A2
Front Range, CO,WY **130** D7
Front Royal, VA **81** B8
Frostburg, MD **38** A2
Fruitland, MD **39** E10
Fryeburg, ME **37** G2
Fullerton, NE **105** C7
Fulton, KY **68** E1
Fulton, MO **103** C5
Fulton, MS **73** B5
Fulton, NY **47** D5
Fundy, Bay of, **28** C9

G

Gabbs, NV **147** D3
Gabbs Valley, NV **147** D3
Gadsden, AL **61** C4
Gaffney, SC **77** A4
Gahanna, OH **109** E4
Gaillard, Lake, CT **33** D4
Gainesville, FL **65** C7
Gainesville, GA **67** B3
Gaithersburg, MD **39** C6
Galax, VA **81** F5
Galena, AK **135** C5
Galena, IL **91** A2
Galesburg, IL **91** C2
Galilee, RI **51** G4
Galion, OH **109** C4
Gallatin, MO **103** B3
Gallatin, TN **79** B5
Gallatin (river), MT **145** E5
Gallinas (river), NM **123** C6
Gallipolis, OH **109** G5
Gallo Arroyo (river), NM **123** E5
Gallup, NM **123** C1
Galveston, TX **127** F9
Galveston Bay, TX **116** F9
Gannett Peak, WY **155** D3
Gantt, SC **76** B2
Garapan, MP **156** C2
Garden City, KS **96** D2
Garden City, SC **77** E9
Garden Peninsula, MI **99** D4
Garden State Parkway, NJ **45** G4
Gardiner, ME **37** G3
Gardner, MA **41** B4
Gardner Lake, CT **33** C6
Gardner Pinnacles, HI **141** F3
Gardnerville, NV **147** D2
Gareloi Island, AK **135** H8
Garland, TX **127** D7
Garner, NC **75** B7
Garnett, KS **97** D9
Garrison, ND **107** C4
Gary, IN **93** A2
Gas City, IN **93** D4
Gasconade (river), MO **103** F4
Gaston, Lake, NC, VA **75** A8
Gastonia, NC **75** C4
Gates, NY **46** D3
Gates of the Arctic N.P. and Preserve, AK **135** B6
Gatesville, TX **127** E6
Gateway N.R.A., NJ, NY **45** D5
Gatlinburg, TN **79** C9
Gauley (river), WV **83** F4
Gauley River N.R.A., WV **83** F4
Gay Head (point), MA **41** F8
Gaylord, MI **99** E6
Genesee (river), NY **46** E3
Geneseo, IL **91** C3
Geneseo, NY **46** E3
Geneva, AL **61** H5
Geneva, NE **105** D8
Geneva, NY **47** D4
Geneva, OH **109** A7
George Rogers Clark N.H.P., IN **93** G1
George Washington Birthplace Nat. Mon., VA **81** C10
George Washington Carver Nat. Mon., MO **103** F2
George, Lake, FL **65** C7
George, Lake, NY **47** C8
Georgetown, DE **35** H6
Georgetown, KY **69** C8
Georgetown, OH **109** G3
Georgetown, SC **77** E9
Georgetown, TX **127** F6
Georgia, Strait of, WA **152** A2
Gering, NE **104** B1
Germantown, MD **39** C6
Germantown, TN **78** D1
Gettysburg, PA **49** F6
Gettysburg, SD **111** B6
Gettysburg N.M.P., PA **49** F6
Gibbon, NE **105** D6
Gila (river), AZ **121** F7
Gila Bend, AZ **121** F4
Gila Cliff Dwellings Nat. Mon., NM **123** F2
Gilford Park, NJ **45** F5
Gillette, WY **155** B8
Glacier Bay N.P. and Preserve, AK **135** F9
Glacier N.P., MT **144** A3
Gladstone, MI **99** D4
Glasgow, DE **35** B4
Glasgow, KY **69** E6
Glasgow, MT **145** B9
Glassboro, NJ **45** G2
Glastonbury, CT **33** B5
Glen Burnie, MD **39** C7
Glen Canyon Dam, AZ **121** A5
Glen Canyon N.R.A., AZ, UT **151** G5
Glen Ullin, ND **107** E4
Glendale, AZ **121** F4
Glendale, RI **51** A3
Glendive, MT **145** C10
Glendo Reservoir, WY **155** E9
Glenns Ferry, ID **143** H2
Glenrock, WY **155** D8
Glens Falls, NY **47** D8
Glenwood, IA **94** E2
Glenwood Springs, CO **139** C3
Globe, AZ **121** F6
Gloucester, MA **41** B8
Gloversville, NY **47** D8
Gold Beach, OR **148** F1
Golden Beach, MD **39** E7
Golden Gate N.R.A., CA **137** E1
Golden Spike National Historic Site, UT **151** A3
Goldendale, WA **153** F5
Goldfield, NV **147** F4
Goldsboro, NC **75** C8
Gonzales, LA **71** G6
Gooding, ID **143** H3
Goodland, KS **96** B1
Goodlettsville, TN **79** B5
Goose (river), ND **107** C9
Goose Creek, ID **143** I3
Goose Creek, SC **77** F7
Goose Lake, CA, OR **137** A4
Goose Point, DE **35** D6
Gordon, NE **105** A3
Gordon Creek, NE **105** B4
Gore Range, CO **139** B4
Gorham, NH **43** D4
Goshen, IN **93** A4
Goshute Mountains, NV **147** C7
Gothenburg, NE **105** D5
Gouverneur, NY **47** B6
Grafton, ND **107** B9
Grafton, WV **83** D6
Graham Lake, ME **37** F5
Grambling, LA **71** B3
Granby, CT **33** A4
Grand (river), MI **99** G6
Grand (river), MO **103** A2
Grand (river), OH **109** A7
Grand (river), SD **111** A3
Grand Canyon, AZ **121** B4
Grand Canyon (canyon), AZ **121** B3
Grand Canyon N.P., AZ **121** B3
Grand Canyon-Parashant Nat. Mon., AZ **121** B3
Grand Coulee (valley), WA **153** C7
Grand Coulee Dam, WA **153** C8
Grand Detour, IL **91** B4
Grand Forks, ND **107** C10
Grand Haven, MI **99** G4
Grand Island, NE **105** D7
Grand Island N.R.A., MI **99** C4
Grand Isle, LA **71** I8
Grand Isle, VT **53** B1
Grand Junction, CO **138** D1
Grand Lake, LA **71** G3
Grand Lake, ME **37** D6
Grand Lake (St. Marys Lake), OH **109** D2
Grand Manan Channel, ME **37** F7
Grand Marais, MN **101** C7
Grand Mesa, CO **139** D2
Grand Portage Nat. Mon., MN **101** B8
Grand Rapids, MI **99** G5
Grand Rapids, MN **101** C4
Grand Staircase-Escalante Nat. Mon., UT **151** G4
Grand Teton N.P., WY **154** C2
Grand Traverse Bay, MI **99** D5
Grand Valley, CO **138** D1
Grand Wash Cliffs, AZ **121** B2
Grand, South (river), MO **103** D2
Grand, South Fork (river), SD **110** A2
Grande Ronde (river), OR **149** A8
Grande Ronde N.W.&S.R., OR **149** A8
Grandfather Mountain, NC **74** B3
Grandview, WA **153** E7
Grangeville, ID **143** D1
Granite City, IL **91** G3
Granite Peak, MT **145** E6
Graniteville, VT **53** D4
Grant, NE **105** D3
Grant Range, NV **147** E6
Grant-Kohrs Ranch National Historic Site, MT **145** D4
Grants, NM **123** D2
Grants Pass, OR **149** F2
Grantsville, UT **151** C3
Grasonville, MD **39** C8
Grasshopper Glacier (site), MT **145** F6
Grays Harbor, WA **152** D1
Grays Lake, ID **143** H6
Gray's Reef National Marine Sanctuary, GA **67** G8
Great Barrington, MA **40** C1
Great Basin, NV **147** B5
Great Basin N.P., NV **147** D7
Great Bay, NH **43** H5
Great Bay, NJ **45** G4
Great Bend, KS **97** C5
Great Dismal Swamp, NC, VA **56** B8
Great Divide Basin, WY **155** F5
Great Egg Harbor (river), NJ **45** G3
Great Egg Harbor N.W.&S.R., NJ **45** G3
Great Falls, MT **145** C5
Great Miami (river), OH **109** D2
Great Pee Dee (river), NC, SC **56** C6
Great Plains, **86** A1
Great Plains Reservoirs, CO **139** E8
Great Pond, ME **37** F3
Great Quittacus Pond, MA **41** E8
Great Sacandaga Lake, NY **47** D8
Great Salt Lake, UT **151** B3
Great Salt Lake Desert, UT **151** D2
Great Salt Plains Lake, OK **125** B7
Great Sand Dunes Nat. Mon. and Preserve, CO **139** F5
Great Smoky Mountains, NC, TN **74** C1
Great Smoky Mountains N.P., NC, TN **74** B1
Great Swamp, RI **51** F3
Greece, NY **46** D3
Greeley, CO **139** B6
Green (river), CO, UT, WY **130** F6
Green Bay, WI **113** E7
Green Bay (bay), WI **113** D7
Green Mountains, VT **53** H2
Green River, UT **151** E6

Green River — Jamestown

Green River, WY **155** G3
Green River Lake, KY **69** D7
Green Swamp, NC **75** E7
Green Valley, AZ **121** H6
Greenbelt Park, MD **39** C7
Greenbrier, AR **63** C4
Greenbrier (river), WV **83** G5
Greencastle, IN **93** E2
Greeneville, TN **79** B10
Greenfield, IN **93** E4
Greenfield, MA **41** B3
Greenfield, OH **109** F3
Greensboro, NC **75** B6
Greensburg, IN **93** F5
Greensburg, KS **97** E4
Greensburg, PA **49** E3
Greenville, AL **61** F3
Greenville, DE **35** A5
Greenville, ME **37** E4
Greenville, MS **73** D1
Greenville, NC **75** C8
Greenville, NH **43** I3
Greenville, OH **109** D1
Greenville, PA **48** B1
Greenville, RI **51** B3
Greenville, SC **76** B2
Greenville, MI **99** G5
Greenway (site), VA **81** D10
Greenwich, CT **33** F1
Greenwood, AR **63** C1
Greenwood, DE **35** G5
Greenwood, IN **93** E4
Greenwood, MS **73** C3
Greenwood, SC **77** C3
Greer, SC **77** B3
Greers Ferry Lake, AR **63** C4
Greeson, Lake, AR **63** E2
Gregory, SD **111** E6
Grenada, MS **73** C3
Grenada Lake, MS **73** C3
Gresham, OR **149** B3
Greybull, WY **155** B5
Greybull (river), WY **155** B4
Greylock, Mount, MA **40** A1
Greys (river), WY **154** D2
Griffin, GA **67** D3
Grinnell, IA **95** D6
Gros Ventre (river), WY **154** C2
Groton, SD **111** B8
Groton, CT **33** D7
Grove, OK **125** B12
Grove City, PA **48** C2
Groveton, NH **43** C3
Guadalupe (river), TX **127** F7
Guadalupe Mountains, NM **123** G6
Guadalupe Mountains N.P., TX **126** E1
Guadalupe Peak, TX **126** E2
Guam (territory), US **156** E1
Guayama, PR **157** I11
Guernsey, WY **155** E9
Guilford, CT **33** E5
Guilford, ME **37** E4
Guilford Courthouse N.M.P., NC **75** B6
Gulf Islands National Seashore, FL, MS **64** B1
Gulf of the Farallones National Marine Sanctuary, CA **137** E2
Gulf Shores, AL **61** I2
Gulfport, MS **73** I4
Gulkana N.W.&S.R., AK **135** D7
Gunnison, CO **139** E3
Guntersville, AL **61** B4
Guntersville Lake, AL **61** B4
Gurdon, AR **63** F3
Guthrie, OK **125** C8
Guyandotte (river), WV **82** G2
Guymon, OK **124** A3

H

H.E. Bailey Turnpike, OK **125** D7
Hackensack, NJ **45** B5
Hackettstown, NJ **45** C3
Haddam, CT **33** D5
Haddonfield, NJ **45** F2
Hagåtña (Agana), GU **156** F1
Hagerman, NM **123** F6
Hagerman Fossil Beds Nat. Mon., ID **143** H2
Hagerstown, MD **39** A5
Hailey, ID **143** G3
Haines, AK **135** F9
Haines City, FL **65** E7
Hal Rogers Parkway, KY **69** D8
Haleakala N.P., HI **141** D8
Hallock, MN **101** A1
Halls Creek, UT **151** G5
Hamburg, AR **63** G5
Hamburg, NY **46** E2
Hamden, CT **33** D4
Hamilton, AL **61** B1
Hamilton, MT **144** D2
Hamilton, OH **109** F1
Hamilton, RI **51** E4
Hammonasset (river), CT **33** D5
Hammond, IN **93** A1
Hammond, LA **71** F7
Hammonton, NJ **45** G3
Hampton, IA **95** B6
Hampton, NH **43** H5
Hampton, SC **77** F5
Hampton, VA **81** E11
Hampton National Historic Site, MD **39** B7
Hams Fork (river), WY **154** F2
Hanahan, SC **77** F7
Hanama'ulu, HI **140** A2
Hancock, MD **39** A4
Hanford, CA **137** F4
Hanford Reach Nat. Mon., WA **153** E7
Hankinson, ND **107** F10
Hanna, WY **155** F7
Hannibal, MO **103** B5
Hanover, NH **43** F2
Hanover, PA **49** F7
Harbeson, DE **35** H6
Harbor Beach, MI **99** F8
Hardin, MT **145** E8
Harding, Lake, GA **67** E1
Hardinsburg, KY **69** C5
Hardwick, VT **53** C4
Harlan, IA **95** D3
Harlan County Lake, NE **105** E6
Harlingen, TX **127** I7
Harlowton, MT **145** D6
Harmony, RI **51** B3
Harney Basin, OR **149** E6
Harney Lake, OR **149** E6
Harney Peak, SD **110** D2
Harpers Ferry N.H.P., WV **83** D10
Harriman, TN **79** B8
Harriman Reservoir, VT **53** I2
Harrington, DE **35** F5
Harris, RI **51** C4
Harrisburg, IL **91** H5
Harrisburg, PA **49** E7
Harrison, AR **63** A3
Harrison, TN **79** D7
Harrisonburg, VA **81** C7
Harrisonville, MO **103** D2
Harrisville, RI **51** A3
Harrodsburg, KY **69** C7
Harry S. Truman National Historic Site, MO **103** C2
Harry S. Truman Reservoir, MO **103** D3
Hart Mountain National Antelope Refuge, OR **149** F6
Hartford, CT **33** B5
Hartford City, IN **93** D5
Hartington, NE **105** A8
Hartland, ME **37** F4
Hartland, VT **53** F4
Hartselle, AL **61** B3
Hartsville, SC **77** C7
Hartwell, GA **67** B4
Hartwell Lake, GA, SC **76** C1
Harvard, IL **91** A4
Harvey, ND **107** C6
Harwinton, CT **33** B3
Hastings, MI **99** H5
Hastings, NE **105** D7
Hatchie (river), TN **78** C2
Hatteras Island, NC **75** B11
Hatteras, Cape, NC **75** C11
Hattiesburg, MS **73** G4
Hau'ula, HI **141** B4
Havasu, Lake, AZ, CA **121** D2
Havelock, NC **75** D9
Haverhill, MA **41** A7
Haverhill, NH **43** E2
Haverhill-Bath Bridge, NH **43** D2
Havre, MT **145** B6
Havre de Grace, MD **39** A9
Haw (river), NC **75** B6
Hawai'i (island), HI **141** E9
Hawai'i Volcanoes N.P., HI **141** F9
Hawaiian Islands Humpback Whale National Marine Sanctuary, HI **141** D5
Hawkeye Point (peak), IA **94** A2
Hawthorne, NV **147** E3
Hayden, ID **143** B1
Hays, KS **97** C4
Hayward, CA **137** E2
Hayward, WI **113** B3
Hazard, KY **69** D10
Hazardville, CT **33** A5
Hazen, ND **107** D4
Hazlehurst, GA **67** G5
Hazlehurst, MS **73** F2
Hazleton, PA **49** C8
Heart (river), ND **107** E4
Heavener, OK **125** D12
Heber City, UT **151** C4
Heber Springs, AR **63** C5
Hebron, NE **105** E8
Helena, AR **63** D7
Helena, MT **145** D4
Hells Canyon, ID **143** E1
Hells Canyon N.R.A., ID, OR **149** A9
Helper, UT **151** D5
Henderson, KY **68** C3
Henderson, NC **75** B7
Henderson, NV **147** H6
Henderson, TN **78** C2
Henderson, TX **127** D8
Hendersonville, NC **74** C2
Hendersonville, TN **79** B5
Henlopen, Cape, DE **35** G7
Hennepin Canal, IL **91** C3
Henniker, NH **43** H3
Henry Mountains, UT **151** G5
Henryetta, OK **125** C10
Henrys Lake, ID **143** F6
Heppner, OR **149** B6
Herbert Hoover National Historic Site, IA **95** D8
Hereford, CO **139** A6
Hereford, TX **127** B3
Hermann, MO **103** C5
Hermiston, OR **149** A6
Hershey, PA **49** E7
Hesperia, CA **137** H6
Hesston, KS **97** D6
Hettinger, ND **107** F3
Hialeah, FL **65** G9
Hiawatha, KS **97** A9
Hibbing, MN **101** C5
Hickory, NC **75** B4
High Bridge, NJ **45** C2
High Desert, OR **149** E5
High Plains, **130** D7
High Point, NC **75** B5
High Point (peak), NJ **45** A3
Highland Lake, NH **43** H2
Highland Lakes, NJ **45** A4
Highmore, SD **111** C6
Hightstown, NJ **45** E3
Hill Country (region), TX **127** H5
Hill Creek, UT **151** D6
Hillsboro, KS **97** D7
Hillsboro, ND **107** D10
Hillsboro, NH **43** H2
Hillsboro, OH **109** F3
Hillsboro, OR **149** B2
Hillsdale, MI **99** I6
Hillsdale Lake, KS **97** C10
Hilo, HI **141** F9
Hilton Head Island (island), SC **77** H6
Hilton Head Island, SC **77** H6
Hinesville, GA **67** G7
Hinsdale, NH **43** I1
Hinton, WV **83** G4
Hiwassee (river), TN **79** D8
Hiwassee Lake, NC **74** C1
Hobart, OK **125** D6
Hobbs, NM **123** G8
Hockanum (river), CT **33** B5
Hockessin, DE **35** A4
Hocking (river), OH **109** F6
Hoisington, KS **97** C5
Holbrook, AZ **121** D6
Holdenville, OK **125** D10
Holdrege, NE **105** D6
Holland, MI **99** H5
Hollandale, MS **73** D2
Hollidaysburg, PA **49** D4
Hollis, OK **125** E5
Holly Springs, MS **73** A4
Hollywood, FL **65** G9
Holston (river), TN, VA **79** A10
Holston, North Fork (river), VA **80** F3
Holston, South Fork (river), VA **80** F3
Holt Creek, NE **105** B6
Holton, KS **97** B9
Holualoa, HI **141** F8
Holyoke, CO **139** A9
Holyoke, MA **41** C3
Home of Franklin D. Roosevelt National Historic Site, NY **47** F8
Homer, AK **135** F6
Homer, LA **71** A3
Homestead, FL **65** H9
Homestead Nat. Mon. of America, NE **105** E8
Homewood, AL **61** D3
Homochitto (river), MS **73** G1
Homosassa Springs, FL **65** D6
Hondo, Rio (river), NM **123** F6
Honey Lake, CA **137** B4
Honolulu, HI **141** C4
Hood River, OR **149** B4
Hood, Mount, OR **149** B4
Hooper Bay, AK **134** E3
Hoopeston, IL **91** D6
Hoosic (river), MA **40** A1
Hoover, AL **61** D3
Hoover Dam, AZ, NV **121** B1
Hopatcong, NJ **45** B3
Hopatcong, Lake, NJ **45** B3
Hope, AR **63** F2
Hope, RI **51** C3
Hope Mills, NC **75** C7
Hope Valley, RI **51** E2
Hopewell, VA **81** D10
Hopewell Culture N.H.P., OH **109** F4
Hopewell Furnace National Historic Site, PA **49** E8
Hopkinsville, KY **68** E3
Hoquiam, WA **152** D2
Horn Lake, MS **73** A3
Hornell, NY **46** E3
Horse Creek, WY **155** G9
Horsehead Lake, ND **107** D6
Horseheads, NY **47** F4
Horsepasture N.W.&S.R., NC **74** C2
Horseshoe Bend, AR **63** A5
Horseshoe Bend N.M.P., AL **61** D5
Hot Creek Range, NV **147** E5
Hot Springs, AR **63** E3
Hot Springs, SD **110** E2
Hot Springs N.P., AR **63** D3
Houghton, MI **99** B2
Houghton Lake (lake), MI **99** F6
Houghton Lake, MI **99** F6
Houlton, ME **37** C6
Houma, LA **71** H7
Housatonic (river), CT, MA **33** D3
Houston, DE **35** F5
Houston, MS **73** C4
Houston, TX **127** F8
Hovenweep Nat. Mon., CO **138** F1
Howard, SD **111** D9
Howland, ME **37** E5
Howland Island (territory), US **156** F3
Hubbard Lake, MI **99** E7
Hubbell Trading Post National Historic Site, AZ **121** C7
Huber Heights, OH **109** E2
Hudson (river), NJ, NY **47** C8
Hudson, NY **47** E8
Hudson, WI **113** D1
Hudson, Lake, OK **125** B11
Huerfano (river), CO **139** F5
Hueytown, AL **61** D3
Hugh Butler Lake, NE **105** D4
Hugo, OK **125** E11
Hugo Lake, OK **125** E11
Hugoton, KS **96** E2
Humacao, PR **157** I11
Humboldt, IA **95** B4
Humboldt, TN **78** B2
Humboldt (river), NV **147** B3
Humboldt Lake, NV **147** C3
Humboldt, North Fork (river), NV **147** A5
Humphreys Peak, AZ **121** C5
Huntingburg, IN **93** H2
Huntingdon, PA **49** D5
Huntington, IN **93** C5
Huntington, WV **82** F1
Huntington, NY **47** H9
Huntington Lake, IN **93** C5
Huntsville, AL **61** A4
Huntsville, TX **127** E8
Hurley, WI **113** B4
Hurlock, MD **39** D9
Huron, SD **111** D8
Huron, Lake, **86** C8
Hurricane, UT **151** H2
Hurricane, WV **82** F2
Hurricane Creek N.W.&S.R., AR **63** B3
Hutchinson, KS **97** D6
Hutchinson, MN **101** F3
Hyannis, MA **41** E9
Hyattsville, MD **39** C7

I

Idabel, OK **125** F12
Idaho Falls, ID **143** G5
Iditarod National Historic Trail, AK **135** E5
Iliamna Lake, AK **135** F5
Ili'ili, AS **156** I1
Ilion, NY **47** D7
Illinois (river), IL **91** E2
Illinois (river), OK **125** B12
Illinois (river), OR **148** G1
Illinois N.W.&S.R., OR **148** F1
Immokalee, FL **65** G8
Imnaha N.W.&S.R., OR **149** B9
Imperial, NE **105** D3
Imperial Valley, CA **137** I7
Independence, IA **95** C8
Independence, KS **97** E9
Independence, MO **103** C2
Independence Mountains, NV **147** B5
Indian (river), FL **65** E9
Indian Head, MD **39** D6
Indian Lake, OH **109** D3
Indian N.W.&S.R., MI **99** C4
Indian Nation Turnpike, OK **125** D10
Indian River Bay, DE **35** I7
Indian River Inlet, DE **35** H8
Indian Springs, NV **147** G6
Indiana, PA **49** D3
Indiana Dunes National Lakeshore, IN **93** A2
Indianapolis, IN **93** E4
Indianola, IA **95** E5
Indianola, MS **73** D2
International Falls, MN **101** B4
Intracoastal Waterway, AL, FL, LA, NC, SC **61** I2
Iola, KS **97** D9
Ionia, MI **99** G6
Iowa (river), IA **95** B5
Iowa City, IA **95** D8
Iowa Falls, IA **95** C6
Ipswich, MA **41** A8
Ipswich, SD **111** B7
Irmo, SC **77** D5
Iron Mountain, MI **99** D3
Irondequoit, NY **46** D4
Ironton, OH **109** H5
Ironwood, MI **99** C1
Ironwood Forest Nat. Mon., AZ **121** G5
Iroquois (river), IL, IN **91** C5
Irving, TX **127** D7
Irvington, NJ **45** C4
Ishpeming, MI **99** C3
Island Falls, ME **37** C5
Island Park, RI **51** D6
Island Park Reservoir, ID **143** F6
Island Pond, VT **53** B5
Isle au Haut, ME **37** G5
Isle Royale, MI **99** A2
Isle Royale N.P., MI **99** A2
Isles of Shoals, ME, NH **37** I2
Itasca, Lake, MN **101** C3
Ithaca, NY **47** E5
Iuka, MS **73** A6
Ivishak N.W.&S.R., AK **135** B7

J

J. Percy Priest Lake, TN **79** B5
J. Strom Thurmond Reservoir, GA, SC **67** C5
Jack Lee, Lake, AR **63** G4
Jackman, ME **37** D3
Jackpot, NV **147** A6
Jacks Fork (river), MO **103** F5
Jackson, AL **61** G2
Jackson, KY **69** D9
Jackson, MI **99** H6
Jackson, MO **103** E7
Jackson, MS **73** F3
Jackson, OH **109** G5
Jackson, TN **78** C2
Jackson, WY **154** C2
Jackson Lake, WY **154** C2
Jacksonville, AL **61** C5
Jacksonville, AR **63** D5
Jacksonville, FL **65** B7
Jacksonville, IL **91** E3
Jacksonville, NC **75** D8
Jacksonville Beach, FL **65** B8
Jaffrey, NH **43** I2
James (river), ND, SD **86** C3
James (river), VA **81** D8
James A. Garfield National Historic Site, OH **109** A7
Jamestown, ND **107** D8

Jamestown — Little Deschutes N.W.&S.R.

Jamestown, NY **46** F2
Jamestown, RI **51** E5
Jamestown, VA **81** D10
Jamestown Reservoir, ND **107** D8
Janesville, WI **113** H6
Jarbidge (river), ID **143** I2
Jarvis Island (territory), US **157** G5
Jasper, AL **61** C2
Jasper, IN **93** H2
Jay Peak, VT **53** A3
Jeanerette, LA **71** G5
Jeannette, PA **48** E2
Jefferson, IA **95** D4
Jefferson (river), MT **145** E4
Jefferson City, MO **103** D5
Jefferson City, TN **79** B9
Jeffersontown, KY **69** B6
Jeffersonville, IN **93** H4
Jekyll Island, GA **67** H7
Jemez, E. Fork N.W.&S.R., NM **123** C4
Jenks, OK **125** B10
Jennings, LA **71** G3
Jericho, VT **53** C2
Jerimoth Hill (peak), RI **51** B2
Jerome, ID **143** H3
Jersey City, NJ **45** C5
Jersey Shore, PA **49** C6
Jerseyville, IL **91** F2
Jerusalem, RI **51** G4
Jesse James Farm and Museum, MO **103** B2
Jesup, GA **67** G6
Jewel Cave Nat. Mon., SD **110** E1
Jewett City, CT **33** C8
Jimmy Carter National Historic Site, GA **67** F2
John D. Rockefeller, Jr. Memorial Parkway, WY **154** B2
John Day, OR **149** C6
John Day (river), OR **149** C5
John Day Fossil Beds Nat. Mon., OR **149** C5
John Day N.W.&S.R., OR **149** B5
John Day, North Fork N.W.&S.R., OR **149** C7
John Day, South Fork N.W.&S.R., OR **149** D6
John F. Kennedy Space Center (site), FL **65** D9
John H. Kerr Reservoir, NC, VA **81** E8
John Martin Reservoir, CO **139** E8
John Muir Nat. Mon., CA **137** D2
John N.W.&S.R., AK **135** B6
John Redmond Reservoir, KS **97** D9
Johnson, VT **53** B3
Johnson City, TN **79** B10
Johnston, RI **51** B4
Johnston Atoll (territory), US **156** E4
Johnstown, PA **49** E3
Johnstown Flood National Memorial, PA **49** D4
Joliet, IL **91** C5
Jonesboro, AR **63** B7
Jonesboro, LA **71** C3
Jonesport, ME **37** F6
Joplin, MO **103** F2
Jordan, MT **145** C9
Jordan Creek, ID **143** H1
Joseph Creek N.W.&S.R., OR **149** A8
Joshua Tree N.P., CA **137** H7
Juan de Fuca, Strait of, WA **152** B1
Julia Butler Hansen Refuge, WA **152** E2
Julian M. Carroll Parkway, KY **68** E1
Jump (river), WI **113** C3
Junction City, KS **97** B7
Junction City, OR **149** D2
Juneau, AK **135** F10
Juniata (river), PA **49** D6
Jupiter, FL **65** F9

K
Ka'ena Point, HI **141** B4
Kadoka, SD **111** D4
Kaho'olawe (island), HI **141** D7
Kahuku Point, HI **141** B4
Kahului, HI **141** C7
Kaibab Plateau, AZ **121** B4
Kailua, HI **141** B5
Kailua, HI **141** F8
Kaiwi Channel, HI **141** C5
Kalae (South Point), HI **141** G8
Kalaheo, HI **140** A2
Kalamazoo, MI **99** H5
Kalamazoo (river), MI **99** H5
Kalaoa, HI **141** F8
Kalaupapa, HI **141** C6
Kalaupapa N.H.P., HI **141** C6
Kalispell, MT **144** B2
Kalkaska, MI **99** E5
Kaloko-Honokohau N.H.P., HI **141** F8
Kamiah, ID **143** D2
Kamuela *see* Waimea, HI **141** E8
Kanab, UT **151** H3
Kanab Creek, AZ, UT **121** B4
Kanawha (river), WV **83** F3
Kane'ohe, HI **141** B5
Kankakee, IL **91** C5
Kankakee (river), IL, IN **91** C5
Kannapolis, NC **75** C5
Kanopolis Lake, KS **97** C6
Kansas (river), KS **97** B9
Kansas City, KS **97** B10
Kansas City, MO **103** C2
Kapa'a, HI **140** A2
Kapa'au, HI **141** E8
Kaskaskia (river), IL **91** F4
Kaskaskia Island, IL **91** H3
Katahdin, Mount, ME **37** D5
Katmai N.P. and Preserve, AK **135** F5
Kaua'i (island), HI **140** A2
Kaukauna, WI **113** E6
Kaulakahi Channel, HI **140** A1
Kaunakakai, HI **141** C6
Kaw Lake, OK **125** A9
Kawich Range, NV **147** E5
Kayenta, AZ **121** B6
Keahole Point, HI **141** F8
Keansburg, NJ **45** D4
Kearney, NE **105** D6
Keene, NH **43** H2
Kekaha, HI **140** A1
Kelleys Island, OH **109** B5
Kellogg, ID **143** C1
Kelso, WA **153** F3
Kemmerer, WY **154** F2
Kenai, AK **135** E6
Kenai Fjords N.P., AK **135** F6
Kenai Peninsula, AK **135** E6
Kendall, FL **65** H9
Kendall Park, NJ **45** D3
Kendallville, IN **93** B5
Kenmare, ND **107** A3
Kennebec, SD **111** D6
Kennebec (river), ME **37** G3
Kennebunk, ME **37** I2
Kenner, LA **71** G7
Kennesaw Mountain National Battlefield Park, GA **67** C2
Kennett, MO **103** G7
Kennett Square, PA **49** F9
Kennewick, WA **153** F7
Kenosha, WI **113** H7
Kenova, WV **82** F1
Kent, CT **33** B2
Kent, OH **109** B7
Kent Island, MD **39** C8
Kenton, OH **109** C3
Kentucky (river), KY **69** B7
Kentucky Lake, KY **68** E2
Kentucky, Middle Fork (river), KY **69** D9
Kentucky, North Fork (river), KY **69** C9
Kentucky, South Fork (river), KY **69** D9
Kentwood, MI **99** G5
Keokuk, IA **95** F8
Keowee, Lake, SC **76** B2
Kern N.W.&S.R., CA **137** G5
Kernersville, NC **75** B5
Kerrville, TX **127** F5
Ketchikan, AK **135** G11
Ketchum, ID **143** G3
Kettering, OH **109** E2
Kettle River Range, WA **153** B8
Keuka Lake, NY **47** E4
Kewanee, IL **91** C3
Keweenaw N.H.P., MI **99** B2
Keweenaw Peninsula, MI **99** B3
Key Largo, FL **65** H9
Key West, FL **65** I7
Keya Paha (river), NE, SD **105** A5
Keyhole Reservoir, WY **155** B9
Keyser, WV **83** C8
Keystone Lake, OK **125** B10
Kiamichi (river), OK **125** E11
Kickapoo (river), WI **113** G3
Kihei, HI **141** D7
Kilauea Crater (site), HI **141** F9
Killeen, TX **127** E6
Killik (river), AK **135** B6
Killington Peak, VT **53** F3
Kimball, NE **104** C1
Kinderhook, NY **47** E8
Kingfield, ME **37** F3
Kingfisher, OK **125** C8
Kingman, AZ **121** D2
Kingman, KS **97** E6
Kingman Reef (territory), US **157** F5
Kings (river), NV **147** A3
Kings Canyon N.P., CA **137** E5
Kings Mountain, NC **75** C4
Kings Mountain N.M.P., SC **77** A4
Kings N.W.&S.R., CA **137** F5
Kings Peak, UT **151** B5
Kingsland, GA **67** H7
Kingsport, TN **79** A10
Kingston, NH **43** H5
Kingston, NY **47** F8
Kingston, PA **49** C8
Kingston, RI **51** F4
Kingstree, SC **77** E7
Kingsville, TX **127** H6
Kingwood, WV **83** C6
Kinsley, KS **97** D4
Kinston, NC **75** C8
Kiowa, CO **139** C6
Kirkland, WA **153** C4
Kirksville, MO **103** A4
Kirkwood, MO **103** D7
Kirwin Reservoir, KS **97** A4
Kiska Island, AK **135** H7
Kissimmee, FL **65** D8
Kissimmee (river), FL **65** E8
Kitt Peak National Observatory, AZ **121** H5
Kittanning, PA **49** D3
Kittatinny Mountains, NJ **45** B2
Kittery, ME **37** I2
Kitts Hummock, DE **35** E6
Kitty Hawk, NC **75** B10
Klamath (river), CA, OR **130** D2
Klamath Falls, OR **149** G3
Klamath N.W.&S.R., CA, OR **137** A1
Klickitat (river), WA **153** F5
Klickitat N.W.&S.R., WA **153** F5
Klondike Gold Rush N.H.P., AK **135** E9
Knife (river), ND **107** D3
Knife River Indian Villages National Historic Site, ND **107** D4
Knoxville, IA **95** E6
Knoxville, TN **79** B8
Kobuk N.W.&S.R., AK **135** C5
Kobuk Valley N.P., AK **135** B5
Kodiak, AK **135** G6
Kodiak Island, AK **135** G6
Kokomo, IN **93** D4
Koocanusa, Lake, MT **144** A2
Kootenai (river), ID, MT **143** A1
Kosciusko, MS **73** D4
Kotzebue, AK **135** B4
Koyukuk (river), AK **135** C5
Koyukuk, North Fork N.W.&S.R., AK **135** B6
Kumukahi, Cape, HI **141** F10
Kure Atoll, HI **140** E1
Kuskokwim (river), AK **135** C6
Kuskokwim Mountains, AK **135** E4
Kuskokwim, North Fork (river), AK **135** D5

L
L'Anse, MI **99** C2
La Crescent, MN **101** H6
La Crosse, WI **113** F3
La Follette, TN **79** B8
La Grande, OR **149** B7
La Grange, GA **67** E1
La Grange, KY **69** B6
La Junta, CO **139** F7
La Moine (river), IL **91** D2
La Perouse Pinnacle (island), HI **141** F3
La Plata, MD **39** E7
La Salle, IL **91** C4
La'ie, HI **141** B4
Laconia, NH **43** G4
Ladder Creek, KS **96** C2
Ladson, SC **77** F7
Ladysmith, WI **113** C3
LaFayette, GA **67** B1
Lafayette, IN **93** D2
Lafayette, LA **71** G4
Lafayette, CO **139** B5
Lafayette, Mount, NH **43** D3
Lafourche, Bayou (river), LA **71** H7
Lahaina, HI **141** C7
Lake Andes, SD **111** F8
Lake Charles, LA **70** G2
Lake City, FL **65** B6
Lake City, SC **77** D8
Lake Clark N.P. and Preserve, AK **135** E5
Lake Erie Beach, NY **46** E2
Lake Geneva, WI **113** H6
Lake Havasu City, AZ **121** D2
Lake Mead N.R.A., AZ, NV **121** C2
Lake Meredith N.R.A., TX **127** A4
Lake Placid, NY **47** B8
Lake Providence, LA **71** A6
Lake Roosevelt N.R.A., WA **153** C8
Lake Village, AR **63** G6
Lakehurst, NJ **45** F4
Lakeland, FL **65** E7
Lakeview, OR **149** G5
Lakeville, CT **33** A2
Lakeville, MN **101** G4
Lakewood, NJ **45** E4
Lakewood, WA **153** D3
Lakin, KS **96** D2
Lamar, CO **139** E9
Lambertville, MI **99** I7
Lambertville, NJ **45** D2
Lamesa, TX **127** D3
Lamlam, Mount, GU **156** G1
Lamoille (river), VT **53** B2
LaMoure, ND **107** E8
Lamprey (river), NH **43** H4
Lamprey N.W.&S.R., NH **43** H5
Lana'i (island), HI **141** D6
Lana'i City, HI **141** D6
Lancaster, CA **137** G5
Lancaster, NH **43** C3
Lancaster, OH **109** E5
Lancaster, PA **49** E8
Lancaster, SC **77** B6
Lancaster, WI **113** G4
Land Between the Lakes N.R.A., KY, TN **68** E3
Land O'Lakes, WI **113** B5
Lander, WY **155** D4
Lanett, AL **61** E6
Langdon, ND **107** A8
L'Anguille (river), AR **63** C6
Lansing, KS **97** B10
Lansing, MI **99** H6
LaPorte, IN **93** A3
Laramie, WY **155** G8
Laramie (river), CO, WY **155** F9
Laramie Mountains, CO, WY **155** E8
Laredo, TX **127** H5
Larimore, ND **107** C9
Larned, KS **97** D4
Larose, LA **71** H7
Las Animas, CO **139** E8
Las Cruces, NM **123** G4
Las Vegas, NM **123** C5
Las Vegas, NV **147** G6
Lassen Volcanic N.P., CA **137** B3
Last Chance, CO **139** C7
Lata Mountain, AS **157** I5
Laughlin, NV **147** I6
Laurel, DE **35** I5
Laurel, MS **73** G4
Laurel, MT **145** E7
Laurens, SC **77** C3
Laurinburg, NC **75** D6
Laurium, MI **99** B2
Lava Beds Nat. Mon., CA **137** A3
Lawrence, IN **93** E4
Lawrence, KS **97** B9
Lawrence, MA **41** A7
Lawrenceburg, IN **93** F6
Lawrenceburg, KY **69** C7
Lawrenceburg, TN **79** C4
Lawrenceville, IL **91** G6
Lawton, OK **125** E7
Laysan Island, HI **140** E2
Layton, UT **151** B4
Le Mars, IA **94** B2
Lead, SD **110** C1
Leadville, CO **139** D4
Leaf (river), MS **73** G5
Leavenworth, KS **97** B10
Lebanon, IN **93** D3
Lebanon, KS **97** A5
Lebanon, KY **69** D7
Lebanon, MO **103** E4
Lebanon, NH **43** F2
Lebanon, OH **109** F2
Lebanon, OR **149** C2
Lebanon, PA **49** E7
Lebanon, TN **79** B5
Lebanon, VA **80** E3
Lee, MA **40** C1
Leech Lake, MN **101** D3
Lees Summit, MO **103** C2
Leesburg, FL **65** D7
Leesburg, VA **81** A9
Leesville, LA **70** E2
Leesville Lake, OH **109** D7
Lehi, UT **151** C4
Lehigh (river), PA **49** C8
Lehua Island, HI **140** A1
Leitchfield, KY **69** D5
Leland, MS **73** D2
Lemhi (river), ID **143** F4
Lemhi Pass, MT **144** F3
Lemhi Range, ID **143** F3
Lemmon, SD **111** A3
Lemon, Lake, IN **93** F3
Lennox, SD **111** E10
Lenoir, NC **75** B4
Lenoir City, TN **79** B8
Lenox, MA **40** B1
Leola, SD **111** A7
Leominster, MA **41** B5
Leon (river), TX **127** E6
Leusoalii, AS **157** I5
Levelland, TX **127** C3
Levisa Fork (river), KY **69** C10
Levittown, NY **47** H9
Levittown, PA **49** E10
Lewes, DE **35** G7
Lewes and Rehoboth Canal, DE **35** G7
Lewis (river), WA **153** F3
Lewis and Clark Lake, NE, SD **111** F9
Lewis and Clark Memorial, MT **144** F3
Lewis Smith Lake, AL **61** B3
Lewisburg, PA **49** C7
Lewisburg, TN **79** C5
Lewisburg, WV **83** G5
Lewiston, ID **143** D1
Lewiston, ME **37** G3
Lewistown, MT **145** C6
Lewistown, PA **49** D6
Lexington, KY **69** C8
Lexington, MA **41** B7
Lexington, NC **75** B5
Lexington, NE **105** D5
Lexington, TN **78** C3
Lexington, VA **81** D7
Lexington Park, MD **39** E8
Libby, MT **144** B1
Liberal, KS **96** F2
Liberty, MO **103** C2
Licking (river), KY **69** A8
Licking (river), OH **109** E5
Licking, North Fork (river), KY **69** B8
Licking, South Fork (river), KY **69** B8
Lihu'e, HI **140** A2
Lillinonah, Lake, CT **33** D2
Lima, OH **109** C2
Limestone, ME **37** B6
Limon, CO **139** D7
Lincoln, DE **35** G6
Lincoln, IL **91** E4
Lincoln, ME **37** E5
Lincoln, NE **105** D9
Lincoln, NH **43** E3
Lincoln Boyhood National Memorial, IN **93** H2
Lincoln City, OR **148** C1
Lincoln Home National Historic Site, IL **91** E3
Lincolnton, NC **75** C4
Lindenwold, NJ **45** F2
Lindsborg, KS **97** C6
Linton, IN **93** G2
Linton, ND **107** F6
Lisbon, ND **107** E9
Lisbon, NH **43** D2
Lisbon Falls, ME **37** G3
Lisianski Island, HI **140** E2
Liston Point, DE **35** C5
Litchfield, CT **33** B3
Litchfield, IL **91** F3
Litchfield, MN **101** F3
Little (river), AR, OK **63** F1
Little (river), KY **68** E3
Little (river), LA **71** D4
Little (river), OK **125** D9
Little Beaver Creek National Scenic River, OH **109** C8
Little Bighorn Battlefield Nat. Mon., MT **145** E8
Little Blue (river), KS, NE **97** A7
Little Colorado (river), AZ **121** D7
Little Compton, RI **51** E6
Little Darby Creek, OH **109** E3
Little Deschutes N.W.&S.R., OR **149** E4

Little Diomede Island — Mio

Little Diomede Island, AK **134** C3
Little Egg Harbor, NJ **45** G4
Little Falls, MN **101** E3
Little Falls, NY **47** D7
Little Humboldt (river), NV **147** B4
Little Kanawha (river), WV **83** D3
Little Lost (river), ID **143** F4
Little Miami (river), OH **109** F2
Little Miami National Scenic River, OH **109** F2
Little Miami, East Fork (river), OH **109** G2
Little Missouri (river), AR, ND, SD **86** C1
Little Missouri, MT **145** F11
Little Missouri N.W.&S.R., AR **63** E2
Little Muddy (river), ND **106** B2
Little Pee Dee (river), NC, SC **77** D9
Little Powder (river), WY **155** B8
Little Red (river), AR **63** C5
Little River Canyon National Preserve, AL **61** B5
Little Rock, AR **63** D4
Little Rock Central High School National Historic Site, AR **63** D5
Little Sac (river), MO **103** E3
Little Salt Lake (dry lake), UT **151** G2
Little Sandy (river), KY **69** B10
Little Sioux (river), IA **94** C2
Little Snake (river), CO **139** A2
Little Tallahatchie (river), MS **73** B4
Little Wabash (river), IL **91** G5
Little White (river), SD **111** F4
Little Wood (river), ID **143** H3
Littleton, CO **139** C6
Littleton, ME **37** C6
Littleton, NH **43** D3
Live Oak, FL **65** B6
Livingston, AL **61** E1
Livingston, MT **145** E5
Livingston, Lake, TX **116** E9
Livonia, MI **99** H7
Llano (river), TX **127** E5
Llano Estacado (plain), NM, TX **116** D5
Lochsa (river), ID **143** D2
Lock Haven, PA **49** C6
Lockport, NY **46** D2
Locust Creek, MO **103** A4
Locust Fork (river), AL **61** C3
Lodgepole Creek, NE, WY **104** C1
Lodi, CA **137** D3
Logan, OH **109** F5
Logan, UT **151** A4
Logan, WV **82** G2
Logan Creek, NE **105** B8
Logansport, IN **93** C3
Lolo Pass, MT **144** D2
Lompoc, CA **137** G4
London, KY **69** D8
Londonderry, NH **43** I4
Lone Grove, OK **125** E8
Long Bay, NC, SC **75** E7
Long Beach, CA **137** H5
Long Beach, MS **73** I4
Long Beach, NY **47** H9
Long Beach Island, NJ **45** G5
Long Branch, NJ **45** D5
Long Island, NY **47** H9
Long Island Sound, NY **47** G9
Long Lake (lake), ME **37** A5
Long Lake (lake), ME **37** B4
Long Lake, ND **107** E6
Long Pond, MA **41** E7
Long Prairie, MN **101** E3
Long Trail, VT **53** D2
Longfellow Mountains, ME **37** F2
Longmont, CO **139** B5
Longview, TX **127** D8
Longview, WA **153** F3
Lonsdale, RI **51** B5
Looking Glass (river), MI **99** G6
Lookout Pass, ID **143** C2
Lookout, Cape, NC **75** D10
Lookout, Point, MD **39** F8
Lorain, OH **109** B5
Lordsburg, NM **123** G1
Loris, SC **77** D9
Los Alamos, NM **123** C4
Los Angeles, CA **137** H5
Los Lunas, NM **123** D4
Los Pinos (river), CO **139** F2
Lost River Range, ID **143** F3
Lostine N.W.&S.R., OR **149** B8
Loudonville, OH **109** C5
Louie B. Nunn Parkway, KY **69** E6
Louisiana, MO **103** B6
Louisville, CO **139** B5
Louisville, KY **69** B6
Louisville, MS **73** D4
Loup (river), NE **105** C7
Loup, Middle (river), NE **105** C5
Loup, North (river), NE **105** B5
Loup, South (river), NE **105** C5
Loveland, CO **139** B5
Lovell, WY **155** A5
Lovelock, NV **147** C3
Loving, NM **123** G7
Lovington, NM **123** G8
Lowell, IN **93** B2
Lowell, MA **41** A6
Lowell N.H.P., MA **41** A6
Lowell, Lake, ID **143** G1
Lower Bay, NJ **45** D5
Lower Peninsula, MI **99** F5
Lower Red Lake, MN **101** B3
Lowville, NY **47** C6
Loxahatchee N.W.&S.R., FL **65** F10
Lubbock, TX **127** C4
Lucedale, MS **73** H5
Ludington, MI **99** F4
Ludlow, MA **41** C3
Ludlow, VT **53** G3
Lufkin, TX **127** E8
Lumber (river), NC **75** D6
Lumber N.W.&S.R., NC **75** D6
Lumberton, NC **75** D7
Luray, VA **81** B8
Lusk, WY **155** D10
Luverne, MN **101** H2
Lyman, WY **154** G2
Lynchburg, TN **79** C5
Lynchburg, VA **81** D7
Lynches (river), SC **77** D8
Lynden, WA **153** A3
Lyndon B. Johnson N.H.P., TX **127** F6
Lyndonville, VT **53** C5
Lynn, MA **41** B7
Lyons, KS **97** D5

M

Machias, ME **37** F7
Machias (river), ME **37** F6
Machiasport, ME **37** F7
Mackinac Island, MI **99** D6
Mackinac, Straits of, MI **99** D5
Mackinaw (river), IL **91** D4
Macomb, IL **91** D2
Macon, GA **67** E3
Macon, MO **103** B4
Macon, Bayou (river), LA **71** B5
Macoupin Creek, IL **91** F2
Mad (river), VT **53** D3
Madawaska, ME **37** A5
Madeline Island, WI **113** A4
Madill, OK **125** E9
Madison, AL **61** A3
Madison, CT **33** E5
Madison, IN **93** G5
Madison, ME **37** F3
Madison, MN **101** F2
Madison, NE **105** C8
Madison, SD **111** D9
Madison, WI **113** G5
Madison, WV **82** G2
Madison (river), WY **154** A1
Madison (river), MT **145** E4
Madison Heights, VA **81** D7
Madisonville, KY **68** D3
Madras, OR **149** C4
Magazine Mountain (peak), AR **63** C2
Magee, MS **73** F3
Maggie L. Walker National Historic Site, VA **81** D9
Magic Reservoir, ID **143** H3
Magnolia, AR **63** G3
Mahoning (river), OH **109** B8
Maia, AS **157** I5
Maine, Gulf of, ME **37** H5
Makawao, HI **141** C7
Malad City, ID **143** I4
Malden, MA **41** B7
Malden, MO **103** G7
Malheur (river), OR **149** D8
Malheur Lake, OR **149** E7
Malheur N.W.&S.R., OR **149** D7
Malheur, North Fork (river), OR **149** D7
Malheur, North Fork N.W.&S.R., OR **149** D7
Malone, NY **47** A8
Malta, MT **145** B8
Malvern, AR **63** E3
Mammoth Cave N.P., KY **69** D5
Manalapan (river), NJ **45** D4
Manasquan, NJ **45** E5
Manassas, VA **81** B9
Manassas National Battlefield Park, VA **81** B9
Manchester, CT **33** B5
Manchester, IA **95** C8
Manchester, MD **39** A7
Manchester, NH **43** H4
Manchester, OH **109** G3
Manchester, TN **79** C6
Manchester Center, VT **53** H2
Mancos (river), CO **138** G1
Mandan, ND **107** E5
Mandeville, LA **71** F8
Mangum, OK **125** D6
Manhattan, KS **97** B7
Manila, AR **63** B8
Manistee, MI **99** F4
Manistee (river), MI **99** F5
Manistee N.W.&S.R., MI **99** F5
Manistique, MI **99** D4
Manitou Islands, MI **99** E4
Manitou Passage, MI **99** E5
Manitowoc, WI **113** E7
Mankato, MN **101** G4
Manning, SC **77** D7
Mannington, WV **83** C5
Mansfield, LA **70** C1
Mansfield, OH **109** C5
Mansfield, PA **49** B6
Mansfield Hollow Lake, CT **33** B7
Mansfield, Mount, VT **53** C2
Manti, UT **151** E4
Manua Islands (islands), AS **156** I3
Manville, RI **51** A4
Many, LA **70** D2
Manzanar National Historic Site, CA **137** F5
Maple (river), ND **107** E9
Maple (river), ND **107** F8
Maquoketa, IA **95** C9
Maquoketa (river), IA **95** C9
Marais des Cygnes (river), KS, MO **97** C10
Marathon, FL **65** I8
Marble Canyon, AZ **121** B5
Marblehead, MA **41** B8
Marcy, Mount, NY **47** B8
Marfa, TX **126** F2
Marianna, AR **63** D7
Marianna, FL **65** A3
Marias (river), MT **145** B4
Marietta, GA **67** C2
Marietta, OH **109** F7
Marinette, WI **113** D7
Marion, AL **61** E2
Marion, IA **95** C8
Marion, IL **91** H4
Marion, IN **93** C4
Marion, KY **68** D3
Marion, OH **109** D4
Marion, SC **77** C8
Marion, VA **80** E4
Marion Lake, KS **97** C7
Marion, Lake, SC **77** E6
Mark Twain Lake, MO **103** B5
Marked Tree, AR **63** C7
Marksville, LA **71** E4
Marlborough, CT **33** C6
Marlborough, MA **41** C6
Marlow, OK **125** E8
Maro Reef, HI **140** F2
Marquette, MI **99** C3
Mars Hill, ME **37** B6
Marsh Island, LA **71** H4
Marshall, MI **99** H6
Marshall, MN **101** G2
Marshall, MO **103** C4
Marshall, TX **127** D9
Marshallton, DE **35** B4
Marshalltown, IA **95** C6
Marsh-Billings-Rockefeller N.H.P., VT **53** F3
Marshfield, WI **113** D4
Marshyhope Creek, DE, MD **35** G4
Martha's Vineyard (island), MA **41** F8
Martin, SD **111** E4
Martin, TN **78** B2
Martin Luther King, Jr. National Historic Site, GA **67** C2
Martin Van Buren National Historic Site, NY **47** E8
Martin, Lake, AL **61** E5
Martins Ferry, OH **109** D8
Martinsburg, WV **83** C9
Martinsville, IN **93** F3
Martinsville, VA **81** E6
Marydel, DE **35** E4
Marys (river), NV **147** A6
Marysville, KS **97** A7
Marysville, OH **109** D3
Maryville, MO **103** A2
Maryville, TN **79** C8
Mascoma Lake, NH **43** F2
Mason, MI **99** H6
Mason, OH **109** F2
Mason City, IA **95** A6
Massabesic Lake, NH **43** H4
Massachusetts Bay, MA **41** B8
Massena, NY **47** A7
Massillon, OH **109** C6
Matagorda Bay, TX **116** F8
Matanuska (river), AK **135** E6
Mattawamkeag (river), ME **37** D6
Matthews, NC **75** C4
Mattoon, IL **91** F5
Maui (island), HI **141** C7
Mauldin, SC **77** B3
Maumee, OH **109** B3
Maumee (river), IN, OH **93** B6
Maumee Bay, OH **109** A3
Maumelle, AR **63** D4
Mauna Kea (peak), HI **141** E9
Mauna Loa (peak), HI **141** F9
Maurepas, Lake, LA **71** F7
Maurice (river), NJ **45** G2
Maurice N.W.&S.R., NJ **45** H2
May, Cape, NJ **45** I2
Mayagüez, PR **157** I9
Mayfield, KY **68** E2
Mayfield Creek, KY **68** E1
Mays Landing, NJ **45** H3
Maysville, KY **69** B9
Mayville, ND **107** C9
McAlester, OK **125** D10
McAllen, TX **127** I6
McCall, ID **143** F1
McCandless, PA **48** D2
McComb, MS **73** G2
McCook, NE **105** E4
McGee Creek Lake, OK **125** E10
McGehee, AR **63** F6
McGill, NV **147** D6
McIntosh, SD **111** A4
McKee Creek, IL **91** E2
McKeesport, PA **48** D2
McKenzie, TN **78** B3
McKenzie (river), OR **149** D2
McKenzie N.W.&S.R., OR **149** D3
McKinley, Mount (Denali), AK **135** D6
McLean, VA **81** A9
McLoughlin House National Historic Site, OR **149** B2
McMinnville, OR **149** B2
McMinnville, TN **79** C6
McPherson, KS **97** C6
Mead, Lake, AZ, NV **121** B2
Meade, KS **97** E3
Meade (river), AK **135** A5
Meadow Valley Wash (river), NV **147** G7
Meadville, PA **48** B2
Mechanicsburg, PA **49** E6
Mechanicsville, VA **81** D9
Medford, MA **41** B7
Medford, OR **149** G2
Medford, WI **113** D4
Medical Lake, WA **153** C9
Medicine Bow (river), WY **155** F7
Medicine Bow Mountains, CO **139** A4
Medicine Lodge (river), KS **97** E4
Medicine Lodge, KS **97** E5
Medina, NY **46** D3
Medina, OH **109** B6
Medora, ND **106** D2
Meeker, CO **139** B2
Meherrin (river), VA **81** E8
Melbourne, FL **65** D9
Melozitna (river), AK **135** C5
Memphis, TN **78** C1
Memphremagog, Lake, VT **53** A4
Mena, AR **63** D1
Menahga, MN **101** D3
Menasha, WI **113** E6
Mendota, IL **91** B4
Mendota, Lake, WI **113** G5
Menlo Park, NJ **45** D4
Menominee, MI **99** E3
Menominee (river), MI, WI **99** D3
Menomonee Falls, WI **113** G7
Menomonie, WI **113** D2
Mentor, OH **109** A7
Mequon, WI **113** G7
Merced, CA **137** E4
Merced N.W.&S.R., CA **137** E4
Mercersburg, PA **49** F5
Mercerville, NJ **45** E3
Meredith, NH **43** F3
Meredith, Lake, CO **139** E7
Meriden, CT **33** C4
Meridian, MS **73** E5
Merrill, WI **113** D5
Merrillville, IN **93** A2
Merrimack, NH **43** I3
Merrimack (river), MA, NH **41** A7
Merritt Island, FL **65** D9
Merrymeeting Lake, NH **43** G4
Mesa, AZ **121** F5
Mesa de Maya, CO **139** G7
Mesa Verde N.P., CO **138** G1
Mesabi Range, MN **101** C4
Mesquite, NV **147** G7
Metairie, LA **71** G8
Meteor Crater, AZ **121** D5
Methow (river), WA **153** B6
Methuen, MA **41** A7
Metolius N.W.&S.R., OR **149** D3
Metropolis, IL **91** I4
Mettawee (river), VT **53** G1
Mexico, ME **37** F2
Mexico, MO **103** C5
Mexico, Gulf of, **56** G3
Miami, FL **65** G9
Miami, OK **125** A11
Miami Beach, FL **65** G9
Miami Canal, FL **65** F9
Michigan City, IN **93** A2
Michigan, Lake, **86** D7
Middleboro, MA **41** D8
Middlebury, VT **53** E2
Middlesboro, KY **69** E9
Middleton, WI **113** G5
Middletown, CT **33** C5
Middletown, DE **35** C4
Middletown, NY **47** G8
Middletown, OH **109** F2
Middletown, RI **51** E5
Midland, MI **99** G6
Midland, TX **127** D3
Midway, DE **35** H7
Midway Islands (territory), US **156** D4
Milaca, MN **101** E4
Milan, NM **123** D2
Milan, TN **78** B2
Milbank, SD **111** B10
Miles City, MT **145** D10
Milford, CT **33** E3
Milford, DE **35** G6
Milford, MA **41** C6
Milford, NE **105** D8
Milford, NH **43** I3
Milford, UT **151** F2
Milford Lake, KS **97** B7
Mililani Town, HI **141** B4
Milk (river), MT **145** B8
Mill Creek, IN **93** F3
Millbrook, AL **61** E4
Millcreek, PA **48** A2
Mille Lacs Lake, MN **101** D4
Milledgeville, GA **67** D4
Millen, GA **67** E6
Miller, SD **111** C7
Millers (river), MA **41** A4
Millington, TN **78** C1
Millinocket, ME **37** D5
Millsboro, DE **35** I6
Millville, NJ **45** H2
Millwood Lake, AR **63** F2
Milo, ME **37** E4
Milton, DE **35** G6
Milton, MA **41** C7
Milton, NH **43** G5
Milton, VT **53** B2
Milton, Lake, OH **109** C7
Milton-Freewater, OR **149** A7
Milwaukee, WI **113** G7
Milwaukee (river), WI **113** F6
Minam N.W.&S.R., OR **149** B8
Minden, LA **70** B2
Minden, NE **105** D6
Mineral Wells, TX **127** D6
Minidoka Internment Camp Nat. Mon., ID **143** H3
Minneapolis, KS **97** B6
Minneapolis, MN **101** F4
Minnesota (river), MN **101** F2
Minot, ND **107** B4
Minute Man N.H.P., MA **41** B6
Minuteman Missile National Historic Site, SD **111** D3
Mio, MI **99** E6

Mishawaka — Odessa

Mishawaka, IN **93** A4
Mission, TX **127** I6
Mission Viejo, CA **137** H6
Missisquoi (river), VT **53** A2
Mississinewa (river), IN **93** D5
Mississinewa Lake, IN **93** C4
Mississippi (river), **56** B2
Mississippi National River and N.R.A., MN **101** F4
Mississippi Petrified Forest, MS **73** E2
Mississippi River Delta, LA **71** I10
Mississippi Sound, AL, MS **73** I5
Missoula, MT **144** C3
Missouri (river), **86** F5
Missouri N.W.&S.R., MT **145** B6
Missouri National Recreational River, NE, SD **105** A7
Misty Fiords Nat. Mon., AK **135** G11
Mitchell, SD **111** E8
Mitchell, Mount, NC **74** B3
Moab, UT **151** F6
Moberly, MO **103** B4
Mobile, AL **61** H1
Mobile (river), AL **61** H1
Mobile Bay, AL **61** I1
Mobridge, SD **111** B5
Modesto, CA **137** E3
Mogollon Rim, AZ **121** E6
Mohave, Lake, AZ, NV **121** C1
Mohawk (river), NY **47** D7
Mohican (river), OH **109** D5
Mojave Desert, CA, NV **130** F4
Mojave National Preserve, CA **137** G7
Moline, IL **91** C2
Moloka'i (island), HI **141** C6
Monadnock Mountain, NH **43** I2
Monahans, TX **127** E3
Moncks Corner, SC **77** F7
Monessen, PA **48** E2
Monett, MO **103** F3
Monhegan Island, ME **37** H4
Monitor Range, NV **147** E4
Monmouth, IL **91** C2
Monmouth, OR **149** C2
Mono Lake, CA **137** D5
Monocacy (river), MD **39** A6
Monocacy N.B., MD **39** B6
Monomoy Island, MA **41** E10
Monona, WI **113** G5
Monongahela (river), PA, WV **28** G1
Monroe, GA **67** C3
Monroe, LA **71** B4
Monroe, MI **99** I7
Monroe, NC **75** C5
Monroe, WI **113** H5
Monroe Lake, IN **93** G3
Monroeville, AL **61** G2
Montauk Point, NY **47** G11
Monte Vista, CO **139** F4
Monterey, CA **137** F2
Monterey Bay, CA **137** F2
Monterey Bay National Marine Sanctuary, CA **137** E2
Montevallo, AL **61** D3
Montevideo, MN **101** F2
Montezuma Castle Nat. Mon., AZ **121** D5
Montgomery, AL **61** E4
Montgomery, WV **83** F3
Montgomery Village, MD **39** B6
Monticello, AR **63** F5
Monticello, IA **95** C9
Monticello, IN **93** C3
Monticello, NY **47** F7
Monticello (site), VA **81** C8
Montpelier, ID **143** I6
Montpelier (site), VA **81** C8
Montpelier, VT **53** D3
Montrose, CO **139** E2
Monument Valley, AZ, UT **151** H6
Moodus, CT **33** D6
Moore, OK **125** D8
Moore Reservoir, NH, VT **53** C5
Moorefield, WV **83** D8
Moores Creek N.B., NC **75** D8
Moorhead, MN **101** D1
Moose (river), VT **53** C5
Moose (river), ME **37** D2
Moosehead Lake, ME **37** D4
Mooselookmeguntic Lake, ME **37** F2
Moosup, CT **33** B8
Moosup (river), RI **51** C2
Mora, MN **101** E4
Mora (river), NM **123** C6
Moreau (river), SD **111** B4
Morehead, KY **69** B9
Morehead City, NC **75** D9
Morgan City, LA **71** H6
Morgan Horse Farm (site), VT **53** D1
Morganfield, KY **68** C3
Morganton, NC **74** B3
Morgantown, WV **83** C6
Moriarty, NM **123** D4
Mormon Reservoir, ID **143** H3
Moroni, UT **151** D4
Morrilton, AR **63** C4
Morris, IL **91** C5
Morris, MN **101** E2
Morristown, NJ **45** C3
Morristown, TN **79** B9
Morristown N.H.P., NJ **45** C3
Morrisville, VT **53** B3
Morton, IL **91** D4
Moscow, ID **143** C1
Moses Lake, WA **153** D7
Mosquito Creek Lake, OH **109** B8
Moss Point, MS **73** I5
Mott, ND **107** E3
Moultrie, GA **67** H3
Moultrie, Lake, SC **77** E7
Moundsville, WV **83** B4
Mount Airy, NC **75** A5
Mount Desert Island, ME **37** G6
Mount Holly, NJ **45** F3
Mount Hope Bay, RI **51** D6
Mount Pleasant, IA **95** E8
Mount Pleasant, UT **151** D4
Mount Rainier N.P., WA **153** E4
Mount Rushmore Nat. Mon., SD **110** D2
Mount St. Helens National Volcanic Monument, WA **153** E4
Mount Vernon, IN **93** I1
Mount Vernon, KY **69** D8
Mount Vernon (site), VA **81** B10
Mount Vernon, WA **153** B4
Mountain Fork (river), OK **125** E12
Mountain Grove, MO **103** F5
Mountain Home, AR **63** A4
Mountain Home, ID **143** H2
Mountain View, AR **63** B5
Mountain View, HI **141** F9
Mountain Village, AK **134** D3
Mountainair, NM **123** D4
Mouse (river) *see* Souris, ND **107** B5
Mt. Carmel, IL **91** G5
Mt. Carmel, PA **49** D7
Mt. Pleasant, MI **99** G6
Mt. Pleasant, SC **77** G7
Mt. Pleasant, TX **127** C8
Mt. Sterling, KY **69** C8
Mt. Vernon, IL **91** G4
Mt. Vernon, OH **109** D5
Mud Lake, ID **143** G5
Mud Lake, MN **101** B2
Muddy Boggy Creek, OK **125** E10
Muir Woods Nat. Mon., CA **137** D2
Mulberry (river), AR **63** B2
Mulberry Fork (river), AL **61** B3
Mulberry N.W.&S.R., AR **63** B2
Mulchatna N.W.&S.R., AK **135** E5
Mullen, NE **105** B4
Mullens, WV **83** H3
Mullett Lake, MI **99** D6
Mullica (river), NJ **45** G3
Mullins, SC **77** C9
Mulvane, KS **97** E7
Muncie, IN **93** D5
Munising, MI **99** C4
Murdo, SD **111** D5
Murfreesboro, AR **63** E2
Murfreesboro, TN **79** B5
Murphysboro, IL **91** H4
Murray, KY **68** E2
Murray, UT **151** C4
Murray, Lake, SC **77** C4
Muscatatuck (river), IN **93** G4
Muscatine, IA **95** E9
Muscle Shoals, AL **61** A2
Musconetcong (river), NJ **45** C2
Muscongus Bay, ME **37** H4
Muskegon, MI **99** G4
Muskegon (river), MI **99** G5
Muskingum (river), OH **109** E6
Muskogee, OK **125** C11
Muskogee Turnpike, OK **125** C11
Musselshell (river), MT **145** D7
Myrtle Beach, SC **77** D9
Mystic, CT **33** D8
Mystic Island, NJ **45** G4
Mystic Seaport (site), CT **33** D8

N

Naches (river), WA **153** E5
Nacogdoches, TX **127** E9
Naknek, AK **135** F5
Namakan Lake, MN **101** B5
Namekagon (river), WI **113** B2
Nampa, ID **143** G1
Nanticoke (river), DE, MD **39** E9
Nantucket, MA **41** F10
Nantucket Island, MA **41** F10
Nantucket Sound, MA **41** F9
Napa, CA **137** D2
Napatree Point, RI **51** G1
Naperville, IL **91** B5
Naples, FL **65** G7
Napoleon, ND **107** E6
Napoleon, OH **109** B2
Nappanee, IN **93** B4
Narragansett Bay, RI **51** E5
Narragansett Pier, RI **51** F4
Nashua, NH **43** I4
Nashua (river), MA **41** B5
Nashville, AR **63** F2
Nashville, IL **91** G4
Nashville, TN **79** B5
Natchaug (river), CT **33** B7
Natchez, MS **73** G1
Natchez N.H.P., MS **73** F1
Natchez Trace Parkway, AL, MS **73** D4
Natchitoches, LA **70** C2
National Park of American Samoa, AS **156** I4
Natural Bridges Nat. Mon., UT **151** G6
Naugatuck, CT **33** D3
Naugatuck (river), CT **33** D3
Nauvoo, IL **91** D1
Navajo, NM **123** B1
Navajo Nat. Mon., AZ **121** B6
Navajo Reservoir, NM **123** A3
Navassa Island (territory), US **157** E11
Nazareth, PA **49** D9
Near Islands, AK **135** G5
Nebraska City, NE **105** D9
Neches (river), TX **127** E8
Necker Island, HI **141** F4
Needles, CA **137** G8
Neenah, WI **113** E6
Nehalem (river), OR **149** A2
Neligh, NE **105** B7
Nelson Island, AK **134** E3
Nelsonville, OH **109** F5
Neosho, MO **103** F2
Neosho (river), KS, OK **86** G4
Nepaug Reservoir, CT **33** B4
Nephi, UT **151** D4
Neptune, NJ **45** E5
Ness City, KS **97** C3
Neuse (river), NC **75** C8
Nevada, IA **95** D5
Nevada, MO **103** E2
New (river), VA **80** F4
New Albany, IN **93** H4
New Albany, MS **73** B4
New Bedford, MA **41** E7
New Bedford Whaling N.H.P., MA **41** E7
New Bern, NC **75** C9
New Braunfels, TX **127** F6
New Brunswick, NJ **45** D4
New Canaan, CT **33** E1
New Castle, DE **35** B5
New Castle, IN **93** E5
New Castle, PA **48** C1
New City, NY **47** G8
New Echota State Historic Site, GA **67** B2
New Fairfield, CT **33** D2
New Hampton, IA **95** B7
New Harmony State Historic Site, IN **93** H1
New Hartford, CT **33** B4
New Haven, CT **33** D4
New Iberia, LA **71** G5
New Ipswich, NH **43** I3
New Jersey Turnpike, NJ **45** E3
New Lexington, OH **109** E5
New London, CT **33** D7
New London, NH **43** G2
New London, WI **113** E6
New Madrid, MO **103** F8
New Martinsville, WV **83** C4
New Milford, CT **33** C2
New N.W.&S.R., NC **75** A4
New Orleans, LA **71** G8
New Paltz, NY **47** F8
New Philadelphia, OH **109** D6
New Richmond, WI **113** D1
New River Gorge Bridge, WV **83** F4
New River Gorge National River, WV **83** G4
New Rochelle, NY **47** H8
New Rockford, ND **107** C7
New Salem, ND **107** E4
New Smyrna Beach, FL **65** C8
New Town, ND **107** C3
New Ulm, MN **101** G3
New York, NY **47** H8
New York State Thruway, NY **47** D4
New, South Fork (river), NC **75** A4
Newark, DE **35** B4
Newark, NJ **45** C4
Newark, OH **109** E5
Newberry, SC **77** C4
Newberry National Volcanic Monument, OR **149** D4
Newburg, OR **149** B2
Newburgh, NY **47** G8
Newbury, VT **53** D5
Newburyport, MA **41** A8
Newcastle, WY **155** C10
Newfound Lake, NH **43** F3
Newfoundland Evaporation Basin (dry lake), UT **151** B2
Newington, CT **33** C5
Newmarket, NH **43** H5
Newnan, GA **67** D2
Newport, AR **63** B6
Newport, DE **35** B5
Newport, KY **69** A8
Newport, ME **37** F4
Newport, NH **43** G2
Newport, OR **148** C1
Newport, RI **51** F5
Newport, TN **79** B9
Newport, VT **53** A4
Newport News, VA **81** E11
Newton, IA **95** D6
Newton, KS **97** D7
Newton, MS **73** F4
Newton, NC **75** B4
Newton, NJ **45** B3
Newtown, CT **33** D2
Nez Perce N.H.P., ID **143** D1
Nez Perce Pass, MT **144** E2
Ni'ihau (island), HI **140** B1
Niagara, WI **113** C7
Niagara Falls, NY **46** D2
Niagara Falls (waterfall), NY **28** D2
Niagara River (river), NY **46** D2
Niangua (river), MO **103** E4
Niantic, CT **33** D7
Niceville, FL **64** A2
Nicodemus National Historic Site, KS **97** B4
Nihoa (island), HI **141** F4
Niles, MI **99** I4
Niles, OH **109** B8
Nine Mile Creek, UT **151** D5
Nine-Mile Prairie, NE **105** D8
Ninety Six National Historic Site, SC **77** C3
Ninigret Pond, RI **51** G3
Niobrara (river), NE, WY **105** A4
Niobrara National Scenic Riverway, NE **105** A5
Niskayuna, NY **47** E8
Nitro, WV **82** F2
Noatak N.W.&S.R., AK **135** B4
Noatak National Preserve, AK **135** B5
Noblesville, IN **93** D4
Nocona, TX **127** C6
Nodaway, East (river), IA **95** E3
Nogales, AZ **121** H6
Nolichucky (river), TN **79** B10
Nolin River Lake, KY **69** D5
Nomans Land (island), MA **41** F8
Nome, AK **134** C3
Nonquit Pond, RI **51** E6
Norfolk, CT **33** A3
Norfolk, NE **105** B8
Norfolk, VA **81** E11
Norfork Lake, AR **63** A5
Normal, IL **91** D4
Norman, OK **125** D8
Norman, Lake, NC **75** B4
Norris Lake, TN **79** B8
Norristown, PA **49** E9
North Adams, MA **40** A1
North Attleboro, MA **41** D6
North Augusta, SC **77** E3
North Bend, OH **109** F1
North Bend, OR **148** E1
North Bennington, VT **53** I1
North Branford, CT **33** D4
North Canton, OH **109** C7
North Cascades N.P., WA **153** A5
North Charleston, SC **77** F7
North Conway, NH **43** E4
North Fork Sprague N.W.&S.R., OR **149** F4
North Grosvenor Dale, CT **33** A8
North Haven, CT **33** D4
North Hero, VT **53** B1
North Hero Island, VT **53** A1
North Island, SC **77** E9
North Las Vegas, NV **147** G6
North Little Rock, AR **63** D4
North Manchester, IN **93** B4
North Myrtle Beach, SC **77** D10
North Ogden, UT **151** B4
North Olmsted, OH **109** B6
North Platte, NE **105** D4
North Pole, AK **135** D7
North Powder N.W.&S.R., OR **149** C7
North Providence, RI **51** B4
North Scituate, RI **51** B3
North Sioux City, SD **111** F10
North Slope, AK **135** B5
North Springfield, VT **53** G3
North Sterling Reservoir, CO **139** A8
North Stratford, NH **43** C3
North Sylamore Creek N.W.&S.R., AR **63** B4
North Troy, VT **53** A4
North Umpqua N.W.&S.R., OR **149** E2
North Vernon, IN **93** G5
North Walpole, NH **43** H1
North Wildwood, NJ **45** I3
Northampton, MA **41** C3
Northern Mariana Islands (territory), US **156** E1
Northfield, MN **101** G5
Northfield, NH **43** G3
Northfield, VT **53** D3
Northwestern Hawaiian Islands, HI **140** E1
Northwood, ND **107** C9
Norton, KS **97** A3
Norton, VA **80** E2
Norton Sound, AK **135** D4
Norwalk, CT **33** F2
Norwalk, OH **109** B5
Norway, ME **37** G2
Norwich, CT **33** C7
Norwich, NY **47** E6
Norwich, VT **53** F4
Norwood, MA **41** C7
Norwood, OH **109** F2
Nottoway (river), VA **81** E10
Nowitna N.W.&S.R., AK **135** D6
Nowood (river), WY **155** B5
Noxontown Pond, DE **35** C4
Noxubee (river), MS **73** D5
Nubanusit Lake, NH **43** H2
Nueces (river), TX **127** G6
Nunivak Island, AK **134** E3
Nuuuli, AS **156** I1

O

O'ahu (island), HI **141** B5
Oahe, Lake, ND, SD **111** B6
Oak Bluffs, MA **41** F9
Oak Harbor, WA **153** B3
Oak Hill, WV **83** G4
Oak Orchard, DE **35** H7
Oak Ridge, TN **79** B8
Oakdale, LA **71** E3
Oakes, ND **107** F8
Oakland, CA **137** E2
Oakland, MD **38** B1
Oakland, ME **37** F3
Oakley, KS **96** B2
Oakville, CT **33** C3
Obed (river), TN **79** B7
Obed N.W.&S.R., TN **79** B7
Oberlin, KS **97** A3
Obion (river), TN **78** B1
Ocala, FL **65** C7
Ocean City, MD **39** E11
Ocean City, NJ **45** H3
Ocean Lake, WY **155** D4
Ocean Pines, MD **39** E11
Ocean Shores, WA **152** D1
Ocean Springs, MS **73** I5
Ocean View, DE **35** I7
Oceanside, CA **137** I6
Ochlockonee (river), FL, GA **65** B4
Ochoco Mountains, OR **149** C5
Ocmulgee (river), GA **67** G4
Ocmulgee Nat. Mon., GA **67** E4
Oconee (river), GA **67** F5
Oconee, Lake, GA **67** D4
Oconto, WI **113** D7
Oconto (river), WI **113** D7
Ocracoke Island, NC **75** C10
Odessa, DE **35** C4

Odessa — Potomac

Odessa, TX **127** E3
Oelwein, IA **95** B8
Ofu (island), AS **156** I3
Ofu, AS **156** H3
Ogallala, NE **105** D3
Ogden, UT **151** B4
Ogdensburg, NY **47** A6
Ogeechee (river), GA **67** E6
Ogunquit, ME **37** I2
Ohio (river), **86** G7
Ohoopee (river), GA **67** F6
Oil City, PA **48** B2
Okanogan (river), WA **153** B7
Okatibbee Lake, MS **73** E5
Okeechobee, Lake, FL **65** F8
Okefenokee Swamp, GA **67** H5
Oklahoma City, OK **125** C8
Okmulgee, OK **125** C10
Okobojo Creek, SD **111** C5
Okolona, MS **73** C5
Olathe, KS **97** C10
Old Faithful (site), WY **154** B2
Old Hickory Lake, TN **79** B5
Old Oraibi (site), AZ **121** C6
Old Orchard Beach, ME **37** H2
Old Saybrook, CT **33** E6
Old Town, ME **37** F5
Olean, NY **46** F3
Olentangy (river), OH **109** D4
Oliver, Lake, GA **67** E1
Olivia, MN **101** G3
Olney, IL **91** G5
Olosega (island), AS **156** H3
Olosega, AS **156** H3
Olympia, WA **153** D3
Olympic Coast National Marine Sanctuary, WA **152** B1
Olympic Mountains, WA **152** C2
Olympic N.P., WA **152** C2
Olympus, Mount, WA **152** C2
Omaha, NE **105** C9
Omak, WA **153** B7
Onalaska, WI **113** F3
Onancock, VA **81** D12
Onawa, IA **94** C2
One Hundred and Two (river), MO **103** A2
Oneida, NY **47** D6
Oneida Lake, NY **47** D6
O'Neill, NE **105** B6
Oneonta, NY **47** E7
Onida, SD **111** C6
Onslow Bay, NC **75** D9
Ontario, OR **149** D9
Ontario, Lake, **28** D2
Ontonagon N.W.&S.R., MI **99** B2
Oologah Lake, OK **125** B10
Oostanaula (river), GA **67** B1
Opelika, AL **61** E5
Opelousas, LA **71** F4
Opp, AL **61** G4
Opportunity, WA **153** C10
Optima Lake, OK **124** B4
Orange, CT **33** E3
Orange, MA **41** B3
Orange, VA **81** C8
Orange City, IA **94** B2
Orangeburg, SC **77** E5
Orchard City, CO **139** D2
Ord, NE **105** C6
Ordway, CO **139** E7
Oreana, NV **147** C3
Oregon, OH **109** A3
Oregon Caves Nat. Mon., OR **149** G2
Oregon City, OR **149** B3
Oregon Dunes N.R.A., OR **148** D1
Orem, UT **151** C4
Orford, NH **43** E2
Organ Pipe Cactus Nat. Mon., AZ **121** G3
Orlando, FL **65** D8
Orleans, MA **41** E10
Orleans, VT **53** B4
Oro Valley, AZ **121** G6
Orofino, ID **143** D1
Orono, ME **37** F5
Oroville Dam, CA **137** C3
Orrville, OH **109** C6
Ortonville, MN **101** F1
Osage, IA **95** A6
Osage (river), MO **103** E3
Osage City, KS **97** C8
Osage Fork (river), MO **103** E4
Osawatomie, KS **97** C10
Osceola, AR **63** B8
Osceola, IA **95** E5
Osgood Mountains, NV **147** B4
Oshkosh, WI **113** F6
Oskaloosa, IA **95** E7
Ossabaw Island, GA **67** G7
Ossabaw Sound, GA **67** G7
Ossipee Lake, NH **43** F4
Oswego, NY **47** C5
Oswego (river), NY **47** D5
Othello, WA **153** E7
Otis Reservoir, MA **40** C1
Ottawa, IL **91** C4
Ottawa, KS **97** C9
Otter Creek (river), VT **53** E1
Otter Creek Reservior, UT **151** F4
Otter Tail (river), MN **101** E1
Otter Tail Lake, MN **101** D2
Ottumwa, IA **95** E7
Ouachita (river), AR, LA **56** D2
Ouachita Mountains, AR, OK **63** D1
Ouachita, Lake, AR **63** D3
Outer Banks (islands), NC **75** C10
Overland Park, KS **97** B10
Overton, NV **147** G7
Owasso, OK **125** B10
Owatonna, MN **101** G4
Owensboro, KY **69** C4
Owl Creek, WY **155** C4
Owosso, MI **99** G6
Owyhee (river), OR **149** D8
Owyhee Mountains, ID **143** H1
Owyhee N.W.&S.R., OR **149** E8
Owyhee, Lake, OR **149** E8
Owyhee, North Fork N.W.&S.R., OR **149** F9
Owyhee, South Fork (river), ID, NV **143** I1
Oxford, MA **41** C5
Oxford, MS **73** B4
Oxford, NC **75** B7
Oxford, OH **109** F1
Oxnard, CA **137** H4
Oxon Cove Park and Oxon Hill Farm, MD **39** D6
Ozark, AL **61** G5
Ozark, AR **63** C2
Ozark National Scenic Riverways, MO **103** F6
Ozark Plateau, **86** G5
Ozarks, Lake of the, MO **103** D4
Ozona, TX **127** E4

P

Pachaug Pond, CT **33** C8
Pacific Crest National Scenic Trail, CA **137** G5
Paden City, WV **83** C4
Padre Island, TX **116** G8
Padre Island National Seashore, TX **127** H7
Paducah, KY **68** D2
Page, AZ **121** A5
Pago Pago, AS **156** I1
Pagosa Springs, CO **139** G3
Pahala, HI **141** F9
Pahranagat Range, NV **147** F6
Pahrump, NV **147** G5
Pahute Mesa, NV **147** F4
Painesville, OH **109** A7
Paint Creek, OH **109** F3
Paint N.W.&S.R., MI **99** C2
Painted Desert, AZ **121** B5
Palatka, FL **65** C7
Palestine, TX **127** E8
Palisades Reservoir, ID **143** H6
Palm Bay, FL **65** E9
Palm Coast, FL **65** C8
Palm Springs, CA **137** H7
Palmer, AK **135** E6
Palmer (river), RI **51** C5
Palmyra Atoll (territory), US **157** F5
Palo Alto, CA **137** E2
Palo Alto Battlefield National Historical Site, TX **127** I7
Palouse (river), WA **153** E9
Palouse Hills, WA **153** D9
Pamlico (river), NC **75** C9
Pamlico Sound, NC **75** C10
Pampa, TX **127** B4
Pana, IL **91** F4
Panama City, FL **65** B3
Pancake Range, NV **147** E5
Panguitch, UT **151** G3
Panorama Point (peak), NE **104** C1
Paola, KS **97** C10
Papillion, NE **105** C9
Paragould, AR **63** B7
Paramus, NJ **45** B5
Paria (river), AZ **121** A4
Paris, AR **63** C2
Paris, IL **91** E6
Paris, KY **69** B8
Paris, TN **78** B3
Paris, TX **127** C8
Park (river), ND **107** B9
Park Falls, WI **113** C4
Park Hills, MO **103** E6
Park Range, CO **139** A3
Park Rapids, MN **101** D3
Park River, ND **107** B9
Parker, AZ **121** E2
Parker, SD **111** E9
Parkersburg, WV **83** D3
Parkston, SD **111** E8
Parkville, MD **39** B8
Parma, OH **109** B6
Parris Island, SC **77** H6
Parsippany, NJ **45** C4
Parsons, KS **97** E9
Pasadena, CA **137** H5
Pascagoula, MS **73** I5
Pascagoula (river), MS **73** H5
Pasco, WA **153** F8
Pascoag, RI **51** A2
Pascoag Lake, RI **51** A2
Paso Robles, CA **137** G3
Passaic, NJ **45** C5
Passaic (river), NJ **45** C4
Passamaquoddy Bay, ME **37** E7
Passumpsic (river), VT **53** C5
Paterson, NJ **45** B4
Pathfinder Reservoir, WY **155** E6
Patoka (river), IN **93** H2
Patoka Lake, IN **93** H3
Patten, ME **37** C5
Patuxent (bay), MD **39** E7
Patuxent (river), MD **39** B6
Pauls Valley, OK **125** D9
Paulsboro, NJ **45** F1
Pawcatuck, CT **33** D8
Pawcatuck (river), CT, RI **33** D8
Pawhuska, OK **125** A10
Pawnee (river), KS **97** D3
Pawtucket, RI **51** B5
Pawtucket Reservoir, RI **51** A5
Pawtuxet (river), RI **51** C4
Payette, ID **143** G1
Payette (river), ID **143** G1
Payette, North Fork (river), ID **143** G1
Payette, South Fork (river), ID **143** G2
Payson, AZ **121** E5
Payson, UT **151** D4
Pea (river), AL **61** G4
Pea Patch Island, DE **35** B5
Pea Ridge N.M.P., AR **63** A1
Peabody, MA **41** B7
Peace (river), FL **65** F7
Peachtree City, GA **67** D2
Peaked Mountain, ME **37** B5
Pearl, MS **73** E3
Pearl (river), LA, MS **71** F9
Pearl and Hermes Atoll, HI **140** E1
Pearl City, HI **141** B4
Pearl Harbor, HI **141** C4
Pearsall, TX **127** G5
Pease (river), TX **127** C5
Pecatonica (river), WI **113** H4
Pecos, TX **126** E2
Pecos (river), NM, TX **116** E6
Pecos N.H.P., NM **123** C5
Pecos N.W.&S.R., NM **123** C5
Peekskill, NY **47** G8
Pekin, IL **91** D3
Pelican Rapids, MN **101** D2
Pell City, AL **61** C4
Pella, IA **95** E6
Pembina, ND **107** A9
Pembina (river), ND **107** A8
Pemigewasset (river), NH **43** E3
Peñasco, Rio (river), NM **123** G6
Pend Oreille (river), WA **153** B10
Pend Oreille Lake, ID **143** B1
Pender, NE **105** B8
Pendleton, OR **149** B7
Penn Hills, PA **48** D2
Penn Yan, NY **47** E4
Penns Grove, NJ **45** G1
Pennsauken, NJ **45** F2
Pennsville, NJ **45** G1
Pennsylvania Turnpike, PA **49** E3
Penobscot (river), ME **37** E5
Penobscot Bay, ME **37** G5
Penobscot, East Branch (river), ME **37** C5
Penobscot, West Branch (river), ME **37** D3
Pensacola, FL **64** B1
Peoria, IL **91** D3
Pepin, WI **113** E2
Pepin, Lake, MN **101** G5
Pequop Mountains, NV **147** B6
Perdido (river), AL, FL **61** H2
Pere Marquette N.W.&S.R., MI **99** F4
Perham, MN **101** D2
Perry, FL **65** B5
Perry, GA **67** F3
Perry, IA **95** D4
Perry, OK **125** B8
Perry Hall, MD **39** B8
Perry Lake, KS **97** B9
Perry's Victory and International Peace Memorial, OH **109** A4
Perrysburg, OH **109** B3
Perryton, TX **127** A4
Perryville, MO **103** E7
Perth Amboy, NJ **45** D4
Peru, IL **91** C4
Peru, IN **93** C4
Peshtigo (river), WI **113** C6
Petal, MS **73** G4
Petenwell Lake, WI **113** E5
Peterborough, NH **43** I2
Petersburg, AK **135** F10
Petersburg, VA **81** D9
Petersburg, WV **83** D7
Petersburg N.B., VA **81** E9
Petoskey, MI **99** D6
Petrified Forest N.P., AZ **121** D7
Petroglyph Nat. Mon., NM **123** D4
Phenix City, AL **61** E6
Philadelphia, MS **73** E4
Philadelphia, PA **49** E10
Philip, SD **111** D4
Philippi, WV **83** D6
Phillipsburg, KS **97** A4
Phillipsburg, NJ **45** C2
Phoenix, AZ **121** F4
Picayune, MS **73** I3
Pickwick Lake, AL, MS, TN **61** A1
Pictured Rocks National Lakeshore, MI **99** C4
Piedmont, AL **61** C5
Piedmont (region), **56** D5
Piedmont Lake, OH **109** D7
Piedra (river), CO **139** F3
Pierre, SD **111** D5
Pigeon (river), IN **93** A5
Pigeon (river), MI **99** D6
Pigeon (river), MN **101** B8
Pikes Peak, CO **139** D5
Pikeville, KY **69** D11
Pine (river), WI **113** C6
Pine Barrens (region), NJ **45** G3
Pine Bluff, AR **63** E5
Pine City, MN **101** E5
Pine Creek, NV **147** C5
Pine Creek, PA **49** B6
Pine Creek Gorge, PA **49** B6
Pine Hill, NJ **45** F2
Pine Mountain, KY **69** E9
Pine N.W.&S.R., MI **99** F5
Pine Ridge, NE **104** A2
Pine Ridge, SD **111** F3
Pinedale, WY **155** D3
Pinehurst, NC **75** C6
Pinelands National Reserve, NJ **45** F4
Pinetop-Lakeside, AZ **121** E7
Pineville, LA **71** D4
Pinnacles Nat. Mon., CA **137** F3
Pioche, NV **147** E7
Pioneer Valley, MA **41** B3
Pipe Spring Nat. Mon., AZ **121** A4
Pipestem Creek, ND **107** D7
Pipestone, MN **101** G2
Pipestone Nat. Mon., MN **101** G1
Piqua, OH **109** D2
Piscataqua (river), NH **43** H5
Piscataquis (river), ME **37** E4
Piscataway, NJ **45** D4
Piscataway Park, MD **39** D6
Pit (river), CA **137** B3
Pittsburg, KS **97** E10
Pittsburgh, PA **48** D2
Pittsfield, IL **91** E2
Pittsfield, MA **40** B1
Pittsfield, ME **37** F4
Pittsfield, NH **43** G4
Pittsford, VT **53** F2
Piute Reservior, UT **151** F3
Plainfield, CT **33** C8
Plainfield, IN **93** E3
Plainfield, NJ **45** C4
Plainfield, VT **53** D4
Plains, GA **67** F2
Plainview, TX **127** C4
Plainville, CT **33** C4
Plainville, KS **97** B4
Plaistow, NH **43** I5
Plankinton, SD **111** E8
Plano, TX **127** D7
Plaquemine, LA **71** F6
Platte (river), NE **105** D9
Platte, SD **111** E7
Platte, North (river), CO, NE, WY **130** D8
Platte, South (river), CO, NE **130** E8
Platteville, WI **113** H4
Plattsburgh, NY **47** A8
Plattsmouth, NE **105** D9
Playas Lake, NM **123** H2
Pleasant Grove, UT **151** C4
Pleasant Prairie, WI **113** H7
Pleasantville, NJ **45** H3
Pleasure Ridge Park, KY **69** C6
Plentywood, MT **145** A11
Plover, WI **113** E5
Plum, PA **48** D2
Plymouth, IN **93** B3
Plymouth, MA **41** D8
Plymouth, MN **101** F4
Plymouth, VT **53** F3
Pocahontas, AR **63** A6
Pocatello, ID **143** H5
Pocomoke (river), MD **39** F10
Pocomoke City, MD **39** F10
Pocono Mountains, PA **49** C9
Pocotopaug Lake, CT **33** C5
Poinsett, Lake, SD **111** C9
Point Hope, AK **135** B4
Point Judith, RI **51** G4
Point Judith Pond, RI **51** F4
Point Pleasant, NJ **45** E5
Point Pleasant, OH **109** G2
Point Pleasant, WV **82** E2
Point Reyes National Seashore, CA **137** D2
Polacca, AZ **121** C6
Polson, MT **144** C3
Pomeroy, WA **153** E9
Pompeys Pillar Nat. Mon., MT **145** E8
Ponaganset (river), RI **51** B2
Ponaganset Reservoir, RI **51** B2
Ponca City, OK **125** A9
Ponce, PR **157** I10
Pond (river), KY **69** D4
Pontchartrain, Lake, LA **71** G8
Pontiac, IL **91** C4
Pontiac, MI **99** H7
Pontoosuc Lake, MA **40** B1
Pontotoc, MS **73** B4
Poplar Bluff, MO **103** F7
Poplarville, MS **73** H4
Popple (river), WI **113** C6
Poquonock Bridge, CT **33** D7
Poquoson, VA **81** E11
Porcupine (river), AK **135** B8
Port Allen, LA **71** F6
Port Angeles, WA **152** B2
Port Arthur, TX **127** F9
Port Charlotte, FL **65** F7
Port Clinton, OH **109** B4
Port Huron, MI **99** G8
Port Jervis, NY **47** G7
Port Lavaca, TX **127** G7
Port Penn, DE **35** C5
Port Royal, SC **77** H6
Port Royal Sound (river), SC **77** H6
Port St. Lucie, FL **65** F9
Port Sulphur, LA **71** H8
Port Townsend, WA **153** B3
Port Washington, WI **113** G7
Portage, IN **93** A2
Portage, MI **99** H5
Portage, WI **113** F5
Portage (river), OH **109** B3
Portal, ND **107** A3
Portales, NM **123** E8
Portland, CT **33** C5
Portland, IN **93** D6
Portland, ME **37** H3
Portland, TN **79** A5
Portland, TX **127** H7
Portland, OR **149** B2
Portneuf Range, ID **143** H5
Portsmouth, NH **43** H5
Portsmouth, OH **109** G4
Portsmouth, RI **51** E6
Portsmouth, VA **81** E11
Post Falls, ID **143** B1
Poteau, OK **125** D12
Potholes Reservoir, WA **153** D7
Potlatch (river), ID **143** D1
Potomac, MD **39** C6
Potomac (river), MD, VA, WV **39** E7

Potomac — Sandstone

Potomac, North Branch (river), MD, WV **38** B2
Potomac, South Branch (river), WV **38** B2
Potsdam, NY **47** A7
Pottstown, PA **49** E9
Pottsville, PA **49** D8
Poughkeepsie, NY **47** F8
Poultney, VT **53** F1
Poultney (river), VT **53** F1
Poverty Point Nat. Mon., LA **71** B5
Powder (river), MT, WY **130** C7
Powder (river), OR **149** C8
Powder Wash, CO **139** A2
Powder, South Fork (river), WY **155** D6
Powell, WY **155** A4
Powell (river), TN, VA **79** A9
Powell, Lake, UT **151** H5
Pownal Center, VT **53** I1
Poygan, Lake, WI **113** E6
Prairie Dog Creek, KS **97** A3
Prairie du Chien, WI **113** G3
Pratt, KS **97** E5
Prattville, AL **61** E4
Prescott, AR **63** F3
Prescott, AZ **121** D4
Prescott Valley, AZ **121** D4
Presidential Range, NH **43** D4
Presidio, TX **126** F2
Presque Isle, ME **37** B6
Presque Isle N.W.&S.R., MI **99** C1
Preston, ID **143** I5
Preston, MN **101** H6
Prestonsburg, KY **69** C10
Pribilof Islands, AK **134** F2
Price (river), UT **151** E5
Price, UT **151** D5
Prichard, AL **61** H1
Priest (river), ID **143** B1
Priest Lake, ID **143** A1
Prince Frederick, MD **39** E7
Prince of Wales Island, AK **135** G10
Prince of Wales, Cape, AK **134** C2
Prince William Forest Park, VA **81** B9
Prince William Sound, AK **135** E7
Princeton, IN **93** H1
Princeton, KY **68** D3
Princeton, ME **37** E6
Princeton, NJ **45** D3
Princeton, WV **83** H4
Princeville, HI **140** A2
Prineville, OR **149** D4
Proctor, MN **101** D5
Proctor, VT **53** F2
Promontory, UT **151** A3
Prospect, CT **33** C4
Prosser, WA **153** F7
Providence, RI **51** B5
Providence, UT **151** A4
Providence (river), RI **51** C5
Provincetown, MA **41** D10
Provo, UT **151** C4
Prudence Island, RI **51** D5
Prudhoe Bay, AK **135** A6
Pryor, OK **125** B11
Pu'uhonua O Honaunau N.H.P., HI **141** F8
Pu'ukohola Heiau National Historic Site, HI **141** E8
Pu'uwai, HI **140** A1
Pueblo, CO **139** E6
Pueblo Bonito (site), NM **123** B2
Puerco (river), AZ **121** D7
Puerco, Rio (river), NM **123** D3
Puerto Rico (territory), US **157** E11
Puget Sound, WA **153** C3
Pukalani, HI **141** C7
Pulaski, TN **79** C4
Pulaski, VA **81** E5
Pullman, WA **153** E10
Pumpkin Creek, NE **104** C1
Punkin Center, CO **139** D7
Punta Gorda, FL **65** F7
Punxsutawney, PA **49** C3
Purcell, OK **125** D8
Purgatoire (river), CO **139** G7
Putnam, CT **33** A8
Putney, VT **53** H3
Puyallup, WA **153** D4
Pymatuning Reservoir, PA, OH **48** B1
Pyramid Lake (river), NV **147** C2

Q
Quabbin Reservoir, MA **41** B4
Quaddick Reservoir, CT **33** A8
Quaker Hill, CT **33** D7
Quakertown, PA **49** D9
Quartzsite, AZ **121** E2
Quartzville Creek N.W.&S.R., OR **149** C3
Queen (river), RI **51** E3
Queets (river), WA **152** C1
Questa, NM **123** A5
Quincy, IL **91** E1
Quincy, MA **41** C7
Quincy, WA **153** D7
Quinebaug (river), CT **33** C7
Quinn (river), NV **147** A3
Quinnipiac (river), CT **33** D4
Quinsigamond, Lake, MA **41** C5
Quitman, GA **67** H4
Quitman, MS **73** F5
Quonochontaug, RI **51** G2
Quonochontaug Pond, RI **51** G2

R
Rabun Gap, GA **67** A4
Raccoon (river), IA **95** C4
Raccoon Creek, OH **109** G5
Racine, WI **113** H7
Radcliff, KY **69** C6
Radford, VA **81** E5
Raft River Mountains, UT **151** A2
Rahway, NJ **45** C4
Rainbow Bridge Nat. Mon., UT **151** H5
Rainier, OR **149** A2
Rainier, Mount, WA **153** D4
Rainy (river), MN **101** B4
Rainy Lake, MN **101** A4
Raisin (river), MI **99** H6
Raleigh, NC **75** B7
Raleigh Bay, NC **75** D10
Rampart Range, CO **139** D5
Ramsey, NJ **45** B4
Randolph, MA **41** C7
Randolph, VT **53** E3
Randolph Center, VT **53** E3
Rangeley, ME **37** E2
Rangeley Lake, ME **37** F2
Rangely, CO **138** B1
Rantoul, IL **91** D5
Rapid City, SD **110** D2
Rapid N.W.&S.R., ID **143** E1
Rappahannock (river), VA **81** C10
Raquette (river), NY **47** B7
Raritan (river), NJ **45** D4
Rat Islands, AK **135** H7
Rathbun Lake, IA **95** F6
Raton, NM **123** A6
Ravenna, NE **105** D6
Ravenswood, WV **83** E3
Rawlins, WY **155** F6
Raymond, NH **43** H4
Raymond, WA **152** E2
Rayne, LA **71** G4
Raystown Lake, PA **49** E5
Rayville, LA **71** B5
Reading, PA **49** E8
Red (river), **116** C7
Red Bank, NJ **45** D5
Red Bank, TN **79** D7
Red Bay, AL **61** B1
Red Bluff Lake, TX **116** E5
Red Bud, IL **91** G3
Red Cedar (river), WI **113** D2
Red Cloud, NE **105** E7
Red Hills, KS **97** E3
Red Lake, AZ **121** C2
Red Lake, MN **101** C3
Red Lake (river), MN **101** B2
Red Lion, PA **49** E7
Red Lodge, MT **145** F7
Red N.W.&S.R., KY **69** C9
Red Oak, IA **95** E3
Red River of the North (river), MN, ND **86** A3
Red Rock, Lake, IA **95** E6
Red Willow Creek, NE **105** D4
Red Wing, MN **101** G5
Red, Elm Fork (river), OK **125** D5
Red, North Fork (river), OK **125** D5
Red, North Fork (river), TX **127** B4
Red, Prairie Dog Town Fork (river), OK, TX **125** E5
Red, Salt Fork (river), OK, TX **125** D5
Redding, CA **137** B2
Redfield, SD **111** C8
Redmond, OR **149** D4
Redmond, WA **153** C4
Redwood Falls, MN **101** G3
Redwood N.P., CA **137** A1
Reedsburg, WI **113** F4
Reedsport, OR **148** D1
Reedy Island, DE **35** C5
Reelfoot Lake, TN **78** B2
Reese (river), NV **147** C4
Rehoboth Bay, DE **35** H7
Rehoboth Beach, DE **35** H7
Reidsville, NC **75** A6
Reisterstown, MD **39** B7
Rend Lake, IL **91** H4
Reno, NV **147** D2
Rensselaer, IN **93** C2
Renton, WA **153** C4
Republic, MO **103** F3
Republic, WA **153** A8
Republican (river), KS, NE **86** F2
Republican, South Fork (river), KS, CO **96** A1
Reserve, NM **123** F1
Reston, VA **81** B9
Rexburg, ID **143** G5
Reynoldsburg, OH **109** E4
Rhinelander, WI **113** C5
Rhode Island (island), RI **51** E6
Rhode Island Sound, RI **51** G4
Rice City, RI **51** D2
Rice Lake, WI **113** C2
Richard B. Russell Lake, GA, SC **67** C5
Richardson lakes, ME **37** F2
Richfield, UT **151** E3
Richford, VT **53** A3
Richland, WA **153** E7
Richland Center, WI **113** G4
Richland Creek N.W.&S.R., AR **63** B3
Richlands, VA **80** E3
Richmond, IN **93** E6
Richmond, MO **103** C3
Richmond, VA **81** D9
Richmond, VT **53** C2
Richmond N.B. Park, VA **81** D9
Richwood, WV **83** F5
Ridgecrest, CA **137** G6
Ridgefield, CT **33** E2
Ridgeland, MS **73** E3
Ridgewood, NJ **45** B5
Ridgway, PA **49** B4
Rifle, CO **139** C2
Rifle (river), MI **99** F7
Rigby, ID **143** G5
Riggins, ID **143** E1
Ringwood, NJ **45** B4
Rio Chama N.W.&S.R., NM **123** B4
Rio Grande (river), CO, NM, TX **116** G7
Rio Grande City, TX **127** I6
Rio Grande N.W.&S.R., NM **123** A5
Rio Grande Wild and Scenic River, TX **127** F3
Rio Rancho, NM **123** D4
Ripley, MS **73** A4
Ripley, TN **78** C1
Ripley, WV **83** E3
Ripon, WI **113** F6
Ritzville, WA **153** D8
River Falls, WI **113** D1
Riverside, CA **137** H6
Riverton, UT **151** C4
Riverton, WY **155** D5
Roan Cliffs, UT **151** E6
Roan Mountain, TN **79** B11
Roan Plateau, CO **138** C1
Roanoke, AL **61** D5
Roanoke, VA **81** D6
Roanoke (river), NC, VA **56** C7
Roanoke (Staunton) (river), VA **81** E7
Roanoke Island, NC **75** B10
Roanoke Rapids, NC **75** A8
Roaring N.W.&S.R., OR **149** B3
Robert South Kerr Lake, OK **125** D12
Robinson, IL **91** F6
Robstown, TX **127** H6
Rochester, IN **93** B4
Rochester, MN **101** G5
Rochester, NH **43** G5
Rochester, NY **47** D4
Rock (river), IL, WI **91** B3
Rock Creek, NV **147** B5
Rock Creek, OK **125** B8
Rock Hill, SC **77** B5
Rock Island, IL **91** C2
Rock Springs, WY **155** G3
Rockcastle (river), KY **69** D8
Rockford, IL **91** A4
Rockingham, NC **75** D6
Rockland, MA **41** C8
Rockland, ME **37** G4
Rockport, ME **37** G4
Rockport, TX **127** H7
Rockville, MD **39** C6
Rocky Ford, CO **139** E7
Rocky Mount, NC **75** B8
Rocky Mount, VA **81** E6
Rocky Mountain N.P., CO **139** B5
Rocky Mountains, **130** A4
Rogers, AR **63** A1
Rogers City, MI **99** D7
Rogers, Mount, VA **80** F4
Rogue (river), OR **149** F2
Rogue N.W.&S.R., OR **148** F1
Rolla, MO **103** E5
Rolla, ND **107** A6
Rolling Fork (river), KY **69** D6
Rome, GA **67** B1
Rome, NY **47** D6
Romney, WV **83** D8
Roosevelt, UT **151** C6
Root (river), MN **101** H6
Roseau, MN **101** A2
Roseau (river), MN **101** A2
Rosebud, SD **111** E5
Roseburg, OR **149** E2
Rosepine, LA **70** E2
Ross Barnett Reservoir, MS **73** E3
Ross Lake, WA **153** A5
Ross Lake N.R.A., WA **153** A5
Roswell, GA **67** C2
Roswell, NM **123** F6
Rota Island, MP **156** D1
Rough (river), KY **69** D4
Rough River Lake, KY **69** C5
Round Rock, TX **127** F6
Round Valley Reservoir, NJ **45** C3
Roundup, MT **145** D7
Roxboro, NC **75** A7
Ruby Mountains, NV **147** C6
Rugby, ND **107** B6
Ruidoso, NM **123** F5
Ruleville, MS **73** C2
Rum (river), MN **101** E4
Rumford, ME **37** F2
Rupert, ID **143** I4
Rush Creek, CO **139** D8
Rushville, IN **93** E5
Rushville, NE **104** A2
Russell, KS **97** C5
Russell Cave Nat. Mon., AL **61** A5
Russellville, AL **61** B2
Russellville, AR **63** C3
Ruston, LA **71** B3
Rutland, VT **53** F2
Rye, NH **43** H5
Rye Patch Reservoir, NV **147** B3

S
Sabine (river), LA, TX **56** E2
Sabine Lake, LA **70** G1
Sable, Cape, FL **65** H8
Sac (river), MO **103** E3
Sacajawea, Lake, WA **153** E8
Saco, ME **37** H2
Saco (river), ME, NH **37** H2
Sacramento, CA **137** D3
Sacramento (river), CA **137** B2
Sacramento Mountains, NM **123** F5
Safford, AZ **121** F7
Sag Harbor, NY **47** G10
Sagamore Hill National Historic Site, NY **47** H9
Sagavanirktok (river), AK **135** B6
Saginaw, MI **99** G7
Saginaw Bay, MI **99** F7
Saguache Creek, CO **139** E3
Saguaro N.P., AZ **121** G5
Saint Albans, VT **53** B2
Saint John (river), ME **37** B4
Saint John, Baker Branch (river), ME **37** C3
Saint John, Northwest Branch (river), ME **37** B3
Saint John, Southwest Branch (river), ME **37** C3
Sainte Genevieve, MO **103** D7
Saint-Gaudens National Historic Site, NH **43** G1
Saipan (island), MP **156** C2
Sakakawea, Lake, ND **107** C3
Sakonnet Point, RI **51** F6
Sakonnet River, RI **51** E6
Salamanca, NY **46** F2
Salamonie (river), IN **93** C5
Salamonie Lake, IN **93** C4
Salem, IL **91** G4
Salem, IN **93** G4
Salem, MA **41** B8
Salem, MO **103** E5
Salem, NH **43** I4
Salem, NJ **45** G1
Salem, OH **109** C7
Salem, OR **149** C2
Salem, SD **111** E9
Salem, VA **81** D6
Salem, WV **83** D5
Salem (river), NJ **45** G1
Salem Maritime National Historic Site, MA **41** B8
Salida, CO **139** E4
Salina, KS **97** C6
Salinas, CA **137** F3
Salinas Pueblo Missions Nat. Mon., NM **123** E4
Saline (river), KS **97** C6
Saline (river), AR **63** E4
Saline (river), IL **91** H5
Saline Bayou (river), LA **71** B3
Saline Bayou N.W.&S.R., LA **71** C3
Salisbury, MD **39** E10
Salisbury, NC **75** B5
Salish Mountains, MT **144** A2
Sallisaw, OK **125** C12
Salmon, ID **143** E3
Salmon (river), CT **33** C6
Salmon (river), ID **143** F3
Salmon Falls (river), ME, NH **37** I2
Salmon Falls Creek Reservoir, ID **143** I3
Salmon N.W.&S.R., AK **135** B4
Salmon N.W.&S.R., ID **143** E2
Salmon N.W.&S.R., OR **149** B3
Salmon River Mountains, ID **143** F2
Salmon, Middle Fork (river), ID **143** F3
Salmon, Middle Fork N.W.&S.R., ID **143** E3
Salmon, South Fork (river), ID **143** F2
Salt (river), AZ **121** E6
Salt (river), KY **69** C6
Salt (river), MO **103** B5
Salt Creek (river), IN **93** G3
Salt Creek, IL **91** E4
Salt Fork Lake, OH **109** D7
Salt Lake City, UT **151** C4
Salt River Bay N.H.P. and Ecological Preserve, VI **157** I8
Salton Sea (lake), CA **137** I7
Saluda (river), SC **77** C4
Salvador, Lake, LA **71** H7
Sam Rayburn Reservoir, TX **127** E9
San Andres Mountains, NM **123** F5
San Angelo, TX **127** E4
San Antonio, TX **127** F6
San Antonio (river), TX **127** G6
San Antonio Missions N.H.P., TX **127** G6
San Bernardino, CA **137** H6
San Blas, Cape, FL **56** F5
San Carlos, AZ **121** F6
San Carlos Reservoir, AZ **121** F6
San Clemente (island), CA **137** I5
San Diego, CA **137** I6
San Francisco, CA **137** E2
San Francisco (river), NM **123** F1
San Francisco Maritime N.H.P., CA **137** E1
San Joaquin (river), CA **137** E4
San Jose, CA **137** E3
San Jose, MP **156** D1
San Jose, Rio (river), NM **123** D2
San Juan, PR **157** H11
San Juan (river), CO, NM, UT **116** B3
San Juan Island N.H.P., WA **153** B3
San Juan Islands, WA **153** B3
San Juan Mountains, CO **139** F2
San Juan National Historic Site, PR **157** H11
San Luis, AZ **121** G1
San Luis Creek, CO **139** E4
San Luis Lake, CO **139** F5
San Luis Obispo, CA **137** G3
San Luis Valley, CO **139** F4
San Manuel, AZ **121** G6
San Marcos, TX **127** F6
San Miguel (river), CO **138** E1
San Pedro (river), AZ **121** G6
San Rafael, CA **137** D2
San Rafael (river), UT **151** E5
Sanak Island, AK **134** H3
Sanbornville, NH **43** F5
Sand Arroyo (river), CO **139** F9
Sand Creek, IN **93** F4
Sand Creek, SD **111** D8
Sand Hills, NE **105** B3
Sand Springs, OK **125** B10
Sandersville, GA **67** E5
Sandpoint, ID **143** B1
Sandstone, MN **101** E5

Sandusky — Stilwell

Sandusky, MI **99** G8
Sandusky, OH **109** B4
Sandusky (river), OH **109** C4
Sandusky Bay, OH **109** B4
Sandwich, IL **91** B4
Sandwich, MA **41** E9
Sandy, UT **151** C4
Sandy Hook (point), NJ **45** D5
Sandy Hook Bay, NJ **45** D5
Sandy N.W.&S.R., OR **149** B3
Sandy Point, RI **51** H3
Sandy Springs, GA **67** C2
Sanford, FL **65** D8
Sanford, ME **37** I2
Sanford, NC **75** C6
Sangamon (river), IL **91** E4
Sangre de Cristo Mountains, CO, NM **130** F7
Sanibel Island, FL **65** G7
Sanpoil (river), WA **153** B8
Santa Ana, CA **137** H5
Santa Barbara, CA **137** H4
Santa Catalina (island), CA **137** I5
Santa Clara, UT **151** H2
Santa Claus, IN **93** H2
Santa Cruz (island), CA **137** H4
Santa Cruz, CA **137** E2
Santa Cruz (river), AZ **121** G5
Santa Fe, NM **123** C5
Santa Maria, CA **137** G4
Santa Monica, CA **137** H5
Santa Monica Mountains N.R.A., CA **137** H5
Santa Rita, GU **156** G1
Santa Rosa (island), CA **137** H3
Santa Rosa, CA **137** D2
Santa Rosa, NM **123** D6
Santa Rosa and San Jacinto Mountains Nat. Mon., CA **137** H7
Santa Rosa Lake, NM **123** D6
Santa Rosa Range, NV **147** A4
Santee (river), SC **77** E8
Santee Dam, SC **77** E7
Sapelo Island, GA **67** G7
Sapelo Sound, GA **67** G7
Sappa Creek, KS **96** A2
Sapulpa, OK **125** B10
Saraland, AL **61** H1
Saranac Lake, NY **47** B8
Sarasota, FL **65** F6
Saratoga, WY **155** G7
Saratoga N.H.P., NY **47** D8
Saratoga Springs, NY **47** D8
Sardis Lake, MS **73** B3
Sardis Lake, OK **125** D11
Sassafras (bay), MD **39** B9
Sassafras Mountain, SC **76** A2
Satilla (river), GA **67** H5
Saugatuck Reservoir, CT **33** E2
Saugus Iron Works National Historic Site, MA **41** B7
Sauk Centre, MN **101** E3
Sault Sainte Marie, MI **99** C6
Saunderstown, RI **51** E4
Savanna, IL **91** B3
Savannah, GA **67** F7
Savannah, MO **103** B2
Savannah, TN **78** C3
Savannah (river), GA, SC **56** D6
Sawtooth N.R.A., ID **143** G3
Sawtooth Range, ID **143** F2
Saylesville, RI **51** B5
Sayre, OK **125** D5
Sayre, PA **49** A7
Sayreville, NJ **45** D4
Scantic (river), CT **33** B5
Scappoose, OR **149** B2
Scarborough, ME **37** H2
Schaumburg, IL **91** B5
Schell Creek Range, NV **147** D6
Schenectady, NY **47** D8
Schuyler, NE **105** C8
Schuylkill (river), PA **49** D8
Scioto (river), OH **109** C3
Scituate Reservoir, RI **51** C3
Scobey, MT **145** A10
Scott City, KS **96** C2
Scotts Bluff Nat. Mon., NE **104** C1
Scottsbluff, NE **104** B1
Scottsboro, AL **61** A4
Scottsburg, IN **93** G4
Scottsdale, AZ **121** F4
Scranton, PA **49** B9
Sea Islands, GA, SC **56** E6
Sea Isle City, NJ **45** I3
Seaford, DE **35** H5
Seaman Range, NV **147** F6
Searcy, AR **63** C5
Searsport, ME **37** F5
Seaside, OR **148** A1
Seaside Heights, NJ **45** F5
Seattle, WA **153** C4
Sebago Lake, ME **37** H2
Sebec Lake, ME **37** E4
Sebring, FL **65** E8
Second Lake, NH **43** A4
Sedalia, MO **103** D3
Sedona, AZ **121** D5
Sedro Woolley, WA **153** B4
Seekonk, MA **41** E6
Seekonk (river), RI **51** B5
Seguam Island, AK **135** H10
Selawik N.W.&S.R., AK **135** C5
Selby, SD **111** B6
Selbyville, DE **35** I7
Seligman, AZ **121** C3
Selinsgrove, PA **49** D7
Selkirk Mountains, ID **143** B1
Sells, AZ **121** H5
Selma, AL **61** E3
Selway (river), ID **143** D2
Seminoe Reservoir, WY **155** F7
Seminole, OK **125** D9
Seminole, Lake, FL, GA **67** I2
Semisopochnoi Island, AK **135** H7
Senatobia, MS **73** B3
Seneca, KS **97** A8
Seneca, SC **76** B1
Seneca Falls, NY **47** D4
Seneca Lake, NY **47** E4
Senecaville Lake, OH **109** E7
Sequatchie (river), TN **79** C7
Sequoia N.P., CA **137** F5
Sespe Creek N.W.&S.R., CA **137** H5
Severn (river), MD **39** C7
Severna Park, MD **39** C8
Sevier (river), UT **151** G3
Sevier Desert, UT **151** D3
Sevier Lake (dry lake), UT **151** E2
Sevierville, TN **79** B9
Seward, NE **105** D8
Seward, AK **135** F6
Seward Peninsula, AK **135** C4
Seymour, CT **33** D3
Seymour, IN **93** G4
Seymour, MO **103** F4
Seymour Lake, VT **53** A5
Shafer, Lake, IN **93** C3
Shaker Heights, OH **109** B6
Shamokin, PA **49** D7
Shannock, RI **51** F3
Sharon, CT **33** B2
Sharon, PA **48** C1
Sharpe, Lake, SD **111** D6
Sharpsburg, MD **39** B4
Shasta Lake, CA **137** B3
Shasta, Mount, CA **137** A2
Shawano, WI **113** D6
Shawnee, OK **125** D9
Shawneetown, IL **91** H5
Sheboygan, WI **113** F7
Sheenjek N.W.&S.R., AK **135** B7
Sheep Range, NV **147** G6
Shelburne, VT **53** C1
Shelburne Falls, MA **40** B2
Shelby, MS **73** C2
Shelby, MT **145** B4
Shelby, OH **109** C5
Shelbyville, IN **93** F4
Shelbyville, KY **69** B7
Shelbyville, TN **79** C5
Shelbyville, Lake, IL **91** F4
Sheldon, IA **94** A2
Shell Creek, NE **105** C7
Shell Rock (river), IA **95** B6
Shelley, ID **143** H5
Shelton, CT **33** E3
Shelton, WA **153** D3
Shenandoah, IA **95** F3
Shenandoah (river), VA **81** A8
Shenandoah Mountain, VA **81** C7
Shenandoah N.P., VA **81** B8
Shenipsit Lake, CT **33** B6
Shepaug (river), CT **33** C2
Sheridan, AR **63** E4
Sheridan, OR **149** B2
Sheridan, WY **155** A6
Sherman, TX **127** C7
Sherman Mills, ME **37** D5
Shetucket (river), CT **33** C7
Sheyenne (river), ND **107** C6
Shiloh N.M.P., TN **78** C3
Shinapaaru, MP **156** D1
Shinnston, WV **83** D5
Ship Bottom, NJ **45** G4
Ship Rock (peak), NM **123** A1
Shippensburg, PA **49** E6
Shiprock, NM **123** A2
Shoshone, ID **143** H3
Shoshone (river), WY **155** B4
Shoshone Mountains, NV **147** D4
Shoshone Range, NV **147** C4
Shoshone, North Fork (river), WY **155** B3
Shoshone, South Fork (river), WY **155** B3
Show Low, AZ **121** E6
Shreveport, LA **70** B1
Shrewsbury, MA **41** C5
Sidney, MT **145** B11
Sidney, NE **104** C2
Sidney, NY **47** E6
Sidney, OH **109** D2
Sidney Lanier, Lake, GA **67** B3
Sierra Nevada, CA **137** C3
Sierra Vista, AZ **121** H6
Sikeston, MO **103** F8
Silicon Valley, CA **137** E2
Siloam Springs, AR **63** A1
Silver City, NM **123** G2
Silver Lake, MA **41** D8
Silver Spring, MD **39** C6
Silver Springs, NV **147** D2
Simi Valley, CA **137** H5
Simpsonville, SC **77** B3
Simsbury, CT **33** B4
Sinclair, Lake, GA **67** D4
Sioux Center, IA **94** A2
Sioux City, IA **94** C1
Sioux Falls, SD **111** E10
Sipsey (river), AL **61** D1
Sipsey Fork N.W.&S.R., AL **61** B2
Sisquoc N.W.&S.R., CA **137** G4
Sisseton, SD **111** A9
Sissonville, WV **83** E3
Sitka, AK **135** F10
Sitka N.H.P., AK **135** G10
Siufaga, AS **156** I4
Siuslaw (river), OR **149** D2
Skagit (river), WA **153** B4
Skagway, AK **135** E10
Skiatook Lake, OK **125** B10
Skillet Fork (river), IL **91** G4
Skowhegan, ME **37** F3
Skykomish (river), WA **153** C4
Skyline Drive, VA **81** C8
Slatersville, RI **51** A3
Slaughter Beach, DE **35** G6
Slayton, MN **101** G2
Sleeping Bear Dunes National Lakeshore, MI **99** E5
Slide Mountain, NY **47** F8
Slidell, LA **71** F8
Smackover, AR **63** G4
Smith Canyon, CO **139** F8
Smith Island, MD **39** F9
Smith Mountain Lake, VA **81** E6
Smith N.W.&S.R., CA **137** A1
Smith, North Fork N.W.&S.R., OR **148** G1
Smithfield, NC **75** C7
Smithfield, UT **151** A4
Smithfield, VA **81** E10
Smoke Creek Desert, NV **147** C2
Smoky Hill (river), KS **96** C1
Smoky Hills, KS **97** B4
Smoky Mountains, ID **143** G3
Smyrna, DE **35** D5
Smyrna, GA **67** C2
Smyrna, TN **79** B5
Smyrna (river), DE **35** D5
Snake (river), ID, OR, WA, WY **130** B3
Snake N.W.&S.R., ID, OR **143** D1
Snake River Plain, ID **143** H4
Snohomish, WA **153** C4
Snow Hill, MD **39** F10
Snow, Mount, VT **53** H2
Snowflake, AZ **121** D6
Snyder, TX **127** D4
Socastee, SC **77** D9
Socorro, NM **123** E3
Soda Springs, ID **143** H6
Soddy-Daisy, TN **79** C7
Sol Duc (river), WA **152** C1
Soledad, CA **137** F3
Solomon (river), KS **97** B6
Solomon, North Fork (river), KS **97** B3
Solomon, South Fork (river), KS **97** B4
Solomons, MD **39** E8
Somers Point, NJ **45** H3
Somerset, KY **69** D8
Somerset, MA **41** E7
Somerset, PA **49** E3
Somerset Reservoir, VT **53** H2
Somersworth, NH **43** G5
Somerville, NJ **45** D3
Songsong, MP **156** D1
Sonora, TX **127** F4
Sonoran Desert, AZ, CA **121** F3
Sooner Lake, OK **125** B9
Souhegan (river), NH **43** I3
Souris (Mouse) (river), ND **107** B5
South (river), NC **75** D7
South Bass Island, OH **109** A4
South Bend, IN **93** A3
South Berwick, ME **37** I2
South Boston, VA **81** E7
South Burlington, VT **53** C2
South Charleston, WV **83** F3
South Hadley, MA **41** C3
South Haven, MI **99** H4
South Hero Island, VT **53** B1
South Hill, VA **81** E8
South Lake Tahoe, CA **137** D4
South Milwaukee, WI **113** G7
South Paris, ME **37** G2
South Pass, WY **155** E4
South Point *see* Kalae, HI **141** G8
South Point, OH **109** H5
South Portland, ME **37** H3
South Sioux City, NE **105** B9
South Yarmouth, MA **41** E10
Southampton, NY **47** G10
Southaven, MS **73** A3
Southbridge, MA **41** D4
Southbury, CT **33** D3
Southern Pines, NC **75** C6
Southington, CT **33** C4
Southport, NC **75** E8
Southwest Harbor, ME **37** G5
Spanish Fork, UT **151** C4
Sparks, NV **147** D2
Sparta, NJ **45** B3
Sparta, TN **79** B6
Sparta, WI **113** F3
Spartanburg, SC **77** B3
Spearfish, SD **110** C1
Spencer, IA **95** A3
Spencer, MA **41** C4
Spencer, WV **83** E3
Spirit Lake, IA **95** A3
Spokane, WA **153** C9
Spokane (river), ID, WA **153** C9
Spoon (river), IL **91** D3
Spooner, WI **113** C2
Sprague (river), OR **149** F4
Spring (river), AR **63** A6
Spring Bay (dry lake), UT **151** A2
Spring Creek, NV **147** B6
Spring Hill, FL **65** D6
Spring Hill, TN **79** C5
Spring Lake, NC **75** C7
Spring Valley, NY **47** G8
Springdale, AR **63** A1
Springer, NM **123** B6
Springer Mountain, GA **67** B3
Springfield, CO **139** F9
Springfield, IL **91** E3
Springfield, MA **41** C3
Springfield, MO **103** F3
Springfield, OH **109** E3
Springfield, OR **149** D2
Springfield, TN **79** A5
Springfield, VT **53** G3
Springfield Armory National Historic Site, MA **41** D3
Springhill, LA **70** A2
Springvale, ME **37** H2
Springville, UT **151** C4
Spruce Knob (peak), WV **83** E7
Spruce Knob-Seneca Rocks N.R.A., WV **83** E7
Squam Lake, NH **43** F3
Squapan Lake, ME **37** C5
Square Lake, ME **37** A5
Squaw Creek N.W.&S.R., OR **149** D4
St. Albans, WV **82** F2
St. Andrew Sound, GA **67** H7
St. Anthony, ID **143** G5
St. Augustine, FL **65** B8
St. Catherine, Lake, VT **53** G1
St. Catherines Island, GA **67** G7
St. Catherines Sound, GA **67** G7
St. Charles, MD **39** D7
St. Charles, MO **103** C6
St. Charles (river), CO **139** E6
St. Clair, MI **99** H8
St. Clair Shores, MI **99** H8
St. Clair, Lake, MI **99** H8
St. Cloud, MN **101** E4
St. Croix (island), VI **157** I7
St. Croix (river), ME **37** D7
St. Croix (river), MN, WI **101** E5
St. Croix Falls, WI **113** C1
St. Croix Island International Historic Site, ME **37** E7
St. Croix N.W.&S.R., MN, WI **113** D1
St. Croix National Scenic Riverway, MN, WI **113** B2
St. Elias Mountains, AK **135** E8
St. Elias, Mount, AK **135** E8
St. Francis (river), ME **37** A4
St. Francis, ME **37** A4
St. Francis (river), AR, MO **63** A7
St. George, UT **151** H2
St. Georges, DE **35** C4
St. Helena Island, SC **77** H6
St. Helena Sound, SC **77** G6
St. Helens, OR **149** A2
St. Helens, Mount, WA **153** F4
St. Ignace, MI **99** D6
St. James, MN **101** G3
St. James, MO **103** D5
St. Joe (river), ID **143** C1
St. Joe N.W.&S.R., ID **143** C2
St. John (island), VI **157** G8
St. Johns, AZ **121** D7
St. Johns, MI **99** G6
St. Johns (river), FL **65** D8
St. Johnsbury, VT **53** C5
St. Jones (river), DE **35** E5
St. Joseph, MI **99** I4
St. Joseph, MO **103** B2
St. Joseph (river), IN, MI **93** A4
St. Joseph (river), IN, OH **93** B5
St. Lawrence (river), NY **47** A6
St. Lawrence Island, AK **134** D2
St. Louis, MO **103** D7
St. Louis (river), MN **101** D5
St. Lucie Canal, FL **65** F9
St. Maries, ID **143** C1
St. Maries (river), ID **143** C1
St. Marys, GA **67** I7
St. Marys, OH **109** D2
St. Marys, PA **49** B4
St. Marys, WV **83** D4
St. Marys (river), FL **65** B7
St. Marys (river), IN, OH **93** C5
St. Marys (river), MI **99** C6
St. Marys City, MD **39** F8
St. Marys Lake *see* Grand Lake, OH **109** D2
St. Matthew Island, AK **134** E1
St. Michaels, MD **39** D8
St. Paul, AK **134** F1
St. Paul, MN **101** F5
St. Paul, NE **105** C7
St. Paul's Church National Historic Site, NY **47** H8
St. Peter, MN **101** G4
St. Peters, MO **103** C6
St. Petersburg, FL **65** E6
St. Simons Island, GA **67** H7
St. Thomas (island), VI **157** G7
Stafford, CT **33** A6
Stafford Pond, RI **51** D6
Staffordville Reservoir, CT **33** A6
Stamford, CT **33** F1
Stamps, AR **63** G2
Stanley, ND **107** B3
Starkville, MS **73** C5
State College, PA **49** D5
Stateline, NV **147** D1
Staten Island, NY **47** H8
Statesboro, GA **67** F6
Statesville, NC **75** B4
Statue of Liberty Nat. Mon., NY **47** H8
Staunton (river) *see* Roanoke, VA **81** E7
Staunton, VA **81** C7
Stayton, OR **149** C2
Steamboat Springs, CO **139** B3
Steamtown National Historic Site, PA **49** B9
Steele, ND **107** E6
Steens Mountain, OR **149** F7
Stellwagen Bank National Marine Sanctuary, MA **41** B9
Stephenville, TX **127** D6
Sterling, CO **139** A8
Sterling, IL **91** B3
Steubenville, OH **109** D8
Stevens Point, WI **113** E5
Stillwater, MN **101** F5
Stillwater, OK **125** B9
Stillwater (river), OH **109** D1
Stillwater Range, NV **147** C3
Stilwell, OK **125** C12

Stockbridge — Waikoloa

Stockbridge, MA **40** C1
Stockton, CA **137** D3
Stockton Lake, MO **103** E3
Stone Mountain (site), GA **67** C3
Stones River N.B., TN **79** B5
Stonewall Jackson Lake, WV **83** D5
Stonington, ME **37** G5
Stony (river), AK **135** E5
Storm Lake, IA **95** B3
Storrs, CT **33** B6
Story City, IA **95** C5
Stoughton, MA **41** C7
Stoughton, WI **113** G5
Stowe, VT **53** C3
Stratford, CT **33** E3
Stratford Point, CT **33** E3
Stratton Mountain, VT **53** H2
Strawberry Reservoir, UT **151** C5
Streator, IL **91** C4
Strong (river), MS **73** F3
Strongsville, OH **109** B6
Stroudsburg, PA **49** C9
Stuarts Draft, VA **81** C7
Stump Lake, ND **107** C8
Sturbridge, MA **41** C4
Sturgeon Bay, WI **113** D8
Sturgeon N.W.&S.R., MI **99** D4
Sturgis, MI **99** I5
Sturgis, SD **110** C2
Stuttgart, AR **63** E5
Sudbury Reservoir, MA **41** C6
Sudbury, Assabet and Concord N.W.&S.R., MA **41** B6
Suffolk, VA **81** E11
Sugar (river), NH **43** G1
Sugar (river), WI **113** H5
Sugar Creek (creek), IN **93** E2
Sugar Creek (creek), IN **93** E4
Sugar Land, TX **127** F8
Sugarloaf Mountain, ME **37** E2
Suitland, MD **39** D7
Sullivan, MO **103** D6
Sullys Hill National Game Preserve, ND **107** C7
Sulphur, LA **70** G2
Sulphur, OK **125** E9
Sulphur Creek, SD **111** C3
Sulphur Springs, TX **127** C8
Summer Lake, OR **149** F5
Summersville, WV **83** F4
Summersville Lake, WV **83** F4
Summerville, SC **77** F7
Summit Lake, NV **147** A2
Sumner Lake, NM **123** D6
Sumter, SC **77** D6
Sun (river), MT **145** C4
Sun City, AZ **121** F4
Sun Prairie, WI **113** G5
Sunapee Lake, NH **43** G2
Sunapee, Mount, NH **43** G2
Sunbury, PA **49** C7
Suncook, NH **43** H4
Suncook (river), NH **43** H4
Suncook Lakes, NH **43** G4
Sundance, WY **155** B10
Sunflower, Mount, KS **96** B1
Sunland Park, NM **123** H4
Sunnyside, WA **153** E6
Sunnyvale, CA **137** E2
Sunset Crater Volcano Nat. Mon., AZ **121** C5
Superior, NE **105** E7
Superior, WI **113** A2
Superior, Lake, **86** B6
Surf City, NJ **45** G4
Surfside Beach, SC **77** E9
Surry Mountain Lake, NH **43** H1
Susanville, CA **137** B3
Susitna (river), AK **135** D6
Susquehanna (river), MD, NY, PA **39** A8
Susquehanna, West Branch (river), PA **49** C5
Susupe, MP **156** C2
Sutherlin, OR **149** E2
Sutton Lake, WV **83** E5
Suwannee (river), FL **65** C6
Swainsboro, GA **67** E5
Swanson Reservoir, NE **105** E4
Swanton, VT **53** A2
Sweet Home, OR **149** D2
Sweetwater, TN **79** C8
Sweetwater, TX **127** D4
Sweetwater (river), WY **155** E5
Sweetwater Lake, ND **107** B8
Swift (river), MA **41** C3
Sycamore, IL **91** B4
Sycan (river), OR **149** F4
Sycan N.W.&S.R., OR **149** F4
Sylacauga, AL **61** D4
Sylvania, OH **109** A3
Syracuse, NY **47** D5
Sysladobsis Lake, ME **37** E6

T
Table Rock Lake, MO **103** F3
Tacoma, WA **153** D3
Taconic Range, MA, NY, VT **47** F9
Tahlequah, OK **125** C11
Tahoe, Lake, CA, NV **137** C4
Tahquamenon (East Branch) N.W.&S.R., MI **99** C5
Taliesin (site), WI **113** G4
Talladega, AL **61** D4
Tallahala Creek, MS **73** G4
Tallahassee, FL **65** B4
Tallahatchie (river), MS **73** C3
Tallapoosa (river), AL **61** E4
Tallassee, AL **61** E5
Talleyville, DE **35** A5
Tallgrass Prairie National Preserve, KS **97** C7
Tallulah, LA **71** B6
Tamaqua, PA **49** D8
Tampa, FL **65** E6
Tampa Bay, FL **65** E6
Tampico, IL **91** B3
Tamuning, GU **156** F1
Tanaga Island, AK **135** H8
Tanana (river), AK **135** D7
Taneytown, MD **39** A6
Tangier Island, VA **81** C11
Tangier Sound, MD **39** F9
Tangipahoa (river), LA **71** E7
Taos, NM **123** B5
Tar (river), NC **75** B8
Tarboro, NC **75** B8
Tarpon Springs, FL **65** E6
Tarrytown, NY **47** G8
Tau (island), AS **157** I5
Tau, AS **156** I4
Taum Sauk Mountain, MO **103** E6
Taunton, MA **41** D7
Taunton (river), MA **41** E7
Tawas City, MI **99** F7
Taylors, SC **77** B3
Taylorville, IL **91** E4
Tazewell, VA **80** E4
Teche, Bayou (river), LA **71** G5
Tecumseh, MI **99** I7
Tecumseh, OK **125** D9
Tekamah, NE **105** C9
Tell City, IN **93** I3
Tellico Lake, TN **79** C8
Telluride, CO **139** F2
Telos Lake, ME **37** C4
Tempe, AZ **121** F4
Temperance, MI **99** I7
Temple, TX **127** E7
Ten Thousand Islands, FL **65** H8
Tenkiller Lake, OK **125** C11
Tennessee (river), AL, KY, MS, TN **56** C4
Tennessee-Tombigbee Waterway, AL, MS **73** B5
Tensas (river), LA **71** C5
Terre Haute, IN **93** F2
Terrebonne Bay, LA **71** I7
Terry, MT **145** D10
Terryville, CT **33** C3
Teton (river), MT **145** B5
Texarkana, AR **63** F1
Texarkana, TX **127** C9
Texoma, Lake, OK **125** F9
Thames (river), CT **33** D7
The Berkshires (hills), MA **40** C1
The Dalles, OR **149** B4
The Everglades, FL **65** H8
The Hermitage (site), TN **79** B5
Theodore Roosevelt Inaugural National Historic Site, NY **46** D1
Theodore Roosevelt Lake, AZ **121** E5
Theodore Roosevelt N.P. (Elkhorn Ranch Site), ND **106** D1
Theodore Roosevelt N.P. (South Unit), ND **106** D2
Thermopolis, WY **155** C5
Thibodaux, LA **71** G6
Thief River Falls, MN **101** B2
Third Lake, NH **43** A4
Thomas Stone National Historic Site, MD **39** D6
Thomaston, GA **67** E2
Thomaston, ME **37** G4
Thomasville, AL **61** F2
Thomasville, GA **67** H3
Thomasville, NC **75** B5
Thompson, CT **33** A8
Thompson (river), IA, MO **103** A3
Thompson Falls, MT **144** C1
Thomson, GA **67** D5
Thornton, CO **139** C6
Thousand Islands, NY **47** B5
Thousand Springs Creek, NV **147** A6
Three Mile Island, PA **49** E7
Three Rivers, MI **99** I5
Thunder Bay, MI **99** E7
Thunder Bay (river), MI **99** E6
Thunder Butte Creek (river), SD **111** B3
Thurmont, MD **39** A5
Ticonderoga, NY **47** C9
Tiffin, OH **109** B4
Tifton, GA **67** G4
Tillamook, OR **148** B1
Tillery, Lake, NC **75** C5
Tilton, NH **43** G3
Timbalier Bay, LA **71** I7
Timber Lake, SD **111** B4
Timberlake, VA **81** D7
Timms Hill (peak), WI **113** C4
Timpanogos Cave Nat. Mon., UT **151** C4
Tims Ford Lake, TN **79** C5
Timucuan Ecological and Historic Preserve, FL **65** A8
Tinayguk N.W.&S.R., AK **135** B6
Tinian (island), MP **156** D2
Tinton Falls, NJ **45** E5
Tioga, ND **106** B2
Tioga (river), PA **49** A6
Tiogue Lake, RI **51** D4
Tippecanoe (river), IN **93** B3
Tishomingo, OK **125** E9
Titusville, FL **65** D8
Titusville, PA **48** B2
Tiverton, RI **51** D6
Tlikakila N.W.&S.R., AK **135** E5
Toana Range, NV **147** B7
Toccoa, GA **67** B4
Toiyabe Range, NV **147** D4
Tok, AK **135** D8
Toledo, OH **109** A3
Toledo Bend Reservoir, LA, TX **70** D2
Tomah, WI **113** F4
Tomahawk, WI **113** C5
Tombigbee (river), MS **73** G6
Tombigee (river), AL **61** G1
Tombstone, AZ **121** H7
Toms (river), NJ **45** E4
Toms River, NJ **45** F4
Tonawanda, NY **46** D2
Tongue (river), MT **145** E9
Tonopah, NV **147** E4
Tonto Nat. Mon., AZ **121** F5
Tooele, UT **151** C3
Topeka, KS **97** B9
Toppenish, WA **153** E6
Toquima Range, NV **147** E4
Toronto, OH **109** D8
Torrington, CT **33** B3
Torrington, WY **155** F10
Touro Synagogue National Historic Site, RI **51** F5
Towanda, PA **49** B7
Towner, ND **107** B5
Townsend, DE **35** D4
Townsend, MT **145** D5
Towson, MD **39** B7
Tradewater (river), KY **68** D3
Trans-Alaska Pipeline, AK **135** C6
Trask (river), OR **148** B1
Traverse City, MI **99** E5
Traverse, Lake, MN, SD **101** E1
Tremonton, UT **151** A3
Trenton, MO **103** B3
Trenton, NJ **45** E3
Trenton, TN **78** B2
Trinidad, CO **139** G6
Trinity (river), TX **127** E8
Trinity Islands, AK **135** G5
Trinity N.W.&S.R., CA **137** B2
Trinity Site, NM **123** F4
Trotwood, OH **109** E2
Troy, AL **61** F5
Troy, MI **99** H7
Troy, NH **43** I2
Troy, NY **47** E8
Troy, OH **109** E2
Trujillo Alto, PR **157** H11
Trumann, AR **63** B7
Trumbull, CT **33** E3
Truro, MA **41** D10
Truth or Consequences, NM **123** F3
Tschida, Lake, ND **107** E3
Tuba City, AZ **121** B5
Tuckahoe (river), NJ **45** H3
Tuckerman, AR **63** B6
Tucson, AZ **121** G6
Tucumcari, NM **123** C7
Tug Fork (river), KY, WV **69** C11
Tugaloo (river), GA, SC **67** B4
Tulare, CA **137** F4
Tularosa, NM **123** F5
Tullahoma, TN **79** C5
Tulsa, OK **125** B10
Tumacacori N.H.P., AZ **121** H5
Tumwater, WA **153** D3
Tuolumne N.W.&S.R., CA **137** D4
Tupelo, MS **73** B5
Tupelo N.B., MS **73** B5
Turkey (river), IA **95** B8
Turlock, CA **137** E3
Turner Turnpike, OK **125** C9
Turners Falls, MA **41** B3
Turtle Mountains, ND **107** A6
Turtle-Flambeau Flowage, WI **113** B4
Tuscaloosa, AL **61** D2
Tuscarawas (river), OH **109** C6
Tuscarora Mountain, PA **49** E5
Tuscarora Mountains, NV **147** B5
Tuscola, IL **91** E5
Tuskegee, AL **61** E5
Tuskegee Institute National Historic Site, AL **61** F5
Tuttle Creek Lake, KS **97** B7
Tutuila (island), AS **156** I1
Tuxedo Park, NY **47** G8
Tuzigoot Nat. Mon., AZ **121** D4
Twin Falls, ID **143** I3
Twin Lakes, CT **33** A2
Two Butte Creek, CO **139** F9
Two Harbors, MN **101** D6
Two Rivers, WI **113** E7
Tybee Island, GA **67** F8
Tygart Lake, WV **83** D6
Tygart Valley (river), WV **83** E6
Tyler, TX **127** D8
Tyndall, SD **111** F9
Tyrone, PA **49** D4

U
U.S. Military Academy, NY **47** G8
U.S. Virgin Islands (territory), US **157** E12
Uhrichsville, OH **109** D7
Uinta Mountains, UT **151** C5
Ukiah, CA **137** C2
Ulysses, KS **96** E2
Ulysses S. Grant National Historic Site, MO **103** D7
Umbagog Lake, NH **43** B4
Umnak Island, AK **134** H1
Umpqua (river), OR **148** E1
Umpqua, North (river), OR **149** E2
Umpqua, South (river), OR **149** F2
Umsaskis Lake, ME **37** B4
Unalakleet, AK **135** D4
Unalakleet N.W.&S.R., AK **135** D4
Unalaska, AK **134** H2
Unalaska Island, AK **134** H2
Uncompahgre (river), CO **139** E2
Uncompahgre Plateau, CO **138** E1
Unimak Island, AK **134** G2
Union, MO **103** D6
Union, SC **77** B4
Union City, NJ **45** C5
Union City, TN **78** A2
Union Springs, AL **61** F5
Union Village, RI **51** A4
Uniontown, PA **48** E2
Unionville, CT **33** B4
University City, MO **103** D7
'Upolu Point, HI **141** D8
Upper Ammonoosuc (river), NH **43** C3
Upper Arlington, OH **109** E4
Upper Darby, PA **49** E9
Upper Delaware Scenic and Recreational River, PA, NY **49** B10
Upper Iowa (river), IA **95** A7
Upper Klamath Lake, OR **149** G3
Upper Mississippi River National Wildlife and Fish Refuge, IA, IL, MN, WI **101** G6
Upper Missouri River Breaks Nat. Mon., MT **145** B7
Upper Peninsula, MI **99** C3
Upper Red Lake, MN **101** B3
Upper Sandusky, OH **109** C4
Urbana, IL **91** E5
Urbana, OH **109** D3
Urbandale, IA **95** D5
USS Arizona Memorial, HI **141** C4
Utah Lake, UT **151** C4
Ute Creek, NM **123** B7
Utica, NY **47** D6
Utukok (river), AK **135** A4
Uvalde, TX **127** G5

V
Vail, CO **139** C4
Valdez, AK **135** E7
Valdosta, GA **67** H4
Valencia, NM **123** D4
Valentine, NE **105** A4
Vallejo, CA **137** D2
Valley, AL **61** E6
Valley City, ND **107** D8
Valley Falls, RI **51** B5
Valley Forge N.H.P., PA **49** E9
Valparaiso, IN **93** B2
Van Buren, AR **63** C1
Van Buren, ME **37** A6
Van Wert, OH **109** C2
Vanceburg, KY **69** B9
Vancouver, WA **153** G3
Vandalia, IL **91** F4
Vanderbilt Mansion National Historic Site, NY **47** F8
Vaughan, MS **73** E3
Vega Baja, PR **157** H10
Venice, FL **65** F6
Ventnor City, NJ **45** H4
Ventura, CA **137** H4
Verde (river), AZ **121** D4
Verde N.W.&S.R., AZ **121** E5
Verdigre Creek, NE **105** B7
Verdigris (river), KS, OK **125** A11
Vergennes, VT **53** D1
Vermilion (river), IL **91** C4
Vermilion (river), IL, IN **91** E6
Vermilion Cliffs Nat. Mon., AZ **121** A5
Vermilion Lake, MN **101** B5
Vermilion N.W.&S.R., IL **91** D5
Vermillion, SD **111** F10
Vermillion Creek, CO **138** A1
Vermillion, Middle Fork (river), IL **91** D5
Vernal, UT **151** C6
Vernon, CT **33** B6
Vernon, TX **127** C5
Vero Beach, FL **65** E9
Versailles, KY **69** C7
Vicksburg, MS **73** E2
Vicksburg N.M.P., MS **73** E2
Victoria, TX **127** G7
Vidalia, GA **67** F5
Vidalia, LA **71** D5
Vienna, WV **83** D3
Vieques Island, PR **157** I12
Villas, NJ **45** I2
Ville Platte, LA **71** F4
Vinalhaven, ME **37** G5
Vincennes, IN **93** G1
Vineland, NJ **45** G2
Vineyard Haven, MA **41** F8
Vineyard Sound, MA **41** F8
Vinita, OK **125** A11
Vinton, IA **95** C7
Virgin (river), AZ, NV, UT **147** G7
Virgin Islands N.P., VI **157** H8
Virginia, MN **101** C5
Virginia Beach, VA **81** E11
Virginia City, MT **145** E4
Virginia City, NV **147** D2
Viroqua, WI **113** F3
Visalia, CA **137** F4
Vivian, LA **70** A1
Volga, SD **111** D10
Voyageurs N.P., MN **101** B5

W
Wabash, IN **93** C4
Wabash (river), IL, IN **86** G7
Waccamaw (river), SC **77** E9
Waccamaw, Lake, NC **75** D7
Wachusett Reservoir, MA **41** B5
Waco, TX **127** E7
Waconda Lake, KS **97** B5
Wadena, MN **101** D3
Wagner, SD **111** F8
Wagoner, OK **125** C11
Wah Wah Mountains, UT **151** F2
Wahoo, NE **105** C9
Wahpeton, ND **107** E10
Wai'ale'ale (peak), HI **140** A2
Waialua, HI **141** B4
Waialua, HI **141** C6
Waikoloa, HI **141** E8

Wailuku — Zuni

Wailuku, HI **141** C7
Waimea (Kamuela), HI **141** E8
Waipahu, HI **141** B4
Wake Island (territory), US **156** E2
WaKeeney, KS **97** B3
Wakefield, RI **51** F4
Walcott, Lake, ID **143** H4
Waldoboro, ME **37** G4
Waldorf, MD **39** D7
Waldron, AR **63** D1
Walhalla, ND **107** A9
Walker, MN **101** D3
Walker Lake, NV **147** E3
Walker, East (river), NV **147** D2
Walkersville, MD **39** B6
Wall, SD **111** D3
Walla Walla, WA **153** F9
Wallenpaupack, Lake, PA **49** B9
Wallingford, CT **33** D4
Wallingford, VT **53** G2
Wallkill (river), NJ **45** B3
Wallops Island, VA **81** C12
Wallowa (river), OR **149** B8
Wallowa N.W.&S.R., OR **149** B8
Wallula, Lake, WA **153** F8
Wallum Lake, RI **51** A2
Walnut (river), KS **97** E7
Walnut Canyon Nat. Mon., AZ **121** D5
Walnut Creek, KS **97** C4
Walnut Ridge, AR **63** B6
Walpole, NH **43** H1
Walsenburg, CO **139** F6
Walt Disney World and EPCOT Center, FL **65** D7
Walter F. George Reservoir, AL, GA **61** F6
Walterboro, SC **77** F6
Walters, OK **125** E7
Wamego, KS **97** B8
Wanaque, NJ **45** B4
Wanaque Reservoir, NJ **45** B4
Wapakoneta, OH **109** D2
Wapsipinicon (river), IA **95** A7
War in the Pacific N.H.P., GU **156** F1
Ware, MA **41** C4
Ware (river), MA **41** C4
Warner Robins, GA **67** E4
Warner Valley, OR **149** G5
Warren, AR **63** F5
Warren, MI **99** H8
Warren, MN **101** B1
Warren, NH **43** E2
Warren, OH **109** B8
Warren, PA **49** A3
Warren, RI **51** C5
Warrensburg, MO **103** C3
Warrensburg, NY **47** C8
Warrenton, VA **81** B9
Warrior, AL **61** C3
Warsaw, IN **93** B4
Warwick, RI **51** D5
Wasatch Range, UT **130** D5
Waseca, MN **101** G4
Washburn, ME **37** B6
Washburn, ND **107** D5
Washburn, WI **113** A3
Washington, GA **67** C5
Washington, IA **95** E8
Washington, IN **93** G2
Washington, KS **97** A7
Washington, MO **103** D6
Washington, NC **75** C9
Washington, NJ **45** C2
Washington, PA **48** E1
Washington Court House, OH **109** F3
Washington Island, WI **113** C8
Washington, Mount, NH **43** D4
Washita (river), OK **125** C6
Washita Battlefield National Historic Site, OK **125** C5
Wasilla, AK **135** E6
Wassuk Range, NV **147** D2
Watch Hill, RI **51** G1
Watchaug Pond, RI **51** F3
Water Valley, MS **73** B3
Waterbury, CT **33** C3
Waterbury, VT **53** C3
Wateree (river), SC **77** D6
Wateree Lake, SC **77** C6
Waterloo, IA **95** C7
Watertown, CT **33** C3
Watertown, NY **47** C6
Watertown, SD **111** C9
Watertown, WI **113** G6
Waterville, ME **37** F4
Watford City, ND **106** C2
Watkins Glen, NY **47** E4
Watonga, OK **125** C7
Watseka, IL **91** D6
Watts Bar Lake, TN **79** C7
Waubay Lake, SD **111** B9
Waukegan, IL **91** A5
Waukesha, WI **113** G6
Waukon, IA **95** A8
Waupaca, WI **113** E5
Waupun, WI **113** F6
Waurika Lake, OK **125** E7
Wausau, WI **113** D5
Wauseon, OH **109** B2
Wauwatosa, WI **113** G7
Waverly, IA **95** B7
Waverly, NE **105** D9
Waverly, OH **109** F4
Wawasee, Lake, IN **93** B4
Waycross, GA **67** H5
Wayne, NE **105** B8
Wayne, NJ **45** B4
Waynesboro, GA **67** D6
Waynesboro, MS **73** G5
Waynesboro, PA **49** F6
Waynesboro, VA **81** C7
Waynesburg, PA **48** E1
Waynesville, MO **103** E5
Waynesville, NC **74** C2
Weatherford, OK **125** C7
Webb City, MO **103** F2
Webster, MA **41** D5
Webster, SD **111** B9
Webster City, IA **95** C5
Weir Farm National Historic Site, CT **33** E2
Weirton, WV **83** A5
Weiser, ID **143** F1
Weiser (river), ID **143** F1
Weiss Lake, AL **61** B5
Welch, WV **83** H3
Weldon (river), MO **103** A3
Wellesley, MA **41** C6
Wellfleet, MA **41** D10
Wellington, KS **97** E6
Wells, ME **37** I2
Wells, NV **147** B6
Wells River, VT **53** D5
Wellsboro, PA **49** B6
Wellsburg, WV **83** B5
Wellston, OH **109** G5
Wellsville, NY **46** F3
Wellsville, UT **151** A4
Wellton, AZ **121** G2
Wenaha N.W.&S.R., OR **149** A8
Wenatchee, WA **153** D6
Wendell H. Ford Parkway, KY **69** D4
Wendover, UT **151** C1
Wentworth, Lake, NH **43** F4
Wessington Springs, SD **111** D8
West (river), VT **53** H3
West Allis, WI **113** G7
West Bend, WI **113** G7
West Chester, PA **49** E9
West Columbia, SC **77** D5
West Des Moines, IA **95** D5
West Fargo, ND **107** D10
West Frankfort, IL **91** H4
West Grand Lake, ME **37** E6
West Hartford, CT **33** B4
West Haven, CT **33** E4
West Helena, AR **63** D7
West Jordan, UT **151** C4
West Kingston, RI **51** F3
West Little Owyhee N.W.&S.R., OR **149** G8
West Memphis, AR **63** C8
West Milford, NJ **45** B4
West Monroe, LA **71** B4
West Okoboji Lake, IA **95** A3
West Palm Beach, FL **65** F9
West Plains, MO **103** F5
West Point, MS **73** C5
West Point, NE **105** B9
West Point, NY **47** G8
West Point, VA **81** D10
West Point Lake, AL, GA **67** D1
West Quoddy Head, ME **37** F8
West Rutland, VT **53** F2
West Seneca, NY **46** D2
West Warwick, RI **51** D4
West Wendover, NV **147** B7
West Yellowstone, MT **145** F5
Westbrook, CT **33** E6
Westbrook, ME **37** H2
Westerly, RI **51** G1
Westerville, OH **109** D4
Westfield, MA **40** C2
Westfield, NY **46** E1
Westfield (river), MA **40** C2
Westfield N.W.&S.R., MA **40** C2
Westfield, Middle Branch (river), MA **40** B2
Westfield, West Branch (river), MA **40** C1
Westminster, CO **139** C5
Westminster, MD **39** A6
Weston, WV **83** D5
Westport, CT **33** E2
Wet Mountains, CO **139** E5
Wethersfield, CT **33** B5
Wewoka, OK **125** D9
Weymouth, MA **41** C7
Wheatland, WY **155** F9
Wheaton, MN **101** E1
Wheeler Lake, AL **61** A3
Wheeler Peak, NM **123** B5
Wheelersburg, OH **109** G4
Wheeling, WV **83** B4
Whidbey Island, WA **153** B3
Whiskeytown-Shasta-Trinity N.R.A., CA **137** B2
White (river), CO, UT **151** D7
White (river), AR, MO **63** A2
White (river), AZ **121** E7
White (river), IN **93** D5
White (river), MI **99** G4
White (river), NE, SD **111** D5
White (river), OR **149** B4
White (river), VT **53** E3
White Butte (peak), ND **106** E2
White City, OR **149** F2
White Earth (river), ND **107** B3
White Hall, IL **91** F2
White Horse, NJ **45** E3
White Lake, LA **71** H3
White Mountains, NH **43** E2
White N.W.&S.R., OR **149** B4
White Oak Lake, AR **63** F3
White Plains, NY **47** G8
White River, SD **111** E5
White River Junction, VT **53** F4
White River Plateau, CO **139** C2
White Rocks N.R.A., VT **53** G2
White Salmon N.W.&S.R., WA **153** F5
White Sands Nat. Mon., NM **123** G4
White Sulphur Springs, WV **83** G5
White Woman Creek, KS **96** C1
White, East Fork (river), IN **93** G3
Whitefield, NH **43** D3
Whitefish, MT **144** B2
Whitefish Bay, MI **99** C6
Whitefish N.W.&S.R., MI **99** C4
Whiteriver, AZ **121** E7
Whiteville, NC **75** D7
Whitewater, WI **113** G6
Whitewater (river), IN **93** F6
Whitman, MA **41** D8
Whitman Mission National Historic Site, WA **153** F8
Whitney, Mount, CA **137** F5
Wibaux, MT **145** C11
Wichita, KS **97** E7
Wichita (river), TX **127** C6
Wichita Falls, TX **127** C6
Wichita Mountains, OK **125** D6
Wichita Mountains Wildlife Refuge, OK **125** D6
Wickenburg, AZ **121** E4
Wickford, RI **51** E4
Wiggins, MS **73** H4
Wilber, NE **105** D8
Wilburton, OK **125** D11
Wild Rice (river), MN **101** C1
Wild Rice (river), ND **107** F9
Wildcat Brook N.W.&S.R., NH **43** D4
Wildcat Creek, IN **93** D3
Wilder, VT **53** F4
Wildwood, NJ **45** I3
Wilkes-Barre, PA **49** C8
Will Rogers Turnpike, OK **125** B10
Willamette (river), OR **149** C2
Willamette N.W.&S.R., OR **149** D3
Willapa Bay, WA **152** E2
Willard, OH **109** C4
Willcox, AZ **121** G7
Willcox Playa (river), AZ **121** G7
William "Bill" Dannelly Reservoir, AL **61** F3
William H. Natcher Parkway, KY **69** D4
William Howard Taft National Historic Site, OH **109** G2
William Preston Lane Jr. Memorial Bridge (Chesapeake Bay Bridge), MD **39** C8
Williams, AZ **121** C4
Williamsburg, KY **69** E8
Williamsburg, VA **81** D10
Williamson, WV **82** G2
Williamsport, MD **39** A4
Williamsport, PA **49** C7
Williamston, NC **75** B9
Williamstown, KY **69** B8
Williamstown, NJ **45** G2
Williamstown, WV **83** C3
Willimantic, CT **33** B7
Willimantic (river), CT **33** B7
Willimantic Reservoir, CT **33** B7
Willingboro, NJ **45** E2
Williston, ND **106** B2
Williston, SC **77** E4
Willmar, MN **101** F3
Willoughby, Lake, VT **53** B5
Willow Creek, UT **151** D6
Wills Creek, OH **109** E6
Wilmington, DE **35** A5
Wilmington, NC **75** D8
Wilmington, OH **109** F3
Wilmington, MA **41** B7
Wilson, NC **75** B8
Wilson Creek Range, NV **147** E7
Wilson Lake, AL **61** A2
Wilson Lake, KS **97** B5
Wilson's Creek N.B., MO **103** F3
Wilton, CT **33** E2
Wilton, ME **37** F3
Wilton, NH **43** I3
Winchendon, MA **41** A4
Winchester, IN **93** D6
Winchester, KY **69** C8
Winchester, NH **43** I1
Winchester, TN **79** D6
Winchester, VA **81** A8
Wind (river), WY **155** C5
Wind Cave N.P., SD **110** E2
Wind N.W.&S.R., AK **135** B7
Wind River Range, WY **155** C3
Windber, PA **49** E4
Windom, MN **101** H3
Window Rock, AZ **121** C7
Windsor, CT **33** B5
Windsor, VT **53** F4
Windsor Heights, IA **95** D4
Windsor Locks, CT **33** A5
Winfield, AL **61** C2
Winfield, KS **97** E7
Winnebag, Lake, WI **113** F6
Winnebago (river), IA **95** A6
Winnemucca, NV **147** B4
Winnemucca Lake, NV **147** C2
Winner, SD **111** E6
Winnfield, LA **71** C3
Winnibigoshish, Lake, MN **101** C3
Winnipesaukee, Lake, NH **43** F4
Winnisquam Lake, NH **43** G3
Winnsboro, SC **77** C5
Winnsboro, LA **71** C5
Winona, MN **101** G6
Winona, MS **73** C3
Winooski (river), VT **53** C2
Winooski, VT **53** C2
Winslow, AZ **121** D6
Winslow, ME **37** F4
Winsted, CT **33** A3
Winston, OR **149** E2
Winston-Salem, NC **75** B5
Winter Haven, FL **65** E7
Winterset, IA **95** E5
Winterthur Museum and Gardens, DE **35** A5
Winthrop, ME **37** G3
Wiscasset, ME **37** G3
Wisconsin (river), WI **113** E5
Wisconsin Dells, WI **113** F5
Wisconsin Rapids, WI **113** E5
Wisconsin, Lake, WI **113** G5
Wishek, ND **107** F6
Wissota, Lake, WI **113** D3
Withlacoochee (river), GA **67** H4
Woburn, MA **41** B7
Wolf (river), WI **113** D6
Wolf Creek, OK **125** B5
Wolf N.W.&S.R., WI **113** D6
Wolf Point, MT **145** B10
Wolf Trap N.P. for the Performing Arts, VA **81** B9
Wolfeboro, NH **43** F4
Women's Rights N.H.P., NY **47** D5
Wood (river), RI **51** F2
Woodall Mountain, MS **73** A6
Woodbine, NJ **45** H3
Woodbridge, VA **81** B9
Woodburn, OR **149** B2
Woodbury, NJ **45** F2
Woodland, ME **37** E7
Woodland Park, CO **139** D5
Woods Hole, MA **41** F8
Woods, Lake of the, MN **101** A3
Woodstock, VT **53** F3
Woodstown, NJ **45** G1
Woodsville, NH **43** E2
Woodward, OK **125** B6
Woonasquatucket (river), RI **51** B4
Woonasquatucket Reservoir, RI **51** B3
Woonsocket, RI **51** A4
Woonsocket, SD **111** D8
Wooster, OH **109** C6
Worcester, MA **41** C5
Worden Pond, RI **51** F3
Worland, WY **155** B5
Worthington, MN **101** H2
Wounded Knee Massacre Site, SD **111** E3
Wrangell, AK **135** G11
Wrangell-St. Elias N.P. and Preserve, AK **135** E8
Wright, WY **155** C8
Wright Brothers National Memorial, NC **75** B10
Wrightsville Beach, NC **75** E8
Wupatki Nat. Mon., AZ **121** C5
Wyaconda (river), MO **103** A5
Wyandotte Cave, IN **93** H3
Wylie Lake, SC **77** A5
Wynne, AR **63** C7
Wyoming, RI **51** E2
Wyoming Range, WY **154** D2
Wytheville, VA **80** E4

X
Xenia, OH **109** E3

Y
Yadkin (river), NC **75** B4
Yakima, WA **153** E6
Yakima (river), WA **153** D6
Yalobusha (river), MS **73** C4
Yampa (river), CO **139** B2
Yankton, SD **111** F9
Yantic (river), CT **33** C7
Yarmouth, ME **37** H3
Yazoo (river), MS **73** E2
Yazoo City, MS **73** E2
Yellow (river), WI **113** D3
Yellow Dog N.W.&S.R., MI **99** C3
Yellowstone (river), MT, WY **145** C11
Yellowstone Lake, WY **154** A2
Yellowstone N.P., ID, MT, WY **154** A2
Yerington, NV **147** D2
Yoakum, TX **127** G7
Yocona (river), MS **73** B3
Yona, GU **156** F1
Yonkers, NY **47** G8
York, AL **61** E1
York, NE **105** D8
York, PA **49** E7
York, SC **77** A5
York (river), VA **81** D10
York Village, ME **37** I2
Yorktown, VA **81** D11
Yosemite N.P., CA **137** E4
Youghiogheny (river), PA **49** F3
Youngstown, OH **109** B8
Ypsilanti, MI **99** H7
Yreka, CA **137** A2
Yuba City, CA **137** C3
Yucca House Nat. Mon., CO **138** G1
Yukon, OK **125** C8
Yukon (river), AK **135** E4
Yukon Delta, AK **134** D3
Yukon-Charley Rivers National Preserve, AK **135** C8
Yuma, AZ **121** G2
Yuma, CO **139** B8
Yunaska Island, AK **135** G10

Z
Zachary, LA **71** F6
Zanesville, OH **109** E6
Zapata, TX **127** H5
Zeeland, MI **99** H5
Zion N.P., UT **151** G2
Zoar, Lake, CT **33** D3
Zuni, NM **123** D1
Zuni (river), AZ **121** D7

Published by the National Geographic Society

John M. Fahey, Jr.
Chairman of the Board and Chief Executive Officer

Timothy T. Kelly
President

Declan Moore
President, Publishing and Digital Media

Melina Gerosa Bellows
Executive Vice President; Chief Creative Officer, Books, Kids, and Family

Prepared by the Book Division

Hector Sierra, Senior Vice President and General Manager
Nancy Laties Feresten, Senior Vice President, Editor in Chief, Children's Books
Jonathan Halling, Design Director, Books and Children's Publishing
Jay Sumner, Director of Photography, Children's Publishing
Jennifer Emmett, Editorial Director, Children's Books
Eva Absher-Schantz, Managing Art Director, Children's Publishing
Carl Mehler, Director of Maps
R. Gary Colbert, Production Director
Jennifer A. Thornton, Director of Managing Editorial

Staff for this book

Priyanka Lamichhane, Project Editor
David Seager, Art Director
Sven M. Dolling, Laura McCormick, Thomas L. Gray, Nicholas P. Rosenbach, Map Editors
Matt Chwastyk, Sven M. Dolling, Steven D. Gardner, Michael McNey, Gregory Ugiansky, Mapping Specialists, and XNR Productions, Map Research and Production
Tibor G. Tóth, Map Relief
Lori Epstein, Senior Illustrations Editor
Martha B. Sharma, Consultant
Martha B. Sharma, Timothy J. Hill, Writers
Stuart Armstrong, Graphics Illustrator
Michelle R. Harris, Researcher
Dan Sherman, Web Page Design
Jennifer Kirkpatrick, Web Page Editor
Kathryn Robbins, Design Production Assistant
Stacy Gold, Nadia Hughes, Illustrations Research Editors
Kate Olesin, Assistant Editor
Lewis R. Bassford, Production Manager
Grace Hill, Associate Managing Editor
Joan Gossett, Production Editor
Susan Borke, Legal and Business Affairs

Manufacturing and Quality Management

Christopher A. Liedel, Chief Financial Officer
Phillip L. Schlosser, Senior Vice President
Chris Brown, Vice President
Nicole Elliott, Manager
Rachel Faulise, Manager
Robert L. Barr, Manager

ISBN 978-0-545-66478-3

12 11 10 9 8 7 6 5 4 3 2 1 13 14 15 16 17 18/0

Printed in the U.S.A. 08

First Scholastic printing, September 2013

Illustrations Credits

Abbreviations for terms appearing below: (t)-top; (b)-bottom; (l)-left; (r)-right; NGS = National Geographic Image Collection; iS = iStockphoto.com; SH = Shutterstock.com

Art for state flowers and state birds by Robert E. Hynes

Locator globe page 16 created by Theophilus Britt Griswold

Front cover, Tibor G. Tóth; (sunflower), Shutterstock; (Mt. Rushmore), Digital Stock; (Statue of Liberty), Punchstock; (eagle), Shutterstock

Back cover (t–b), FloridaStock/SH, Peder Digre/SH, Lou Ann M. Aepelbacher/SH, Olga Lyubkina/SH

Front of the Book

2 (l–r), Freerk Brouwer/SH; PhotoDisc; Brandon Laufenberg/iS; Richard Nowitz/NGS; 3 (l–r), Joel Sartore/NGS; Jeremy Edwards/iS; Eileen Hart/iS; PhotoDisc; 4 (l), PhotoDisc; 4 (r), Brian J. Skerry/NGS; 4–5, Lenice Harms/SH; 5 (l), italianestro/SH; 5 (r), James Davis Photography/Alamy; 5 (b), Digital Stock; 11 (t–b), Lane V. Erickson/SH; Elena Elisseeva/SH; SNEHIT/SH; Nic Watson/SH; FloridaStock/SH; Sai Yeung Chan/SH; TTphoto/SH; 12 (l) Lowell Georgia/NGS; 12 (r), NASA; 14 (l–r), George F. Mobley/NGS; Skip Brown/NGS; Jan Brons/SH; Michelle Pacitto/SH; Tammy Bryngelson/iS; 15 (l–r), Carsten Peter/NGS; Mark Thiessen/NGS; Michael Nichols/NGS; Steven Collins/SH; Robert Madden/NGS; 18, Ira Block/NGS; 20 (t), Penny de los Santos; 20 (bl), Steven Clevenger/Corbis; 20–21, Sarah Leen/NGS; 22 (l), Marcelo Piotti/iS; 22–23, Jim Richardson/NGS; 23 (r), Sorin Alb/iS; 24, PhotoDisc; 24–25, PhotoDisc; 25 (t), L. Kragt Bakker/SH; 25 (b), Lori Epstein/National Geographic Stock.

The Northeast

30 (bl), Rudi Von Briel/Photo Edit; 30 (br), Les Byerley/SH; 30–31 (t), Michael Melford/NGS; 30–31 (b), Tim Laman/NGS; 31 (t), Donald Swartz/iS; 32 (both), David L. Arnold/NGS; 33, Catherine Karnow/NGS; 34 (bl), Kevin Fleming/NGS; 34 (br), Stephen R. Brown/NGS; 34–35, Stephen St. John/NGS; 36 (b), iS; 36–37, PhotoDisc; 37 (b), Roy Toft/NGS; 38 (t), Jeremy Edwards/iS; 38 (b), Justine Gecewicz/iS; 39, James L. Stanfield/NGS; 40 (t), Sarah Leen/NGS; 40 (b), Tim Laman/NGS; 41, Darlyne A. Murawski/NGS; 42 (t), Medford Taylor/NGS; 42–43, Steven Phraner/iS; 43 (t), Richard Nowitz/NGS; 44 (t), Richard Nowitz/NGS; 44 (bl), Iconica/Getty Images; 44 (br), Matt Rainey/Star Ledger/Corbis; 44–45, Mike Derer/Associated Press; 46 (t), Glenn Taylor/iS; 46 (b), James P. Blair/NGS; 47, Kenneth Garrett/NGS; 48 (t), Kenneth Garrett/NGS; 48 (b), Jeremy Edwards/iS; 49, William Albert Allard/NGS; 50 (t), Todd Gipstein/NGS; 50 (b), Onne van der Wal/Corbis; 50–51, Ira Block/NGS; 52, Michael S. Yamashita/NGS; 52–53, David McLain/Aurora/Getty Images; 53, Daniel W. Slocum/SH.

The Southeast

58 (t), Klaus Nigge/NGS; 58 (bl), Tyrone Turner/NGS; 58 (br), Richard Nowitz/Corbis; 58–59, Skip Brown/NGS; 59 (t), Raymond Gehman/NGS; 59 (b), Robert Clark/NGS; 60 (t), Raymond Gehman/NGS; 60 (b), Richard Nowitz/NGS; 62 (t), Harrison Shull/Aurora/Getty Images; 62 (b), Joel Sartore/NGS; 63, Cary Wolinsky/NGS; 64 (t), David Burnett/NGS; 64 (b), Brian J. Skerry/NGS; 64–65, NASA; 66 (tl), NGS; 66 (tr), PhotoDisc; 66 (b), Michael Melford/NGS; 68, Melissa Farlow/NGS; 69, Randy Olson/NGS; 70 (t), Tyrone Turner/NGS; 70 (b), Jason Major/iS; 72 (t), William Albert Allard/NGS; 72 (b), Ira Block/NGS; 73, Elena Vdovina/iS; 74 (l), Jack Fletcher/NGS; 74 (r), Pete Souza/NGS; 75, Raymond Gehman/NGS; 76, Terry Healy/iS; 76–77, Annie Griffiths Belt/NGS; 77, Raymond Gehman/NGS; 78, Melissa Farlow/NGS; 79 (t), Dennis R. Dimick/NGS; 79 (b), Jodi Cobb/NGS; 80 (t), Robert Clark/NGS; 80 (b), Richard Nowitz/NGS; 80–81, Medford Taylor/NGS; 82 (t), James L. Stanfield/NGS; 82 (b), Joel Sartore/NGS; 83, Robert Pernell/SH.

The Midwest

88 (t), James L. Stanfield/NGS; 88 (b), Jim Richardson/NGS; 88–89, NGS; 89 (tl), Nadia M. B. Hughes/NGS; 89 (tr), Sean Martin/iS; 89 (b), Aga/SH; 90 (t), Chas/SH; 90 (b), Jenny Solomon/SH; 90–91 (t), Lenice Harms/SH; 92–93 (t), iS; 92–93 (b), Melissa Farlow/NGS; 94 (t), Joel Sartore/NGS; 94 (b), Madeleine Openshaw/SH; 95, Tom Bean/NGS; 96, Cotton Coulson/NGS; 97, Phil Schermeister/NGS; 98 (t), Kevin Fleming/Corbis; 98 (b), Vince Ruffa/SH; 99, Geoffrey Kuchera/SH; 100 (t), Joel Sartore/NGS; 100 (b), Medford Taylor/NGS; 101, Lawrence Sawyer/iS; 102, Phil Schermeister/NGS; 102–103 (b), PhotoDisc; 103, Sarah Leen/NGS; 104 (both), Joel Sartore/NGS; 105, Sarah Leen/NGS; 106 (t), Farrell Grehan/NGS; 106 (b), Beverley Vycital/iS; 107, Annie Griffiths Belt/NGS; 108 (t), PhotoDisc; 108 (bl), Weldon Schloneger/SH; 108 (br), Robert J. Daveant/SH; 110, Peter Digre/SH; 111, Dan Westergren/NGS; 112 (t), Paul Damien/NGS; 112 (b), PhotoDisc; 112–113 Medford Taylor/NGS.

The Southwest

118 (t), Joseph H. Bailey/NGS; 118 (b), Penny de los Santos; 118–119, Anton Folton/iS; 119 (t), Chih Hsueh Tseng/SH; 119 (b), Joel Sartore/NGS; 120 (t), Joel Sartore/NGS; 120 (b), George Burba/SH; 122 (tl), James P. Blair/NGS; 122 (tr), italianestro/SH; 122 (b), Lynn Johnson/NGS; 124, Joel Sartore/NGS; 125, Annie Griffiths Belt/NGS; 126 (t), Sarah Leen/NGS; 126–127, Diane Cook & Len Jenshel/NGS.

The West

132 (both), PhotoDisc; 132–133, Digital Stock; 133 (t), Phillip Holland/SH; 133 (bl), Joel Sartore/NGS; 133 (br), Digital Stock; 134 (t), Joel Sartore/NGS; 134 (b), PhotoDisc; 136 (t), PhotoDisc; 136 (b), Randy Olson/NGS; 138 (both), PhotoDisc; 140, PhotoDisc; 141, Frans Lanting/NGS; 142 (b), Joel Sartore/NGS; 142–143, Michael Melford/NGS; 143 (r), J. Cameron Gull/SH; 144 (b), William Albert Allard/NGS; 145, SH; 146 (b), Sam Abell/NGS; 146–147, Andy Z./SH; 147 (b), Raymond Gehman/NGS; 148 (t), Jennifer Lynn Arnold/SH; 148 (b), Peter Kunasz/SH; 150 (b), Digital Stock; 150–151, PhotoDisc; 152 (l), PhotoDisc; 152 (r), Digital Stock; 154 (t), Michael Rubin/SH; 154 (b), Digital Stock; 155, PhotoDisc.

The Territories and Back of the Book

158 (l), Kendra Nielsam/SH; 158–159 (t), James Davis Photography/Alamy; 158–159 (b), Ira Block/NGS; 159 (t), VisionsofParadise.com/Alamy; 159 (b), Gerry Ellis/Minden/Getty Images; 160, SH.

Map Acknowledgments

2–3, 26–27, 54–55, 84–85, 114–115, 128–129, Blue Marble: Next Generation NASA Earth Observatory; 12–13, climate data adapted from Peel, M. C., Finlayson, B. L., and McMahon, T. A.: Updated world map of the Köppen-Geiger climate classification, Hydrol. Earth Syst. Sci., 11, 1633–1644, 2007; 14–15, data from Billion Dollar Weather Disasters 1980–2007 (map), NOAA's National Climatic Data Center (NCDC); 18–19, data from Center for International Earth Science Information Network (CIESIN), Columbia University, and Centro Internacional de Agricultura Tropical (CIAT), 2005. Gridded Population of the World Version 3 (GPWv3): Population Density Grids—World Population Density, 2005 (map). Palisades, New York: Socioeconomic Data and Applications Center (SEDAC), Columbia University. Accessed October 2007. Available at sedac.ciesin.columbia.edu/gpw; 20–21, United States Atlas of Renewable Resources, National Renewable Energy Laboratory; 22–23, U.S. Census Bureau, Census 2000 Redistricting Data (PL 94-171) Summary File, Population Division.